IMMIGRATION

IMMIGRATION

An American History

CARL J. BON TEMPO

HASIA R. DINER

Yale

UNIVERSITY PRESS

New Haven and London

Published with assistance from the foundation established in memory
of Philip Hamilton McMillan of the Class of 1894, Yale College.
Yale University Press books may be purchased in quantity for
educational, business, or promotional use. For information, please
e-mail sales.press@yale.edu (U.S. office)orsales @yaleup.co.uk
(U.K. office).

Printed in the United States of America.

Library of Congress Control Number: 2021946779
ISBN 978-0-300-22686-7 (hardcover : alk. paper)

A catalogue record for this book is available from the British Library.

10 9 8 7 6 5 4 3 2

For our parents:
Carl P. Bon Tempo, Eileen S. Bon Tempo,
Esther Kite, and Moshe Schwartzman

My heart is filled with optimism
My dreams are so close to coming true
But the same cannot be said for others.

—KAELA AALTO, "Eyes of an Immigrant"

Contents

Acknowledgments

KAELA AALTO, NOW AN undergraduate student at New York University, visited Ellis Island as a youngster in the fifth grade. Inspired by the lesson she received at that historic place, she turned to poetry to reflect on what she had seen. A few of her amazing words, preserved on an internet site, serve as the epigraph for this book. Her verse testifies to the fact that history does matter and that right now, in these tumultuous times, the history of immigration in particular has much to say to the American public. Our thanks to Ms. Aalto for permitting us to use her poetry to open this book.

Yale University Press must have agreed with that assessment, and we owe it a great thanks for having asked us to prepare a book on this always fascinating and profound aspect of American life. Sarah Miller at the Press first helped us conceive of the project. Adina Popescu Berk, our extraordinary editor, provided wise and patient counsel as we wrote and revised—and during a global pandemic at that! The rest of the Yale Press team, especially Ash Lago, have been so helpful as we worked through the production of the book.

A special note of thanks to the wonderful Hannah Zaves-Greene, a talented historian in her own right, who helped us find the images and make the charts in this book. Thanks as well to the Goldstein-Goren Center for American Jewish History for providing funding for parts of the research and writing. Thank you also to the History Department at SUNY Albany for funding to cover part of the indexing and proofreading of the book.

This book is built on the work of so many gifted scholars of immigration and the United States. We owe special thanks to the three anonymous readers who commented on the manuscript, helping us sharpen our arguments and analysis and saving us from many silly errors. Many others took time from their own work and lives to read parts, or all, of the manuscript or to answer questions. Thanks also to Kristin Celello, Sarah Coleman, Rebecca Erbelding, Nicole Eustace, Susan Ferber, Libby Garland, Adam Goodman, Ryan Irwin, Maddalena Marinari, Edward Murphy, Christopher Nehls, Jason Scott Smith, Aaron Sheehan-Dean, Barry Trachtenberg, Philip Wolgin, and Hannah Zaves-Greene.

Co-authoring a book can be a challenge. We are happy to report that it was a thoroughly enjoyable experience. It was a joy to share the project with each other. We challenged and supported each other through the writing and the revisions and came out to the other side as colleagues and friends. Co-authors cannot ask for much more than that.

A final thanks to our families. Kristin Celello and Teo Bon Tempo have been equal parts supportive and enthusiastic as Carl worked on the book. Steven Diner, as always, pitched in, asked great questions, read and edited the full manuscript, and shared parts of it with his undergraduate students at Rutgers University–Newark, giving them a chance to see and comment on an unpublished, and indeed unrevised, manuscript.

INTRODUCTION
Immigration: An American History

A YOUNG MAN WITH FEW skills, fewer resources, and no real prospects at home, John W. Nordstrom left his hardscrabble farm in Alvik Neder Lulea in northern Sweden in 1887. He headed to the United States. After some early struggles, he and a friend from back home decided to take laborers' jobs in an iron mine in Stambaugh, Michigan. "We knew we could get jobs there," he recalled. "They always needed men," he remembered, and "greenhorns like us were the only ones" the mine operators "could get," as "no American would work there."[1] Nordstrom eventually found his way to Seattle, Washington, where he opened a successful shoe store. He and his heirs turned that enterprise into a high-end department store, Nordstrom, a staple of large shopping malls in the latter part of the twentieth century.

Achut Deng, at first glance, shared little with John Nordstrom. Born in Southern Sudan in the 1980s and orphaned at age six during a civil war, she fled to refugee camps in Kenya and then Ethiopia. In 2000 a U.S. government program for Sudanese orphan refugees brought her to America. She went to college and ended up in Sioux Falls, South Dakota, working at a massive Smithfield pork processing plant. She started on the processing line, using a knife to cut fat from the hanging carcasses, and advanced to shift manager, a less physically taxing and more lucrative position. Eventually earning over eighteen dollars an hour, plus overtime, she gave her three boys a life she could only have dreamt of as a child. "It's not a perfect world. I'd make it perfect for them," she noted as she reflected on her efforts with pride and satisfaction. But then, in the spring of 2020, her workplace experienced a massive outbreak of coronavirus, which exposed Deng and so many others to the lethal virus. She got sick and the plant shut for weeks. When it reopened, Deng returned to work. She needed the money, but all the while she worried about her health, her finances, and the future. "I cannot afford to stay home for a long time."[2]

Nordstrom and Deng, two different people from different parts of the globe at different times and facing different challenges, both came to the United States to craft better futures for themselves. For them, and the tens of millions of others whose stories unfold in these pages, the United States represented a new start. Many came with dreams of economic security, hoping to match their industriousness to economic opportunities in the United States. Others came to escape religious or political persecution and aimed to enjoy privileges that the United States offered. For still others, the aftershocks of natural disasters played decisive roles in pushing them outward. Finally, many newcomers came to reunite with family members who had preceded them to the United States.

The chance that Nordstrom or Deng or any of the others could in fact accomplish their migration goals depended on their ability to navigate multiple, intersecting dynamics both in the places they sought to leave and in the place they hoped to enter, the United States. Governments, motivated by a mix of popular cultural and social attitudes, economic imperatives, and foreign policy concerns, could make it easier or harder for immigrants to leave or enter. Immigrants called on the latest in communications technologies to learn of opportunities in the United States and to arrange their travels and resettlement plans. They also depended on transportation networks at both ends of their journeys to ease their passage across borders and facilitate their resettlement.

Whether in the mid-nineteenth century, when John Nordstrom grabbed a shovel in Michigan, or the early twenty-first, when Achut Deng picked up her meat cleaver in the pork plant in South Dakota, and indeed in centuries earlier, immigrants stoked the material, physical, social, and cultural development of the United States. The vast growth of the American economy depended on the willingness of individuals to leave their homes elsewhere and exchange their physical strength and mental acuity for pay. The kinds of work they performed changed, but the recognition that without them the work could not get done persisted. Away from their jobs, in their communities every day, those same immigrants brought much to America's social fabric, both reinforcing and reinventing it.

Yet at the same time, Americans consistently articulated deep fears that every new contingent of immigrants threatened the United States. Such arguments might seem inconsistent with historic realities, but at each moment in time, some Americans expressed the opinion, stating it as fact, that newcomers took work away from Americans by selling their labor for low rates of pay. They likewise, throughout this long history, deemed all or some immigrants to be less desirable, more dangerous, and more markedly defective than the ones who came before. At various times Americans feared and reviled the political beliefs, religious practices, and physical appearances of the newcomers. Some Americans abhorred immigrants as speakers of languages other than English, as bearers of cultures that seemed to jar with American ways of living, and as women and men still tied to their faraway communities.

And yet, women and men from around the world voted for America with their feet. If they could make their way to America, they did. In the colonial period, indentured servants recruited from England, Scotland, Ireland, and various German-speaking states arrived, women and men who provided the labor to farm the soil of North America. In the nineteenth century, men from Ireland, central, eastern, and southern Europe, Mexico, China, and India entered the United States, willing to dynamite the earth, blast away at the mountains, and lay the tracks to build a network of canals, roads, and railroads. They were joined by Irish Catholic women who labored in the homes of Americans, cooking, cleaning, and tending children. In the twentieth century, immigrants, largely from Europe, worked the industries that spat out mammoth amounts of textiles, garments, machines, rubber, steel, and automobiles, while newcomers, many from Mexico and the Caribbean, harvested and processed the food that found its way to dinner tables across the country. In the twenty-first century, Chinese, Indian, Mexican, and

Central American newcomers continue to do some of the most difficult and least desirable, but absolutely crucial, work in the country.

These are only some of the stories of the newcomers who inhabit this book. As these examples suggest, we give primary significance to economic matters in explaining the United States' immigration history. The declining chances of women and men of particular classes and regions to make a living at home motivated many to leave their current place of residence. North America's labor needs, meanwhile, drew them in particular to the United States. All this occurred within, and often because of, the interconnected global economy that knit together people and regions around the world.

The economic context was, and remains today, a vital driver of immigration to the United States. But it was not the only one. Families—wives and husbands, parents and children—immigrated in order to reunite with loved ones. Even here, though, the labor imperative was not far away: individuals often reunited with their family who had come to the United States earlier for work. Other troubling conditions, including religious, political, and racial persecution back home, also propelled them outward. That dynamic connects central Europeans in the 1840s, eastern European Jews in the late nineteenth century, German Jews in the 1930s, Indochinese in the 1970s, and today's Central Americans across the breadth of immigration history. But even for individuals who suffered persecution, the inability to make a living in one place and the possibility of doing so in the United States influenced individual, family, and community choices more profoundly.

If work and the nation's labor needs stand as one pillar at the heart of this book, then the state—the local, state, or federal governments—emerges as the other key pillar. The federal government facilitated John Nordstrom's options, since as a young man defined both by law and by common practice as "white," he faced no legal restriction or impediments to immigration. He arrived before the government of the United States restricted which "whites" from Europe, and how many, could immigrate, when, and how, and if they could remain permanently and become citizens. Nordstrom in 1887 handily fit, and benefited from, the dictates of the still relevant Naturalization Act of 1790, which defined as eligible for citizenship anyone deemed to be a free white person of good character.

For people coming from any part of Europe until the 1920s, immigration, though increasingly regulated, proceeded without a numerical ceiling or any quotas based on place of origin. The millions who took advantage of that comparatively free flow across the Atlantic experienced immigration as a personal choice relatively unfettered by the actions of the U.S. government. State-based rules that demanded the deportation of paupers, real or potential, colored the experiences of some immigrants, and they demonstrate that the United States never had a completely open door to newcomers. But enforcement of these laws and policies was kept at a minimum, and, in the big picture, they did not stem the movement of tens of millions.

But five years before Nordstrom's arrival, the Chinese Exclusion Act of 1882 did exactly what its name declared. The federal government made it impossible, with minor exceptions, for individuals from China to immigrate to the United States. Three years later, Congress legislated against the immigration of contract labor, directed also against potential Chinese immigrants and Italians, though without explicitly naming either. From then on, Congress defined new categories of women and men as ineligible to immigrate, whether on the basis of class, gender and sexuality, physical and mental disability, or political affiliation. By the 1920s this restrictionist impulse reached its apogee with federal legislation that created a quota system for immigrants that was based on national origin. Congress ended the national origins quotas in 1965, but the new system it crafted placed numerical restrictions on immigration from the Western Hemisphere for the first time. After that year, government policies categorized newcomers in new ways, for instance for the first time declaring some to be refugees entitled to entry and others denied that label and barred from access.

As various states and then the federal government sought to regulate and sometimes restrict immigration, they created administrative and bureaucratic structures to oversee enforcement. The mechanisms of enforcement at times took on law enforcement or military trappings, as armed agents stood, often literally, at the borders. At other times, a web of courts and administrative bodies passed judgment on whether a newcomer could enter the United States. Finally, the United States, especially in the twentieth century, built what one historian has called "the deportation machine" to remove newcomers under a variety of political and legal pretexts.[3]

The changing role of local, state, and federal governments brought immigration squarely into the fractious realm of politics, parties, and public opinion, where it had been even in the pre–National period. The ways in which Americans, particularly native-born whites, responded to the new arrivals, and how these responses left their mark on political and public life, emerge as a theme in this book. In that history of politics, the public, and immigration, Americans have simultaneously welcomed and rejected, lauded and reviled immigrants. They have debated and divided over issues such as whether immigrants strengthen or harm, enrich or impoverish the nation. Could immigrants become American, and how and what did that mean? At different times, Irish, Chinese, Italians, and Mexicans loomed especially menacing in the popular imagination. Their sheer presence, according to some Americans, seemed to jeopardize the very nature of the social, cultural, and political order. Fear of these immigrants caused the American public and the state to respond with force.

The state played another noteworthy role in immigration: it took up the task of counting newcomers. But the seemingly straightforward assignment of noting who and how many arrived in the United States—and from where—was not such a simple proposition. Nor was it simple to determine how to label those newcomers. Were they refugees, immigrants, asylees, or nonimmigrant visitors, to name just a few of the bureaucratic categories that the federal government developed over the years?

Still, the federal government tried. In 1819 it began to require masters of ships carrying immigrants to the shores of the new nation to declare the number of immigrants they had carried across the Atlantic. But ship companies and captains fulfilled this obligation haphazardly, and federal officials only haphazardly enforced it. Moreover, the law did not specify clearly who was an immigrant and what that meant. Instead, information told essentially where ships had come from but little about where the individuals had lived before making the voyage. Later in the nineteenth century, with the opening of the immigrant-receiving stations at the ports of New York, Philadelphia, Boston, and elsewhere, figures became somewhat more reliable—but not completely so. For example, only women and men traveling in steerage and third class, the least expensive tickets, were listed as immigrants. Those whose family members already in the United States could afford to send them tickets for second-class accommodations were not counted as such. Some immigrants, then, eluded the attention of officials gathering the data at the ports of disembarkation. In the twentieth century, the federal government, and the public, became more concerned with unauthorized migration, but this raised a vexing question: how do you count individuals who are not supposed to be in the United States and who do not present themselves to border officials or census takers? The U.S. government and a variety of nongovernmental organizations devised statistical methods to estimate this unauthorized population, but these approaches are hardly infallible. Even good statistical estimates remain estimates, after all.

The federal government's reports and publications on immigration admit the sketchiness of the available numbers and the inability to truly answer questions about how many and from where. The *Historical Statistics of the United States*, issued by no less authoritative a body than the U.S. Census in 1949, reported that "since 1820," the first year after the passage of the Steerage Act, "official immigration statistics have changed considerably in completeness and in the basis of reporting," implying the incompleteness of the whole body of data.[4] For historians, then, guesswork, interpretation, and informed judgment calls have had as much to do with making sense of immigration statistics as do the official figures that we also rely on.

No history of immigration would be complete without thinking about the ongoing conversations between sending and receiving societies. Once immigrants settled in America, they sent back news and money, in the form of remittances, to family members who had stayed put. The information and funds fostered further migration as immigrants earmarked some part of their wages, no matter how paltry, to bring over loved ones to join them in America. In America they found ways to re-create elements of their old homes, albeit in new forms.

Not every newcomer stayed in the United States. Some immigrants returned to their places of origin. Some traveled back and forth, crossing borders repeatedly. Whether they went for brief visits or they hoped to settle down permanently in their home countries, they carried knowledge, goods, and often money from America. Those items and people traveled faster as technologies of communication and transportation improved, quickening the pace of immigration to the United States from across the globe. This dynamic relationship between sending and receiving countries and regions shaped every immigrant's experiences and the places they came to and from.

No sending-receiving relationship in American immigration history is more important than the one between the United States and Mexico. The migration history between the two countries, as much as the more familiar story of European migration, stands at the center of American immigration history. Large portions of what is now the United States belonged to Mexico until the mid-nineteenth century. The peoples of that region, whether "Mexican," "American," or indigenous, moved fairly freely across that territory, often in search of work, but also to visit and reunite with family. A unique American-Mexican-Native hybrid society developed that deeply influenced all aspects of life—and immigration. Those well-worn tracks continued into the twentieth century, as more Mexicans desired to come to the United States and as Americans sought to employ them. That migration grew even as the U.S. government began to guard and fortify its border with Mexico. The development of a more tangible border set in motion other dynamics, such as the bulking up of the Border Patrol, attention to a so-called illegal immigration problem, and new patterns of immigration and settlement that did much to shape culture in the United States.

All this also points to the global nature of the United States' immigration history. Immigration functioned as one very important way that the colonies, and then the United States, interacted with the rest of the world. United States diplomacy, military interventions, and foreign economic relations sometimes eased, sometimes impeded, and sometimes even sparked immigration to the United States. Unsurprisingly, the country's immigration history is deeply embedded in the country's history as a continental and overseas empire.

Building the American empire required disposing of Native Americans and then encouraging immigrants to repopulate and transform that territory. The United States' overseas holdings, won in the late nineteenth and early twentieth centuries, proved just as important. Individuals in those near and far-flung colonies and territories, such as Puerto Rico and the Philippines, entered more easily than they would have otherwise, taking advantage of their place in the American empire. But, as imperial subjects and racial minorities, these newcomers still found themselves in a subordinate position compared especially to European immigrants.

Thus, the history of immigration to America cannot be disassociated from the nation's long and abiding obsession with race, another theme of our narrative. The history of race and the changing definitions of that word for the most part fell along a white-nonwhite divide. Immigrants from Europe—from Ireland and Italy, the Balkans and the Baltics, the Austro-Hungarian and the czarist empires—encountered discrimination and endured ugly rhetoric that depicted them variously as criminal, ignorant, primitive, defective, and wild. But as people defined by law as white, they had access to citizenship and state protections. Even the harsh laws of the 1920s that assigned them low entry quotas allowed some, however limited the numbers, to enter the United States as legal immigrants and to pursue naturalization.

Not so women and men defined by the state as nonwhite. Millions sought to emigrate from a region designated in 1917 by Congress as the Asiatic Barred Zone, which defined these human beings as literally inadmissible. Race shaped the realities of immigration, but non-European, nonwhite immigrants nevertheless chose America. While aware of rampant racism, people from China, Japan, Korea, the Indian subcontinent, and the West Indies yearned to enter America, as its economic lure outweighed that painful knowledge. No doubt this history of racism, which continues to the present day, weighs heavily still on the minds of newcomers choosing to come to the United States. It also makes their prominence in contemporary immigration that much more remarkable. Indeed, if one considers European immigration the story of the eighteenth and nineteenth centuries, and Mexican immigration the story of the twentieth century, some recent trends point to immigration from Asia perhaps emerging as the story of the twenty-first century.

It behooves us to say something about what related and crucial topics this book will not include, although not including them does not deny their centrality to the American historical narrative. It will not explore ethnicity, the complex, multigenerational undertaking by which immigrants, and their descendants, built communities and fashioned novel cultural practices and identities in their new land. Other works have addressed this vital phenomenon in great detail, building careful histories of how immigrant communities took root and were transformed over time in the United States. This book for the most part stops at the point of arrival and earliest settlement, focusing most intently on the comings, and sometimes goings, of various newcomers and the economic forces, political structures, and familial and personal imperatives that attracted them. We do consider how elements of ethnic culture, such as immigrant institutions in the United States, facilitated further movement of family, friends, and others from home communities. In that vein, we pay attention to immigrant aid societies, religious groups, ethnic banks, and cultural and legal institutions that welcomed and sheltered their new arrivals.

Additionally, *Immigration: An American History* explores the experiences of the women and men who had some ability to shape their own migrations. The people whose stories appear here exercised a degree of agency as they faced difficulties and dwindling opportunities. They not only chose to emigrate, but often could determine when to go, how, and where. In many, but not all, instances, they could determine which family members went, in what order and combination, if others would follow, and who among them. That some decided to return home also reveals that they exercised an element of control over their own circumstances. Not all these immigrants had the same degree of agency, of course. Women and children often had fewer opportunities to participate in these discussions about immigration choices, and they had fewer choices about where and when to go, how to get there, and how to resettle. The same limitations held for immigrants of color and those from the Global South, as well as individuals fleeing political, religious, or social persecution who probably and accurately felt they had too little control over their migration choices. Achut Deng, the refugee from Sudan via Kenya and Ethiopia, embodies the complicated, historically contingent hierarchy of immigrant agency that is a key component of the book. Deng had limited choices about where she might go, but she could choose among some options or she might have remained put, no matter how difficult that environment. Moreover, once in the United States, she could move to a new locale, as she did by finding her way to South Dakota.

By telling the story of what scholars used to call "voluntary immigrants," we purposely do not include the millions of Africans who arrived in North America as slaves. Their story, and that of their ancestors, might be the most fundamental one to U.S. history. But a bright and stark distinction separates the compelled migrations of the enslaved from the movement with some choice of the immigrants. Slavers forcibly and violently removed Africans from homes and families. Enslaved Africans had no choice about whether to go or to remain, no choice about timing or destination or transport, nor obviously could they choose to return or move to a new location, whether in the United States or elsewhere. These individuals lacked even the circumscribed options of Achut Deng and others from Africa, the Caribbean, or the larger global Black diaspora, starting in the late nineteenth century and continuing into the twenty-first. They after all chose the United States, while the enslaved, by virtue of their forced migration, had no choices.

At the heart of this book, as the title declares, lies the drama of immigration to America, told through the stories of women and men from the seventeenth through the twenty-first centuries who decided that their homes held out little for them and that America offered them opportunities unavailable if they stayed put. It circumnavigates the globe, starting in a small corner of the north Atlantic, and ultimately spans the planet to include people from every habitable continent. These women and men, after weighing and balancing their life chances at home, immigrated to America. Once there, they created a country and shaped a nation.

Further Reading

We will conclude the chapters that follow with a short "Further Reading" section that identifies some key scholarly works addressing that time period. For this introduction, though, we offer some vital primary sources that we hope prove helpful to our audience.

Center for History and New Media. *Bracero History Archive.* http://bracero archive.org.

Center for Jewish History. https://www.cjh.org.

Densho Digital Repository. http://ddr.densho.org.

Department of Homeland Security. *Yearbook of Immigration Statistics.* https:// www.dhs.gov/immigration-statistics/yearbook and https://catalog.hathi trust.org/Record/002973860.

Ellis Island Foundation. *Ellis Island Passenger Search.* https://heritage.statueof liberty.org/passenger.

Harper's Weekly (anti-immigrant cartoons). https://www.harpweek.com/ 09Cartoon/SelectThemeReturn.asp?Theme=Theme&TopicID=119 &Topic=Irish%20Americans and https://immigrants.harpweek.com/ Default.htm.

Museum of Chinese in America. https://www.mocanyc.org.

National Park Service. *Ellis Island Virtual Tour.* https://www.nps.gov/hdp/ exhibits/ellis/Ellis_Index.html?html5=prefer.

ProPublica and WNYC. "The Waiting Game," April 23, 2018. https://projects .propublica.org/asylum/.

University of Minnesota. *Digitizing Immigrant Letters.* https://ihrca.dash.umn .edu/dil/.

University of Washington Libraries. *South Asian Oral History Project.* https:// content.lib.washington.edu/saohcweb/index.html.

U.S. Census Bureau. *Statistical Abstracts of the United States, 1878–2012.* https:// www.census.gov/library/publications/time-series/statistical_abstracts .html.

CHAPTER ONE

Founding Immigrants

Seventeenth- and Eighteenth-Century America

JOHN HARROWER, FORTY YEARS old, a shopkeeper in Lerwick in Scotland's Shetland Islands, lamented the growing poverty and withering possibilities for making a living at home. He left his family to search out work, setting off in January 1774 for London. With no clear plan, he considered himself "like a blind man without a guide." He wandered the capital city, hitting dead ends everywhere he turned. "Being reduced" to his "last shilling," he happened upon a friend who offered advice that changed everything. Find a ship sailing across the Atlantic, his friend suggested, and then locate the agent of someone from any of Britain's colonies in North America who would pay his fare in exchange for some set years of service.

In a letter he sent home and also copied into his diary, he wrote, "I . . . was obliged to engage to go to Virginia for four years as a schoolmaster for Bedd, Board, washing and five pounds during the whole time." Along with seventy-one other men, all with indenture certificates in hand, he boarded a ship, sailed the ocean, and, upon landing safely, began his American life as a tutor for the sons of a Colonel Daingerfield, owner of an estate, Belvidera, near Fredericksburg.[1]

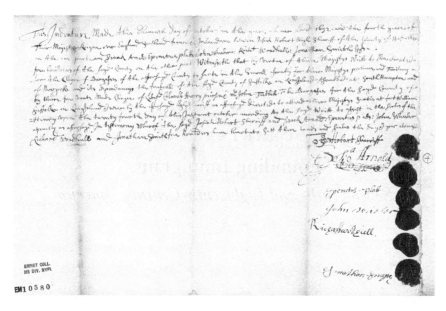

Indenture contract, 1692. New York Public Library, New York.

The details and tone of John Harrower's story would have resonated with the hundreds of thousands from Scotland, Ireland,
Wales, England, and various German-speaking regions who joined
the emigration to any one of Britain's thirteen North American colonies. His descriptions of the dangers he faced and the risks he took
would have echoed in their experiences.

Crowding and poor sanitation during the eight- to twelve-week
journey spawned high levels of onboard mortality. Scurvy and dys-
entery ran rampant. Storms at sea during the sailings, which typically commenced during the summer, cast many ships into the ocean
waters. Immigrants brought their own supplies. No shipping lines
existed with published schedules, or fixed sailing dates and prices.
Sometimes groups consisting of people who knew each other, or
just of individuals who met while congregating for weeks on end at
the ports, negotiated with ship captains, haggling over the cost of
the trip.

Despite the difficulties, from the seventeenth century until
the American Revolution in 1776, men first, then women joining
them, learned that they could remake their lives in America. With

little settlement policy directed by the Crown or Parliament, they peopled the territory between the Atlantic Seaboard and the eastern edge of the Appalachian Mountains, the founding beachhead of the United States.

Different Empires, Different Settlement Policies

As the territory occupied by the United States expanded piecemeal, it incorporated the descendants of women and men who had immigrated to North America through imperial projects launched by Spain, France, and the Netherlands. These European nations believed that they, like Britain, had the right to conquer and occupy territory where Native peoples lived, using the land of others to enrich themselves. They too sent over administrators, clergy, military, and settlers. All these European nations engaged in settler colonialism, deliberately populating spaces on which others had lived with their own people, to do the bidding of their empires.

Britain's North American colonies resembled these. But differences existed. Europeans, regardless of religion or place of origin, who wanted and had necessary funds to immigrate to Britain's North American colonies could do so. The other empires fostered more organized, state-directed, and selective settlement programs than the British, who cared little about who settled and where so long as they worked, did not cost the state much, and participated in the common defense. The British approach left many policies undefined, which allowed administrators in America and investors to decide much about immigration.[2]

The other empires pursued more restrictive policies, whether in Mexico, French Canada, New Netherlands, Florida, or the other colonies. State authorities in Madrid, Paris, and Amsterdam exerted greater authority than their London equivalents. In 1685, for example, King Louis XIV promulgated the Code Noir, banning all non-Catholics from settling in any of France's colonies, and expelled the few Jews there. The Spanish Empire, based in Mexico and extending through the southwestern region of the future United States, transported the Inquisition to the New World to root out Jews, former Jews known as *conversos* or *marranos*, and other non-Catholics.

Dutch officials in New Amsterdam wanted to expel a group of twenty-three Jews who arrived in 1654; though the Dutch West Indies Company, which governed the colony, objected, it denied Jews the right of public worship or trading outside the city in the larger New Netherlands. Ten years later the British took over, renamed the colony New York, and wiped out the restrictions.

Encouraging Immigration and
Doing Nothing to Discourage It

Britain's policy did not reflect an ideology of tolerance or a belief in pluralism. It put profits first, placing few obstacles in the way of individuals who got themselves over the ocean and worked. Individuals contemplating immigrating to British North America, like John Harrower, never dealt with state officials, negotiating instead on their own with shipowners and the agents of colonial employers.

British policy makers valued emigration as a way to syphon off young people, individuals and families whose increasing poverty might cause them to become troublesome at home and render them financial burdens on their communities. Those same women and men, once residing in North America, would produce goods and services to benefit the empire.

The British state did try to play some role in the emigration process, although never consistently or rigorously. Potential emigrants had to get permission from local authorities to leave, and British officials from the onset demanded that Englishmen going to the colonies promise to remain loyal. In the 1630s immigrants sailing from Bristol had to show papers signed by a member of the clergy, attesting to their good character.

At various times, officials in some British towns collaborated with immigration recruiters, allowing them to pluck men and women out of prison and ship them off to the colonies. This worked for the recruiters who got paid by how many bodies they brought over and for the town officials who no longer had to provide for the prisoners. It was a practice unpopular among the British residents of the colonies, and local Virginia officials in 1697 refused to allow the docking of convict transport ships. Parliament, however, saw the matter differently and wanted the practice to continue. In 1718 it enacted the Transportation Act, which sought to create a more rational approach to keep the system alive. In the three-quarters of a century culminating in 1775, over 20,000 felons disembarked in Virginia.

The groundswell for immigration grew with economic changes in Britain. Growing numbers of people could not adjust to economic changes brought about by early industrialization and the demise of common grazing lands that had existed for centuries. True, some immigrants came from England's better-off classes. A small coterie received patents or grants of land from the Crown, many of whom settled in the southern colonies. They became the owners of plantations. They then recruited larger numbers of poorer women and men who negotiated labor contracts and immigrated to America, hoping to achieve a more livable life.

The story of America in the centuries under British rule constitutes an immigration story. Everyone of European background owed their lives in America to immigrant origins, whether their own, their parents', or their grandparents'. All exercised a degree of choice in their decision to opt for the British colonies of North America. Even convicts, at times, had a choice, inasmuch as judges and other carceral personnel offered them the option of going to America or languishing in prison.

Some small numbers came as members of religious communities, emigrating together, including Calvinists bound for Massachusetts, Quakers who went to Pennsylvania, and French Huguenots who built communities in New York, New Jersey, and the Carolinas, joined there by German Pietists and Anabaptists. But even they considered the economic promise of America.

Colonial officials, investors, wealthy landowners, ship captains, importers, and exporters on both sides of the Atlantic all had a keen interest in bringing over, by whatever means, streams of men and women to the colonies, ensuring that those who arrived worked. But as more people left their homes and settled in the North American colonies, the more attractive life became there. An idea spread throughout Europe of America as a place where persons of humble means could, despite uncertainties, end their lives more comfortably situated than when they had started out. Though embodying a common story across the long history of immigration, this era presented some distinctive characteristics.

The Native Peoples of North America and the Immigrants Who Met Them

Colonial-era immigration differed from that of later eras because of the proximity and active presence of multiple nations of Native peoples, erroneously called Indians by Europeans. Native peoples lived on and defended territory that Britain claimed as its domain and opened up for immigrant settlement. European newcomers understood that they had migrated to a vast battle zone, punctuated by sporadic fighting, sparked by Native peoples' resistance to the loss of their homelands. Fear of attack hung over the immigrants' heads, particularly in the seventeenth century and beyond that in the western fringes of the colonies.

That danger influenced policies enacted by colonial officials as they considered immigration recruiting. Decision makers, particularly locally elected representatives, believed that planting immigrant settlements in the western regions of the colonies could subdue the Native population by inhabiting the territory between seaboard port cities and the farms and towns closer to the coast and the deeper interior. Pennsylvania officials considered Protestant immigrants from Ulster, the northern part of Ireland, particularly suited for life in the far western mountainous region. Colonial elites in Philadelphia, adherents to the pacifist Quaker faith, could not themselves pick up arms to fight the Leni-Lenape, Iroquois, Tuscarora, and others. But they wanted others to go to the frontier, work, and stave off Indian attacks. They encouraged the Ulster newcomers, people not burdened by such religious principles, as perfect buffers.

Immigrants came from a variety of places; Englishwomen and Englishmen made up the dominant core, although the label *English* obscured premigration differences. Most English immigrants who went to the northern colonies of New England starting in the middle of the seventeenth century emigrated from East Anglia, while those who opted for Virginia hailed from the south of England.

Many English immigrants bound for the middle colonies, like Delaware, originated in England's Midlands, whereas at the end of the seventeenth century immigrants from the north of England and the Celtic fringe went to the backcountry at the edge of the Appalachian Mountains. Each brought distinctive foodways, modes of agriculture, marriage patterns, language, accents, religious practices, and architectural styles for houses and barns.[3]

The Importance of Place: The Northern Colonies

Immigrants in this period as in later centuries moved along family and kinship chains, favoring particular destinations over others. Each region had its own immigrant mix.

The more northern British colonies attracted the least varied immigrant pool. Massachusetts, New Hampshire, Rhode Island, and Connecticut consisted primarily of people from England, as well as some from Wales, Scotland, and Ulster, known as Scotch-Irish. Though they hailed from the British Isles, they did not identify as English. Immigrants from England, likewise, did not consider that they all shared a common place of origin. Non-English immigrants constituted about 30 percent of the population of the region that in the eighteenth century came to be known, perhaps accurately, as New England.

The initial immigrants to Massachusetts and the other northern colonies, small independent farmers whose descendants would become America's elite, came primarily from East Anglia. Their decision to immigrate starting in the 1620s reflected the pressures of overpopulation, the enclosure of common lands, and escalating land prices, which prevented young men from settling down as farmers and young women from marrying. This first immigrant generation paid its own fare. Few arrived as indentured servants. Some single women who immigrated worked briefly in domestic service, then married men who owned their own small farms.[4]

America's national narrative, consumed most powerfully every November at Thanksgiving, focuses on the Pilgrims, who called themselves Separatists and arrived in Plymouth in 1620. It depicts them as seekers of religious freedom, not as economically motivated immigrants. So, too, American collective memory has described the settlement of New England in general as driven by religiously motivated Puritans who chose the rigors of Massachusetts over persecution in England.

But that story defies historical fact. The 20,000 or so who arrived in Massachusetts between 1628 and 1642 came under the aegis of a royal charter, granted to the Massachusetts Bay Company. Attracted to a place graced with a fine natural harbor, these people of middling economic circumstances from southwestern England gambled like others that despite many difficulties, migration to America offered greater economic prospects than staying put.

The place to which they moved shaped the region's colonial-era migrations. Its relatively poor, rocky soil kept farms from expanding dramatically. They needed few nonfamily laborers. Nonfarming enterprises such as coastal water fishing also did not require sizable pools of workers. Those colonies invested little in immigrant recruiting.

Full families migrated. Women and men arrived in relatively equal numbers. Populations grew steadily as the region enjoyed relatively low mortality and high fertility. The bumper crops of children born and surviving infancy then labored alongside parents, doing work that elsewhere depended on laborers. Some sons inherited parents' farms and married, while non-inheritors pressed farther west, looking for cheap or even free land, on which Mohegans and Wampanoag lived.

Immigration to this region continued modestly after the initial Great Migration of the 1620s and 1630s. Nearly all newcomers came as East Anglian chain migrants, relatives and townspeople of those men and women already living there, so the ethnic makeup changed little with time.

The Mid-Atlantic

The mid-Atlantic colonies of New York, New Jersey, and Pennsylvania attracted the greatest number and variety of immigrants. In 1700 fewer than half of the residents of New York and New Jersey, and less than one-quarter of Pennsylvanians, traced their lineage to

England. Micro-regions of the mid-Atlantic drew from women and men who had come from the Netherlands, Ulster, other parts of Ireland, France, and, in Pennsylvania in particular, certain German states and created scattered enclaves.[5]

The mid-Atlantic became such a powerful immigrant magnet in part because the key Atlantic ports, New York, Philadelphia, and Baltimore, served as gateways for merchants, craftsmen, and seamen from all over Europe. Though Italian immigration to the United States would not commence until centuries later, some handful of Italian speakers already lived in New Amsterdam even before it became New York in 1664, and Philadelphia housed a small Italian community on the eve of the American Revolution.

Though mid-Atlantic cities boasted multiple immigrant communities, most immigrants moved west to the hinterlands. The second quarter of the eighteenth century saw the largest influx of German and Dutch newcomers: 80,000 arrived between 1710 and 1775 and spread out in the interior from the port of Philadelphia. By the 1750s immigrants from German states made up almost one-third of Pennsylvania's population.

Emigrants from southwestern Germany's Rhine Valley and others from Switzerland and the Low Countries participated in a vast global migration. American recruiters actively sought them out. News of America spread among family and friends as those already working in Pennsylvania or any of the mid-Atlantic colonies wrote home, stimulating a vigorous flow across the Atlantic. Referred to as "the frivolous itch of emigration," this movement outward concerned local officials in some eighteenth-century German states, who worried that as more left, particularly the young and able-bodied, the more restive those who remained would become. Although they hoped to do so, government officials could do little to restrain those yearning for *Bintzel-vannier,* what they called Pennsylvania. That powerful "itch" inspired some hopeful immigrants to create formal immigration societies to collectively handle the many details involved.[6]

Most new immigrants to the middle colonies moved beyond the coast, finding cheap and fertile land, perfect for small family farms that could grow and prosper. Many who started as indentured servants became owners of comfortable, even profitable farms. One of these immigrants dubbed Pennsylvania "the best poor man's country."[7]

Immigrants, regardless of place of origin, could work for someone else, pay back the fare, and transition to independent farming. Indenture contracts offered cash or land in exchange for completing the term of service, and, once liberated from employment, the immigrant could take the cash and move farther west to cheaper land. Few became wealthy, but families could achieve landownership and better living.[8]

Even less expensive, often free, land existed in the backcountry. Between 1700 and 1775, 200,000 immigrants, mostly Protestants from Ulster, flocked to Pennsylvania. Substantial numbers spread farther south to Virginia and the Carolinas. They gravitated to the foothills of the Appalachian region, and some over time even penetrated the mountains themselves. Originally known simply as Irish, in later centuries they called themselves Scotch-Irish to distinguish themselves from the Catholic Irish who arrived in massive numbers in the mid-nineteenth century.

These immigrants might be considered the quintessential frontier people, the first European occupants of a zone of land that at the end of the nineteenth century the historian Frederick Jackson Turner would pinpoint as the central space of American history and culture, the "meeting point between savagery and civilization." According to Turner, newcomers from Ireland, poor and landless upon arrival, gave America its national character, bequeathing it with its "coarseness and strength combined with acuteness and acquisitiveness." Turner asserted that these immigrants originated Americans' fierce commitment to individualism.[9]

More than others, Ulster immigrants came into direct contact and conflict with Native peoples. They fought the Indians, defenders of their homelands, engaging in battle from New Hampshire to Carolina. In Pennsylvania they fought against the Iroquois, pressing the ruling Philadelphia Quakers for more resources to subdue the enemy. Ulster frontiersmen also served as middlemen in the highly lucrative global trade in pelts and timber and in land negotiations between merchants in the east and the various Native nations. These transactions, handled by Scots-Irish immigrants, produced great profits for London business interests.

Backcountry Ulster immigrants also shaped American independence. They smarted from King George III's decision to limit western expansion beyond the crest of the Appalachian Mountains. The Proclamation of 1763 banned settlement in the territory Britain had won from France during the French and Indian War (1754–1763). Considering that it infringed on their freedom, these immigrant residents of the backcountry rallied against it. The Declaration of Independence listed this as one grievance against the king.

Immigrants to the Southern Colonies

A line ran through the southern colonies, dividing them into upper and lower regions, both with distinctive immigration histories. The upper colonies included Maryland and Virginia, while Georgia, and both North and South Carolina, which had been a single colony until 1712, constituted the lower ones. Neither attracted many non-English immigrants. Relatively few from outside England chose the South.

Immigrants to the Upper South divided unequally between the second and third sons of British aristocrats, called "Cavaliers," who made up the small elite, and a much larger population of indentured servants. The latter far outnumbered the former, and by the American Revolution, they and their immediate descendants made up over 75 percent of the southern population. They shared premigration geographic origins with their social and economic betters, but in so many other ways they differed.

The elite, adherents to the Church of England and supporters of the royalists, came first. Many fled England in the 1650s, the period of Puritan rule under Oliver Cromwell. They sat at the top of the Upper South's social, political, and economic hierarchy, having seized the most fertile swathes of land in the Tidewater region. They established large holdings on valuable acreage astride transportation routes along the region's rivers. They grew the region's single crop that defined and shaped it, tobacco.

As early as the 1620s, Chesapeake planters in Virginia and Maryland began cultivating the "stinking weed," selling it in England to an increasingly addicted public. Tobacco rapidly depleted the soil.

Growers needed to expand their holdings on new, fertile soil, which then called for an ever-expanding labor force. That call determined the region's history.

The importation of Africans commenced in 1619. The first did not come as chattel slaves, but as indentured servants, but that changed by the middle of the seventeenth century. As of the 1680s the system of perpetual, hereditary slavery took root, whereby skin color was the defining line between freedom and enslavement.

Planters in Virginia, Maryland, and Carolina also hoped to recruit in England, preferring white workers with contracts. Between 1619 and 1680 about 5,000 men and a few women, the first of whom disembarked in Williamsburg in 1619, arrived at the request of Edwyn Sandys, treasurer of the Virginia Company. Most of the immigrants came via the port of Bristol, having been recruited by Chesapeake landowners. The number of relatively poor English people willing to emigrate as indentured servants bound for Virginia and Maryland declined in the 1660s in reaction to news that land values in these colonies had climbed so high that servants, when their service ended, could not expect to become economically comfortable landowners.

Those who wanted to leave England turned instead to remote areas of Pennsylvania and the Carolinas, leaving the Chesapeake's tobacco-growing elite with a critical labor shortage, which in turn made the forced importation of Africans more attractive. By the latter decades of the seventeenth century perpetual, hereditary slavery for Africans became the norm, and skin color provided southern society's essential cleavage. For white European immigrants, regardless of poverty level, employers' harshness, arduousness of work, length remaining on their contracts, and even place of origin, whiteness meant everything.

Colonial officials accepted and even looked for non-English immigrants. A handful of German colonies sprang up in Virginia and Carolina. In 1712 and 1714 Governor Alexander Spotswood of Virginia invited some German speakers to the colony's frontier region both to serve as defenders against local Indians allied with the French and to develop an ironworks. Spotswood named the unsuccessful colony Germanna.

Few Germans found the region attractive. Like other Europeans, they recognized that, unable to compete with the large-scale planters who enslaved their workers, they could never experience meaningful mobility. As African slavery became a fundamental regional institution, European immigrants avoided the South.

The Lower South proved somewhat more alluring to white immigrants. English immigrants steadily immigrated there, and they and their children accounted for just under half the population by 1750. Scots-Irish, Scots from the Highland region, and French Huguenots settled in South Carolina, along with English immigrants who had lived previously in various British colonies in the Caribbean, particularly Barbados. A contingent of Jews of Spanish and Portuguese background opted for South Carolina and Georgia, forming communities in Savannah and Charleston.

These immigrants gravitated to those two port cities. With economies based on the lucrative Atlantic trade that linked Europe, North America, Africa, the Caribbean, and the rest of the world, Charleston and Savannah offered opportunities to newcomers with capital, appropriate skills, and business contacts.

The hinterland areas did not begin to draw in immigrants until the middle decades of the eighteenth century. Once settled on small farms, they grew foodstuff to feed the Tidewater plantations, which concentrated on regional cash crops, rice, indigo, and tobacco.

Georgia's founding provides an illustrative colonial-era immigration story. In the 1730s James Oglethorpe, a retired British army officer, appalled by the hordes of poor people roaming London's streets and then landing in debtors' prisons, formulated a plan to found a North American colony. He would name it for the newly crowned King George III and settle it with men and some women who might prefer America over an English jail. He sold the king on the idea of Georgia as a buffer between South Carolina and Native peoples, who lived close by on territory occupied by the empires of Spain, to the south in Florida, and France, based in Louisiana and beyond, along the Mississippi River. Oglethorpe and the colony's trustees envisioned American life transforming poor English debtors into hardworking, self-reliant farmers. The founders banned rice cultivation, alcohol consumption, and the importation and use of African slaves, believing that slavery made white men lazy. Though the ban lasted less than a decade, Oglethorpe's efforts transported the debtors and stimulated other migrations. Officials of London's Bevis Marks Synagogue, concerned about poor Polish Jews flooding England, convinced Oglethorpe to take some of their charity cases to America as well; thus was created Savannah's Jewish community. Oglethorpe established a village outside Savannah for German Lutherans and welcomed French Huguenots during the colony's first years.

Cities and the Backcountry

Savannah and Charleston, like the other three large Atlantic coast cities—New York, Philadelphia, and Newport, Rhode Island—experienced immigration differently from the hinterlands. In the port cities workers loaded the backcountry's lumber, fur, agricultural products, and mineral riches onto oceangoing vessels, bound mostly for England. On their return journeys, those ships brought finished goods and people, immigrants and slaves. The port cities (the predominantly English Boston an exception) attracted immigrants from a wide geographic net.

Jews also came to the five cities with immigrant populations. Made up of two distinct populations, they differed from the overwhelmingly Christian majority. Jews of Spanish and Portuguese background, Sephardim, whose families had previously migrated to Amsterdam, London, and the West Indies, came first. Valued by the colonial elite for the extensive global trade they pursued with kin around the world, these merchants dominated the Jewish communities. But the majority of colonial-era Jews came from German-speaking lands, including parts of the defunct Kingdom of Poland annexed by Prussia. These Ashkenazim, meaning Germans, supported themselves as artisans and small-scale shopkeepers. Both gained rights and respect beyond those of their coreligionists back home.

In these cities, all relatively small in physical size, immigrants from different places lived near each other and had to interact. They did not create dense enclaves. Rather, the city streets resounded with multiple languages. Women and men, immigrants from many places, lived cheek-by-jowl, needing to accommodate each other and the English. Artisans, operators of small businesses serving the broad public, and domestic servants, they needed English to communicate with employers, customers, and coworkers. Urban life fostered Anglicization at the same time that individual immigrant populations fashioned their community institutions, churches in particular.

The backcountry and rural areas differed in terms of immigrant commingling. From north to south, immigrants from Ulster, Scotland, and the German-speaking lands formed relatively separate communities. Here people from particular towns and regions back home clustered close to each other, keeping alive language, diet, and religion, living somewhat isolated from others.[10]

But wherever immigrants of this era settled, city, country, or frontier, they did not have to appeal to or curry favor with a long-resident population that claimed roots that lay deep in the soil. North America's longest residents, the Native people, did not constitute an elite wherever they came from and had to beg for permission to settle. Though privilege and class mattered greatly in differentiating some immigrants from others, those who came first and gained access to the most resources acknowledged their dependence on immigrants and helped enable their arrival.

As in other settler societies born of European colonialism, immigrants to British North America removed by whatever means they could the people who had lived there for millennia. Their approach fully consistent with the ideology of the age, these foreigners came to America, defined it as theirs, and pushed away anyone blocking them, making this immigration era different from later ones. Likewise, the nature of work and patterns of labor rendered it distinctive.

Labor and Immigration: From Free to Bonded

Fewer than half of the immigrants came freely, in the sense that they were not bonded to someone else upon arrival. A tiny fraction had been well-off before migration, but most were not. Those migrating as families generally paid their own fares and came with no obligation to an employer or ship captain. Many of these headed for

New England, but every colony attracted some able to fund their own journeys and with enough money to allow them to immediately strike out on their own as farmers, artisans, or entrepreneurs. Able to take advantage of local economic opportunities, and with wives, husbands, and children all contributing to the project of making a better living in America than they could at home, they really could prosper as immigrants in the new place.

At the other end of the spectrum, Africans arrived as involuntary laborers, shackled to their employers, referred to as "owners." Having experienced the harrowing ordeal of capture, they endured transportation across the ocean, undergoing the harrowing Middle Passage. They took their first American steps in some Caribbean island, such as Jamaica, where planters "seasoned them." From there slavers transported them to the mainland of British North America. Sold at auction and unprotected by contract, they worked in every colony, and in places even as far north as Rhode Island they outnumbered white bonded laborers. Everywhere they shaped economic realities. Many northern farmers, fishermen, shipbuilders, and artisans derived their livelihoods, whether growing crops, running households, or manufacturing goods, on the backs of the enslaved.

That system created a society that linked being nonwhite to a lack of freedom and whiteness to freedom. But freedom existed along a spectrum. In some colonies, at times, the law put white immigrant indentured servants and enslaved Africans on the same footing, yet even the least-free white immigrants derived some modicum of legal protection from their whiteness, their contract, which fixed the term of their service, and the conditions of their immigration.

As early as the 1610s and extending to the Revolution, England offered some convicts the choice of remaining in prison at home or transportation to North America. This freed local communities from the expense of housing and feeding prisoners, and it reflected new ideas about punishment, the possibilities for rehabilitation under better circumstances, and the critical shortage of laborers in the colonies. About 50,000 convicts, imprisoned mostly for petty property thefts, unpaid debts, or subversive activities, agreed to go to America, hoping for physical freedom and economic improvement.

Some other immigrants crossed the ocean by less than voluntary means. Ship captains, eager to fill their vessels with bodies, hired kidnappers to pluck unsuspecting men out of taverns or off streets. Local authorities in England, disturbed by hordes of vagrants clogging the roads, allowed merchants to round them up and dump them on ships bound for the colonies.

But most chose to go, considering life in the colonies a reasonable choice. Reservoirs of men and women in England, elsewhere in the British Isles, and the German-speaking lands decided that only a new place would allow them to support themselves. Mostly young, they could not afford to marry or, if married, could not sustain their families. Disadvantaged by powerful economic upheavals that undercut long-standing ways of making a living, and rising birth rates, swelling numbers of people responded to spreading knowledge of American possibilities, immigrating through labor recruiting.

The colonies' need for labor fueled their decisions. Immigrants got their fares paid and had work waiting for them upon arrival. Earning no money while in service, they knew that upon the contracts' completion, employers had to compensate them. The indenture contract detailed the required work and stipulated the employer's obligations, specifying how much food, the kind of shelter, and other necessities he promised to provide. The law protected both parties, although punishments faced by servants who ran away or did not fulfill their chores far exceeded those handed down to employers who stinted on food or reneged on payment.

Most British immigrants arrived with contract in hand, knowing in advance the name of the employer and the terms of service. Parliament passed several pieces of legislation that theoretically, at least, spared them the many abuses faced by other, non-British immigrants. Those coming from Europe, particularly from German-speaking lands in the eighteenth century, came as redemptioners. With no legal contract and unprotected by British legislation, these immigrants indebted themselves to shippers who brought them over. They negotiated the terms of employment only after landing. Potential employers gathered at the docks, hiring workers as they disembarked, then taking them away. The immigrant had to work to first pay off, or redeem, the cost of the fare.

Shipowners held much power in this process, and abuses were rampant. An immigrant might arrive with a promise of work, but if the employer failed to show up at the dock, the captain could sell him off to the highest bidder. The newcomers stood on auction blocks, naked, inspected, and judged for their ability to work.

German-speaking men, once established in America, turned to these same companies to bring over wives, sons, daughters, and other relatives, agreeing to pay the fares. The shippers attempted to wring as much profit as they could from this travel-now-pay-later system of transporting human cargo to America.

Free and self-financed immigrants, enslaved and compelled Africans, and quasi-free indentured servants and redemptioners did colonial work. Except for the few company and government administrators stationed temporarily in the colonies, all who lived in British North America owed their presence to a demand for workers to generate profits, a goal of the British colonial project.

Colonial Immigration and Global Politics

Beyond providing a source of labor for the colonies, immigrants fit into Britain's global political strategy. Some of its North American colonies bordered on territories flying the flags of rival empires. Immigrants in the northern reaches of Massachusetts, New Hampshire, and Vermont lived at the edge of the French Empire, while those in Georgia had the Spanish colony of Florida as a neighbor. These empires vied with Britain for dominance all over the world. The immigrants to British North America, whether from England, from other parts of Great Britain, Ireland, or Scotland, or from German-speaking lands, had to defend British interests.

Spanish and French colonial practices differed from those of the British. While they did recruit immigrants for their colonies, such as New France, they did so less actively or extensively than the British. At the same time, they worked more ably with Native peoples, stimulating less hostility than the British, who considered immigration a solution to problems of poverty, displacement, religious dissent, political dissent, overpopulation, and mass incarceration at home.

The various Indian nations in turn had fewer reasons to fear the French and the Spanish. The British encroached on Indians' lands, felled their forests, established towns and villages, and turned hunting grounds into farmlands for permanent settlement. The French and Spanish governments viewed their North American colonies more as places from which to extract natural resources, which demanded more positive relationships with indigenous peoples. The French and Spanish colonies witnessed higher levels of intermarriage between European men and Native women, a practice that created a different dynamic from that which characterized the British zone.[11]

British administrators and investors worried constantly about Indian attacks, sure that the French and Spanish deliberately armed the Indians, who engaged in local wars to defend themselves against British settlement. The welcome extended to the women and men of Ulster, viewed by the English as primitive, wild, and warlike, reflected a desire to populate the frontier with white people ready and able to fight the Indians, equipped with weapons by Britain's rivals.

Immigrants to British North America experienced four major colonial wars, starting in the 1680s and extending until the 1760s, including the French and Indian War, known also as the Seven Years' War, from 1754 to 1763. Such struggles flared around the world during this era as European nations, using their economic and military forces, confronted each other on nearly every continent.

While most of this struggle for empire involved three nations, England, France, and Spain, other empires also participated in the colonization of North America, planting settlements and peopling them with immigrants. Both the Netherlands and Sweden, for example, scrambled to conquer an area along the Delaware River. Dutch families along with Swedes, a majority from Finland, took up land in the 1630s around what would become Wilmington, Delaware. Though neither the Dutch nor the Swedes could compete with the British for the possession of North America, their brief competition demonstrated the importance of immigrants to European imperial dreams.

An episode from the 1650s shows how imperial concerns affected immigrant settlement. In 1654 a small group of Jews who had lived in Recife, in northern Brazil, fled north when Portugal seized control from the Dutch. Unable and unwilling to live under this Catholic power, which in the previous century had expelled the Jews, twenty-three of them fled north to New Amsterdam. The Jews enjoyed protection and prosperity in Dutch colonies like

Suriname, Curaçao, and Recife before the Portuguese arrived, and they expected to be welcomed in another of their colonies. Instead, Peter Stuyvesant, the governor general, refused them for religious reasons, as he considered Jews blasphemers, deniers of Christ, and members of an "accursed race," as well as for security reasons. He fretted over their Iberian origins, considering them potential spies or agents of the rival Spanish. The Dutch West India Company, which owned the colony, instructed Stuyvesant to allow them to stay but denied Jewish men the right to serve in the guard, again questioning their loyalty.

The story highlights the ways immigration in the colonial period reflected the worldwide European race for colonies. People shifted among the colonies, but usually within an empire, however far-flung. Many white people from England who immigrated to South Carolina came there from Barbados and other British Caribbean locales. Some Huguenots settled first in Nova Scotia, under British rule, and then made their way to New York, New Jersey, Delaware, and Virginia.

Transatlantic immigration entered the strategy of British imperial policy makers. The backers of the colonies, encouraged by the government, which gave investors a fairly free hand in peopling the colonies, believed that extensive agriculture, fur trapping, foresting, and mining would ensure a victory in the global scramble for riches and empire. Britain calculated that it would secure the greatest wealth and establish dominion over the largest possible territory by settling its North American colonies with people to work and fight. Although authorities in London preferred English immigrants, they simply could not find enough of those whom they desired, and they therefore began to scan a wider geography to find people to settle the land, form frontier outposts, produce wealth, and defend the empire.

The French and Indian War demonstrated how immigration patterns formed over the course of the previous century affected the global politics of England and its rival France. France's North American empire, centered primarily in Canada, had fewer than 60,000 settlers, almost exclusively French Catholics. Britain's mainland colonies boasted a population of approximately 2 million residents, of diverse premigration backgrounds. The French relied heavily on allied Indian nations to fight for them—hence the war's name—alongside the regular French army, a force stretched thin around the globe. The British fought with contingents of local men, originally from Scotland, Ulster, and the European continent. These American soldiers of diverse backgrounds fought primarily under the command of their own officers, such as the Virginian George Washington.

England won the war, expelled France from Canada, and vastly augmented its North American territory. The military victory altered administrative and fiscal policies, as the Crown and Parliament demanded greater control over colonial affairs. The colonists increasingly saw themselves as Americans, having formed a new identity that combined identification with the places they or their progenitors had come from and their diverse religious backgrounds.

Religion and Immigration

Religion shaped this era's immigration. Some advocates of immigration hoped that it would help spread Christianity among the Native peoples. As early as the sixteenth century a proponent of British colonization, Richard Hakluyt, predicted that if thriving English colonies cropped up in North America, "the salvation of those poor people which [have] been sitting in the darkness and in the shadow of death" would ensue. As Protestant English families came to North America, he predicted clergymen would surely immigrate as well. They could minister both to the immigrants and to the Indians, those he described as "sitting in the darkness."[12]

The English colonies accomplished little in the conversion of the Indians to Christianity, as compared to the Catholics under the French and Spanish. Those empires made Christianization of the Indians priorities of state policy. This reflected the reality that France and Spain maintained centralized control of the colonies and dictated matters of religious practice. France disallowed the settlement of Jews or Huguenots (French Protestants of a Calvinist theological orientation) in New France.

England, however, left religious matters up to the companies and proprietors of each individual colony. Those running the colonies, whether administrators sitting in London or their agents in North America, could decide whose religion might keep them from settling down and what limitations might be placed on adherents to minority faiths.

The English did not prevent religious dissenters, women and men persecuted and restricted at home, from immigrating to the American colonies. Huguenots, despite being French speakers, settled comfortably in places like New York, New Jersey, and various colonies farther south, where the Church of England enjoyed official, established status. Quakers, who experienced serious persecution in England, settled in many of the North American colonies besides Pennsylvania, founded by William Penn, a Quaker.

Colonial Protestantism existed along a wide denominational spectrum. Protestants divided among adherents to the Church of England, Congregationalists, later Presbyterians, Methodists, Lutherans, Quakers, and Baptists. Immigrants from England included communicants of the Church of England, who predominated in the South, and Calvinists, who flocked to New England. Scots, as well as immigrants from Ulster and Wales, brought their particular churches with them, whereas German speakers were divided among Lutherans, Pietists, and Anabaptists, also referred to as Mennonites.

Religion dovetailed somewhat with the various immigrants' place of origin. During much of the era, immigrants from specific places, with their distinctive religious traditions, tended to form enclaves, particularly those who settled outside the more residentially jumbled cities. Here they lived apart from others of different religious and cultural backgrounds. In the rural and frontier regions they mostly retained denominational commitments, worshipping in the languages familiar from their premigration homes. Wherever the various Protestant European immigrants came in contact with each other, they expressed hostility and disdain for the others. Whereas Peter Stuyvesant of the Dutch Reformed Calvinist religion ruled that Jews could remain but could not pray in public, he expressly forbade Lutherans from praying even in the confines of their own homes.

However wide the Protestant spectrum in terms of beliefs, rituals, languages, and places of origin, they shared a revulsion to Catholicism. In the seventeenth and eighteenth centuries hatred of the Catholic Church—its beliefs, priests, and global structure—determined who could settle and where, in addition to civil rights status. Only Delaware, Pennsylvania, Maryland, and Virginia maintained no, or few, civil disabilities against Catholics. All the other colonies had some limitation on Catholic settlement. Some did not allow the consecration of Catholic churches. Georgia granted freedom of worship to all in its bylaws, but it stipulated, "except papists." South Carolina did the same. In 1700 Massachusetts banned Catholic priests from entering the colony, stipulating that they could face imprisonment and possible execution if they did.

Such legislation reduced the numbers of Catholics willing to immigrate to British North America. The few Catholics who did tended to be English, and some Irish Catholics joined the small trickle. Knowing they faced restrictive legislation and periodic explosions of mob violence, even in colonies that did not legally disable them, stymied their immigration. The first census of the United States, conducted in 1790, put the population at about 4 million, with fewer than 65,000 Catholics estimated among them.[13]

Jews, whether of Iberian derivation from England, the Netherlands, and the various islands of the Caribbean, or from German lands, mostly of Polish background, experienced the era differently, although they also immigrated in small numbers. By the American Revolution about 1,500 to 2,000 lived in the colonies, enduring varying degrees of political disability but no real overt hostility, in word or deed, compared to Catholics. In some colonies, though this changed over time, they could not vote or hold public office. Other colonies, however, enacted few civic restrictions, and nowhere did the law bar them from settling down, doing business, and, if they wanted, creating congregations.

Distance from European centers of Jewish life hampered their immigration. No rabbis came to North America. They faced difficulties accessing services they needed, including getting kosher meat, circumcision for male infants, and religious education for the young.[14]

All the colonies, except Rhode Island, maintained an established church, whether Congregationalism in Connecticut or Church of England in Virginia, which received tax support as the official religion. But labor needs trumped creed when it came to encouraging immigrants and fostering settlement. Colonies needed workers. Getting them settled mattered more than religious homogeneity. If Lutherans, Presbyterians, Huguenots, Anabaptists, and Jews would immigrate and enrich Pennsylvania, Maryland, South Carolina, or Georgia, then however offensive their religions, the colonies' bottom line, profit, took precedence. If immigrants, whether they believed in infant or adult baptism, for example, defended the colony, then the elites and investors valued and welcomed them.

Xenophobia in British North America

Yet hostility toward immigrants, from one place or another, flourished. Despite the reality that all Europeans had themselves immigrated from someplace, or their parents or grandparents had, each batch of newcomers confronted nasty words, defamatory images, and random violence. Common immigrant histories and shared whiteness did not prevent xenophobia and the belief, expressed everywhere at some time, that the most recent arrivals did not measure up to the imagined qualities of the earlier ones. Class played a role in this. As the colonies developed economically and needed continuous replenishments of their labor forces, indenture, redemption, and convict immigration became more common. Colonial and town officials worried that poor people disembarking at the ports would become public charges. Unable to support themselves, they would drain resources from public coffers. Modeling their policies on recently enacted British poor laws, colonial administrators limited relief to those whom they considered deserving of help, widows and orphans. They placed residency requirements on public assistance, making it impossible for newly arrived immigrants who, as a result of circumstances beyond their control, needed help. Officials dealt with immigrants who had fallen on hard times by expelling them. The numbers cannot be estimated, but commentators at the time lamented the growing number of vagrants on the roads, whom the public feared and associated with the fact of their being immigrants.

Immigrants tried to protect their newly arrived brethren from being labeled burdens to society. Philadelphia's German Society raised funds to erect a shelter for German immigrants, hoping to provide temporary lodging, pay off debts incurred by redemptioners, and quell animosity toward Germans.

The eminent founder of the American nation, Benjamin Franklin, commented on life in Pennsylvania and offered words about the Germans, "the Palatine Boors." Franklin, son of an immigrant father and grandson of an immigrant woman who arrived as an indentured servant, published an article in 1751, "Observations Concerning the Increasing of Mankind, Peopling of Countries, &c." He bemoaned the influx of Germans flooding "our Settlements." These "swarthy" immigrants refused, he declared, to learn English, read only German-language newspapers, put up German signs where they lived, and with their growing numbers would soon sit in the colonial assembly, usurping the rightful places of those who deserved to hold office.[15]

Those whose recent forebears had immigrated from elsewhere created a narrative that contrasted immigrants of the past with those in the present. One Virginia official complained bitterly that his colony, once the destination for second and third sons of the British elite, now served as "a sink to drain England of her filth and scum."[16]

That "filth and scum" increasingly considered moving to America, which caused a reaction in Great Britain. In 1773 rumors swirled around England purporting that Parliament planned to vote on a bill halting all immigration to the thirteen North American colonies. One newspaper of the day, while probably exaggerating, captured the moment, noting that Parliament feared that "so great a number of useful inhabitants, of the United Kingdom," were "daily emigrating to the American colonies," as to cause harm at home and deprive Britain of the labors of its "useful inhabitants."[17]

Such legislation never passed, but talk about it reflected the reality that many, like John Harrower, saw few chances of making a living at home, but saw immigration to America as an attractive alternative.

Further Reading

Bailyn, Bernard. *The Peopling of British North America: An Introduction* (1986).
Fisher, David Hackett. *Albion's Seed: Four British Folkways in America* (1989).

Fogleman, Aaron Spencer. *Hopeful Journeys: German Immigration, Settlement, and Political Culture in Colonial America, 1717–1775* (1996).

Miller, Kerby, ed. *Irish Immigrants in the Land of Canaan: Letters and Memoirs from Colonial and Revolutionary America, 1675–1815* (2003).

Rana, Aziz. *Two Faces of American Freedom* (2010).

Smith, Abbot E. *Colonists in Bondage: White Servitude and Convict Labor in America, 1607–1776* (1947).

Tomlins, Christopher. *Freedom Bound: Law, Labor, and Civic Identity in Colonizing English America, 1580–1865* (2010).

CHAPTER TWO

Opening the Door to
Europe's People

RENCH-BORN HECTOR ST. JOHN de Crèvecoeur lived in
New York during the American Revolutionary era. Married
to an American woman, he farmed a sizable estate, Pine
Hill, in Orange County and traveled the region as a land
surveyor. His work demanded that he study the topography of the
emerging independent country, but it also allowed him to observe
its people. He had much to say about them in his 1782 *Letters from
an American Farmer: Describing Certain Provincial Situations, Manners, and Customs, Not Generally Known: and Conveying Some Idea of
the Late and Present Interior Circumstances of the British Colonies of
North America*. He introduced his European readers to the "great
American asylum," birthplace of a "new man," a "European, or the
descendant of a European, hence the strange mixture of blood,
which you will find in no other country. I could point out to you a
family," he offered, "whose grandfather was an Englishman, whose
wife was Dutch, whose son married a French woman, and whose
present four sons have now four wives of different nations. *He* is an
American." In the name of these Americans with their amalgamated
ancestries, Crèvecoeur wrote, "Welcome to my shores, distressed
Europeans; bless the hour in which thou didst see my verdant fields.

... If thou wilt work, I have bread for thee; ... I will give thee fields to feed and clothe thee."[1]

He symbolically extended his hand to Europeans only. So too did the white Protestant men, almost all of British origins and who authored the nation's basic texts, consider free Europeans the potential beneficiaries of the institutions they created. Their documents crafted the country's governmental structures, which then formulated its immigration, naturalization, and citizenship policies. Although few immigrants chose the new United States in the years from the 1770s through the 1820s, the rhetoric and guidelines, including those specified in the U.S. Constitution, greatly influenced subsequent eras when immigration soared and the United States emerged as the world's most powerful immigration magnet.

The openhanded policy for European immigrants, regardless of home country or religion, highlighted the power of skin color and slavery's chains that shaped America. Although white Americans, both the elite and ordinary people, considered some European immigrants better or worse than others, the legally recognized whiteness of all new European arrivals opened doors for them.

Policy makers thought little about those parts of the world where white people did not predominate, such as Asia, despite the presence of a handful of Chinese merchants who lived in port cities like New York and the growing importance of trans-Pacific trading and the Muslim world of North Africa and the Middle East. Immigrant meant white and European.

Class certainly mattered. State lawmakers, particularly in New York, Maryland, and Massachusetts, fretted over the arrival of poor newcomers whose poverty they feared would burden taxpayers. Those same state and local officials, however, also worried about the native-born poor who they similarly thought would drain resources. Federal policy and national discussions, though, connected whiteness and immigrant status but had little to say about wealth or poverty.

The image of the United States as a welcoming place for ordinary Europeans took hold in the late eighteenth and early nineteenth centuries. American writers, orators, and public figures articulated it broadly. George Washington described the new nation in 1783 to Joshua Holmes: "The bosom of America is open to receive not only the opulent and respectable stranger, but the oppressed and persecuted of all nations and religions; whom we shall welcome to a participation of all our rights and privileges, if by decency and propriety of conduct they appear to merit the enjoyment."[2]

On his way to accepting the presidency, he comforted members of the small Jewish community of Newport, Rhode Island, who were anxious about the fate of Jews in the new, overwhelmingly Christian nation. Washington promised that "happily the Government of the United States gives to bigotry no sanction, to persecution no assistance, requires only that they who live under its protection should demean themselves as good citizens, in giving it on all occasions their effectual support."[3]

These words of the man who might have been king read as a blanket statement to Europeans contemplating immigration to America. Such rhetoric captured the imaginations of writers, poets, political activists, and increasing numbers of women and men who felt their homes offered few prospects for making a living. The Jewish poet Heinrich Heine, born in Frankfurt, put it powerfully: "Even if all Europe should become a single prison, there is still another loophole of escape, namely America, and, thank God! the loophole is after all larger than the prison itself."[4]

Some architects of the United States envisioned immigration as key to establishing a solid economic basis. Most famously, Alexander Hamilton, an immigrant from the Virgin Islands and eventually Washington's secretary of the Treasury, founded the Society for Establishing Useful Manufactures in 1791 to attract skilled workers to America. In his "Report on Manufactures," Hamilton linked economics, immigration, and religious freedom. "Men reluctantly quit one course of occupation and livelihood for another, unless invited to it by very apparent and proximate advantages," he wrote, predicting that individuals who wanted to better their circumstances would find the United States attractive, with its "greater cheapness of provisions and raw materials, of an exemption from the chief part of the taxes burthens and restraints, which they endure in the old world . . . greater personal independence and consequence, under the operation of a more equal government, and . . . what is far more precious than mere religious toleration—a perfect equality of religious privileges." They, he contended, "would probably flock from Europe to the United States to pursue their own trades or professions." Good for both individuals and the nation, it would behoove "the United States to open every possible [avenue to] emigration from abroad."[5]

Individuals and companies agreed, and they proceeded to organize immigration schemes. Few accomplished much, but their efforts indicate how the United States had captured European attention as a place burgeoning with opportunities and how enthusiastically some Americans viewed potential immigration. Joel Barlow, an American diplomat and poet whose book-length *Visions of Columbus* rhapsodized about America as Europe's antidote, traveled to France as a representative of the Scioto Land Company to bring French immigrants to Gallipolis, a town built from the ground up on the banks of the Ohio River in 1790. Within two years Gallipolis folded and the immigrants scattered. Like many orchestrated immigration projects, outright fraud, mismanagement, and outsize expectations probably doomed it from the start.

Other native-born white Americans raised questions about the liabilities and dangers immigrants could pose to the United States. A fierce partisan storm raged about the harm immigrants might inflict: they would probably retain loyalties to their former lands, thereby threatening the independence of the newly sovereign country. Such concerns began smoldering during the Revolution and continued through the period of the Articles of Confederation and into the era of the early republic, escalating in the last years of the eighteenth century as the United States got caught up in the global wars between England and France. Members of Congress, journalists, and others asked whether immigrants would drag the nation out of its blessed isolation into the turmoil of the old world.

Despite the debates, unlimited and unregulated European immigration won out. The trickle of arrivals, even in this period of slow immigration, from both familiar and new European sources gave the United States one of its most distinctive characteristics.

Modest Numbers

Glowing rhetoric about America circulated around Europe. One popular English guidebook of 1819 made it clear: "Wages in America are better," the pamphlet claimed, and there, more "than in any other country, work can be had." Though it did not promise great riches, it noted that "the living is reasonable, so that labourers can live very comfortably and save a little."[6]

Despite such promise, only modest numbers of women and men crossed the Atlantic. Optimal conditions for mass emigration did not yet exist. As Europe and the British Isles experienced the disruptions caused by altered landholding patterns, declining domestic manufacturing, and overpopulation, the masses could not go. Constant warfare, particularly at sea, hampered transatlantic shipping. Young men, prime candidates for emigration, faced conscription into their home country armies.

The policies of local and national governments in a variety of European places also quashed large-scale movement. Phineas Bond, the British consul in Philadelphia in the 1780s, noted that "an almost total stop has lately been put to the migration hither [America] from the Palatinate and other parts of Germany so that the few who now came hither from that country get into Holland by stealth."[7] The British Parliament in 1788 banned the emigration of skilled artisans from Ireland. Earlier it had blocked opportunities for this same class to leave England, Scotland, and Wales. In the 1803 Passenger Act it slashed the number of immigrants allowed to sail on any British vessel, reducing the profits shipowners could make from the immigrant trade.

Several jurisdictions in the German-speaking lands as well as Swiss towns and cantons imposed taxes on those who wanted to leave and forced prospective emigrants to renounce their right to return. The British Parliament decreed that emigrants could not take tools with them. They could not even tuck into their valises or pockets scraps of paper with drawings of machinery and sketches of manufacturing plants.

Samuel Slater of Belper, Derbyshire, fifth of eight children born into a hardscrabble farming family, started working at age ten in a local cotton mill using the most advanced technology, the Arkwright water frame. In 1789, after mastering the cotton weaving process, Slater, known in England as "Slater the traitor," left for the United States. He evaded the law by storing the banned information in his brain, having systematically memorized details of the entire process and of the machines' designs. In 1793 Slater opened America's first water-powered roller spinning textile mill in Rhode Island.

Slater, dubbed "the Father of the American Industrial Revolution," opened his factory the same year as the invention of the cotton gin by Eli Whitney. Whitney's cotton gin resulted in the expansion of southern slavery and a vast increase in the cultivation of cotton, much of which went for processing to towns in Rhode Island, Massachusetts, and other New England states.

Samuel Slater, an immigrant driven to leave his home because of a dearth of economic opportunities, set off a chain reaction that transformed America. By introducing a mechanized means to produce fabric, he provided mill work for the daughters of New England farmers, facilitated the spread of the cotton kingdom, made white Americans even more dependent on the labor of enslaved Africans, and provided the United States with a solid basis for its economic expansion, which increasingly after the 1820s drew multitudes of immigrants.

Few other immigrants affected America as did "Slater the traitor," but despite their anonymity and lives of struggle, they collectively helped launch the United States. The successful entrepreneur's story illustrates how American conditions had to be ripe as well to stimulate immigration. With the end of the wars in Europe in 1815, American trade blossomed, as did American manufacturing. The opening of wide swathes of land after the French departed following the 1803 Louisiana Purchase and the British retreated from North America (other than Canada) opened the floodgates of immigration.

The exact numbers of immigrants before the 1820s remain elusive. Until 1820, shipmasters did not have to list names or nationalities of their passengers, how many they dropped off at some American port, or whether they intended to stay. No federal or state bureaucracies monitored the disembarking passengers. Some historians have estimated that between 250,000 and 400,000 immigrants cast their lot with America between 1783 and 1820, though numbers dipped during the peak war years in Europe and its American offshoot, the War of 1812.[8]

Of those who did immigrate, Protestants from the northern part of Ireland predominated, and German speakers were a close second, diluting the English origins of the population. In 1790, with the first federal census, mandated by the Constitution, people of mixed British origin, including the English, constituted just under 60 percent of the white population, about 3 million people all together; those identifiable as German constituted more than 8 percent.

Politics sent some immigrants to America. Some Ulster immigrants and Catholics from Ireland left because of their anti-English activities. French immigrants initially came to the United States from the ranks of the aristocratic foes of the French Revolution of 1789. After them, partisans of the Revolution fled in the face of the political reaction that followed. In 1791 other French immigrants came via Saint-Domingue, the island where Toussaint L'Ouverture led a revolution of enslaved people. The rebellion saw the exodus of nearly the entire white population. Some headed for France, but most opted for the United States. The French immigration added to America's linguistic diversity and stimulated Catholic institution building in the Protestant land. Sympathetic members of Congress passed a bill in 1794 to provide financial relief to these immigrants, fellow slaveholders whose flight from insurrection mirrored their own anxieties of living with and depending on enslaved Black people.

While political upheavals abroad spurred immigration, most of the quarter million immigrants had been small farmers, agricultural workers, and artisans uprooted by combinations of low wages, disastrous harvests, soaring birthrates, early industrialization, and the consolidation of estates by the well-to-do. These factors operated differently in different regions, but all stimulated families to consider immigration. As women and men from England, for example, went to new communities in Ohio, or those from Wales to Pennsylvania, or the Palatines to North Carolina, they spurred further migration of kin, friends, and neighbors to those same places.

Their enclaves caught the attention of native-born white Americans. Charles Woodmason, an Anglican minister, having traveled the Carolina backcountry, described the region and its Ulster Presbyterians in decidedly negative tones. "There is not a cabin but has ten or twelve children in it," he remarked with the unmistakable disdain most Americans of English origin harbored for the Ulstermen. He continued, "When the boys are eighteen and the girls fourteen they marry—so that in many cabins you will see ten or fifteen children . . . and the mother looking as young as the daughter."[9]

German speakers also went to specific places where they found relatives and townspeople. Some, and the numbers defy accurate enumeration, stayed in cities such as New York, Baltimore, and Philadelphia. Others headed to the interior, creating German-speaking enclaves in hinterland towns. In 1802, for instance, immigrants published German-language newspapers in Lancaster, Reading, Easton, York, Harrisburg, and Norristown, Pennsylvania, disseminating news from back home and providing information about their new country.

Few white European immigrants after the 1780s came as indentured servants or redemptioners, and none came as convicts. Most moved as free people, traveling on their own resources. If they received any assistance, as most did, it came from family members. Immigrants from Europe believed, and probably rightly, that they could expect to secure employment upon landing. That work did not pay spectacular wages or lead to great wealth. But they did get paid. Their wages enabled them, whether living in port cities, small towns, or farms, to scrape by. For the most part, that work allowed them to put food on their tables and set up households. Most important, they considered that they lived better than they had at home.

Those who went to cities could rely, at moments of crisis, on formal immigrant aid associations. Benevolent groups, consisting of relatively successful merchants, professionals, and artisans, either immigrants themselves or the children of immigrants, provided direct assistance to the needy newcomers. Their help reflected the bond they felt toward their fellow German speakers, fellow emigrants from Ireland, or fellow Jews. These community leaders also worried that their own comfortable place in America might suffer because the poverty of the new arrivals would stigmatize and jeopardize the status of the group as a collective.

The new immigration complicated American religious patterns. Catholics started showing up in increasing numbers, including those among the Irish and the German speakers, who now hailed from regions other than the Palatinate. Among the Jews, Ashkenazim, of central and eastern European origin, particularly from Polish lands recently acquired by Prussia, predominated. Each shift in the source of immigration complicated what it meant to be Irish, German, or Jewish in America.

New York's only Jewish congregation, Shearith Israel, strained to meet its obligations to assist newly arriving Jewish immigrants from Prussia, as did Philadelphia's Mikveh Israel. In 1802 New York's Jews founded a charitable society, Hebra Hased va-Emet, directing its resources at the newest arrivals. Baltimore's Irish residents, fairly prosperous Protestant merchants, created the Hibernian Society "to do all such . . . as shall be necessary, for the purpose of affording charitable assistance and advice to such emigrants from, or natives of Ireland arriving at, or residing in any part of the State of Maryland as may be in want and deemed worthy." The German Society of Maryland, founded in 1783, shouldered similar responsibilities for those coming from Hesse, Bohemia, and Bavaria.[10]

The city of Baltimore, second only to New York as an immigrant port of arrival, provided some funding to both the Hibernian Society and the German Society. By subsidizing these immigrant aid associations, the city reckoned, it did not have to provide services. Alarmed by the swelling crowds of immigrants landing in Baltimore, city officials encouraged the aid societies to disperse the new immigrants to farming lands beyond the Chesapeake. The city's health inspector, Samuel B. Martin, lamented that "the more able part" of the immigrants "pass on to the interior, but the *pauper* part are left in our hands."[11]

In Need of Labor

Martin erred. Immigrant men with marketable skills and women willing to work in domestic service generally stayed in Baltimore and other cities. Struggling to get by, as many did, did not make them paupers. They differed little, in fact, from most city residents, non-immigrants who lived at the margins of the economy. Americans like Martin might have seen immigrants as paupers, but they got it wrong.

Among those who arrived in these years, an uncountable number moved inland from the ports, either right away or after some time in the cities. Some newcomers went into farming, buying land white Americans had given up on as too small or too depleted, or moving farther west to areas even beyond the Appalachian Mountains.

Immigrants flocked to holdings once farmed by these Americans. Guidebooks emphasized the greater opportunities awaiting "a person who comes to America," and who then decided to move "from the seaports, they being very full of people," while "labourers in agriculture and many trades are sure of work in the Western country."[12]

Nonagricultural work in the interior also beckoned. Irish men found opportunities, although hard and dangerous ones, in digging canals and laying roads. Immigrant men made America's great canal age possible. The twenty-seven-mile Middlesex Canal of Massachusetts, begun in 1794 and completed by 1810, represented the most ambitious of these engineering feats and depended on immigrant labor. Of even greater consequence, the 363-mile Erie Canal, which linked the nation and the world in spectacular ways, opened in 1817. Its building and functioning required male immigrant muscle.

Referred to as "Clinton's Folly" or "Clinton's Ditch," the Erie Canal became fully functional in 1835. It connected New York City and its port to the Hudson River at Albany and the Great Lakes,

Artist's rendition of the Erie Canal, 1829. New York Public Library, New York.

providing access to the resources of the Midwest. Envisioned as early as the 1780s by Governor Dewitt Clinton and other New York backers, it entailed the labor of thousands. Gangs of men digging, blasting, hauling away dirt, and laying the canal's foundations caused the population to surge across western New York State, transforming small villages such as Rochester, Syracuse, Schenectady, Rome, and Utica into booming cities. The presence of Irish canal workers during the building process and beyond fostered the flourishing of the canal cities and the surrounding countryside, stimulating business opportunities, driving up the value of farmland, and begetting work of all sorts.

Once finished, the canal revolutionized the American economy. Barges floated down its waters, laden with iron ore from Michigan and Minnesota, wheat and other grains from Illinois and Wisconsin, as well as timber and other minerals, which were loaded onto oceangoing vessels departing from New York. Its full significance would be felt after the 1820s, but immigrant workers of the 1810s set the stage for the explosive growth of New York City and America's emergence as a world economic power.

Thanks to the many canals crisscrossing the United States, as well as the new roads, such as the National Road, which immigrant men began to construct in 1811 to link the Potomac and Ohio Rivers, lumber, agricultural products, and minerals of the hinterlands arrived at markets. Cotton picked in southern slave fields, processed in the mills of Pawtucket, Rhode Island, Lowell, Massachusetts, and other textile towns, then sewn by tailors and seamstresses—themselves immigrants—eventually ended up on the backs of consumers. This chain needed immigrant labor to tunnel through mountains, clear forests, dig canals, plank logs, and keep building roads for the expanding population and developed territory.

During the decades between the American Revolution and the 1820s, while still predominantly rural and based on small family farms, the nation experienced the first stirrings of the industrial revolution. Samuel Slater's mills launched this, as did the introduction of a fully automatic mill for grinding flour, and Eli Whitney's cotton gin. These enterprises joined agriculture with commerce, stoking a need for labor that fired dreams of America for immigrants looking for work.

Few of those immigrants came close to equaling Slater's success or that of John Jacob Astor, born in the Palatinate in 1763, the youngest son of a butcher. As a young man, Astor decided to leave home to improve his lot. After a short stint in England, he came to New York in 1784, expecting his butchering skills to support him. But a different, vastly more lucrative path presented itself, which used the animals' outer, rather than inner, assets. Astor developed a mighty empire selling hides and furs from the frontier's teaming herds. All steps in the process, including hauling skins and furs from frontier outposts to towns and cities, processing and tanning them, loading them onto boats at the port, and finally shipping them to England and the Continent, required workers. Immigrants provided much of that workforce.

Astor's stupendous fortune also derived from New York City real estate. He bought up land and erected buildings of all sorts, including block after block of dwelling places to house immigrants who worked the docks, shipyards, abattoirs, tanneries, clothing shops, and the streets as vendors of sundry goods.

The shortage of laborers available to Astor and the other builders and entrepreneurs demonstrated to middle- and upper-class white Americans the need for European immigrants to stoke economic development and help them make personal profits. The outbreak of the Napoleonic Wars in Europe in 1803 and the War of 1812 in the United States illustrated to policy makers that the nation needed to strive for economic self-sufficiency. International shipping suffered, and Americans realized that they had to churn out manufactured goods for themselves and stop relying on imported finished products from England. The ability to produce, though, depended on the availability of hands to tend machines, whether machines that made other machines or machines that produced cloth, shoes, flour, nails, or whatever.

Natural growth through reproduction could not begin to fulfill these needs. It could not generate enough people to tap the resources of land, animals, minerals, and lumber of the land of the original thirteen colonies, let alone the much larger territory purchased from France in 1803, and Florida, acquired from Spain in 1819.

Women and men, Catholic, Jewish, and Protestant, adherents to many denominations, speaking English, German, French, Dutch, and other European languages, learned about America's hunger for labor. They learned through newspapers, guidebooks, posters, speeches, and letters from friends and family already in the United States that their languages and religions would not prevent them from trying to improve their lives by leaving home and going to America. They learned that the newly crafted laws and policies of the early nineteenth century did not handicap them, whatever their tongue and faith, in that scramble to succeed.

Laws and Documents, Texts and Politics

The new nation took much of its shape from the influx of immigrants, if in modest numbers, landing on its shores. The issue of immigration to the colonies had appeared among the grievances that the revolutionaries lodged against the king and his Privy Council: they stated in the Declaration of Independence that the king tried "to prevent the population of these states" from growing. Those calling for independence pointed to the Proclamation of 1763, which blocked westward settlement at the crest of the Appalachians and refused to recognize naturalization acts passed by various colonial assemblies. These naturalization acts extended citizenship rights to white men born abroad, but not in England.

Word of the Declaration and the Revolution spread to Europe, disseminating the idea that this American nation consisted of "one people." Though the fledgling nation's citizens consisted entirely of white men, they came from a variety of origins and collectively became something new—Americans. That more than half had arrived less than free but still merited inclusion in the category of "the people" spoke volumes about the ideology of the nation and the possibilities for immigrants someday to become insiders. The words "all men are created equal," so marked and marred by the existence of slavery and the reality that women and men of African origin did not count as equal, spoke to Europeans.

The Congress, which formed after the Declaration and governed under the Articles of Confederation until the 1789 adoption of the Constitution, acted on this vision of integrating outsiders as it contemplated acute labor shortages and the need to populate the land and to neutralize the Indian nations living there. Article 4 of this first national document dealt with related matters, without discussing immigration or citizenship directly. But it ensured that naturalized foreigners would be at no disadvantage and that those born on United States soil would have no privileges that those born abroad did not. It stated, departing dramatically from pre-Revolutionary policies, that anyone naturalized in one state would have the same rights in every other state and that "the free inhabitants of each of these States, paupers, vagabonds, and fugitives from justice excepted, shall be entitled to all privileges and immunities of free citizens in the several States." By referring to those who had undergone naturalization, Article 4 meant immigrant without using the word, but since birth automatically conferred rights in that place, only those born abroad had to become naturalized.[13]

Under the Articles, Congress passed one particular piece of legislation that demonstrated the importance of immigration as a settlement policy for new territory under American control. Codified on July 13, 1787, the Northwest Ordinance, formally "An Ordinance for the Government of the Territory of the United States, North-West of the River Ohio," seemingly had nothing to do with immigration. Rather, it set the standards by which the chunk of land that was eventually divided into Ohio, Michigan, Indiana, Illinois, and Wisconsin would be incorporated into the nation. Among its stipulations for the acquisition of territorial and then state status, the Northwest Ordinance both banned slavery and other forms of "involuntary servitude" and promised unfettered religious freedom. Given the tight association in the colonial era between European place of origin and religion, and the reality that most of the original thirteen states still maintained an established church, with the Northwest Ordinance Congress made a statement about immigration. Its decision to make the Northwest Territory different from, say, Massachusetts and Connecticut, with their official churches, ensured that all white Europeans would be comfortable in the west and set a standard for the future. If and when sectarian friction flared in the states without established churches, between immigrants from a variety of countries and adherents of competing denominations, such disputes did not involve state officials or state policies. Additionally, its ban on slavery was not based on moral reasons. Rather,

Congress recognized that immigrants did not find places where they had to compete with landowners who relied on involuntary labor particularly attractive.

Deliberations in Congress concerning the Northwest Ordinance focused on the importance of filling the region with Europeans, which perforce meant stimulating immigration. No one raised the issue of where immigrants would come from, so long as they arrived as free people with white skin. Participants in the discussions instead linked the prospect of European immigration and the settling of the newly opened lands with the matter of religion. James Madison noted that "that part of America which has encouraged [immigrants] most, has advanced most rapidly in population, agriculture and the arts," a statement linked to Hamilton's observation that "a perfect equality of religious privileges will probably cause [immigrants] to flock from Europe to the United States."[14]

Powerful individuals, Madison and Hamilton chief among them, considered the Articles of Confederation an ineffective instrument to govern the new nation. They called for a Constitutional Convention in 1787 and helped draft a new document, writing the most enduring text of its kind in the world. The U.S. Constitution, ratified in 1789, had little to say about immigration. The words *immigrant* and *immigration* never appeared in its original form or in any of the amendments passed since 1790. But in not saying anything on the subject, it spoke volumes about it.

The Constitution gave Congress, not the states, the power in Article 1, Section 8, "To establish an uniform Rule of Naturalization," providing no guidelines on the details. The Constitution furthermore stipulated only minor distinctions between the native-born and naturalized foreign-born. It declared that in order to serve in the House of Representatives, one had to have been a citizen for seven years, and for nine years to serve in the Senate. As for the executive branch, the Constitution limited the office of president to natural-born citizens.

The Constitution's stance on religion bears greater evidence of the Framers' vision and the welcome they proffered to European immigrants, whether Catholics, Jews, Protestants of any denomination, or even nonbelievers. By mandating in Article 6 that no religious test be set for federal officeholding, the framers declared that a white man could serve the nation whether he worshipped in a Lutheran church with a German liturgy or a Reformed church where he heard Dutch sermons, hymns, and prayers, or attended and belonged nowhere. By its silence, the Constitution decreed that the government would collect no information on who believed in what or was affiliated with which church.

The Constitution's openness regarding religion demonstrated its countenance of a broad European immigration. A rainbow of religious denominations flourished, and though a few of the new states, derived from the British colonies, did maintain tax support for an established church, other faith communities representing non-English places of origin found homes in the new United States. Uncoupling religion and state, the document's authors understood, would enhance the attractiveness of America to potential immigrants who carried their many religious affiliations with them.

That uncoupling went even further in the First Amendment to the Constitution, appended to the document immediately upon its completion. Well into the twenty-first century, scholars, activists, judges, and policy makers debate the exact meaning of the late eighteenth-century words, "Congress shall make no law respecting an establishment of religion, or prohibiting the free exercise thereof."

But for ordinary European women and men, committed to their religions but experiencing dwindling economic prospects, these words meant something concrete. They could know that deciding to emigrate to America would not hamper their observing the precepts of their faiths and that their religious institutions would be able to act according to their ideas about truth, God, salvation, and community. If they came to the United States, regardless of their religion, they could fulfill creedal obligations with no state interference, something quite different from what prevailed in Europe. Whether they came from places where their religion enjoyed state support or if, like Catholics in Ireland or Jews in German-speaking lands, they suffered disabilities because of their religious affiliations, potential immigrants from Europe recognized that they would not have to compromise on their faiths and beliefs in the United States.

The Constitution and the First Amendment also meant that, unlike the case in their old homes, their religious institutions would not have to conform to laws made by the state. Their ministers would never receive salaries from the government, and their congregations and denominations would depend only on the consent and approval of the members, which would allow adherents of the various creeds to shape the kinds of practices they wanted. The inner lives of the denominations, brought over from a variety of places, came to reflect the basic structure of the United States' governmental system.

The issue of who could become an American also surfaced in the earliest years of the republic. Congress, during its first session and following the ratification of the Constitution, took up the matter of naturalization in the Naturalization Act of 1790. The act declared that naturalization could be attained by all "free white persons of good character"; "persons" were assumed without debate to be male. From a negative standpoint, the law disallowed the naturalization of the "unfree," asserting that convicts, indentured servants, and those fettered to an employer did not qualify. Enslaved people certainly could not expect naturalization. By 1790 arriving unfree mostly meant being defined as nonwhite, and without saying so explicitly, the law rendered free Black persons ineligible, as well as America's Native people, Asians, and anyone else whom the law and custom perceived and categorized as lacking whiteness.

The representatives who sat in Congress and crafted this legislation did not debate among themselves the whiteness, or lack thereof, of people from Wales or Ireland, of Jews, whether from Lithuania or Bavaria, or indeed of any other immigrants, actual or potential. Representative John Page of Virginia addressed this issue on the floor of the House of Representatives, although he referred to religion rather than place of origin in arguing for the broad naturalization of white men. Page declared:

> We shall be inconsistent with ourselves, if, after boasting of having opened an asylum for the oppressed of all nations, and establishing a Government which is the admiration of the world, we make the terms of admission to the full enjoyment of that asylum so hard as is now proposed.
>
> It is nothing to us whether Jews or Roman Catholics settle amongst us; whether subjects of Kings or citizens of free States, wish to reside in the United States, they will find

it in their interests to be good citizens, and neither their religious nor political opinions can injure us, if we have good
laws, well executed.[15]

Neither the white Christian men, like Page, who sat in Congress
and argued for expansive naturalization, nor those who pressed for
more restrictive standards, fretted over who qualified as white as
they emphatically barred nonwhites from naturalization. They
clearly assumed all Europeans to be white and capable of attaining
citizenship. If they harbored negative views of Jews or Irish Catholics, of Italians or Poles, they did not associate such people with a
lack of whiteness.

Europeans, regardless of place of origin or religion, merely had
to reside someplace in the United States as a measure of their "good
character" for two years, after which they could go to any court-
house, file a Petition for Naturalization, take an oath promising to
support the Constitution, and then the clerk of the court would
make a record, and "thereupon such person shall be considered as a
citizen of the United States."[16]

The Naturalization Act, which would be amended in 1795, 1798,
and 1802, as Congress lengthened and then shortened the number
of years of residence, set a standard for the future. By ensuring that
any European man could become a citizen, and that his children
occupied an equal footing with all those born in the United States,
it confirmed a prevailing logic about the new nation.

Page offered these words as Federalists and Democrats, the two
parties, confronted the immigration issue. Their debates over immigration took place against the background of the French Revolution, sparking the nation's first sputtering of xenophobia.

Immigration's First Political Crisis

Native-born Americans, perhaps no different from other people,
viewed new immigrants with suspicion. Evidence of hostile comments and deprecatory imagery goes back to colonial times. Benjamin Franklin's diatribe against the German speakers in Pennsylvania offers a case in point. Samuel Adams of Massachusetts, one of

the great Patriots of the American Revolution, reflected the broad anti-Catholicism pervading all thirteen colonies, writing in 1768, "I did verily believe, as I do still, that much more is to be dreaded from the growth of popery in America, than from the Stamp Act, or any other acts destructive of civil rights." The only way for "popery" to have grown would have been immigration of women and men of the Catholic faith.[17]

Before national independence, each colony decided for itself how, when, or if new arrivals would get rights similar to those enjoyed by colonists with longer roots in that particular place. Each colony set the standards of naturalization, officeholding, voting in local elections, property ownership, and the other privileges that Adams would have included under the rubric of "civil rights."

After national independence, while states retained some power in these matters, for the most part authority shifted to Congress on the federal level. In the emerging party system, which pitted the Democrats (also known as the Democratic-Republicans), aligned with Thomas Jefferson, against the Federalists, linked to Alexander Hamilton and John Adams, immigration, immigrant rights, and criteria for citizenship became a political battleground, as two different ideas about these matters opposed each other.

That political battle took shape initially after the French Revolution erupted in 1789. The New England–based Federalists, committed to fostering a strong central government and highly skeptical of mass democracy, worried that violence such as that inflaming France could spread across the Atlantic. Federalists considered that French immigrants and newcomers from other European countries who sympathized with the revolutionaries there had fomented a number of local episodes of political unrest, such as the Whiskey Rebellion of 1791 in western Pennsylvania. They recognized that most immigrants were aligned with the Democratic Party, and according to Federalists in Congress and President John Adams, Jefferson and his allies had stirred up the immigrants to challenge the power of the elites, those most likely to be Federalists.

Federalist-dominated Congresses then passed several acts reflecting their fear of alien radicals, particularly those associated with the Democratic Party. The Naturalization Acts of 1795 and 1798 extended the time an immigrant had to wait until he could become a citizen, moving from the 1790 legislation's two years to five, and then to fourteen years. It included a "notice time," or a period during which immigrants had to wait until they could legally declare their intention to apply for citizenship, something not in the original legislation. In addition, and for the first time, the two Naturalization Acts required states to keep records of immigration and place of domicile in order to keep track of when the white immigrants had initially arrived and how long they had been present. This marked the first time that the federal government insisted on documenting place of birth in conjunction with the acquisition of citizenship. Congress also passed the Alien Friends Act, giving the president power to deport any noncitizen deemed "dangerous to the peace of the United States," as well as the Alien Enemies Act, which authorized him to deport any citizen of a hostile nation, aged fourteen years or older, during wartime. (The three 1798 laws, in addition to the Sedition Act, are commonly known as the Alien and Sedition Acts.)

These pieces of legislation and the debates surrounding them exposed the complex intersection of fears some Americans felt when they considered the nation under attack from the outside and their sense of vulnerability in the international arena, contributing to the demonization of immigrants as agents of subversion. A set of events on the world stage set this in motion. France, one of Europe's great colonial nations, engaged the small, new United States in an undeclared war dubbed the Quasi-War. The diplomatic fiasco that became known as the XYZ Affair of 1798, in which the French government demanded a hefty bribe just to meet with three American diplomats, exposed America's weakness in relation to the Continental superpower. Federalists used this event to their partisan advantage. They argued that the nation could be dragged into a real war against France, and that in such a confrontation, the latter would surely win and the United States could easily surrender its recently gained independence.

In short order this line of thinking transformed a set of diplomatic maneuvers into a political argument, made by the Federalists, claiming that immigrants who sympathized with France posed a threat. French immigrants felt this sting, as did those from Ireland. Irish revolutionaries at home and in the United States looked to France for help against Britain, and, indeed, they entered into agreements with the French to use its raging battles with England as an opportunity to liberate them from English domination. A Connecticut congressman, Joshua Coit, predicted that "we may very shortly be involved in war," and the "immense number of French citizens in our country" would aid America's enemy.[18] The Federalists pointed to the Democratic Party, with its pro-French orientation and its solid immigrant electoral base, as a source of danger. This talk of national vulnerability exposed anti-immigrant sentiment.

That sentiment catapulted the Federalists to power in the nation's new capital city, Washington, D.C. It flared in the halls of Congress, in the White House, and in the public arena in a battle of words in broadsides, speeches, and the press. William Smith Shaw, John Adams's nephew and personal secretary, aptly captured the Federalists' outlook when he wrote to Abigail Adams that "the grand cause of all our present difficulties may be traced . . . to so many *hordes of Foreigners* imigrating to America." Shaw deliberately turned George Washington's vision of America on its head, warning, "Let us no longer pray, that America may become an asylum to all nations."[19]

The Federalists' legislation, which reflected their hope to redefine the United States to make it less hospitable to "hordes of Foreigners," did not survive the Democratic victory of 1800 that gave Jefferson's party the majority in Congress and the presidency to him. An 1802 law under Jefferson's Democratic administration rolled back the fourteen-year residency requirement for citizenship to the five years mandated in 1795, but the country never returned to the two years stipulated in 1790.

However intense the public debate about immigrants as bearers of subversive ideas, and however intense the concern that immigrants threatened the viability of the young nation, Federalist legislation never contemplated halting the flow of women and men from Europe to America. The debate centered on formal matters of citizenship and naturalization, rather than free movement to the United States, which would include those who expected to remain. Harrison Gray Otis, a Federalist congressman from Massachusetts, made that clear when he argued in favor of the more elaborate naturalization procedure, saying, "If some means are not adopted to prevent the indiscriminate admission of wild Irishmen and others to the right of suffrage, there will soon be an end to liberty and property." Congressman Otis did not advocate restricting the admission of immigrants, including "wild Irishmen," to the physical space of the United States, but he questioned the wisdom of giving them the "right of suffrage."[20]

In a new nation, with an as yet unformed identity and a less than clear idea of what "American" meant, standards for inclusion in the political process weighed heavily on those holding power. The Federalists formulated their legislation as nearly all the thirteen original states continued to maintain property qualifications for voting and officeholding, limiting the right to govern to white men with financial means regardless of how long their families had resided in North America or their lands of origin. Most states restricted officeholding to those who would swear an oath on a King James Bible, thereby excluding Catholics, Jews, and nonbelievers who could not do so. Several states, such as Maryland, forbade Jews from serving as public officials.

At the same time, though, a country with expanding physical territory, desperately wanting labor, did not define immigration as intrinsically harmful. Hence, the legislation did not seek to restrict it. Instead, it set obstacles in front of foreign-born men before allowing them to take their places as equal citizens in matters of state.

Whether considering the liberal standards mandated in 1790, or the restrictive ones of 1798, one criterion remained consistent and formative. Only free, white men of European background could take advantage of the opportunity to become—politically—"American," while only free, white, property-owning men could become enfranchised and hold elected office. Naturalization in this era involved white males whose skin color rendered them worthy of national inclusion. Being European offered to immigrants the chance to seize within a few years after arrival—two, five, or fourteen—the benefits of citizenship and participation in public life. It granted them a voice in deciding the fate of all Americans at ballot boxes, on juries, and in the halls of government.

Did partisan jostling in America influence potential European immigrants who weighed and measured their decisions regarding whether to emigrate to the United States? Did they care how long they would have to wait until they could naturalize? By all evidence, the idea of America as a place where Europeans would be more likely to make a living than if they stayed at home resonated even when Federalists unleashed ugly words about immigrants and passed legislation making citizenship harder to obtain. That rhetoric and political action did little, or nothing, to stymie immigration.

Rather, circumstances at home, less-than-robust opportunities in America, and the difficulties of travel all reduced the numbers of people who took to the roads, boarded ships, and journeyed westward. But the end of the European wars in 1815 stimulated mass movement to America. So, too, simultaneous innovations in transportation enabled those who wanted to leave to do so. Not until the late 1810s did the first railways penetrate into the English, Scottish, and German countrysides, bringing growing numbers to ports of embarkation. By the close of that decade, sailing ships leaving the harbors of Liverpool and Hamburg offered printed schedules of the sailings and widely advertised set prices. In 1818 a group of New York merchants founded the Black Ball Line, launching their packet ship operation, which now facilitated efficient immigrant transportation. The ships traveled westward with human cargo, the women and men bound for America. In reverse they sailed eastward with cotton, grain, timber, and the rest of the bounty of the American continent, now possible because of the transportation revolution in the United States. With the Black Ball Line in the lead, other companies formed, adding an element of competition to what became the big business of immigrant transportation and launching a new era in world history.

The mass movement of European immigrants felt the pull from the American side as a result of new realities in the waning years of the 1810s. Britain's defeat in 1815 meant that it would not reconquer its rebellious colonies. The United States was here to stay. The removal of the British, along with the Louisiana Purchase of the previous decade, opened up unimaginable stretches of land that called for people to exploit its vast untapped resources, farm it, and launch it on its first steps into the industrial age. Immigrants from 1820 onward served as the shock troops of America's economic transition from being Europe's Atlantic outpost to emerging as a force for global change.

Further Reading

Bartlett, Richard A. *The New Country: A Social History of the American Frontier, 1776–1890* (1974).

Baseler, Marilyn C. *"Asylum for Mankind": America, 1607–1800* (1998).

Berkin, Carol. *A Sovereign People: The Crises of the 1790s and the Birth of American Nationalism* (2017).

Erler, Edward J., John Marini, and Thomas G. West. *The Founders on Citizenship and Immigration: Principles and Challenges in America* (2007).

Kenny, Kevin. *Peaceable Kingdom Lost: The Paxton Boys and the Destruction of William Penn's Holy Experiment* (2009).

Tucker, Barbara M., and Kenneth H. Tucker. *Industrializing Antebellum America: The Rise of Manufacturing Entrepreneurs in the Early Republic* (2008).

CHAPTER THREE

From Two Continents, Bound
for Two Coasts, 1820–1882

ARY McBRIDE FROM COUNTY Sligo joined the mass exodus from Ireland at the height of the devastation wrought by the Great Famine of the late 1840s. Like many of her compatriots, she disembarked first in St. John's, in Canada's New Brunswick province, and then headed south to the United States. She and one of her sisters arrived in Boston, and, as she wrote in 1847 to a friend back home, they did not like it there, so they moved on to nearby Newburyport. Now, she reported, they enjoyed good health, and "have got an excellent situation," working for "a fine Master and Mistress." The two managed to save a pound a week from their salaries as domestic servants, and with what they could squirrel away, they intended to "send you money enough" to bring over another sister and brother.[1]

A year later on the continent's other side, Chum Ming, a San Francisco storekeeper, heard the news of the discovery of gold some miles away in California's American River. Energized by the possibility of making money, he communicated right away with a cousin in the Chinese province of Canton (Guangdong), Cheong Yim, urging him to round up some other men and join him. Four months later the group met up with Chum Ming in goldfields and began to seek their fortunes in the Mother Lode, known to the Chinese as the Gold Mountain.[2]

From the 1820s to the 1920s ceaseless immigration of women and men defined the life of the American nation, shaping its society, politics, and culture. It enabled the launch of the United States from a relatively minor place to a global leader in production and consumption. Mass migration propelled the vast expansion of the United States across the North American continent, making possible mining, farming, logging, and industrial development on a scale that transformed the planet. White, Protestant English speakers of British origin defined American culture in 1820. Over the course of the century that followed, Catholics challenged that hegemony. Jewish immigrants, while smaller in number, also upended the idea of America as a Christian nation, and immigrants from Asia further shook up comfortable assumptions about the meaning of being American. Throughout the country, German, Swedish, Czech, French, Polish, Cantonese, Italian, and Spanish, among other tongues, emerged as languages of everyday life. They resounded on city streets and in smaller communities.

Mass migration transformed the United States and shook up the world, primarily Europe but other places as well. As transportation allowed people to leave their many homes in response to dwindling opportunities in their long-standing places of residence, they had someplace to go where comparatively few laws impeded their entry and where the possibility of work abounded. The steady outward movement of individuals and families from specific towns and regions gained steam. The idea of immigration to America gained traction. Whole towns, regions, and countries felt the profound effect of the out-migration of their young people. One Irish commentator asserted a sentiment echoed in multiple languages: "Indeed the regret belongs rather now to those who stay behind and those who watch the unceasing flow of the hardiest and most vigorous of our race."[3]

The *Telegraph*, a newspaper in the Welsh city of Merthyr, described the "excessive course of depletion" of the local population as it chronicled the outward flow of local youth bound for America in the 1860s. This coal-mining region, like farming areas across western and central Europe, Ireland, and the Pearl River Delta in China, witnessed the steady movement of the young and able to engage in difficult physical labor, whom another Welsh publication described as "our best men," who were smitten by the "contagion" of emigration.[4]

Like Chum Ming and Mary McBride, emigrants sent back remittances to parents and siblings, and they described in letters the details of wages, work, and personal choices they found. In these simple quotidian familial acts, they redefined how those left behind understood their own lives.

Immigration to America from 1820 through 1882 proceeded apace. It took its shape from the fact of the U.S. physical expansion over the continent, as it ingested lands farther and farther away from the Eastern Seaboard. Deeply affected in the 1840s by the U.S. conquest of land owned by Mexico, immigration from Europe and China pivoted toward the future states of Texas, Arizona, New Mexico, and California, populated by Spanish speakers born under Mexican rule. In that vast swathe of land, indigenous people such as the Comanche ruled over their own empires, trading widely north and south of the Rio Grande. Only in 1875 did they suffer final defeat.

As for those women and men who had been residents of Mexico, the United States came to them when war altered the borders of their homelands. The 1848 Treaty of Guadalupe Hidalgo ended the Mexican War, undertaken in large measure at the encouragement of the Southerners who hoped to expand territory for cotton cultivation by the enslaved, and extended American citizenship to about 60,000 Mexican residents. Despite having citizenship and family ties to people living on either side of the new national boundary, they and their descendants would participate in the constant migrations so common among Americans, journeying from place to place, state to state, countryside to city, and because of the war, nation to nation, in search of work and opportunity.

An Immigration Watershed: 1820

In 1820, for the first time, the federal census began to collect immigration statistics. While it did not regulate, restrict, or legislate any of the details of immigration, it did start counting. The numbers tell a story of constant growth (table 3.1). In the 1820s, 150,000

Table 3.1. Immigrants and Major Countries or Regions
of Origin, 1840s–1910s

Decade	Immigrants (millions)	Major Countries or Regions of Origin
1840s	1.4	Ireland, Great Britain, Germany
1850s	2.8	Ireland, Great Britain, Germany
1860s	2.1	Germany, Great Britain
1870s	2.7	Germany, Great Britain, Ireland
1880s	5.2	Germany, Great Britain, Scandinavia
1890s	3.7	Italy, Russia, central Europe
1900s	8.2	Italy, Russia, central Europe
1910s	6.3	Italy Russia, central Europe

Source: U.S. Bureau of the Census, *Statistical Abstract of the United States, 1944–45*
(Washington, D.C., 1945), 109, 111.

immigrants came to America, whereas in the 1830s the number qua-
drupled to 600,000. The 1840s overshadowed everything that had
come before, with 1,400,000 newcomers. By the 1850s that number
would have seemed small when compared to the 2,800,000 people
who disembarked at some American port intending to make a living
in the United States. More people chose to immigrate between 1820
and the Civil War than had lived in the United States in 1790, and
the nine years from 1845 to 1854 witnessed the single largest flood
of newcomers to American shores to that date.

The outbreak of the Civil War in 1861 caused a temporary decline in immigration, but even with four years of war, the decade
still saw 2,100,000 immigrants arrive. The 1870s, punctuated by a
terrible economic downturn that lasted from 1873 until 1879, still
saw 2,700,000 immigrants attracted to America.

These numbers cannot convey the complex individual human
stories that lay at their core. But regardless of place of origin, they
had three things in common, namely, that circumstances at home
did not prevent them from leaving, that they could make use of new
technologies of communication and transportation that allowed
them to move, and that favorable conditions in America, despite xenophobia, continuing anti-Catholicism, and the national stress that
emanated from the ongoing debate over slavery, did not prevent
them from entering. A kind of balance existed between the deficits

of their familiar homes and the positive conditions of the settings to which they went. Such a synergy connected millions of the world's peoples to the United States through the flow of knowledge and the transportation networks that brought them here.

No single story encapsulates the breadth of the immigration experiences of these decades. A few personal narratives might, however, convey something of their texture. Leonora Kearney came to America with her parents in 1852, at age three, from Ireland's County Cork. They settled in Pierrepont, New York, where her father farmed a small holding. She did not experience poverty in America until after the death of her husband, William Barry, also an immigrant from Ireland. She then had to work to support her children. Securing employment in a hosiery factory, she encountered the realities of unregulated American industrial capitalism, its grueling work conditions and low pay. Known as Leonora Barry, she rose to be the only woman to serve as an officer in the Knights of Labor, a union that reached across racial and ethnic boundaries and sought to restructure the American economy.

Hans Mattson arrived in the United States in 1851. A native of Önnestad in the Swedish province of Scania, he left his family's impoverished farm, journeying to America with a friend. He settled initially in an all-Swedish community in Illinois and within a year had saved enough money to bring his family from Sweden. Together with some of his fellow Swedes he moved to Minnesota, eventually settling in Red Wing, where he served as a local official. In 1861 Mattson raised a company of Swedish-born men to fight for the United States during the Civil War. He lived and functioned in a profoundly Swedish environment in the United States; Swedish was the common language of daily life. Yet he became an avid American patriot. He hoped to stimulate even more Swedish immigration to America and took a position as an agent with the Saint Paul and Pacific Railroad, greeting new arrivals from Sweden and Norway and helping them find work and places to live in the upper Midwest. In 1866 he convinced Minnesota officials to create a Board of Immigration to promote even more immigration to his American state from his Swedish homeland.

Levi Strauss left his home in Franconia, in Bavaria, in 1847, arriving in New York, where he joined his brothers. Together with his family, he moved west to San Francisco, the center of the Gold Rush, where, like many of his fellow Jewish immigrants, Strauss established a wholesale dry-goods business. His business prospered, selling a wide range of goods, including bedding, mirrors, combs, purses, as well as tents to the miners—perhaps even Chum Ming and his friends—who came from around the United States, Europe, China, and South America, lured by promises of gold, silver, and the other riches of the Pacific region. He also sold pants made of denim, and for more than 150 years since then consumers around the globe have recognized the first name of this immigrant by the label "Levi's" and the brass rivets on the back pockets of their jeans.

The Homes They Left

They left homes scattered throughout Europe, although Chum Ming's story broadens the geography of emigration to China's Pearl River Delta. They left homes now labeled Germany, Sweden, Denmark, Norway, Ireland, and China, among others. These familiar names obscure the complexities of language, religion, and ethnic identity in these places, and the reality that families and individuals came to America from very specific regions within. The borders of these countries changed during these decades, and over time immigrants from any of these nation-states came from shifting geographies within, which complicated ideas about the places they left.

Each migration seems unique, particularly if described by country of origin. Each one seemingly had a narrative of its own. But circumstances in the many sending communities resembled each other, and their commonalities offer a more compelling story than that which emphasizes uniqueness. For example, the mass migration of Irish Catholics, like Mary McBride, largely has been told as the desperate flight of Irish peasants in response to the devastation of the much-depended-on potato crop. From 1845 until 1849 this vast ecological crisis, the result of the spread of non-photosynthetic algae, *Phytophthora infestans*, killed 1 million people, about a quarter of the population of Ireland. According to the conventional telling of the history, the famine impelled the emigration of another million, halving the Irish population. British colonial policies had rendered the Irish a people who daily lived on potatoes, so the cataclysm of the 1840s left them bereft.

Yet the potato famine, Ireland's "Great Hunger," can just as easily be called the European "Great Hunger" or "the Hungry Forties." The blight encompassed nearly all of northern Europe, destroying potato crops across a wide region. It hit the Scottish Highlands even worse than it did Ireland. It rampaged through Belgium, Denmark, Sweden, Prussia, the Netherlands, and elsewhere, moving as far south as Spain and Portugal, affecting these societies as it did Ireland, causing mass deaths by starvation and disease. Wherever it struck, it reduced fertility, upended landholding patterns, and stimulated emigration.

Emigration from Ireland, like that from all these places, involved more than a frenzied simple flight from famine. Though the movement of emigrants during the late 1840s transformed Ireland and America, it followed on the arrival of Irish Catholics in North America that had commenced during the late colonial and early national periods. Those leaving Ireland even during the worst of the famine had some capital, coming from the least poor and destitute of their communities mostly in the west of the island. Women in particular left Ireland in droves for decades well after 1849. Not merely victims of the famine's scourge, they understood that their transformed home communities offered only limited chances for either marriage or earning a living. Only in the United States could they expect to do either, or possibly both.[5]

The history of Germany as a nation complicates thinking about the immigration of mid-nineteenth-century German speakers, who in these years constituted less than one-quarter of all immigrants to America, whereas in 1860 they accounted for more than one-third of America's foreign-born. But Germany did not exist as a unified nation until the Prussian ruler Otto von Bismarck engineered it in 1871. Before then, German speakers arrived in the United States from a number of independent states, each with its specific economic, social, and political realities.

The narrative of German immigration to America tends to explain the draw of the United States in terms of the failed liberal revolution of 1848. That year protests flared over the German-speaking lands, inspiring high hopes for a new and more democratic order. Within two years the revolution collapsed, and some of the defeated revolutionaries from throughout the German lands set sail for America. But the collapse of the revolution played no part in the mass exodus.

German speakers from the various regions, like the Irish, Swedish, Chinese, Czech, Québécois, and the many others who immigrated in the mid-nineteenth century, mobilized their personal and familial resources as they faced new economic realities in home communities that could no longer accommodate them.

Most had to cope with overpopulation. In the late eighteenth century a precipitous drop in the death rate began in northern Europe, spreading eventually to the east and south. That decrease in mortality did not bring about any downward adjustment in fertility, and ordinary people underwent a process that social scientists have labeled "the demographic transition." Put simply, the various locales that sent immigrants to America contained too many people competing for dwindling opportunities.

This population growth went hand in hand with new practices in agriculture, landholding, and manufacturing. Most people lived in rural areas. Farming occupied nearly all, and their lives changed, as did their basic way of making a living. In these decades, the displacement of millions of rural people disrupted life throughout western and central Europe. The enclosures of common land and the consolidation of estates by landowners seeking more efficient methods of cultivation threw off the land massive numbers of people, whose forebears had labored as peasants, serfs, tenants, or hired hands with little or no rights. The abolition of serfdom in the czarist empire in 1861 created a vast contingent of landless laborers, which intensified competition for any work in the countryside. This pushed young people out of their home communities and created a first wave of emigrants from the affected regions.

This agricultural transformation occurred in tandem with industrialization and globalization. The rise of factories, even small ones, meant that shoes, clothing, cloth, and other goods could be made more cheaply and efficiently by machines in towns and cities, which undermined home production, another way that for many decades rural families had sustained themselves. For generations, European peasants had supplemented their farm earnings by making things in their homes, which in turn they, or an agent or contractor, sold.

Mills and factories, using the latest technology, could by the early nineteenth century churn out goods more quickly, more cheaply, and at a higher volume than rural families could manage, jeopardizing a crucial source of income for families in England, Scotland, Wales, and the European continent.[6]

This happened slowly. Areas closest to cities and towns felt it first, but over time changes extended to rural regions, directly and powerfully. The development and expansion of the United States played a decisive role in smashing European patterns of life. As Americans moved farther west, they produced bumper crops of agricultural goods. Facilitated by the complex railroad system launched in 1827 with the opening of the Baltimore and Ohio Railroad, they could get their produce onto ships bound for Europe. Those ships transported wheat, rye, corn, and so many more crops, and in the decades after the Civil War, finished goods as well, to Europe. From northern and western European ports, railroads chugged into the cities and hinterlands, bringing ordinary people American products.

Gender mattered greatly as people experienced these economic disruptions. Generally, men migrated first, followed by women. Whether the order of migration consisted of single men, then women, or husbands, then wives, decisions about immigration reflected the economic challenges at home and work opportunities in America. Immigrants who imagined establishing themselves as farmers in America came as full families, husbands, wives, and children, all able to participate in the enterprise.

Age also lay at the heart of immigration. Young people felt the sting of change more acutely than older ones. They recognized that the new order made it impossible for them to get a start in life, earn a living, marry, and take their places as adults in their home communities.

Immigrants, particularly in the earliest stages, tended to live closest to both rail lines and ports of embarkation. The first sizable contingent of Chinese emigrants bound for the United States in the 1840s, like Chum Ming and his friends who joined him in the goldfields, came from a region with easiest access to the harbor on the South China Sea, primarily from the Cantonese counties Sam Yup, Sze Yup, and Xiangshan. The region experienced overpopulation, and its people had been on the move for decades. American and

European business interests clustered in coastal port cities, as did labor recruiters and missionaries who spread knowledge of America to the people living along the tributaries of the Pearl River.

Similarly, after the population of rural Quebec mushroomed by 400 percent between 1784 and 1844, while available farming land shrank, and the first railroad line linked Quebec to other parts of Canada and to the United States in the late 1830s, as droves of young people headed for the mill towns and farms of New England.

The Economic Origins of Immigration

The economic bases of *all* migrations undermine familiar tales of political and religious oppression as the prime forces that catalyzed millions to leave their homes. They challenge the narratives of Germans seeking freedom after their revolutions failed, of Poles embittered by the lack of an independent country, and of Jews fleeing religious persecution. Famines and other crises certainly had a role in pushing migrants out, but they occurred in places where outmigration had already begun and where it would continue for some time, after adverse conditions had settled down.

The first emigrants from Balestrand, in Norway's Sogn province, for example, came from the ranks of the middle class. Nothing forced them out in desperation. In the 1840s they had some choices as they confronted changing local realities. After the first Balestranders planted communities in the upper Midwest, poorer people from the region followed, going to the same places in America.

The most destitute men from Cantonese towns and villages did not join the first contingents of immigrants who started out in the 1840s. The British governor of Hong Kong described those leaving in the 1850s as "respectable people" of a "superior class" and, importantly, as "self-supporting, paying their own passages and making all the necessary provisions from their own or their family resources for their departure."[7]

Young Irishwomen who could not obtain the dowries that they needed in the 1850s to marry instead opted to "travel," as they called it, to leave Ireland, which offered no options for industrial and urban employment. This class of young women, who had usually just enough money to pay their fares, found America attractive. Their immigration in turn profoundly affected Irish life, largely because, through the money sent back home, they made possible the further emigration of sisters, cousins, and other family members, giving them the financial means to sail the Atlantic.

These immigrants, like the others, would over the course of their lives in America contribute money in the form of remittances to the families and villages they had left, which allowed parents and siblings to move from being renters to landowners and augment the size of their farms. Their money enabled siblings to acquire educations and helped pay their fares, so they too could immigrate. This migration, like the others, decreased population in the sending societies. It also enhanced the value of labor and raised wages for those left behind.

The young men and women considering immigration from Ireland and all the other places may not have been the most impoverished, but they worried that economic disruptions would with time drag them down, subjecting them to futures of destitution. The communities where they lived offered no solutions to their worries, but the United States did.

Some immigrants during these years did decide to leave, in part, for noneconomic reasons, particularly those who lived as religious and linguistic minorities, whose distinctive life experiences as outsiders made America particularly appealing. Jews hailing from Alsace to Lithuania made their way to America. So too did Mennonites, German speakers who had lived in czarist Russia since the sixteenth century. Adherents to religious traditions at odds with the official churches in the Netherlands, Sweden, and various locales in central Europe also saw America as a place where they could worship freely and form communities of their own. They also, however, considered the economic limitations at home and the possibilities in the United States as they made their decisions.

The year 1820 was not so much a clear start of a new era, but it can be seen as a highly charged moment of change. It brought about a numerically enhanced continuation of earlier, less dramatic movements to North America. It ushered in several decades that witnessed an escalation of trends that had already been in the works, as immigrants from Switzerland or Sweden, from the Netherlands,

Alsace, Wales, China, or Ireland arrived in the United States, joining others who spoke their languages, understood their circumstances, and shared their religious traditions. Those settled family members and friends provided immediate aid to the newcomers, offering relief in moments of distress and linking them up to work and housing opportunities, serving therefore as helpful resources for the newly arrived to start their American lives.

Making Migration Possible

In the six decades between 1820 and 1880, several forces coalesced abroad to make enlarged migration possible. Government policies in the sending societies shifted priorities from preventing to encouraging emigration. As of the 1820s policy makers in many countries worried about the effect of overpopulation and lifted old rules that blocked the paths of those who would leave. Britain in 1827 wiped away all legal impediments that prevented individuals, including skilled craftsmen, from emigrating. The German states had no single policy, but the 1848 uprisings and the increasing number of rural people moving off the land into cities convinced lawmakers that the stability of society depended on opening the floodgates and letting those unhappy with their situations at home go. The Swedish government in 1840 repealed an anti-emigration law promulgated in 1768, in the hope that those who could not adjust to new economic realities would not become paupers and thus burdens to their communities.

Government officials seeing the overpopulation and the onus placed on public coffers by the growing numbers of the impoverished, allowed people to leave without paying the long-standing "going away" tax. Having to pay to leave would certainly have challenged the majority who wanted to go but had only enough resources to buy their tickets. Enforcing the rules would have kept them from going, but by changing the law or ignoring violations, governments indirectly encouraged potential emigrants to leave for the United States.

Other state actions helped make emigration possible. In the mid-1840s several local Swiss councils offered cash incentives, about 400 Swiss francs, equivalent to six months' wages, to those who would leave, on the condition that they never return. If they did come back, they had to repay the money, and with interest. German communities also nudged out those they deemed undesirable, paying their fares and hoping that their departures would lighten the burden of poor relief on taxpayers. Landlords eager to consolidate their holdings offered to pay their tenants' fares to America, and a range of benevolent societies considered helping the poor get to the United States an act of Christian charity.

The exact number who left this way cannot be accurately tracked, but in fact most immigrants paid for themselves, with or without the help of family. Few depended on the funding of landlords, emigration societies, or governments. The existence of such schemes, however, shows that the vision of America as a destination, a place where superfluous women and men could make something of themselves, rippled through European society.

The flow of information from America to Europe informed potential immigrants of what to expect and how to get there. The European press abounded with accounts of America's possibilities. Potential emigrants could learn about the various destinations in America to consider, and information about the prospects for work appeared in many publications. The German-language Jewish newspaper, the *Allgemeine Zeitung des Judentums*, hailed America as "the garden of the Lord," invoking "the majestic blessed American coast."

Its readers and those of other contemporary publications probably cared little about the coastline or about Edenic landscapes. Rather, as a writer for the *Allgemeine* reported, a "Bavarian Israelite" had shown him "a letter received from his brother, who had migrated to New York. . . . He highly extols his present situation and his trade [he is a shoemaker] guarantees him an ample livelihood even if not wealth."[8]

The steady improvement of postal systems around the world did much to facilitate the spread of information across the ocean. The cost of postage also dropped and information sped up. The letters became such fixtures of everyday life that they came to be called "America letters."

Ann Whitaker and her husband, who probably left Leeds, England, sometime between 1839 and 1841, tried farming in Monroe County, Illinois. Despite their English urban roots, their efforts in

America proved reasonably successful. She wrote home in 1851: "We have a good prospect of a plentiful harvest which will soon be on. We have about 30 acres in wheat and no much less in corn." After enumerating then their yields of potatoes, turnips, beets, cherries, and apples, Whitaker concluded her letter of June 24: "We have the right to praise and thank God. For we have seen many of our fellow beings suffer in many ways whilest we enjoy plenty of every thing and above all other blessings good health." An Irish emigrant seamstress in Connecticut wrote to her folks back home and declared, "I am getting along spending and likes [*sic*] my work. . . . It seems like a new life. I will soon have a trade and be more independent. . . . You know it was always what I wanted so I have reached my highest ambition." We cannot know if she exaggerated, but this letter made its way across the ocean and to the home of her kin.[9]

In a letter sent from Wisconsin to Sweden, Gustaf Unonius reported, "I can tell you that here we do not live frugally, but one has eggs and egg pancakes and canned fish and fresh fish, and fruit of all kinds." He went on, "It is different from you who have to sit and suck herring bones." Unonius, founder of a small Swedish colony in Pine Lake, may have wanted to encourage folks back home to join him in the Wisconsin Northwoods with tantalizing tales of pancakes and fruit.[10]

Food loomed large in immigrant letters, as they described the United States as a place where working people could consume meat, sugar, white bread, coffee, and other foods associated with the upper classes in their places of origin. In 1871 a British industrial laborer who lived in the United States wrote that "you get pies and puddings" here.[11]

Not all letters expressed such positive views. Complaints about loneliness, disappointment, and difficult working conditions ran through the letters. An immigrant from Württemberg living in Johnstown, Pennsylvania, wrote home in 1877 to tell his "dear mother, brother, grandparents, dear sisters and all relatives" that he found himself "really ill, very ill," as a result of the "miserable air" that he breathed in "from 6 in the morning until 6 at night."[12]

But that so many letters contained remittances may have mattered more than either tales of pie and pudding or complaints about work. By 1880 America money made its way back to Ireland, for example, at a staggering level, given the fact that most of it came from single women working as domestic servants. One study undertaken in Ireland in the 1870s estimated that one-third of all money in circulation came from women in America. The remittances advertised American possibilities.[13]

As the immigrants formed ethnic communities, they created more formal means to transmit the money. The Emigrant Industrial Savings Bank, founded in New York in 1850 by eighteen Irish members of the Irish Emigrant Society, enabled working-class women and men to save their money and enhance their lives in America, but it also streamlined the process of sending funds across the Atlantic. Within the first year of Chinese settlement in San Francisco, merchants in the community forged an association, and though it did not last long, a network of district and clan associations provided crucial services to the newcomers, including mediating disputes among members, providing interpreters for the newly arrived, securing jobs and places to live, and facilitating the always crucial flow of remittances back home. In smaller enclaves scattered around the United States, regardless of place of origin, immigrants turned to merchants in their ethnic communities to serve as intermediaries to transmit dollars back home.

The laying of the Atlantic cable in late 1858 played a powerful role in hastening further immigration. The telegraph linked Europe to America as never before. The cable made it easy to send money, at lightning speed, from anyplace in America to anyplace in Europe and became a multiplier of migrations.

Technological and commercial advances of transoceanic shipping, including the development of steamships, made travel less expensive and dangerous, and dramatically faster. After the 1810s, with the cessation of Europe's seemingly endless wars, Atlantic commerce grew. It began in the 1820s with the development of the North American timber trade. Increasing numbers of sailing ships brought cotton, tobacco, and other American products eastward to Europe. The ships, whether going to and from Liverpool, the numerous smaller ports in Ireland, Wales, and Scotland, or continental port facilities in Bremen, Le Havre, Rotterdam, and

Hamburg, returned westward carrying emigrant cargo traveling in the empty spaces, called steerage.

Steerage offered the cheapest and the worst possible conditions of travel. In these dirty, dark, and vermin-infested quarters, immigrants had to contend with disease and abuse meted out by crew members. Great Britain passed legislation in 1828 to protect its people from the worst of the practice, but, spottily enforced, such laws did little, and only in the late 1860s did emigrants from British ports receive any meaningful protection. Irish immigrants and those leaving the Scottish Highlands at the height of the great potato famine, in the late 1840s, endured the most dangerous experiences on the "coffin ships," the least expensive and least safe vessels plying the waters of the North Atlantic. High onboard mortality and the appearance of typhus among those who disembarked in New York and elsewhere reflected the reality of dismal shipboard conditions and stoked fears about immigrants as bearers of disease. New York, which became the chief port of entry, launched a variety of public health initiatives because of the constant influx of immigrants whom the public considered, and not without cause, as bearing infectious diseases.

One of the biggest businesses of the nineteenth century, the immigrant trade expanded when it became regularized, publishing and disseminating set schedules to potential passengers. Sailing lines opened ticket offices beyond the ports, in interior cities, synchronizing their sailings with the expanding railroad networks and increasingly penetrating the once remote hinterlands. They hired agents who oversaw advertising in local newspapers and informed potential emigrants about the journey to the ports, the dates of the voyages, and the costs.

The more the railroads connected the women and men of the landlocked regions with ports and the more the sailing lines competed with one another, the more precipitously the ticket prices dropped, bringing them increasingly within the reach of poorer and poorer people, compared to those who had emigrated earlier. People of humbler means could, as the trade developed, consider their lives and those of their children in the context of the possibilities of emigration. Especially as they benefited from remittances from

America, they could decide whether or not to go with an ease that would have been impossible in earlier decades. As the sailing ship companies like the Black Ball Line, founded in 1818, along with state and private railroad companies that fanned out across the European continent, sought profits, they ignited "America fever."

The age of sail began to give way to the age of steam in the 1840s. With the development of the Cunard, Red Star, Inman, and other lines, which by the late 1850s dominated transatlantic traffic, the journey dropped from six or seven weeks when powered by sail to six or seven days by steam. Ships got bigger, carrying more people who were increasingly poorer and from remoter regions of their homelands.

Steamships shaped emigration out of China as well. Several forces, including the development and refinement of the technology, the founding of companies like the Pacific Mail and Steamship Company in 1848, and the discovery of gold in California that same year, encouraged the first substantial contingents of Chinese emigrants to the United States, sailing onboard vessels like the S.S. *California*. The Pacific Mail ran steamships up and down California's Sacramento and San Joaquin rivers, allowing immigrants from the Pearl River Delta to get from San Francisco to *Gum Shan*, or Gold Mountain.

In this first phase of mass emigration, some American companies began to recruit directly from regions already sending emigrants, hoping to stimulate further movement to the United States. Wisconsin and Michigan, among other newly admitted states to the Union, eagerly sought out individuals and families willing to work in farming, mining, or shipping on the Great Lakes. After the end of the Civil War, almost every northern and western state advertised in European newspapers touting the attractiveness of this state or that.

That southern states tried as well, and failed, to get in on the scramble for immigrants testifies to the economic basis of the migration. Immigrants for the most part did not consider the slave states attractive destinations. The high cost of land, less robust urban development than in the North, and firm control of the politics and economics of the region wielded by slaveowners made it a poor alternative to the Middle West, whose economy was based on free labor.

The South recognized that immigration from abroad served the interests of the North, in terms of numbers and industrial prowess. The northern and midwestern states grew in the decades leading up to the Civil War, and most immigrants had settled in the cities and farmlands that in 1861, with the outbreak of the war, constituted the Union. These immigrants had dug the coal, mined the ore, built the railroads, and forged the steel, thereby giving the North the advantage in material. One of every four soldiers in the U.S. Army, which took on the Confederacy, had immigrated from someplace in Europe, and another huge chunk, almost half, had at least one immigrant parent, which gave the Union a larger supply of men to send to the battlefields. During the war, with the Southerners absent from Congress, the United States passed various pieces of legislation that further encouraged immigration.[14]

During Reconstruction, in the 1870s, some southern planters attempted to recruit laborers from Canton to the cotton region of the Mississippi Delta, and small numbers came. Within a few years they struck out and became shopkeepers rather than agricultural workers. In the main, though, the South largely lacked free or cheap land and offered few industrial opportunities, while the continuing impoverishment of the masses, Black and white, meant that immigrants would have had little hope of making a living in small businesses, one typical strategy that they adopted elsewhere. Similarly, Reconstruction brought Jewish immigrants from Lithuania to the South, working as pack peddlers and eventually opening up stores throughout the region. But for the most part, the South with its particular economy and racial dynamics did not draw in many immigrants who had many choices about where to go.

Their American Lives

The immigrants of the middle decades of the nineteenth century, like nearly all immigrants, came to places where they had friends and family. Participants in chain migrations, they flocked to those cities, towns, and rural communities where those whom they knew

Cartoon celebrating immigration, 1880. Library of Congress, Washington, D.C.

from back home already lived. Those who went before them pulled them to America with information and assistance in the crucial task of finding work or, for those bound for farming, land.

For the small number who took advantage of assistance packages provided by American employers, or who had been lured by state recruiters, where they went had been, to a degree, predetermined. But these played a minor role in the immigrant draw to America.

The mid-nineteenth century saw the formation of some formal colonization schemes, hatched in Sweden, Bohemia, and parts of Germany, in which participants banded together, emigrated as a group, settled in tight and closed communities, and maintained for some time relatively isolated and homogeneous enclaves. In the 1840s and early 1850s, about two thousand followers of Erik Jansson of the Swedish Evangelical Lutheran Augustana Synod made their way to western Illinois and founded Bishop's Hill, their Heaven on the Prairie. Three shiploads of Dutch Catholics made their way to Wisconsin in 1848 under the direction of a priest, Theodore J. van den Broek, forming colonies in Green Bay, Little Chute, and Little Holland Township. The Adelsverein, the Society for the Protection of German Immigrants in Texas, assisted the emigration of thousands to the Lone Star State, establishing enclaves in Fredericksburg and New Braunfels.

Such schemes undertaken by any number of groups represented just a tiny fraction of the millions who came to America in these years, but their efforts reflected the availability of inexpensive land. All over the country, with the exception of the South, some immigrants sought out places where they could make a living in agriculture. Their whiteness aided them greatly. Despite their lack of U.S. citizenship, they qualified for government—both state and federal—land grants. This draw of the land and the desirability of farming gained much from the passage of the Homestead Act of 1862 during the Civil War. In this highly successful program, Americans of modest means, including millions of immigrants, acquired almost 10 percent of the landmass of the United States.

Though some immigrants headed directly to the frontier, most purchased farms abandoned by Americans who had headed west to virgin land. Immigrants from Sweden, the Netherlands, Wales, the German-speaking lands, and Bohemia set their sights on the Middle West, staking their claims near each other and taking up holdings that others had considered not attractive enough.

Nearby towns reflected the immigrant origins of the women and men who came there to shop, go to church, and attend school. The town of Lindsborg, Kansas, founded in 1869 by immigrants from Värmland, Sweden, served the many Swedish-speaking farmers homesteading in surrounding McPherson County.

Farming alone did not bring immigrants to America's rural regions and to the towns that cropped up across the country. Mining required large numbers of relatively unskilled laborers, and all over the North immigrants gravitated for work to regions opened up for the extraction of iron ore, copper, coal, zinc, lead, or whatever other riches lay buried deep in the American soil. Men from Cornwall headed for southwestern Wisconsin, settling in and around the town of Mineral Point in the early 1840s. In a few years they constituted over half the population. Starting in the early 1870s, hundreds of thousands of Finnish immigrants settled in Michigan's Upper Peninsula, spilling out to the iron ore counties of Wisconsin and Minnesota.

The dramatic story of the discovery of gold in California in 1848 generated a movement of masses eager to try their hand and strike it rich. Men from France, Chile, Italy, Ireland, Peru, the German lands, China, and many more places joined the numerous Americans who made their way to the port at San Francisco and then on to the goldfields. Though an untold number went home, either with money in their pockets or not, the Gold Rush nevertheless paved the way for the growth of the population of California and the crucial development of its commercial agricultural potential by immigrants from abroad.

Immigrant miners, wherever they came from and wherever they went to search for their American livelihoods, differed little from the majority of this era's immigrants who went to cities. The cities of mid-nineteenth-century America, the large, older ones of the East Coast, and newer frontier cities, Buffalo, Chicago, Detroit, St. Louis, Cincinnati, Cleveland, Kansas City, and as far west as San Francisco, grew rapidly as commercial hubs and manufacturing centers, as places of industrial production linked by railroads.

The particular origins of the immigrant population varied from city to city, although the very largest, New York, Chicago, Baltimore, and Philadelphia, attracted immigrants from the full range of European sending societies. Immigrants often stayed for some period in the port cities where their ships had landed, making their homes in New York, Boston, Philadelphia, Baltimore, and New Orleans in large numbers.[15]

In some cities single industries dominated and created distinctive employment and entrepreneurial niches, while in other cities with more diversified economies, a range of factories and workshops provided opportunities for immigrants. Since immigrants helped bring each other over along family and community chains, those already in America and in very specific places, such as St. Louis, Milwaukee, Seattle, Pittsburgh, and more, informed their folks back home as jobs opened up in their workplaces when their employers needed more workers to expand their businesses.

This, then, meant people from particular places clustered, coalescing around particular work sites. In 1858 Joseph Schlitz, a German-born bookkeeper living in Milwaukee, married the widow of August Krug, a local brewer, also a German. The newlywed

Mr. Schlitz took over Krug's beer manufacturing plant, founded a decade earlier, and renamed it Schlitz, over time known worldwide as "the beer that made Milwaukee famous." Milwaukee, with its booming German population, emerged as a beer town, as did St. Louis and Cincinnati; German-owned breweries drew in men from the German-speaking regions, which made these cities heavily German into the end of the nineteenth century. Brewers encouraged the continuous immigration of their fellow Germans to work for them, considering home-country newcomers likely to be loyal and hardworking, deferential and unlikely to cause trouble.

Generally, the larger the employer, the more diverse the workforce it employed. Bethlehem Steel, founded in 1857 as the Saucona Iron Company, used immigrants from multiple places of origin, as did the shipyards at American ports. The meatpacking plants in Chicago, as well as its slaughterhouses like the Union Stockyards, which opened in 1865, brought together men from Ireland, Sweden, Bohemia, the German states, Wales, and elsewhere. The hiring practices of these employers resulted in the creation of towns and cities where people from different places, speaking different languages, lived close to each other. Sometimes everyday cooperation, friendships, and marriages took place as a by-product of these encounters. At the same time, competition, friction, and distrust took hold as well.

The tendency of immigrants to resent others different from themselves, newcomers from strange places, speakers of unintelligible languages, and adherents of unfamiliar faiths, sporadically sparked conflict and violence, particularly when it involved workplaces. Railroad crews, canal building gangs, mining camps, and factory floors became scenes of skirmishes pitting immigrants against immigrants. Mobs of Welsh-born miners who labored in the anthracite coalfields attacked newly arrived Irish immigrants hired as strikebreakers. In Worcester, Massachusetts, working men, divided between Swedish and Irish immigrants, repeatedly clashed. New Yorkers witnessed riots in which Irish Protestants and Irish Catholics fought over labor issues and matters of honor, cast in terms of religion and who had the right to claim being truly Irish.

In New York, as elsewhere, German Catholics and Irish Catholics avoided each other. Despite their shared communion in the universal church, they emphasized their differences rather than their commitment to a common faith and liturgy. German Catholics, the minority, called for female and male religious orders based in Germany to send nuns and priests to America to serve them in German, creating their own schools, hospitals, and parishes. Resentful of the more numerous and institutionally dominant Irish, they wanted Catholicism to come to them in their own language.

Lutherans created separate churches and national synods that were based on their German, Swedish, and Norwegian language loyalties, whereas Jews in larger cities created synagogues for Bavarians, Bohemians, those from the Province of Posen, and, in the 1850s with the influx of Lithuanian Jews, Russians.

Nevertheless, immigrants rolled cigars, sewed garments, stoked blast furnaces, slaughtered cattle, loaded and unloaded ships, filled vats with hops, paved city streets, laid sewer and gas lines, created the infrastructures for streetcars, and, by the end of this era, electrified public and private spaces. Their physical work connected America by roads, canals, and railroads. The many dangerous steps they had to undertake to fell forests, make shoes, dig mines, spin cotton into textiles, blast rocks, and lay train tracks depended primarily on men from China, Ireland, Wales, Bohemia, and many other places.

Some immigrants with skills in weaving, pottery making, brewing, distilling, furniture production, ironworking, and the like launched manufacturing enterprises, becoming entrepreneurs in America, often, like the German brewer Joseph Schlitz, employing large numbers of men from their home communities.

The moment that perhaps best symbolizes the nation's reliance on immigrant labor, a ceremony held on May 10, 1869, took place at Promontory Point, Utah. Teams of primarily Irish men working from east to west, and work groups with a substantial number of Chinese men working from west to east, met and drove the "golden spike" into the ground. In so doing, they opened up America's transcontinental railroad, at once a symbol and a reality of a networked nation.

Immigrant women helped launch America's industrial revolution as well. They found work defined as appropriate to women, in a narrower range of places, laboring in cigar factories, textile mills, garment shops, and other work settings defined as "light industry."

These workshops tended to employ fewer workers and required less capital.

But one occupation, domestic service, proved paramount in the immigration of women and shaped their American lives. Middle-class native-born households desperately craved "help" and turned mostly to women from Ireland, but also those from Sweden and the German lands, who immigrated to work in American homes, cooking, cleaning, and tending children.

From the middle of the nineteenth century, work in domestic service propelled Irish women to leave home and come to America. One 1870s immigrant guidebook written by an Irish Catholic priest, the Reverend Stephen Byrnes, stated, "Servant girls in America get from eight to sixteen dollars a month—sometimes as high as twenty." He calculated for them that "if they save half of that amount every year, and place it at interest, they will have acquired a considerable sum at the end of ten years. Many of them . . . have in the course of twenty or thirty years . . . become owners of from three to five thousand dollars."[16]

Freed from the day-to-day drudgery of laundry, sweeping, food preparation, and child care, middle-class American women turned their attention to reform and charitable work. They created a vast enterprise of philanthropic projects, both religious and nondenominational, that sought to remake America and the world. Some of those women, not needed at home to prepare the meals, scrub the floors, and wash the clothes, pursued self-improvement, while others joined movements to free slaves, end drunkenness, relieve poverty, convert non-Christians at home and abroad, and even extend rights to women.

The influence of the arrival of millions of foreigners, increasingly Catholic and increasingly of non-British origins, continually surfaced in public discussions. Native-born and more recently arrived Americans argued over their merits and demerits, generating an intense discussion in the decades before and after the Civil War. They asked, simply put, whether the value of the work that these women and men provided balanced out the threat that some claimed the newcomers posed to the nation's basic values.

Further Reading

Bergquist, James M. *Daily Life in Immigrant America, 1820–1870* (2008).

Cohn, Raymond L. *Mass Migration under Sail: European Immigration to the Antebellum United States* (2008).

Eifler, Mark A. *The California Gold Rush: The Stampede That Changed the World* (2016).

Miller, Kerby. *Emigrants and Exiles: Ireland and the Irish Exodus to North America* (1985).

Sinn, Elizabeth. *Pacific Crossing: California Gold, Chinese Migration, and the Making of Hong Kong* (2013).

CHAPTER FOUR

Americans React, Regulations Begin, 1820–1882

THE MIGRATIONS OF THE mid-nineteenth century took place in the context of a world with few legal barriers to movement. Immigrants increasingly left homes where their governments put up few obstacles to their leaving and even saw emigration as a solution to domestic problems. These immigrants only had to pay their fares; no papers or passports were required. They did not have to apply to anyone for permission to come to the United States, as no laws restricted their entry.

During the nineteenth century, for the most part those who wanted to immigrate to the United States could do so at will because they had no legal need to prove their worth or demonstrate their abilities. Earlier in the nineteenth century, some Atlantic seaboard states sought to bar the arrival of paupers, those who they feared would be unable to support themselves and end up as public charges. Until the end of the 1870s, congresses and presidents did not advocate, pass, or sign any legislation to halt the steady flow of women and men, from anywhere, to help settle the land and do the necessary work.

During this era the passage of the Fourteenth Amendment to the United States Constitution, adopted in 1868 as one of the innovations of the Reconstruction era, added an especially positive element that seemed to announce the openness of the United States to immigrants. The amendment read, "All persons born or naturalized in the United States are citizens of the United States and enjoy any of the privileges" that flow from that fact. Having been born elsewhere did not deprive an individual, so long as he happened to be a white male of European background and not deemed to be a pauper, the chance to enjoy whatever benefits derived from the federal and state governments, whether in the political sphere or, for example, in the chance to get in on the cheap land being offered for sale in the West. Their children enjoyed birthright citizenship. Their parents' status would not matter at all.

This national policy, which normalized immigration, attaching no legal barriers to it, did not mean, however, that all Americans viewed those born abroad positively. Rather, some of them, coalescing in this era, launched a national debate. Could all immigrants truly become American? What about the Chinese, whom Americans decidedly considered nonwhite? What defects did Americans consider that some immigrants could bring? Who among them would be good for America and who would harm it? Nativists considered that they had a duty to protect the nation from dangerous foreigners, particularly from the growing numbers of Catholics, speakers of non-English languages, and those who seemed to be the bearers of alien cultures, however defined.

Despite the constant agitation from the vociferous and politically charged forces of anti-Catholicism, which culminated in the Know-Nothing, or Native American, Party—which after 1855 shortened its name to the American Party and was founded earlier that decade—masses of immigrants flocked to the United States unchecked by meaningful restrictions. Indeed, toward the end of the Civil War, in response to a decline in the volume of immigration due largely to the hostilities consuming the United States, and set against the continued goal of expanding the nation's economic output, Congress passed a contract labor law in 1864 encouraging companies to pay the passage of immigrants in exchange for their labor. Although it was repealed in 1868, the embrace of such a policy by the federal government indicated that the thirst for workers, particularly Europeans, seemed unquenchable. President Lincoln had addressed Congress in 1863 on this matter, sounding the note that "a system for the encouragement of immigration" ought to be established, as the United States faced "a great deficiency of laborers in every field of industry, especially in agriculture, and our mines, as well as of iron and coal, as of the precious metals" needed the able-bodied willing to relocate to America.[1]

The 1864 legislation, as envisioned in Lincoln's speech, did little to stimulate immigration. Neither did the activities of the many employers and state and territorial governments that sent agents to Europe, fanning out to towns and villages to recruit immigrants, or the southern planters who actively looked for laborers in China. Those who wanted to come to the United States and could get to a port and pay their fare did so without incentives or recruitment. They knew that the federal, state, and local governments of the United States, employers, and the press considered immigration an economic boon to the nation, helping it expand the economy and fulfill its mission, its "manifest destiny," to spread across the continent. This required people, or immigrants.

Nativism Becomes Political

Yet anxiety was growing, articulated by Protestant Americans of British origin, that Catholics from Ireland in particular would, as they became too numerous, alter the basic character of the nation. That would change it decidedly for the worse.

Popular hatred toward Irish immigrants dominated much of mid-nineteenth-century American life. Anti-Catholic, anti-Irish sentiment expressed in print, on the stage, and in sermons from the pulpits of churches resounded in large cities and small towns. Mob violence, including the burning of churches, attacks on nuns and priests, and anti-Catholic political organizing pervaded much of the electoral and social agenda of the nation. Protestants believed that the nation belonged to them by virtue of their having been here the longest, as a result of their having founded it, and by virtue of their upholding basic American values, something Catholics could not do.

Many Americans, like Protestants in Europe, believed that Catholicism constituted an evil, satanic religion, calling it the "Scarlet Woman." They also considered it incompatible with American ideals of democracy, liberty, and individualism. Catholic immigrants could never be good Americans since they took their orders, presumably, from some foreign potentate, the pope. They slavishly followed the rulings of their priests, who told them what to do. The Catholic Church, according to American Protestants, stood in the way of progress and opposed modern ideas. Catholicism, they considered, imprisoned its adherents in ignorance and poverty.

Americans who opposed the flourishing of Catholicism in their land took to the streets and rioted. They threw stones at priests and nuns and burned down Catholic churches. An enraged mob burned down a convent of the Ursuline nuns in Charlestown, Massachusetts, in 1834, just one of such acts intended to purify the Protestant nation of the stain of "Romanism," and to convince the Catholics that they had no place in America. Ten years later, an enflamed mob in Ellsworth, Maine, fell upon a Catholic priest, tarred, and feathered him.

Some who identified Irish Catholics as dangerous to the nation hoped to remake them, to civilize the "Papists" and get them to change their religious beliefs. Lyman Beecher, a well-known minister, published *A Plea for the West* in 1835, advocating that Catholics, a code word for Irish, be excluded from settlement in the territories opening up for white settlement. Meanwhile, the widely published political cartoonist Thomas Nast repeatedly depicted Catholic prelates as crocodiles, sneaking into the United States with their jaws wide open, ready to snap up and destroy American liberty. Charles Loring Brace, a mid-nineteenth-century New York philanthropist, devised a scheme to ship Irish Catholic orphans out of the city to live on farms with Protestant families who would, he believed, transform them into healthy Protestant Americans.[2]

Americans associated Irish Catholic immigrants with rowdiness, ignorance, drunkenness, and poverty. Calls for public education and temperance, both powerful mid-nineteenth-century reform movements, owed their popularity in part to Americans' anxiety that the immigration of Irish Catholics threatened the nation. Advocates of these and other movements sought to minimize the growing influence of these aliens in public life. Public schools, for example, according to their proponents, would operate as an antidote against the evils of Catholicism. Temperance would render them sober and industrious.

That Irish Catholic men in New York, Boston, Pittsburgh, San Francisco, and other cities flocked to the Democratic Party and emerged as a visible and energized bloc in urban politics did not help them either, at least in the eyes of native-born Americans, many of whom were of Irish background themselves, but Protestant in religion. The pursuit by Irish men of street-, ward-, and city-level politics went hand in hand with charges of corruption, vote buying, and influence peddling, all described as antithetical to the American Protestant ideal of politics as service. It mattered little that American machine politics predated the arrival of the Irish or their entry into the political fray. As native-born Americans, particularly those associated with the Whig and then the Republican Party, saw it, the Irish had poisoned American politics.

Americans' rhetoric against Irish immigrants bore a racial inflection, transferred to America from England, where for centuries the Irish seemed a breed apart. The Irish, with their overconsumption of alcohol, volatility, pugnaciousness, and feckless behaviors, represented, on both sides of the Atlantic, a lower form of human life. Americans associated Irish immigrants and their enclaves with disease, bred primarily by the filthy conditions in which they chose to live. One New Yorker, Philip Hone, wrote in his diary in 1832 that "they [the Irish] have brought the cholera this year and they will always bring wretchedness and want." He went on to note that the claim "that our country is an asylum for the oppressed in other parts of the world is very philanthropic and sentimental, but I fear that we shall before long derive little comfort from being made the almshouse and refuge for the poor of other countries."[3]

Cartoonists typically portrayed the Irish with sloping and protruding foreheads and pug noses, more apelike than human. Irish men, ubiquitously labeled "Paddy," and Irish women, "Bridget," brandished crude weapons and fists poised to strike, while clutching bottles of alcohol. American image makers vacillated between seeing the Irish as defective in nature and viewing them as defective in circumstance. Either way, the Irish immigrants in conjunction with their Catholicism did not measure up to American ideals.

Americans, middle-class, Protestant, and native-born, saw the Irish as paupers and slum dwellers, as domestic servants, cartmen, longshoremen, factory workers, ditchdiggers, and casual laborers, and they assumed these occupations to be their permanent and hereditary fate. Those who worried about the Irish newcomers associated the meteoric growth in numbers of these new immigrants in urban areas with unhealthy slums, the spread of crime, and the increase in public disorder.

American commentators fixated on the Irish as the worst of the immigrants and as standing for all the problematic "foreign populations" changing the face of America. One doctor from Providence, Rhode Island, declared in 1851 that "as a class, in this city, and in other cities in this country," immigrants "are under entirely different sanitary influences then the American population." He ticked off the various diseases running rampant in the tenement houses, a distinctive new form of urban residential architecture of the mid-nineteenth century.[4]

The specter of Irish poverty, more than problems associated with any other group, shaped immigration policy and politics. A few East Coast states, particularly New York and Massachusetts, took steps to regulate immigration by ensuring that paupers not disembark at their doors, although these measures had little effect on numbers.[5] In 1847, the second year of the great famine in Ireland, the State of New York created a first for the nation, a Board of Commissioners on Immigration. It established the Marine Hospital on Staten Island and another facility on Ward's Island to care for immigrants coming with infectious diseases, hoping to prevent sick newcomers from infecting the population as a whole. The next decade it opened an employment bureau in lower Manhattan and in 1855 transformed a fort, then a popular concert hall at Castle Garden, into a receiving station, through which all the immigrants landing in New York would traverse. The arrival of immigrants, Irish in particular, and the anxieties of Americans surrounding this, thus paved the way for the emergence in the mid-nineteenth century of city and state agencies of regulation and social service.

New York State and Massachusetts, both magnets for the Irish immigrants in the famine years, legislated that shipmasters had to pay bond on any people being transported who state officials decided might become paupers, and therefore drains on public resources. The state legislation gave the commissioners the power to determine whom to send back to their countries of origin. These states started requiring ship captains to provide documents, and they put in place procedures and enforcement mechanisms so state officials could determine who could stay and who could not. Designed to devise standards of acceptability or lack thereof among the masses, these state laws authorized the appointment of America's first immigration officials.

Even before the creation of the Board of Commissioners, New York State passed a law that declared that shipmasters had to report the names of those who had traveled on their vessels and post bond for those who the captains considered would become public charges. The U.S. Supreme Court, in the 1837 decision *Mayor of the City of New York v. Miln*, validated the law as constitutional. New York instituted a head tax on immigrants, lest any become dependent on the resources of the state. The *Passenger Cases* of 1849, however, overturned *Miln*, and a subsequent case in 1876, *Henderson v. Mayor of New York*, further impeded the actions of states to regulate immigration and tax ship captains.

The numbers deported or assisted to leave financially by individual states paled in comparison to the number of those who disembarked and then entered the country, with the right to naturalize, settle wherever they liked, and pursue livelihoods. Between 1837 and 1845, 33,436 immigrants arrived in Massachusetts, which sent only 715 back to Ireland. But a preponderance of Americans perceived that many of the newcomers came from the ranks of the poor and that their poverty harmed America; those perceptions, combined with the actions of the Supreme Court that undermined state-level action, led to growing calls for the federalization of immigration policy. What New York and Massachusetts had considered local problems came by the 1880s to be reconsidered national problems, in need of national solutions.[6]

New York's opening of Castle Garden took place amid a public outcry about allegations of the diseases and disorder immigrants brought with them. But the actions of New York State authorized little in the way of surveillance of immigrants, and the few officials

stationed there did not stem immigration or regulate it in any meaningful way. Castle Garden, in fact, ran a range of reception services.
Immigrants who went through its portals availed themselves of
places to buy a meal and take a bath, and even a communal kitchen
to prepare some food for themselves. Officials, all volunteers, focused their energy on protecting the immigrants from those who
would prey on them, in particular, "runners" from hotels who lured
them with promises of places to stay, as well as fraudulent employers
claiming to be looking for workers and agents of transportation services offering to help them get to their final destinations who stole
from the immigrants the meager funds they had with them.

The arrival of the immigrants, coupled with outbreaks of cholera and other infectious diseases, pushed cities and states to become
partners in aiding those in distress, something previously left to charitable institutions, particularly those immigrant societies founded to
care for their own. At times immigrant-based institutions asked the
state to help them support the newly arrived. In 1850, for example,
the Hibernian Society of New Orleans successfully petitioned the
city to assign two police officers, both Irish, to stand guard at the
dock to protect Irish immigrant women from the procurers who
tried to trick single female immigrants, a typical feature of Irish immigration, into prostitution.

City by city, state by state, governments decided that they had
to manage the situation, responding to complaints by native-born,
middle-class, white Americans who believed that hordes of poor,
wild, and diseased newcomers threatened their well-being. Governmental bodies created a set of carceral institutions to keep the so-
called problematic elements of the immigrant population away from
the public.

The arrival of new immigrants, the anti-immigrant discourse,
and the increased actions of cities and states prompted the various
immigrant communities, one by one, to respond. They established
their own agencies to provide services to the newcomers and to
circumvent the actions of governmental bodies. In 1871 the president of the Charitable Irish Society of Boston addressed potential
donors among the increasingly large number of comfortable Irish
immigrants of the city to "call your attention to the want of a fund
to temporarily assist distressed Irishmen arriving in this city." To

him, the honor and welfare of his community depended on such philanthropy, as "the Scotch, and the British, and Welsh, and other nationalities, have their homes where a poor strange wayfarer can be accommodated . . . but the friendless Son of Erin, has none to shelter or give him food!" In trying to persuade Boston's Irish to give, he contrasted their lack of generosity, as he saw it, with the more impressive record of Protestants, who often sparred with Irish immigrants over jobs and politics.[7]

But the process of government intervention proceeded apace, and a subtle but important shift to the federal level moved forward. By the middle of the 1850s, federal oversight ratcheted up. Congress charged the U.S. Customs Service with collecting statistics on the number of immigrants, and in 1864 it established a Bureau of Immigration to count them. In 1867 it transferred responsibility for these tasks to the Treasury Department.

The Know Nothings and Their Moment in the Spotlight

The emergence of state supervision of immigration cannot be disassociated from the rise of nativist politics. The American Republican Party emerged in New York in 1843 and spread to other states, taking the name of the Native American Party and then shortening it to the American Party. Within a year of its founding the party began to garner considerable political clout, capturing sizable numbers of votes in Pennsylvania and winning elections, including a congressional seat for one of their own. It and such patriotic societies as the Order of the Star Spangled Banner and the Order of United Americans appealed mostly to native-born, white, Protestant men, some wealthy, most above average in income, few poor or unskilled, who lived primarily in cities. Some Germans and some Jews, including Lewis Charles Levin, the first Jew elected to Congress, representing Pennsylvania's First District, joined the overwhelmingly Protestant, anti-Catholic movement.

These groups coalesced and by the early 1850s they fused into a political party. Reflecting its origins as a secret society, the party went by the name the "Know Nothings." It dominated the Massachusetts legislature in the 1854 election and embarked on a campaign to undermine Irish Catholic participation in the political life of the state. In 1855 newly elected Mayor Levi Boone of Chicago, standing for the nativists, barred all immigrants from securing government jobs.

Yet, within a year or two of its electoral glory, the party and the movement faded. The issue of slavery and the increasingly harsh sectional divide over it ripped the party apart. Those members of the Know Nothing Party who opposed slavery joined the newly formed Republican Party in the wake of the landmark 1857 Supreme Court case *Dred Scott v. Sandford*, which not only declared that the U.S. Constitution did not include Black people as citizens, but also wiped away the sectional boundary between free and slave as legislated in the Missouri Compromise of 1830.

The history of the Know Nothing Party and its moment in the sun can be read several ways. On the one hand, it demonstrated the discomfort white, native-born Americans felt about immigration, as it resembled the anti-immigrant sentiments that flared in the years of the early republic at the time of the Alien and Sedition Acts. They saw immigrants as outsiders who by virtue of their growing numbers threatened the supremacy of the nation's rightful guardians. Poor immigrants who arrived in droves, they believed, drained public resources, which were paid for by the taxes contributed by real (meaning white), native-born Americans. So, too, many nativists claimed, poor immigrants searching for work took any jobs they could, willingly accepting lower wages than those real Americans used to command. Immigrants therefore depressed the rate of pay that these insider Americans deserved. They associated immigrants with the increasing trend toward industrial production, in which goods once made by skilled American artisans now spewed out of factories, as craftsmen were left behind and degraded.

But the Know Nothings did not call on the federal government to ban immigration. They sought instead to make it harder for immigrants to become naturalized in a bid to prevent them from dominating politics. Nativists worried about the increasing political muscle flexed by the Irish and the tendency of immigrants to vote partly in response to what they considered their group interests. If these immigrants, the nativists reasoned, had to wait longer to become citizens, they would enter the political process tamed and educated to act in harmony with American values.

The party also hoped to combat Catholicism directly. The Know Nothing–dominated Massachusetts legislature mandated the reading of the King James Version of the Bible in public schools, which was anathema to Catholics. It also created a high-level commission to investigate supposed rampant sexual immorality in Catholic convents, responding to a long-held Protestant fantasy.

A drawn-out struggle developed between John Hughes, an Irish-born priest who became New York's first archbishop in 1842, and the nativist fears of New Yorkers of encroaching Catholic power. Hughes argued that the Protestant-based Public School Society should cease operating in the city's schools because it exposed Catholic youngsters to texts that harmed their souls and demeaned their religion. Having failed in this, he then demanded that the state fund the growing number of Catholic parochial schools that served immigrant children.

Irish immigrants, as individuals and through their communal institutions, responded to the hostility. They formed social, political, educational, and religious institutions that insulated and protected them. They built schools, churches, newspapers, and a rash of political and cultural associations, both formal and informal, to sustain ethnic group life in America.

They demonstrated their presence regardless of the nativism. In 1853, as one very bold example, Hughes, after his combat with New York over the school issue, announced plans to build a cathedral that would by its size and splendor announce to New Yorkers that the Irish and their religious tradition had come to stay. He hired the renowned American architect James Renwick to design the cathedral, St. Patrick's, named for Ireland's patron saint. He chose a site atop a hill on Fifth Avenue, which would, according to Hughes, show Americans that his flock, made up of immigrants and their children, were, "worthy," having among them "ever increasing numbers, intelligence, and wealth." They were entitled to be seen "as a religious community . . . in this metropolis of the American continent," along with all others. He rightly predicted that as the city grew and spread northward, the spot he had chosen would tower over one of New York's most prestigious sections, where elite Protestants would live and daily would have to see the cathedral of the hated Papists and constantly confront the Catholics' permanence in the nation that reviled them.[8]

The cathedral arose in 1853 as the political arena resounded with nativist rhetoric and action, but the failure of the Know Nothings reflected the unwillingness of most Americans in the nineteenth century to call for the wholesale end of immigration, and to freeze the population or to eliminate further newcomers, at least European ones. Even as a few state legislatures in the East attempted to make it harder for immigrants to naturalize and vote, states in the West and Midwest liberalized their processes.

The state of Wisconsin, for example, allowed immigrants to vote in 1846, even if they had merely filled out their papers declaring their naturalization intentions. In 1850 Michigan granted immigrants resident only two and a half years in the United States the right to vote. These actions showed how power over this matter still resided in the hands of states and not at the federal level.

The Republican Party, a party tightly tied to business interests and to which some nativists flocked upon the demise of the Know Nothings, included in its 1864 platform a statement that "foreign immigration which in the past has added so much to the wealth, resources, and increase of power to this nation—the asylum of the oppressed of all nations—should be fostered and encouraged by a liberal and just policy." The next two national Republican platforms repeated these sentiments.[9]

Indeed, immigration kept going, even during the nativists' brief moment in the limelight of American politics. Potential immigrants were oblivious to the rhetoric and the victories registered by the xenophobes. That so many immigrants arrived after having received letters and remittances from relatives in the United States puts the clout of the Know Nothings in perspective. That those who had settled in the United States earlier continued their efforts to encourage loved ones to join them indicates that their experiences in America, the salaries they earned and their ability to feed themselves and articulate hopes for the future, withstood the nativist assault.

Between 1841 and 1850, approximately 1,400,000 new immigrants made their way to the United States. The next ten years saw that number exceed 2,800,000. We cannot know if the numbers would have been even higher had there been no, or less, anti-immigrant political action, but clearly the economic imperatives of leaving Europe and prospects of work in America offset for millions the moments of street violence and the proliferation of words and deeds demonizing the immigrants as threats to American society. The numbers indicate the degree to which the European migration of the nineteenth century constituted a movement of women and men looking for livelihoods better than those they could access at home, and not the movement of people swayed by America's political rhetoric, with its promises of citizenship and freedom.

Nativism beyond the Irish

The Know Nothing Party and the movement that fed it highlighted one group in particular, the Irish, pointing them out as the most problematic among the many immigrants of the time. According to the nativists, their Catholicism represented one of the most reprehensible aspects of their culture, something that rendered them unfit for inclusion in the nation. The brief but tumultuous life of the Know Nothings reflected the particular way in which Irish Catholic immigrants served as the paramount symbols and targets of nativist fears in the period, up until the 1880s.

Other immigrants, including Germans, Swedes, Bohemians, French Canadians, Jews, and others, did not escape derisive stereotyping in the press and on the stage. They too endured the experience of being mocked on the street for their accents and lack of English. In the ordinary course of their American lives they had to contend with hostile comments hurled at them in schoolyards and on public conveyances. The German-born Henry Morgenthau, a Jew, who would go on to a notable career in banking and diplomacy, recalled how as a child growing up in Brooklyn he had suffered anti-Jewish name-calling: "I had my little difficulties in school," he commented. Rabbi Bernard Drachman, born to parents from Galicia and Bavaria, remembered his Jersey City boyhood as a time when he got called "sheeny" and "Christ killer."[10]

Americans, whether themselves children of immigrants of earlier decades or not, lavishly dipped into a lexicon of names for

HARPER'S WEEKLY.

A
JOURNAL OF CIVILIZATION.

WITH THE DICKENS SUPPLEMENT

VOL. XIV.—No. 718.]   NEW YORK, SATURDAY, OCTOBER 1, 1870.   [SINGLE COPIES TEN CENTS.
                                                                        [$4.00 PER YEAR IN ADVANCE.

"THE PROMISED LAND," AS SEEN FROM THE DOME OF SAINT PETER'S, ROME.—[SEE PAGE 630.]

Anti-Catholic cartoon, 1870. Library of Congress, Washington, D.C.

immigrants, including "micks" for the Irish, "krauts" for Germans, "frogs," "Canucks," and "pea-soupers" for the migrants from Quebec, "Bohunks" for the Czech speakers from Bohemia, as well as "sheeny" and "kike" for Jews. These derisive monikers and many ugly images, which appeared in newspapers and magazines, did not, however, translate into state action to stymie the movement of yet more of these people. The proliferation of these images and words also did not keep the immigrants and their children from fulfilling the personal and familial goal of the migration, namely, making a living.

At times, though, how immigrants made their livings put them in conflict with other Americans. German immigrants heavily involved in the production and purveying of alcohol, saloon keeping, and ownership and patronage of beer gardens drew criticism from those Americans worried about the evils of drink. Political campaigns in which the temperance issue surfaced, particularly on the municipal level in cities where large numbers of Germans lived, such as Milwaukee, St. Louis, Cincinnati, and Buffalo, tended to pit Germans against native-born Americans. Though less severely stigmatized than the Irish as drunkards, Germans bore the brunt of a public discourse that blamed them for trafficking in alcohol, harming others as they pursued business. But rarely did these disputes escalate into the kind of xenophobia that fueled the crusade against the Irish.

Municipalities and states passed ordinances against peddling, one of the most common occupations pursued by Jewish men, doing so at the behest of shopkeepers who disliked the competition and in the name of preserving order. Such actions linked the Jews' economic niche to the spread of hostility toward them as foreigners and adherents to a strange, non-Christian religion. The notion that clever, sharp-tongued Jews bearing goods on their backs and in wagons, traversing country roads and city streets and bent on profiteering, could easily induce Americans to buy things that they did not need enjoyed a certain currency. When General U. S. Grant issued Order Number 11 in 1862, expelling all the Jews living in Kentucky as a response to their supposedly traitorous business dealings with the Confederate enemy just across the border, he capitalized on a long-standing image of Jews as disloyal money-grubbers who lined their pockets but did not care about the nation. An image hardly limited to nineteenth-century America, it reached back into Christian Europe's medieval past. For the most part, though, it caused little harm to Jews, even those affected by Grant's actions. President Lincoln speedily rescinded his general's order, and Jewish immigrants to America overall experienced the middle decades of the nineteenth century undisturbed, free to trade where they wanted and able to build communities as they wished.

How many immigrants shunned occupations, employers, and neighborhoods because they believed that they would be stigmatized and treated poorly cannot be answered accurately. In an uncountable number of newspaper advertisements, the phrase "No Irish Need Apply" appeared, letting potential job seekers of Irish origins know that they would never be hired. The *New York Sun* printed forty-two such notices in 1842 alone. In 1833 another newspaper, the *Truth Teller*, printed a notice of an employer looking for "a woman, that understands cooking, and to assist in the work generally . . . also a girl to do chamber work. *Irish People* need not apply, nor any one that will not rise at 6 o'clock." Such advertisements, however, belied the reality that domestic service in Protestant homes constituted a ubiquitous Irish female experience in America.[11]

Such rhetoric, in job advertisements and other kinds of public documents, surely shaped the behavior of Catholics. Many Irish and German Catholic families sent their children to parish schools, both to avoid the highly Protestant tone of public schools and perhaps because they believed that teachers and administrators there would demean them. Their embrace of Catholic schools, a practice parish priests heartily encouraged, involved both a protective reaction to perceived ill-treatment by Protestant Americans in public schools and a belief that in the parochial schools, children would become more fully and profoundly enculturated into the faith of their parents, which many Irish Catholic families highly desired.[12]

This anti-immigrant rhetoric and hostile popular action took place without governments—city, state, or federal—involved in any substantive manner. And all this state inaction benefited Europeans, women and men defined by law as white.

Turning of the Tide

Until the early 1880s, Americans in public office at the federal level and in the private sphere did little to check the free, unregulated, and unrestricted entry of immigrants into the United States. Few American government policies impeded immigrants' ability, especially if white, to decide, while still back home, if they should or should not come to America and how. Such matters lay, for the most part, in their own hands as they measured the benefits and liabilities of staying put or going, and indeed where to go as other global destinations became available.

But by the late 1870s the tide had begun to turn, and America set itself on a course of action that in the next five decades would severely limit the freedom of Europeans to migrate when and how they wanted. The 1870s represented the first noticeable, but subtle, geographic shifts in the sources of European immigration, including a quickening of the movement to America of Jews and Christians from eastern Europe, from the Austro-Hungarian and Russian empires, as well as from the newly formed nation of Italy. Immigrants from Norway, which became independent in 1905, began to outpace those from Sweden in the 1870s. Immigrants from Japan began arriving first in 1867 in Hawaii, already heavily dominated by American business interests. They went there as contract laborers, but many of these, over the course of the next few decades, made their way to the mainland.

Like the initial Japanese immigrants in California, they turned their attention to farming. That first group, made up of twenty-two men and one woman, disembarked in 1869 in San Francisco and headed for Gold Hill Ranch, which they transformed into a colony and a business, the Wakamatsu Tea and Silk Farm. While the colony folded within a few years, reports of the initial success of this enterprise launched a wider emigration from Japan, constituting about 100,000 women and men. They came primarily from small towns in Japan's southern regions and gravitated to the Pacific Rim of the United States; agriculture provided the biggest draw, along with commercial fishing.

The penetration of railroads into these regions, the stirrings of industrial development, the changing landholding patterns, the opening of ports, the desire of governments to see the exodus of excess populations, and the remittances sent back by the earliest of family members who made the journey all converged to send immigrants from these new places.

While these migrations would skyrocket numerically in the early twentieth century, the 1870s represented a clear starting point, as Americans began to confront new forms of difference in terms of immigrant origins. In part Americans, here understood as native-born, white, and Protestant, began to sour on immigration during the 1870s as a result of an unprecedented upsurge in labor radicalism and what many considered the emergence of class warfare. Between the mass unemployment that gripped the nation with the Panic of 1873, reports of violence perpetrated by the Molly Maguires, an Irish secret society with a strong presence among Irish miners in Pennsylvania's anthracite coalfields in 1875, and the founding of the Socialist Labor Party in 1878 with a robust German membership base, Americans began to wonder if the nation had reached its limit in terms of welcoming more and more immigrants to its shores. If they had previously embraced the idea of immigration as a crucial source of labor, then a discourse about unemployment, poor wages, and the potential of a revolution from the bottom up caused them to question well-worn, often-repeated truths.

The year 1877 may have been most pivotal in putting the nation, its lawmakers, and the native-born public more generally on the road toward restriction. What began as a local strike against the Baltimore and Ohio Railroad in Martinsburg, West Virginia, flared into nationwide labor action against the entire railroad system. Often referred to as the "Great Upheaval," the strike pitted against each other on the one side an alliance of state governments, with their police forces and militias, the federal government, as President Rutherford B. Hayes called in the national guard, and the railroads, which employed their own private armies, and on the other side workers, mostly immigrants, who revolted against drastic cuts in wages. Violence spread across the nation, and for over forty-five days it seemed as though the immigrant laborers, drawn from many different European homes, threatened the railroad, the nation's lifeline; the civic order; and no less than the American way of life and its deep belief in private property and the sanctity of capitalism.

Ironically, though, the move toward the restriction of European immigration grew and gained momentum as a result of popular agitation and state decisions to end the flow of immigrants from another continent, China.

Chinese Exclusion Led the Way

Chinese immigrants resembled all other immigrants, with the exception that their transoceanic voyages took them across the Pacific, not the Atlantic, and they disembarked primarily in one port, San

Anti-Chinese immigrant cartoon, 1880. Library of Congress, Washington, D.C.

Francisco. They tended, unlike most of the European immigrants of the mid-nineteenth century, to migrate in male groups, accompanied by relatively few women and families. But like their counterparts from Germany or Ireland, Sweden or Quebec, they chose America because of its economic possibilities as measured against the economic dislocations and constrictions at home that caused them to see immigration to America as a wise life choice. Like European immigrants, Chinese newcomers tended to hail from the particular towns and regions experiencing economic changes most acutely and offering access to newly developing means of transportation and communication.

The first Chinese immigrants, a few hundred Cantonese men, responded to news of the 1848 Gold Rush. Within a few years 20,000 more Chinese immigrants worked around California, focusing on mining and on providing services to the miners.[13] They established businesses that served their own population and also other Americans. Californians, for the most part, exhibited initially little hostility to them, and Governor John McDougal of California in 1852 placed them among the "most worthy classes of our newly adopted citizens."[14] As letters from America, often containing money to buy steamship tickets, sailed across the Pacific, Chinese immigrants' numbers grew, and by the 1870s, when anti-Chinese agitation became a fact of life in California and beyond, the U.S. census enumerated 63,000 individuals born in China. Ten years later, at the start of the decade that saw passage of the 1882 Chinese Exclusion Act, the census showed that the number had grown to 105,000.

Despite the warm words of praise heaped on the Chinese in California by the governor, their presence exposed anew what had never been hidden—namely, an obsessive concern with color as a line sharply demarcating good and bad peoples. The same year that Governor McDougal sang their praises, Chinese miners found themselves targeted by the state legislature and subjected to a tax on their earnings. The legislators imposed a special tax on any miner who had not been naturalized, and since the Chinese could not claim whiteness and therefore eligibility for naturalization, they particularly suffered from the tax. Seven years later, in another legislative move, state lawmakers in Sacramento passed a bill designed to lessen competition on "Free White Labor" by "Coolies." That the Chinese miners had not been contracted by anyone and arrived as free as any other worker did little to prevent the unfolding of legislation against them, as the bill further stipulated that it had been passed in order to "discourage the Immigration of the Chinese into the State of California."

Economic fears grew in tandem with racial ideas about what constituted an American and who could not fit into that category, as defined by white California. In 1860 the California Supreme Court rendered the decision *People v. Hall*, which stipulated that Chinese men could not testify in court against white men.

Over the course of the next decades, white revulsion toward Chinese workers, whether laboring on railroads, in agriculture, or in cigar, shoe, or garment making, erupted in violence as white workers fought for their primacy. They fought, lobbied, and agitated in the name of whiteness, some forming in 1877 the Order of Caucasians.

The year 1877 also witnessed the founding in San Francisco of the Workingman's Party by Dennis Kearney, an immigrant from Ireland who linked together ideas about Chinese immigration, the unfair competition they posed to white workingmen, and the evils of capitalism. In the most famous speech delivered by this eloquent speaker, "The Chinese Must Go," he declared, "We propose to rid the country of cheap Chinese labor as soon as possible and by all means in our power, because it tends still more to degrade labor and aggrandize capital."[15]

Kearney, an immigrant cartman who hauled goods around the city in his wagons, envisioned ridding not just California, but the entire nation, of the Chinese. He set his sights on federal policy, and within a few years his vision would triumph. Even before Kearney began declaiming from San Francisco's sandlots, the U.S. Congress had begun to train its sights on the Chinese and the problems posed by their immigration into the United States.

Congressional scrutiny took off when in 1870, in the spirit of the Reconstruction era, the national legislative body redrafted the Naturalization Act, first passed in 1790. Now the standards used to determine who might be naturalized would be extended to "aliens of African nativity and to persons of African descent." But despite the objections of a few, Congress excluded the Chinese, rendering them and others from Asia ineligible for membership in the nation. Though their American-born children did qualify for citizenship on the basis of the Fourteenth Amendment's guarantee of birthright citizenship, fathers could not. They could be present but they could never be, according to the law and echoing the ideology behind the *People v. Hall*, fully included in the legal concept of *American*.

Then in 1875 Congress passed the Page Act, the first piece of prohibitive immigration law at the federal level. It used the word *undesirable*, positing that any immigrant from Asia who had been compelled to emigrate fell into that category, regardless of the particular circumstances of the migration. It expressly forbade entry to any Asian woman who might, according to lawmakers, while in the United States, engage in prostitution. Enforced vigorously, it worked on the assumption that any Chinese woman might become so employed, and therefore made it very difficult for Chinese men already in America to bring over their wives or for Chinese women to migrate on their own.

Then, in the year of Kearney's speeches and during the year of violence as clashes spread across America and armed troops fought striking railroad workers, Congress took up for the first time a proposal to ban Chinese immigration. President Hayes considered their arrival not a case of immigration, since, after all, that phenomenon referred to Europeans. Rather, he accepted ideas about the problems posed by Chinese immigration and endorsed the prospect of finding means to prevent their further arrival.

Yet Hayes in 1879 vetoed legislation passed by Congress that restricted steamships coming from China to carrying no more than fifteen passengers. His veto stemmed in large measure from his recognition that the law violated the terms of an earlier diplomatic agreement, the Burlingame-Seward Treaty, with China. He vetoed it not because he believed that all immigrants enriched America and that whiteness or European origins did not make some immigrants better than others. Rather, he vetoed it because of trade and foreign policy concerns.

The reprieve proved short-lived, and the 1882 passage of the Chinese Exclusion Act ushered in a new era in American immigration history. From then on Americans, both government officials and the public at large, began more explicitly and forcefully to discuss the merits and demerits of one group or another, and the advisability of their immigration. The American discourse on immigration shifted from one that assumed that immigrants would somehow integrate and, more important, perform productive labor to one that defined immigration as a deep problem that was based on the fundamental character of those immigrating, their putative inability to integrate, and the degree to which they harmed the United States, draining it of its economic strength and threatening its cultural essence. And in the course of that evolving discussion, the nation moved toward restriction.

Further Reading

Anbinder, Tyler. *Nativism and Slavery: The Northern Know Nothings and the Politics of the 1850s* (1992).

Billington, Ray Allen. *The Protestant Crusade, 1800–1860: A Study in the Origins of American Nativism* (1938).

Gyory, Andrew. *Closing the Gate: Race, Politics, and the Chinese Exclusion Act* (1998).

Hirota, Hidetaka. *Expelling the Poor: Atlantic Seaboard States and the Nineteenth-Century Origins of American Immigration Policy* (2017).

Kenny, Kevin. *Making Sense of the Molly Maguires* (1998).

CHAPTER FIVE

The Masses Arrive as the Door
Starts to Close, 1882–1921

A T THE TIME OF its publication and for decades to come, Mary Antin's 1912 memoir, *The Promised Land*, attracted legions of avid readers. Among them, President Theodore Roosevelt declared the book evidence that immigrants could become Americans. Born in 1881 in Polotsk, in Belarus, a part of the Russian Empire and in the Pale of Settlement to which Jews like the Antins had been consigned, Antin described her father's 1891 departure for America and the struggles of her mother, Hannah Hayye, while awaiting the tickets that would allow her and the children to join him.

After three years of waiting, one day the steamship tickets arrived. Antin recounted, perhaps with exaggeration, how "before sunset the news" spread. Hannah Hayye could now join the millions moving to America. "They began to come. Friends and foes, distant relatives and new acquaintances, young and old . . . a steady stream of them poured into our street, both day and night, until the hour of our departure." All wanted Hannah Hayye, now "the heroine" of Polotsk, to show them the documents that would change her life.

The family settled in Boston's West End, the city's Jewish enclave. Hannah Hayye operated a grocery store. The family lived in a space behind the store so she could be housemaker and shopkeeper at the same time. She eked out just enough money so her daughter could go to school and become a writer.[1]

Thakar Singh Johl, called Tuly, born in the Punjab region of British-ruled India in 1878, did not leave a memoir and received less acclaim in his lifetime or posthumously than Mary Antin. But his story contains other details of immigration to the United States in the last two decades of the nineteenth century and into the first two of the twentieth. Those details expose both the pull of the United States as an immigrant destination and the meaning of race as a legal category connected to ideas about color.

Married and a father, twenty-eight-year-old Johl immigrated with a group of male friends, all adherents of the Sikh religion. They crossed the Pacific, getting work in the lumber industry of Canada's far western province, British Columbia. From there they easily crossed the U.S. border to do the same kind of work in Bellingham, Washington. Drawn farther south, the group showed up in Sutter County, California, employed by the Southern Pacific Railroad. Bill Eager, a local farmer, then hired Johl and his friends to tend his cotton fields and orchards. Tuly rose to foreman, managing the farm and, most significantly for the history of immigration, recruiting other Punjabis to work for the Eager Ranch. Despite the passage of California's Alien Land Law in 1913, which prohibited noncitizens from buying land, and the fact that Punjabis, defined as nonwhite, could never become citizens, Johl brought dozens over from his region.

In the years from the 1880s through the 1910s, when the Antin family came to Boston and Tuly Singh Johl arrived with his friends in California, immigration shaped the United States. Argentina, Brazil, Canada, and Australia also drew in millions, but the United States, the world's largest immigrant sponge, absorbed the most and accepted the greatest variety in terms of places of origin, languages, and religions.

Approximately 23,400,000 immigrants, mostly Europeans, arrived in those decades, although, as we see in the story of Tuly Singh Johl and his Punjabi co-immigrants, some came from Asia to the United States as well. The majority of newcomers to the United States made their way through the port of New York and its immigrant-receiving station at Ellis Island. But whether they had booked passage through that port or through Boston, Philadelphia, Baltimore, New Orleans, Galveston, or San Francisco, all of which had immigrant-receiving stations by the early twentieth century, their decision to immigrate affected nearly every aspect of American life and left its mark on the nation's economic, political, cultural, and social makeup. America looked radically different at the end of 1910s from the way it did in the 1880s, and immigrants settling in every city and region did much to shape these changes.

Beyond just showing up and being there, the labor of immigrant women and men fueled American industry and energized the labor movement; and as they defended their rights and advocated for their homelands, immigrants made their distinctive voices heard in politics. American vernacular culture came to reflect their voices and sensibilities as well.

Their arrival in the millions and the upheavals they wrought made immigration the subject of heated debate. Did these immigrants benefit or harm America? Did they measure up to previous immigrants, whose smaller numbers and whose national origins, in retrospect, seemed less alien to many Americans who continued to think of the nation's core as based on British, Protestant values? These new immigrants appeared to be bearers of very strange cultural repertoires, and Americans asked themselves if the United States could continue to welcome them in these numbers. Such issues dominated the legislative, judicial, and intellectual life of the nation in the decades after the 1880s to a greater degree than they had before. Legislators, presidents, judges, political analysts, journalists, and members of scientific and learned bodies had much to say about these immigrants as they sought to answer questions about them and about America.

The number of immigrants would actually have been greater than the millions who did arrive had the United States, like much of the Western world, not experienced a severe economic depression from 1893 to 1897. Potential immigrants seriously calculated the likely prospects for their livelihoods, at least in the short run, in America as less attractive than before. Relatives in America, facing economic difficulties, sent home thinner envelopes with less cash, meaning that family members could not pay their passage. Without much chance of finding work in the United States, where levels of unemployment inched up to 18 percent, those who might have immigrated opted to stay put or go elsewhere.

Another four-year period even more profoundly suppressed immigration. From 1914 to 1918 war ravaged Europe, disrupting transportation and subjecting young men, the typical immigrants, to military service. In the years before World War I, millions of men—husbands, fathers, and sons—had gone to America, leaving wives and children back home and expecting to bring family members over when they could. The war put such plans on hold.

World War I also reconfigured the makeup of the American population. The movement of people across the Rio Grande from Mexico had been continual for over a century. In the 1890s employers in agriculture and mining based in the rapidly developing U.S. Southwest, a region once part of Mexico, increasingly considered Mexican men good workers, willing to labor hard, demand little, and then return home. The development of a railroad system in Mexico, along with instabilities caused by a decade-long civil war from 1910 to 1920, hastened the flow outward. But World War I proved pivotal in attracting Mexicans to places beyond the Southwest and the border—Chicago, Detroit, and Gary, Indiana, among them. The cessation of European immigration and the need for workers in American industries inspired men, women, and entire families from Mexico to come to the United States, where they like all other immigrants created communities and facilitated the migration of kin and townspeople.

So, too, during the war, responding to unmet labor needs, immigrants began to arrive from the Caribbean, joining smaller numbers who had moved here since the beginning of the twentieth century. The descendants of African slaves, about 230,000 from Jamaica, Barbados, the Bahamas, and other islands, responded to the possibilities of work in the United States between 1900 and 1920.[2]

An Era of Lawmaking

The road to immigration restriction moved along inexorably from 1882 to the 1920s. Its progress seemed unstoppable, and though the leaders of the various immigrant communities wrote, lobbied, and organized to stem the tide, their efforts had no real effect. From the adoption of the Constitution in 1789 until the passing of the 1875 Page Act, the federal government eschewed any meaningful management of the constant flow of immigrants to the nation's shores, but after 1882 it changed course.

The Page Act, which severely constrained the immigration of Chinese women, opened the path as the federal government embarked on a step-by-step journey, moving from regulation to control and restriction. This process of selection and restriction stemmed from a growing belief in eugenics, endorsed by scientists and much of the American public, which proposed that all people can be understood by virtue of the race or group into which they are born, and—more significantly here—that groups can be described in mental and moral terms, and that some groups are inherently defective. No matter the circumstances of their experiences, they can pass their fundamental defects on to future generations. Indeed, the term *eugenics*, coined by the British naturalist and statistician Sir Francis Galton, appeared for the first time in 1883, months before Congress passed the first piece of immigration legislation that rested on the basis of race thinking.

The history of restriction began most decisively with the 1882 passage of the Chinese Exclusion Act, which initially suspended the immigration of Chinese laborers for ten years and decreed that Chinese men, no matter their occupations or wealth, were ineligible for citizenship. Ten years later, the Geary Act excluded nearly all Chinese from entry into the United States, though it offered a few loopholes that allowed potential admission to merchants, ministers, students, and teachers, as well as wives and children of naturalized American citizens. Those seeking admission through these categories had to prove their qualifications, which required certification from the Chinese government.

Validated by the U.S. Supreme Court in the 1889 case *Chae Chan Ping v. U.S.*, the Chinese Exclusion Act remained the law until 1943. It and its 1902 extension identified men and women from China not just by place of birth but by phenotype (that is, observable characteristics).

Such laws and court cases left a profound mark on Chinese immigrants and their children. First, because they could not naturalize, they became more dependent on community leaders, the heads of the various district and clan associations who mediated between them and U.S. government officials, in contrast to immigrants of other backgrounds who had multiple avenues to accomplish the goals of their migration. Second, while the parents could not naturalize, their children born in the United States were citizens. Confirmed by the U.S. Supreme Court in *U.S. v. Wong Kim Ark*, the principle derived from the Fourteenth Amendment gave children a profound advantage over their parents. If the parents wanted to buy land for farming, for example, they had to do so with their children as the official owners. All immigrants lived life differently from their children, who grew up in the United States and felt more comfortable navigating its culture, but the families of Chinese immigrants—and in fact all Asian immigrants—experienced the generation gap more acutely.

All immigrants after 1882, regardless of where they came from or their future rights to naturalize, had to contend with a head tax, collected upon the moment of arrival. Intended to pay for the increasing number of bureaucrats and facilities necessary to control immigration, the tax rose repeatedly over the next decades as the bureaucracy grew. The system of regulation required buildings, personnel, supplies, and equipment, and prevailing wisdom asserted that if all these people wanted to come to America, they should pay for it themselves. The law also excluded paupers, criminals, and those lumped into a category called lunatics. The poorest, who could not pay the head tax, found the doors closed irrespective of place of origin, although throughout much of the period, they could enter via Canada or Mexico.

The legislative process continued in 1885. Congress passed the Foran Act, also known as the Contract Labor Law, barring employers from paying the fare to the United States of laborers whom they intended to employ. It sought to keep the U.S. labor market from being flooded by indigent immigrants induced by promised jobs. Like the head tax, its jurisdiction did not extend to those coming in by land.

An 1891 immigration act created the Office of the Superintendent of Immigration, housed in the Treasury Department. It authorized the hiring of a team of inspectors to be stationed at the various ports of disembarkation along the Atlantic coast. The act instituted a procedure by which government officials, charged with collecting the manifests of the arriving ships carrying immigrants, questioned newcomers one by one. Among other issues, the inspectors sought to identify those traveling on a ticket prepaid by an employer, a violation of the Foran Act.

The following year Congress set aside funds for the construction of the immigrant-receiving station at Ellis Island, a monumental facility in New York's harbor, through whose portals millions streamed in. Uniformed staff members recorded names, asked questions, and tested new arrivals on their physical and mental health. Ellis Island, like its smaller counterparts in Philadelphia, East Boston, Baltimore, New Orleans, and later Galveston, received the immigrants. Most passed the tests, gaining admission.

Angel Island opened in San Francisco in 1910, handling ships and passengers from across the Pacific Ocean. Primarily monitoring women and men from Asia—China, Japan, Korea, and other countries—this facility existed to exclude and send back, not receive, although officials distinguished between immigrants coming from Asia, whom they subjected to long and detailed interrogations, and those from New Zealand and Australia, phenotypically white. They experienced the island differently.

The government agents stationed at Angel Island interrogated Chinese women and others from Asia who claimed to be married to men who had become citizens. The Americans assumed them to be prostitutes. Some Chinese men on Angel Island declared that their fathers had become naturalized, and inspectors tried to ferret out those they believed had made fraudulent claims, calling them "paper sons." Given the harshness of exclusion, immigrants from China relied on ruses to get in, and the American men who sat on the Board of Special Inquiry asked the prospective immigrants questions involving minute details of their homes, family relationships, and other trivial facts of their lives before they had set sail. Those seeking to get in developed a system of memorizing appropriate answers, which helped them evade being sent back.

The Bureau of Immigration could never handle the volume of people coming through the receiving stations, and in 1903 the newly created Department of Commerce and Labor took over. In

1906 it began handling naturalization matters also, and as a result it became the Bureau of Immigration and Naturalization. In 1914, when Commerce and Labor split off into separate government departments, immigration fell into the domain of the latter.

Paralleling the rise of the immigration bureaucracy, Congress designated new classes of people deemed inadmissible. Each new category of the disallowed raised the admissions bar higher. These included anarchists, epileptics, bigamists, and beggars, who as of 1903 could be screened out and sent back. The list, with its origins in laws passed in 1882 and 1891, then expanded in 1907 to include the physically and mentally defective, carriers of tuberculosis, and unaccompanied children. Inspectors considered homosexuals mentally flawed, and as such they were excluded.

In 1907 the U.S. government entered into an agreement with Japan, another landmark in American immigration history. The former agreed to ensure that San Francisco would not segregate Japanese children in its public schools, while the latter agreed to curtail drastically the number of exit permits it issued to its people.

The decision of the United States to enter into the 1907 "Gentleman's Agreement" with Japan, a rising military and economic world power, reflected the U.S. government's calculation that its immigration policies could harm its diplomatic and geopolitical agenda. But that did not stop Congress in 1922 from legislating that anyone born in Japan could not acquire citizenship.

The acts of Congress and the decisions of courts about immigration took place in the context of national and global political matters. Political parties, elected officials, and their constituents framed the debates and the outcomes.

But each one of these laws affected ordinary people, women and men in homes around the world who aspired to come to the United State. They faced difficulties and limitations in their home communities and had been exposed to the knowledge that the United States offered them a chance to live better and more freely. Untold millions contemplated emigrating to America, saving money to pay their fares and calculating when and how to go so that their plans could become realities.

Many had family already living in the United States, siblings, spouses, and other kin who had gone to America and worked long hours in arduous labor to squirrel away the money they had earned on the assumption that their efforts would ensure that their family members could join them. To the men and women on both sides caught up in the drama of late nineteenth- and early twentieth-century immigration, these acts of the U.S. government blindsided their plans and threatened to shatter their dreams.

The flow of letters across these many national borders, in response to the emerging structure of restriction, began to include not just remittances and information about jobs, but also counsel about how to evade the law. They suggested the right answers to give to the questions asked by immigration officials. They offered advice on what do, how to look, how to present oneself while being scrutinized by Americans who had the power to decide the fate of individuals and thus families.

A family traveling with a son, a daughter, or some other relative who at the port of disembarkation received a diagnosis from the doctor on call of lung disease or trachoma, or had been listed as manifesting signs of retardation or some mental illness, for example, faced an excruciating dilemma. Should only that one family member go back? What if that person was a child? Should everyone go back or just the individual deemed inadmissible? Should someone able to get through the process instead accompany the rejected family member and return as well?

Each family had to navigate these choices on their own, and though relatively few European immigrants were denied entry, the ever-present possibility of failing the inspection hung over their heads. The ethnic communities in the United States, made up of immigrants who had arrived earlier, all organized in one way or another to negotiate for or provide guidance for individuals from their homelands who encountered such difficulties. Their newspapers chronicled the distress, appealed for aid, and reached out to members of Congress who represented the districts where they lived, often in large enough numbers that their votes would matter in coming elections.[3]

But despite the anxieties of ordinary people set against the continuing lure of life in the United States, the road to restriction continued along its trajectory. A bipartisan joint congressional commission, chaired by Vermont Senator William P. Dillingham, formed in

The men of the Dillingham Commission. Library of Congress, Washington, D.C.

1907 to study and resolve the matter of immigration, which many white, native-born Americans felt constituted a serious problem.[4] The forty-one-volume report the Dillingham Commission issued in 1911 confirmed what seemed so clear to many, namely, that contemporary immigration from southern and eastern Europe indeed threatened the nation's vitality.

Following suit, Congress acted and passed the Literacy Act in 1917, which excluded from entry to the United States all immigrants over the age of sixteen who could not pass a mandated literacy test. It also expanded the number of excludable categories; more significantly, it created the Asiatic Barred Zone, which shut the doors to anyone from Asia and the broader Pacific region, with the exception of those seeking admission from any of the territories annexed by the United States, mostly as a result of the Spanish-American War of 1898. Many in the public endorsed this bill, but President Woodrow Wilson vetoed it. Congress then overrode him, codifying this law.

Despite the headlong movement toward restriction in these decades, most European immigrants coming into the United States met with welcome. Government-issued guidelines for detention or even deportation did not single out any one national group, and officials sent back very few of those who went through Ellis Island.

The criteria used did not mention any European nationality as un-welcome, though it put in bold relief the difference between being deemed white and not white.

A New Immigration?

Critics of immigration identified late nineteenth- and early twentieth-century immigration as "new." They believed that it represented a departure from the immigrations of an earlier era, ignoring the reality that immigrants continued to come from those old places as well. Irish, German, Norwegian, and Swedish immigrants came to America, traveling at times on the same ships as women and men from Italy, Greece, the Balkans, and the Baltic lands. Annie Moore, a fifteen-year-old girl from Ireland, had the honor of being the first immigrant to step onto Ellis Island at its 1892 opening, followed by a man from the Austro-Hungarian Empire.

Like Annie Moore, Irishwomen, speakers of English, still attracted by jobs in domestic service, were joined by immigrants bound for other occupations. Speakers of Polish, Hungarian, Yiddish, Czech, Serbo-Croatian, Ukrainian, Romanian, Greek, Italian, and other languages stood in the same lines of the immigrant-receiving stations. This blurred the difference between new and old.

But a geographic shift in the source of the largest number of immigrants had occurred. By the 1870s and 1880s masses of people from places in Europe and elsewhere that had previously sent out few began to immigrate. Increasing numbers of individuals and families left homes in southern and eastern Europe for the United States. They left the eastern parts of the Habsburg Empire, the Balkans, including Greece, and the czarist lands. Huge numbers from Italy, particularly the south and Sicily, also made their way to America, as did some from parts of the Ottoman Empire. Mexicans arrived from across the southern border, as did men and some women from the Philippines, an archipelago in the Pacific captured by the United States in the Spanish-American War. In the early twentieth century immigrants from Japan, Korea, and the Indian subcontinent, like Tuly Singh Johl, also sought economic opportunities in America, and, before the Gentleman's Agreement and then the creation of the

The Imperator, *a steamship, with immigrants.*
Library of Congress, Washington, D.C.

Asiatic Barred Zone, they entered the United States, labored, and formed communities.

Solid Catholic majorities dominated most of the European sending societies, particularly Italy and the lands of eastern Europe. The latter region included within its borders millions of Jews and adherents to the Eastern Orthodox rite who also joined the flow. Unlike those entering before the 1880s, few of the newcomers arrived with a command of the English language, although newly arriving immigrants from Ireland did, as did some from the British-ruled Punjab, like Johl, and immigrants from the American-occupied Philippines. But since the earlier decades had included millions of Irish immigrants who spoke English, the newest newcomers seemed more foreign.

Yet in terms of class, skill level, and reasons for migration, they resembled each other more than they differed. All these global migrations stemmed from the same set of pressures that had swept through western and central Europe earlier, the twin forces of overpopulation and economic change brought by industrial development and the infusion of global capital, which disrupted familiar ways of making a living. The spread of the railroad into regions previously isolated from cities, markets, and international ports of embarkation, as well as shifting agricultural realities, the destruction of home production, and the continuing growth of the big business of transatlantic shipping, converged after the 1880s to send out so many millions from these new places.

As in centuries past, during the decades from 1882 through the 1910s, news of America stimulated individuals to believe that they could escape limitations and difficulties at home. The migrations of some brought about the subsequent migrations of others, husbands, wives, children, siblings, other relatives, friends, and townspeople. All immigrants had their own personal and family stories about this transition in their lives. Some left written accounts. Most did not.

Perhaps the labor organizer and writer Louis Adamic, born Alojz Adamič, can speak for those whom we can never hear. Adamic, born in the Austro-Hungarian Empire in 1898 in a small town in the region of Lower Carniola, which after World War I would become part of Yugoslavia, came from a peasant family. He remembered how at about age five or six he learned that from his hometown "a poor peasant clad in homespun, with a mustache under his nose and a bundle on his back" had gone to America. The man returned, "a clean-shaven *Amerikanec*," now dressed in "a blue serge suit . . . a black derby, a shiny celluloid collar, and a loud necktie." His words resembled those of young Irishwomen in the 1860s and 1870s who had marveled at the clothes worn by some "returned Yank," one of their own who had labored in America as a servant and came back attired in a fine dress, with matching shoes, gloves, umbrella, and bag. Adamic moved to the city of Ljubljana as a youngster to attend school, got involved with politics, spent some time in jail, and decided, at age fifteen, that a better life awaited him in America. Despite his age, he resolved, "I am going to America." He had no idea yet how, "but I knew that I would go," he recounted in his 1932 autobiography, describing his 1913 immigration.[5]

His awareness of American possibilities perhaps differed little from those of Hannah Hayye's neighbors in Polotsk when they saw the tickets she held. Stories like Adamic's and Antin's resounded throughout eastern and southern Europe and those parts of Asia that potential immigrants left. But immigrations from such a range of places also reflected many special circumstances.

The commonalities of these immigration stories stand alongside the particularities of place and community. The immigrations of the post-1880 period included people from the Balkans and regions within the Ottoman Empire, such as Armenians, best considered refugees. Their homes became battlegrounds between warring empires and nationalities, where winning armies expelled people on the basis of their group identity, and where mass murders, as in the case of Armenians, left traumatized survivors seeking refuge. Some of those who endured these upheavals made their way to America, and the horrors they had endured at the hands of the Turks remained with them in memory and community politics, shaping their immigration histories.

Immigrants from Italy did not bring with them memories of such murderous upheavals, but their experiences also reflected specific conditions. Over 4 million Italian immigrants came to the United States, particularly from places in the south negatively affected by the creation of a unified Italian nation-state in 1870. Well-off, educated, urban Italians, mostly northerners, led the *Risorgimento*, a movement to create a consolidated nation with a central government, an army, and a modern infrastructure. These ambitions required money, which would come from taxes. Landowners expected their tenants and the renters of small plots of land to pay, and these much poorer people found it difficult, if not impossible, to do so. They turned to emigration. New railroads and the opening up of Italian ports for transatlantic shipping facilitated their decisions.

Men left first, many expecting to return. About one-third did so. But with time, particularly after the restrictions of the 1920s, women left as well. They had not emigrated so much as Italians but as people from specific locales. In America immigrants from Sicily, Calabria, Abruzzo, Apulia, and elsewhere settled near each other, forging neighborhoods and social institutions with others from their former regions, villages, and towns. Once in America, though, this evolved. Americans, ignorant of the variations in language, customs, and loyalties, considered them all Italians. The immigrants started to recognize how much, despite these differences, they actually shared with others from various Italian provinces and regions.

Each country and region had its own inner dynamic in terms of the size, structure, and timing of the migration. The case of men whom Americans identified as Greek, who spoke the Greek language, and who adhered to the Greek Orthodox religion points

Newly arrived immigrants at Ellis Island, 1912.
Library of Congress, Washington, D.C.

to the interplay between place of origin and immigration to America, and the mix of economic and political realities. About 450,000 came to the United States between 1890 and 1914. Men constituted 90 percent of these immigrants, as opposed to about 60 percent of those from Italy. Greek men, mostly from southern Greece and Laconia and Arcadia on the Peloponnese peninsula, hoped to earn enough money in the United States to buy land when they returned home. But the upheavals in the Balkans with the displacement of millions of Christians from the Ottoman Empire meant that many could not go back. Stripped of their former citizenship, they had little choice but to stay, apply for naturalization, and use their newly acquired American citizenship to bring over family members.

The immigration of the almost 3 million Polish speakers, mostly Catholics, who arrived primarily after the 1880s also reflected particular conditions. Poland did not then exist as a country. Poles left homes divided among three empires. Their emigrations had begun in the 1870s, and the first came from regions in the German part such as Posen, closest to the Baltic ports. By the 1880s and 1890s recruits from the Habsburg Empire and provinces like Galicia made up a second Polish wave. Only later, with the penetration of the railroad into the Russian Empire, did Poles come to America from eastern sections of what in the 1920s was united into an independent Poland.

Like most immigrants, these small farmers, whether owners or renters, could not make it in the age of commercializing agriculture. They contended with overpopulation, and their home industries died in the face of industrial production. At home and once in America, they hoped to see a restored Polish homeland, and they considered that their German, Austrian, and Russian overlords demeaned and oppressed them. They found it easier to organize and agitate for Polish independence from Chicago, Milwaukee, Buffalo, and Detroit than from their hometowns, which were divided by imperial boundaries.

Tens of thousands, possibly more, left for America from Bosnia, Serbia, Montenegro, Croatia, Bulgaria, Macedonia, Albania, Herzegovina, and Slovenia in the Balkans. They came for the same set of economic reasons as all others, joining townspeople and relatives already in the mining and steel towns of Pennsylvania, Ohio, and elsewhere in the Midwest. Cleveland in the early twentieth century housed the world's third-largest concentration of Slovenes, smaller only than Trieste and Ljubljana. Many of them, mostly men, hoped to go home after laboring in America's heaviest industries. The First and Second Balkan Wars, in 1912–1913, increased the numbers of people leaving and brought women over, as dreams of going home faded. This largest wave of Balkan immigration took place after the 1890s, when the United States government had started registering immigrants by country of origin, so they appeared on official forms as Austro-Hungarian, Greek, or Turkish, obliterating their places of origin.

Likewise, Americans identified an immigrant population of "Russian Jews," but in fact few of the Jews who came from the czarist empire hailed from Russia. Rather, they lived, and not by choice, in the Pale of Settlement, created in 1791 and encompassing non-Russian regions of the empire, including Lithuania, Belarus, Moldova, Latvia, and Ukraine; the actual borders changed over time. Jews from the Austro-Hungarian province of Galicia and other regions of the future Poland also came to the United States, but to Americans they all seemed "Russian."

Until the 1910s most Jews from the czarist empire left the poorest, most crowded, and most overpopulated region, Lithuania. Situated on the Baltic, Lithuania enjoyed railroads and good access to ocean ports. After that decade the geographic sources of Jewish emigration shifted to the south and east of the empire, as railroads came there too, enabling Jews from Ukraine, Belarus, Bessarabia, and Moldova to join the exodus to America.

Eastern European Jewish immigration took place in the context of pogroms, violent outbursts against Jews, which flared from 1881 to 1882, from 1903 to 1906, and then at the end of World War I and the early 1920s. The bloodiest and most extensive spate of pogroms, that of the early 1920s, coincided with the waning years of open and unrestricted immigration to the United States. The horrendous murders, rapes, and widespread destruction of Jewish property, signatures of the pogroms, associated with places such as Kishinev and Odessa, however, do not explain the mass immigration of over 2 million Jews after the 1880s. After all, Lithuania experienced relatively little of this mayhem, and Jews from the Austro-Hungarian province of Galicia also endured little anti-Jewish violence. But they emigrated in large numbers as well.

Rather, the historic role of Jews as artisans, particularly tailors, and petty merchants fell victim by the end of the nineteenth century to the same forces of change that engulfed the region as a whole. Jews had long made their livings selling goods to rural people as peddlers, whether on the road, in shops, or at stalls in the weekly markets when peasants came to town to exchange agricultural products for finished goods. As the peasant economy fell apart and threw millions off the land, and as factory-made goods came to the countryside by train, the Jews' economic role crumbled.

Jews migrated in their particular ways, as did all others: married men arrived first in America with their older children, including daughters, and later sent for their wives and younger children. Among Jews, substantial numbers of young, single women immigrated as well.

Other migrations followed different patterns. Slovenians and other Balkan men migrated to jobs in heavy industry. Therefore, they went alone, in all-male groups or with sons. Italians and non-Jews from the Slavic lands also traveled this way, as many went to steel towns and mining camps where little work existed for women, as opposed to Jews who headed for New York's garment factories, where women could earn money.

Conversely, women made up a substantial proportion of the immigrants from a region of the Ottoman Empire designated as Mount Lebanon, sometimes referred to as Syria. The presence of large numbers of widows among the Syrian immigrants starting in the 1890s, though not as large a percentage as Irishwomen or eastern European Jewish women in their migrations, tells a particular story. Widows, sometimes with small children in tow, must have determined that the dearth of opportunities to support themselves at home, as single women responsible for youngsters, called for decisive action. Immigration, whether to the United States—or to South or Central America, to which many went—constituted a solution to a problem that could not be addressed had they stayed put.

Like the Syrians, whether male or female, and the small number of Muslim Bengalis, most of whom became peddlers of silks and other fine wares in these decades, many immigrants to America came from places other than Europe. The Punjabi immigration to the lumber mills and farms of the West Coast offers a prime example, as does the arrival of newcomers from China, Japan, and Korea.

But the arrival of immigrants from two places in this new era of immigration signaled America's changing role in the world beyond its forty-eight states. Between April and August 1898, the United States waged, in the words of President Theodore Roosevelt, a "splendid little war" against Spain. In its first overseas military foray, the Spanish-American War, America won handily and acquired noncontiguous colonies, including Puerto Rico and the Philippines. The immigration from those newly acquired lands demonstrated the complexity of U.S. immigration, especially its laws and citizenship protocols and the processes by which people arrived and were incorporated into the nation.

Small enclaves consisting overwhelmingly of political radicals who had fled Puerto Rico to escape Spanish repression formed in New York in the middle of the nineteenth century. After the 1898 war, movement from the island picked up substantially, and the

U.S. Treasury Department, then managing immigration, declared in 1902 all Puerto Ricans "foreigners," despite their living in an American territory. One young woman, Isabel González, arrived in New York that year intending to marry her fiancé, who already resided in the city. Immigration officials detained her and all the other Puerto Ricans onboard her ship at Ellis Island, labeling them aliens. González, they argued, ought to be refused entry because she had an out-of-wedlock child and as a pregnant unmarried woman, she must be a disreputable person and would probably be a future financial burden on the city. But rather than return home, González challenged the ruling, and the U.S. Supreme Court in the case *Gonzales v. Williams* declared that she and all other Puerto Ricans were not aliens who could be denied entry to the United States. Instead, it created a category of "non-citizen nationals" whose movement into the United States would not constitute a foreign immigration. With the outbreak of World War I and the abrupt cessation of immigration from Europe, which stopped the flow of laborers, Congress passed the Jones-Shafroth Act, giving Puerto Ricans American citizenship, so they would not need passports to travel to and from the United States. The combination of the Jones Act, the industrial needs of World War I, and worsening island conditions propelled the beginnings of a mass migration to New York, as well as Philadelphia and Chicago, which would grow dramatically after the 1920s.

Migration from the Philippines, also won by the United States during its brief but transformative 1898 war, grew out of America's colonial aspirations. The United States occupied the Philippines while suppressing a popular armed uprising. As part of America's "civilizing" mission, thousands of teachers, medical personnel, and others went to the Philippines to elevate their "little brown brothers," in the words uttered by William Howard Taft, governor-general of the newly annexed islands and a future president. Defined as nationals by the United States, residents of the Philippines could, without the benefits of citizenship, immigrate to the mainland and to Hawaii, yet another relatively recent U.S. territory, at will. Although Filipinos were considered Asians, the Asian Barred Zone did not keep them out.

The arrival of the United States in the Philippines stimulated a substantial exodus of young men in particular, bound for a variety of industrial jobs, many to canneries in the West. Called the "*manong*," an Ilocano term meaning firstborn son or older brother, by their families, they resembled the Greeks, Slovenians, and Italians who also participated in male-heavy migrations.

Those who left the Ilocos Region in northern Luzon and those emigrating from the Visayan Islands of the central Philippines, however, differed from those from southern Europe in one crucial way. They came already exposed to English and had a familiarity with other aspects of American culture, thanks to their encounters with teachers, sailors, doctors, nurses, missionaries, and other Americans who went to the Philippines with the occupation.

The story of one region, one town, or one group of people cannot stand for all the millions of immigrant stories of these decades of mass migration. But whether they arrived from a clearly demarcated nation-state with long-recognized boundaries or came from one of the polyglot empires, America offered them opportunities to work, and, as one Slavic commentator in Johnstown, Pennsylvania, said, the chance to eat "bread with butter."[6] A young Sicilian immigrant laboring on a Louisiana sugarcane plantation described America as a place where, though "the life is hard, the bread is soft," also employing food as a marker of the improvement in the standard of living that these two individuals and millions of others experienced after immigration.[7]

The dynamic economy needed streams of unskilled workers, both women and men, to labor long hours at low pay, churning out the products fueling American capitalism, namely, clothing, machines, iron, rubber, household goods, textiles, and by the end of these decades, automobiles sold in global markets, on every inhabited continent. As American cities grew, significantly because of immigration itself, municipalities and local businesses embarked on ambitious projects of residential and commercial building, public transportation, electrification, extension of sewer and gas lines, and all the other accoutrements of modern life. Immigrant labor dug tunnels, laid tracks, built skyscrapers, hung electrical wires, constructed bridges, erected electrical poles, and created transit systems above and below ground.

Their low pay made consumer goods more affordable for working-class Americans, including non-immigrants, and created wealth for those at the top, propelling further economic development. The arrival of millions of unskilled workers raised the economic level of those who had come earlier. Having acquired American skills, the earlier immigrants and their children now earned their incomes as middle managers, shop stewards, and supervisors of the work crews of newcomers who performed lower-level labor. The daughters of Irish immigrants of the 1850s and 1860s by the 1890s taught in public schools in New York, Chicago, Boston, San Francisco, and elsewhere, earning their living by educating the children of the new immigrants. The economic activity generated by new immigrants facilitated the movement of other Americans into the middle class.

Immigrant Communities in the Age of Restriction

Immigrant communities aided their most recent arrivals, banding together to help them navigate American life, whether assisting in finding jobs and places to live, or coping with American institutions, such as courts, hospitals, and public schools. Families provided much of the support. But hometown societies, cousins' clubs, and other groups that provided sociability and mutual aid also pitched in, using what resources they commanded.

Some immigrants, when necessary, turned to the consulates of their home countries for protection and advocacy. After a mob lynched eleven Sicilian immigrants in New Orleans in 1891, leaders of the local Italian community enlisted the aid of the Italian consul to lodge their outrage and demand protection. Mexican immigrants in Los Angeles and Chicago implored consular officials to intercede for them with unscrupulous employers and American government officials. The Chinese vice consul in San Francisco, a white American hired by the Chinese government, handled the 1884 case of Mamie Tape, a young girl whose parents had emigrated from China. Tape's mother did not want her daughter to attend a school reserved for Chinese children. Tape won her case in the landmark decision *Tape v. Hurley*, decided in March 1885. The California legislature responded by passing a bill establishing separate facilities for "Mongolians."

Immigrant organizations led and funded by the better-off with knowledge of English and American culture addressed ongoing immigration problems, one by one. The Armenian Colonial Association, for example, founded in 1909 by Armenians already settled in the United States, stationed agents at Ellis Island to steer their fellow Armenians getting off the ships to nearby Armenian communities, helping them reunite with relatives, townspeople, and others who spoke their language and shared their cultural repertoires. Fiorello La Guardia, the son of immigrants from Apulia and Trieste who would become a congressman and then mayor of New York, worked for the U.S. Bureau of Immigration as an interpreter at Ellis Island from 1907 to 1911, guiding newly arrived Italian speakers through the bureaucratic maze conducted in English.

The Hebrew Immigrant Aid Society (HIAS), founded in 1881, and the National Council of Jewish Women (NCJW), founded in 1893, also put workers at Ellis Island and the other immigrant-receiving stations. Officially recognized by the government, NCJW and HIAS workers, mostly volunteers, looked for Jewish immigrants who arrived without family to greet them or to solve problems they faced at the hands of immigration officials. In 1907 the Jewish banker Jacob Schiff used his not inconsiderable political resources to convince President Theodore Roosevelt to open an immigrant port and depot in Galveston, Texas. Schiff hoped that Jewish immigrants would stay in the West and Midwest and steer clear of New York, where so many lived. He thought that their doing so would lessen anti-Semitism. At the turn of the twentieth century, well-off Jews in New York, including Schiff, created the Industrial Removal Office, a nationwide agency to help Jewish immigrant men resettle in smaller cities and towns.[8]

Chinese community leaders in San Francisco, merchants who led the Six Companies, also known as the Chinese Consolidated Benevolent Associations, used their resources to advocate for those detained and those slated for deportation. Even before Angel Island opened, San Francisco's Chinese elites went to administrative hearings and courtroom trials to advocate for those seeking to enter the United States. Articles and editorials in *Sai Yat Po* documented the names of those being held and asked the paper's readers to help them. Though the percentage of the Chinese who did get sent back far surpassed the percentage of Europeans similarly treated, the figure would have no doubt been higher but for the work of the organized Chinese community.[9]

The Catholic Church, although divided over the politics of immigration, directly served its immigrants in need at ports of disembarkation and around the country. Beyond providing for newcomers at the parish level, the Extension Society, founded in 1905, and the National Conference of Catholic Charities, organized in 1910, assumed responsibility for immigrants. The National Catholic Welfare Conference created a Bureau of Immigration to do port work, after receiving official status at Ellis Island. It provided loans to immigrants to launch small businesses and interceded in behalf of individual immigrants facing detention or possible deportation.

Immigrant communities, locally and nationally, created organizations, newspapers, and political entities, all of which participated in the immigration debate. They mounted strenuous defenses of their people against what they considered unfounded attacks against them. In their community newspapers, written in Yiddish, Italian, Polish, Greek, Chinese, Hungarian, and the like, writers, editors, and publishers documented the progress of the group in America, exposing the baselessness of their critics' words. *Sai Yat Po*, the San Francisco Chinese-language newspaper launched in 1900; *Svoboda*, published in Ukrainian since 1893 in Jersey City, New Jersey; the Armenian *Hayrenik*, from Watertown, Massachusetts, published as of 1899; and thousands more like them advised immigrants on how to deal with American realities and taught them about their rights.

They also chronicled developments back home, making it possible for those in the United States to be informed and involved in home-country politics from afar. Immigrant communities, Irish, Polish, eastern European Jewish, Mexican, Italian, Greek, and the others, divided over political disputes agitating their homelands but also raised mammoth funds to advance the interests of the places they had left.

One Armenian immigrant, for example, documented the political parties that flourished in his community, noting that the political groups "occupy an important place in the life of these people. It must be understood that these parties have no connection with and take no direct interest whatever in American politics." Rather, he wrote, "they are solely concerned with their own national affairs, the main issue of which is the liberation of the Armenian people from the oppression of the Turks and the realization of absolute Independence."[10]

Many Americans found such rhetoric disturbing, sure that immigrants cared more about their old countries than about their new one. The lead-up to U.S. entry into World War I in 1917 made this a highly charged public matter. Many Irish Americans called for neutrality, not wanting the United States to fight on the side of Britain, the hated colonial occupier of their homeland. Polish communities in the United States, however, clamored for America to enter against Austria-Hungary, expecting an independent Poland afterward. Americans believed that many Germans harbored divided loyalties, their sympathies lying really with their old home.

The campaign against Germans in America in the years leading up to U.S. entry into the war and during the war itself demonstrated the ease with which Americans moved from tolerating difference to demonizing it. Communities around the country banned the speaking of German, the federal government suppressed the publication of German-language newspapers, vicious propaganda labeled Germans, regardless of U.S. citizenship, as dangerous and depraved monsters, and acts of violence became, if not commonplace, not unusual. On April 3, 1918, Robert Prager, a German national living in a small coal-mining town in Illinois, who had already applied for citizenship, found himself surrounded by a mob, which demanded he sing patriotic songs and kiss the flag. As the throng got larger and increasingly enraged over the course of the next two days, some declared that Prager ought to be tarred and feathered, but not finding any tar, they decided instead to hang him. They did so with a group of local people watching.

While public officials did not encourage such criminal behavior, they stoked popular anger against Germans and indeed chided all immigrants who continued to identify with their places of origin. They declared, like former president Theodore Roosevelt and the sitting president, Woodrow Wilson, that hyphenated Americans could not be real Americans, and that the nation demanded full and undivided loyalty. Expressing opinions about the interests of the places they had left, Wilson determined, precluded total love for the United States.

Ethnic communities addressed the larger public to disprove such accusations. They produced texts and staged events to tell Americans about themselves, how long they had been in the United States, their contributions to American society, and why more women and men from their country would enrich, and not harm, America.

Wealthy Italians in New York, for example, collected and donated money to the city in 1892 to pay for a giant statue to arise on 59th Street to honor Christopher Columbus, the Genoese explorer who "discovered America." A year after the New Orleans lynching, these community notables convinced officials to rename Grand Circle, part of Frederick Law Olmsted's plan for Central Park, Columbus Circle, hoping that New Yorkers and tourists entering or leaving the park, or walking up and down Broadway, would look up and remember that an Italian had made America, as they knew it, possible. Farther west, Angelo Noce and Siro Mangini, immigrants in Denver, persuaded city authorities in the first decade of the twentieth century to stage a grand parade on October 12 to honor the Italian navigator, declaring the day a holiday. Americans, they argued, should not see the small but growing Italian population in their midst as made up solely of poor, uneducated manual laborers, but rather as the nation's founders.

Immigrant communities also developed political strategies. They voted, aligned with local political organizations, and, when they could, ran for office. Wherever they settled, they forged relationships with local politicians, many of them Irish Americans who had achieved local power. Immigrants, once they became citizens, used their growing numbers to secure jobs and contracts and extract other favors to enhance their lives. Operatives for local political machines, in most cities under the banner of the Democratic Party, maintained close ties to judges and congressmen able to help individuals with immigration problems. In exchange, newly enfranchised immigrant men had to demonstrate their loyalty to the machine, work for it, and vote for it on Election Days. Leaders of these political machines recognized how immigrants clustering in particular wards and districts made them important players in winning elections, and they made winning over immigrant voters a high priority.

But the overwhelmingly negative view of these immigrants, the Italians, Poles, and Jews, among so many others, ran too deeply in the nation, and arguments that they constituted a new, dangerous element in American life held too much sway for the words of immigration advocates and supporters to stem the tide.

Further Reading

Bayor, Ronald H. *Encountering Ellis Island: How European Immigrants Entered America* (2014).

Benton-Cohen, Katherine. *Inventing the Immigration Problem: The Dillingham Commission and Its Legacy* (2018).

Lee, Erika. *The Making of Asian America: A History* (2015).

Ngai, Mae M. *Impossible Subjects: Illegal Aliens and the Making of Modern America* (2014).

Zahra, Tara. *The Great Departure: Mass Migration from Eastern Europe and the Making of the Free World* (2016).

CHAPTER SIX

What Americans Said about
the Immigrants, 1882–1921

T HE LAST DECADES OF the nineteenth century witnessed an almost lockstep movement from the nation's nearly unregulated and unrestricted immigration of the past to, in 1921, the passage of the Emergency Quota Act, which limited the number of immigrants who could lawfully enter each year; slots were assigned to people on the basis of where they came from. America's long history of relatively open and free immigration came to be replaced by a creeping new reality, as the federal government created a system of exclusion, detention, and denial of admission, sending people back. These momentous years from the 1880s onward saw political, economic, cultural, and racial concerns converging to launch a new chapter in the history of the United States and indeed of the world beyond.

Did this inexorable journey toward immigration restriction accurately reflect how Americans saw immigrants? Who endorsed this emerging system, and who did not? What arguments did the critics of late nineteenth-century immigration offer to justify this historic reversal, and how did other Americans respond?

The Rationale for Restriction

Those who advocated for this kind of restriction considered the masses of newcomers from a variety of perspectives, but all perceived that certain characteristics rendered them unworthy and unable to become American as they defined it. To some critics the new immigrants came from primitive societies, places removed from the values of Western civilization. They came with no ability to understand and adopt American ideals. Whether characterizing all immigrants in these terms, or commenting specifically on Italians, Greeks, or Poles, the critics identified them as peasants dumbly searching for bread. They represented the worst classes of their places of origin. The presence of these individuals, defined as defective, eugenicists and advocates of restriction declared, would reverse America's progress.

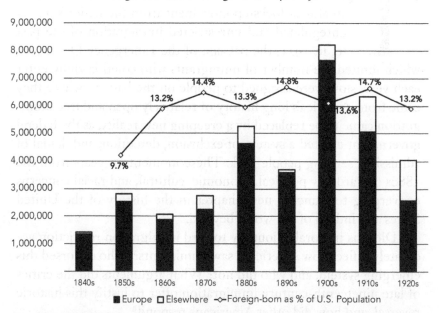

Origins of U.S. Immigrants, 1840s–1920s

Sources: U.S. Bureau of the Census, Census of Population, 1850–2000; U.S. Bureau of the Census, American Community Survey, 2010; U.S. Bureau of the Census, *Statistical Abstract of the United States*, 1944–45 (Washington, D.C., 1945).

They condemned immigrants for settling in cities, big, noisy, dirty places, as few chose agriculture. Those flooding America from eastern and southern Europe, the argument ran, fundamentally altered the character of the country. These immigrants pushed America away from its rural and small-town roots and transformed it into an urban nation, something confirmed by the 1920 census, which showed that a majority of Americans then lived in cities.

The foes of the most recent immigrations likewise found it problematic that so many immigrants arrived as single men, without women. They saw this as a sexual threat to America's moral life. They worried for the safety of American women, white women, who might fall prey to the predations of hordes of single men, wild, uncivilized, and prone to excessive drinking. Living without the taming influence of their own women would unleash the dangerous proclivities of the foreign men let loose on American city streets. Congress indeed passed the Expatriation Act of 1907, which declared that if a woman with U.S. citizenship married a noncitizen, she lost hers.

Likewise, critics linked the immigrants' maleness to the reality that many returned home after working some number of years. They had immigrated for the wrong reasons, lacking a desire to transform themselves, to adopt American values. Never intending to become American, they had no loyalty to the nation and would never blend in.

Their arguments continued. The newcomers, whether men or women, never would or could learn English, leave their immigrant enclaves, and meld into the American people. They did not send their children to school, forcing them instead into factories and mines, ensuring that they would never rise above their parents' degraded level and improve themselves. Their daughters in particular had low rates of school attendance, thereby ensuring that they would just replicate their mothers' conditions, subject to the men who kept them ignorant and bound to pre-migration family practices.

The condition of immigrant women drew the attention of restrictionists. They expressed much anxiety over the fact that immigrant families manifested high birthrates, exceeding those of middle-class, white, native-born women. They claimed that immigrants bred too rapidly, which threatened to make real Americans a minority in their own land. They opined that immigrant fertility directly suppressed that of American women.

Critics of immigration believed all this. Yet the anti-immigrant discourse of the late nineteenth century, which asserted profound differences between the purported problematic new and the good old immigrants, rested on faulty assumptions. Most immigrants who arrived before 1880 also headed to cities where jobs abounded, labored in factories, and created Swedish, German, and Irish enclaves, differing little from Italian, Greek, and Ukrainian neighborhoods of later decades.

As for the draw of agriculture for earlier immigrants, critics of the late nineteenth century ignored the fact that free or inexpensive land had ceased to be available. By 1871 the federal government stopped giving portions of public domain lands to railroads, so in turn railroads mostly stopped giving away land to anyone, whether new immigrants or the American-born. The 1890 census also demonstrated that the frontier, a region where settlers might once have found land for the taking, no longer existed. The consolidation of big agricultural business in the late nineteenth century further made farming a poor economic choice for people with limited means.

The fertility issue also shows the flawed thinking of those who feared and abhorred the new immigrants. These immigrants, like those before, tended to be young and in their childbearing years. For many, immigration to America represented the chance to marry and start families, something circumstances back home prevented. But the American population on the eve of the new immigration represented the full age spectrum, including those too young to have children and those too old. Simultaneously, many white, middle-class, native-born Protestant women received extensive educations and developed skills for white-collar and professional work. Spending some years studying and earning money, they deferred marriage, having therefore fewer years to bear their children. Some, including the most highly educated, decided against marriage at all, instead pursuing professional ambitions and achieving personal autonomy outside traditional family life. Those who married and had children opted for smaller families, hoping to provide more care and greater resources for their children.

Immigration in the Age of Scientific Racism

Post-1880s immigrants arrived when Americans, like their counterparts in England, France, Germany, and elsewhere in Europe, embraced scientific racism. A proposition, articulated by scholars and widely discussed in magazines and newspapers, asserted that all people fell into distinct racial groups. Each group could be understood in terms not only of its own distinctive physical characteristics, but also and of equal importance of its inherent mental and moral ones. Those fixed traits included their intelligence levels, criminal proclivities, sexual passions, and basic temperaments, impulsive and emotional or sober and rational, and could not be altered. Each group constituted a distinctive type of human being, and scientists, agreeing that the types existed in nature, decided how those types could be arrayed from most admirable to most depraved.

According to these thinkers, some of them increasingly holding prestigious positions in the newly emerging American universities, the multiple races of the world originated and lived within clearly demarcated national boundaries. The books they wrote, issued by some of the best-known publishing houses, received the acclaim of their professional peers and were read widely by white, affluent, native-born Americans. These works discussed the distinctive characteristics of the "Celtic" race, the "Alpine" race, the "Slavic" race, the "Nordic" race, the "Hebrew" or "Semitic" race, as well as races they labeled "Anglo-Saxon," "Teutonic," "Latin," "Asiatic," "Negroid," and the like. Race scientists differed on the exact definitions and labels and precise placement of the various European races in relationship to each other on the scale of ability and worth. They had no doubt, however, that the European races stood higher on the scale than those of the rest of the world, classified as Asian and African.

They also debated in scholarly publications and in the pages of magazines whether the presence of people from inferior races would drag down superior ones, or if the superior ones would triumph over the inferior. William Z. Ripley, author of *The Races of Europe* in 1899, and Madison Grant, who published *The Passing of the Great Race* in 1916, did not agree on all these matters but converged in the alleged scientific truth that races existed, that people belonged to one race or another, and that each race demonstrated specific behaviors and temperaments.

Not surprisingly, the fair-skinned races, as defined by the discourse, of northern and western European origins, often labeled "Anglo-Saxon," showed the highest examples of virtue, intelligence, good character, and an orientation toward progress. "Anglo-Saxonism," a term the scholars used, had shaped the nation and its core values, understood as progressive, acquisitive, and rational. Brave and hardworking by nature, Anglo-Saxons deserved the right to govern. The other races, by nature of their essential characters, as evidenced by their phenotype, tended toward laziness, criminality, immorality, impulsivity, and stupidity.

Madison Grant and other advocates for an end to immigration on the basis of national origins participated in the political debate over restriction. Senator Ellison DuRant Smith of South Carolina quoted Grant directly on the floor of the U.S. Senate, asking his colleagues in 1921: "Who is an American? Is he an immigrant from Italy? Is he an immigrant from Germany?" Smith continued his rhetorical questioning, "Would it be the son of an Italian immigrant, the son of a German immigrant, the son of any of the breeds from the Orient, the son of the denizens of Africa?" Then answering himself, he suggested that "members of the Senate . . . read that book just recently published by Madison Grant, *The Passing of the Great Race*. Thank God," he went on, "we have in America perhaps the largest percentage of any country in the world of the pure, unadulterated Anglo-Saxon stock, certainly the greatest of any nation in the Nordic breed."[1]

Decades earlier, in 1894, a group of New Englanders, well-off, politically connected descendants of the immigrants of the prenational era, had formed the Immigration Restriction League. Presided over by a Harvard professor, Charles Warren, the Boston group soon established chapters in New York, San Francisco, and Chicago. It advocated for a drastic numerical limitation in the annual number of immigrants who could enter and a literacy test to keep out the "wild motley throng," a phrase penned by the poet Thomas Bailey Aldrich, a member of the group, in "The Unguarded Gates."

The distinguished magazine of which Aldrich was editor, the *Atlantic*, published the poem, which declared that the "Men from the Volga and the Tartar Steppes,/Featureless figures" constituted invaders who brought to America "the Old World's poverty and scorn." The Immigration Restriction League issued reports, placed articles in newspapers and magazines, and lobbied Congress to silence, through restrictive legislation, the "accents of menace alien to our air."[2]

The elite nativists of the Immigration Restriction League, like the scientists, intellectuals, and academicians who asserted the inherent inferiority of contemporary immigrants, argued that the mere presence of immigrants had a negative effect on the native-born. Francis A. Walker, a professor at Yale and later the president of the Massachusetts Institute of Technology, preeminent in the field of statistics, weighed in on the fertility issue, asserting with authority that white, native-born Americans had decided to forgo having children because they did not want "to bring forth sons and daughters who should be obliged to compete in the market for labor and in the walks of life with those whom they did not recognize as of their own grade and condition." He continued, warning that "the entrance into our political, social, and industrial life of such vast masses of peasantry" should concern all Americans. The immigrants, "beaten men from beaten races," he wrote, "have no history behind them which is of a nature to give encouragement. They have none of the inherited instincts and tendencies which made it comparatively easy to deal with the immigration of the olden time."[3]

The racial ideas of the late nineteenth century differed from prevailing beliefs of earlier decades. Previously those who found immigrants repugnant and uncivilized subscribed to a republican optimism that held that no matter how degraded people, particularly Europeans, were when they arrived, they could change and improve. In the late eighteenth and the early nineteenth centuries, values associated with the Enlightenment about human mutability through better conditions, including education, still held sway. Even the Irish, so despised, could be weaned of their worst traits by schooling them in cleanliness, sobriety, and, with any luck, Protestantism.

But with the emergence of social Darwinism in the 1870s, which was based on principles of natural selection, survival of the fittest, and the inevitability of the struggle for resources, a scientific consensus about race and biology shifted the discussion. The new way of thinking accepted as true and accurate, as scientific, the notion that race functioned as a matter of fixed characteristics that could not be changed no matter the level of their exposure to more enlightened and progressive ideas. The nation had to defend itself against the invasion of alien and defective peoples.

The newly hatched eugenics movement picked up on this call for self-defense, demanding that the state ensure that inferior peoples did not reproduce. Many Immigration Restriction League members belonged also to the American Breeders Association, which in turn in 1911 created a special immigration committee devoted to hastening restriction. The ABA, along with other eugenics organizations and sympathetic individuals who believed in "good birth," a concept that aptly summarized the central ideas of eugenics, also worried about African Americans and poor white people from long generations of American life as defectives who jeopardized the health of the nation. But in the press and in their publications, they hammered away at the perils of immigrant defectiveness and fecundity.

Talk like this wafted through American society as a kind of consensus. It became obvious common sense, conventional wisdom. Americans whose ancestors hailed from northern and western Europe, the British Isles in particular, had the right stuff and deserved to be the majority, while those from other places should be excluded and relegated to lower places.

During World War I, as millions of American men served in the military, officials administered newly minted intelligence tests to them. The scientists who perfected these tests wanted to show the differences between the races and got the results they expected; they demonstrated with scientific accuracy that those who themselves had immigrated recently, or whose parents had, scored lower than other white people. They did better than only African Americans. Their lower scores, according to the psychologists and statisticians who collected and analyzed the data, proved their point. Intelligence reflected innate abilities, not environment or education, and intelligence varied by race. New immigrants could never do better.

Other Calls for Restriction

Clamors to restrict immigration by number and type resounded far beyond scientific and elite circles. A revitalized Ku Klux Klan emerged in 1915, spreading far beyond the South, the home of the first Klan of the post–Civil War era. This incarnation concerned itself with Jews, Catholics, and immigrants, the ones from southern and eastern Europe. It raised millions of dollars and recruited members in New Jersey, Maine, New York, Massachusetts, New York, Indiana, Ohio, and elsewhere. In the 1920s the Klan scored some electoral victories and gained respectability. Governor Clifford Walker of Georgia, a Klansman himself, addressed the 1924 Klan national convention and urged his members to advocate for a "wall of steel, as high as heaven" to keep America for Americans and keep immigrants out.[4]

Calls for shrinking immigration also came from the working class. The American Federation of Labor, led by Samuel Gompers, a Jewish immigrant from England whose parents had originally come from Poland, decried the immigrant flood that he and many of the A.F. of L. members believed lowered the American standard of living. They asserted that newly arriving unskilled laborers, desperate for employment, worked for lower wages than Americans. Employers used immigrants as a way to destroy the craft system and deskill conditions of labor. Gompers took an especially active role in the campaign to ban Chinese immigration in particular, and labor unions expressed specific hostility toward the fact that industrial employers turned to new immigrants as strikebreakers, who made it impossible for American workers to mobilize against low pay and poor working conditions.

Calls for restriction also came from some Catholic publications and prelates. Ironically, the Catholic population in America grew greatly because Catholics constituted the large majority of the newcomers. This growth enhanced its influence and visibility as never before, and Catholic schools, hospitals, and charitable societies took up the needs of the immigrants. But some within the church publicly criticized the new immigrants, despite their shared faith. They worried that the Protestant public would even more toxically than in the past associate Catholicism with poor aliens and backward foreigners, stoking old anti-Catholic hatreds. Cardinal James Gibbons of Baltimore declared, "The country it seems to me, is overrun with immigrants and a word of caution should be spoken to them." One writer in *America*, a Catholic publication, mused, "If we can greatly restrict immigration and especially immigration from Catholic countries, so-called, we may be able to catch our breath for a few years and begin to do something in an intelligent way toward mending our fences," implying that immigrants made too great a demand on the church's resources, economic and political.[5]

One broad fear of immigrants reflected the industrial strife of the late nineteenth century, associating immigrants with labor activism and political radicalism. Americans mostly evinced little sympathy for unions and trembled over radical politics from the left, while the federal and state governments endorsed employers' wishes to stymie unionization, particularly of unskilled workers in large industries.

But these years saw intense and visible activity to challenge the status quo in which the state collaborated with employers to keep workers from organizing. A strike in 1886 of the Union Pacific Railroad, the 1892 Homestead lockout, the Pullman strike of 1894, the uprisings in the anthracite coalfields in 1902, the 1909 "Uprising of the 20,000" shirtwaist workers, and the 1910 "Great Revolt" by cloak makers drew public attention to workers' discontent and their calls to unionize. Violent strikes among textile workers in Lawrence, Massachusetts, in 1912 and of the silk workers in 1913 in Paterson, New Jersey, pitted immigrant workers against their employers. In 1916 miners in the Mesabi Iron Range went out on strike, and steelworkers across the country followed suit in 1919. Americans read in their newspapers how immigrants, energized in some of these uprisings by the Industrial Workers of the World, or the Wobblies, took to the streets to demand their employers pay them a living wage. They challenged American beliefs in laissez-faire capitalism, thereby threatening the stability of the economic order.

Chicagoans, for example, in 1886 lived through the Haymarket riot. Striking workers, many immigrants, staged an action with the support of the Knights of Labor to protest conditions in the plants run by the McCormick Harvester Company, one of the city's largest employers. They gathered on May 4 to demand higher pay and what must have been shocking then, an eight-hour day. The demonstration brought out battalions of police, ready to take on the strikers and their allies. A fracas ensued. A bomb went off, proven later by historians to have been set by law enforcement to discredit the strikers. Several police lost their lives. Numerous strikers sustained injuries. The police arrested eight men reputed to be anarchists, five of them German immigrants, who the state claimed had started the riot. A jury found the men guilty on flimsy evidence, and the State of Illinois hanged five, including August Spies, a German-born upholsterer.

The press fed the American public a steady diet of stories of immigrants imperiling the nation's stability. On September 6, 1901, an anarchist named Leon Czolgosz, born in Alpena, Michigan, to Polish-speaking immigrant parents, shot President William McKinley, who died from his wounds. What more compelling evidence did Americans need to show that the advocates of restriction had it right?

They also read about the work of an Irish immigrant, Mary Harris Jones, known as Mother Jones. An advocate for the rights of workers, she achieved her greatest fame as the "miners' angel," working in and around the coalfields of West Virginia, Pennsylvania, and Colorado, vociferously demanding that the companies recognize the humanity of the immigrant miners. In 1903 she marched with the children of striking miners from Pennsylvania to Oyster Bay, New York, gathering them in front of President Theodore Roosevelt's home. The president refused to see her or meet the children, and she earned another title, "the most dangerous woman in America."

Others instead considered that Emma Goldman deserved that label. Born in Lithuania, she immigrated to the United States as a teenager in 1885, one of the millions of Jews coming from the czarist empire. In her young adulthood she embraced anarchism as the most effective way to address the plight of the working class. In 1892, during the violent suppression of a strike in Homestead, Pennsylvania, Goldman, along with her fellow immigrant and anarchist Alexander Berkman, tried to assassinate the businessman Henry Clay Frick. In the ensuing years, Goldman was in and out of jail and wrote and lectured about anarchism. In her magazine launched in 1906, *Mother Earth*, she advocated for birth control, then illegal and considered immoral, and for women's right to sexual freedom.

Her opposition to the U.S. entry into World War I landed her in prison in violation of the Espionage Act. Deported by federal authorities in 1920, along with 249 others classified as immigrant radicals, Goldman the anarchist ended up in the Soviet Union. Tales of Emma Goldman and Mother Jones and other immigrant labor activists circulated widely, corroborating the idea that immigrants stood ready to destroy the American way of life.

Such stories agitated ordinary white, middle-class Americans, who yearned for the stability and homogeneity that they believed had prevailed in the past. Not alone in defining immigrants as foreigners who imperiled their interests, they found common ground with some African Americans, but from a very different perspective.

Booker T. Washington, arguably the dominant figure in African American community life in the early twentieth century and certainly the one most acceptable to white people, declared that the continuing influx of European immigrants harmed his people. In the early twentieth century, southern states formed exploratory commissions to see if they could bring European immigrants to the region to work in agriculture. Louisiana had, for example, successfully recruited Sicilian laborers to work at low pay and under harsh conditions in the sugarcane plantations. Washington, a vigorous advocate for the economic advancement of African Americans, declared in a speech he delivered in 1895 at the Atlanta Cotton Exposition that the South should not "look to the incoming of those of foreign birth and strange tongue and habits for the prosperity of the South." Instead, the region's political and business leaders should remember and do better by those "who have, without strikes and labour wars," long served the South, namely, the Black women and men for whom he spoke.[6]

Seemingly rational arguments offered against immigrants, whether based on scientific, economic, or moral reasons, went hand in hand with popular culture imagery. Negative images of immigrants abounded in popular texts, on the stage, in music, in print, and, by the early twentieth century, in film. The dumb "Bohunk," the "inscrutable" Chinese, the "greedy" Jew, the "stiletto-wielding" Italian criminal who operated within a shadowy underworld of the "black hand" all took their places on the American stage alongside the drunken Irishman, a stock character forged in the earlier immigration era. Americans across backgrounds consumed these images on a quotidian basis, probably believing them to be true.

Acceptance of these images as accurate, buttressed by science and included in the daily reportage of newspapers, turned the majority of the American public into a solid mass that supported restriction. By the 1920s, in the aftermath of World War I, restriction advocates convincingly argued that people from particular countries, those that had been sending immigrants in the largest numbers since the 1880s, could never be good Americans, and their immigration had to be most severely curtailed.

In all the talk and political action surrounding immigration and the problems it wreaked on American society and culture, however, no one called for policies to strip European immigrants, regardless of place of origin or religion, of their rights to citizenship. As white people, they came protected and endowed with the potential for naturalization, with the promise that they would secure the full bundle of rights of all Americans. Certainly, in the immediate aftermath of World War I, the United States government took away the citizenship of a few hundred defined as political radicals, and, as it did to Emma Goldman, deported them. The millions of immigrants in the United States, whether already naturalized or not, did not suffer such a fate, but still they lived in the shadow of the move to more extensive restriction, something that would affect their families and that besmirched the good name of their communities.

In Defense of the Immigrants

Not all Americans shared the racialist perspective that took as its goal curtailing immigration and increasingly restricting immigration on the basis of national origins. Some articulated counterarguments, exposing the fallacies in the nativists' pronouncements, and in the process advocated for immigrants and immigrant rights. Whether defending Chinese or Italian immigrants specifically, or assembling their evidence to show that forces other than inherent group traits explained differences, advocates for the immigrants, some of them women and men who commanded much respect in American life, could still not undo the power of nativism.

Americans across the nation, amid the growing calls for restriction and the constant discussion in the press and courts about the newcomers' defects, decided to provide services and support as they could. The projects they undertook at times reflected prevailing discourse about the immigrants' defects and accepted as true elements of the anti-immigrant discourse. Yet everywhere, some white, middle-class Americans, native-born and Protestant, stepped up to assist.

Sarah Wool Moore believed that she should do something for newly arrived Italian immigrants. An artist, Moore lived in Brooklyn, New York, and in 1900 helped found the Society for the Protection of Italian Immigrants. Initially the group focused on preventing the unscrupulous runners for boardinghouses from fleecing newly arrived immigrants who did not know English. The organization, with Moore in the lead, warned immigrants about men who posed as potential employers promising work but then hauled them off to work sites under conditions of near servitude. The society raised funds to hire Italian-speaking agents to wait at Ellis Island and steer unsuspecting immigrants away from those eager to exploit them. Moore realized that Italian immigrants succumbed to such chicanery for the simple reason that they did not know English, so in 1902 she published an English-Italian reader to help them overcome this linguistic deficiency. In 1905 she opened an English school for Italian immigrant men laboring and living in a Pennsylvania mining camp town, Aspinwall. Recognizing then that her efforts alone could not accomplish much, she turned to the state legislature for more funds to hire more teachers. Moore branched out, creating similar schools in various towns in New York State, including Wappinger Falls, Brown's Station, Valhalla, and other places where groups of Italian men quarried rocks, excavated reservoirs, and engaged in other jobs in which their lack of English, as she saw it, prevented them from being able to negotiate on their own behalf.

On the other side of the country, Margaret Culbertson and Donaldina Cameron served as superintendents of the Presbyterian Mission Home of San Francisco, founded in 1877 to rescue Chinese women from brothels. The assumption that all Chinese women had been forcibly brought to America to work as prostitutes gripped American public consciousness and led to passage of the Page Act in 1875, which effectively prevented their entry into the United States.

Some Chinese women, however, did work as prostitutes, and the mission, during Cameron and Culbertson's years as superintendents, from the 1870s into the early twentieth century, led raids on brothels, provided the women they liberated with a place to live, and, probably most important, offered job training so that they could support themselves.

The Presbyterian Mission that served the Chinese women started as a denominational project, and Moore's efforts for Italian men enjoyed the support of the YMCA, the Young Men's Christian Association. These Protestant churches may have hoped to convert the Chinese, very few of whom were Christian before coming to America, or the Italians, mostly Catholics, but they did not make conversion a prerequisite for assistance. Rather, they and countless others around the country embraced the idea that immigrants deserved the help of Americans. That help would provide practical assistance, would equip them with skills they needed to succeed, and would in the end lessen antipathy toward them and make America a more welcoming place.

Individuals associated with the settlement house movement participated in this effort, simultaneously spurring the growth and professionalization of the field of social work. These included women like Jane Addams, who founded Chicago's Hull House in 1889, a novel kind of institution that served immigrants living on Chicago's Near West Side, close to the slaughterhouses and garment factories, as well as her associates Sophonisba Breckinridge, Grace and Edith Abbott, and their counterparts in other cities who observed the day-to-day lives of immigrants in their neighborhoods. They gathered statistics and investigated the work, housing, schooling, and sanitary conditions the immigrants had to put up with, showing how powerful forces combined to exploit immigrants and keep them in poverty.

These women, mostly the daughters of native-born Protestant families possessing long roots in America, educated, and socially committed, lectured widely and published books such as *Hull House Maps and Papers*, which documented the conditions of the immigrants. They pointed out to government officials and the public at large that contemporary immigrants faced unique problems not of their own making, spawned by mass industrialization, greedy employers, low wages, and corrupt politicians who worked hand in glove with factory owners. The problems plaguing the immigrants did not reflect defects in their characters or the inevitability of racial inheritance. Rather, those problems reflected the defects of American industrial capitalism.

Many reformers like Addams worried in particular that the American-born children of the immigrants would be caught in a tug-of-war between their parents' traditional ways and the lure of American popular culture, which appealed to many immigrants, the young in particular. These reformers, including Florence Kelley, Lillian Wald, and the Abbott sisters opposed the increasingly loud chorus of voices that claimed that immigrants and their descendants could not become American and that they harmed society.

Addams lived among the immigrants in the converted mansion that she bought. She translated the needs of the residents of the neighborhood to the city's elite and powerful. In addition, she offered the immigrants a way to showcase their skills. In 1901 she created what may have been a first in the nation, a Labor Museum, where the immigrant women who lived around Hull House could display their handicrafts. In her first report, a document written for the wealthy donors who supported her work, she described how the Italian women of the Back-of-the-Yards, the Hull House area, had before migration "spun and wove the entire stock of clothing for their families," the older ones still using "the primitive form of spindle and distaff." Why not, Addams asked, set up a museum exhibiting these works, once done by hand and requiring great skill, but obliterated by the industrial production of textiles and garments? Addams expected that the exhibition of fabrics made by the older Italian women would "have an indirect social result. The children, and more ambitious young people of the colony, are inclined to look down on the simpler Italians who possess this skill . . . because they consider them uncouth and un-American."[7]

The work of Hull House easily transformed into the founding in 1908 of the Immigrants' Protective League (IPL), a service for all new immigrants to Chicago, not just those living in the Back-of-the-Yards neighborhood. Grace Abbott, one of the women associated with Hull House, served as the IPL's first director, and she oversaw its activities investigating abuses by people who lurked around the train station preying on unsuspecting new arrivals, unfamiliar with

English and lacking anyone local to help them out. The IPL handled the cases of immigrants living in Chicago whose relatives faced the threat of deportation while still at East Coast ports. It also marshaled its resources to lobby before Congress against the impending immigration restriction legislation.

In other cities individuals and organizations did similar kinds of work. Emily Greene Balch, a sociologist and reformer, published *Our Slavic Fellow Citizens* in 1910 in response to the increasing demonization of immigrants from the Slavic lands amid the voluble calls to restrict their immigration. The title of her book emphasized her vision of the fundamental commonality between the millions of immigrants laboring in steel mills, coal mines, meatpacking plants, and other industries and their "fellow" Americans. She used the pronoun *our* to denote the ideal relationship between the immigrants and other Americans.

The newly organized Russell Sage Foundation commissioned a six-volume survey in 1907 of conditions immigrants in Pittsburgh faced, setting out to prove that the industrial situation rather than any supposed defects in the immigrants' character contributed to the city's many ills. Each volume of the Pittsburgh survey detailed how steel mill owners, like the other industrialists, put maximizing profits over the quality of life for all, both the immigrants and the middle class.

Margaret Byington wrote volume 4 of the Pittsburgh survey. Titled *Homestead: The Households of a Mill Town*, the book opened with a discussion of the city's stark class divide:

> On the slope which rises steeply behind the mill are the Carnegie Library and the "mansion" of the mill superintendent, with the larger and more attractive dwellings of the town grouped about two small parks. Here and there the towers of a church rise in relief. The green of the parks modifies the first impression of dreariness by one of prosperity such as is not infrequent in American industrial towns. Turn up a side street, however, and you pass uniform frame houses, closely built and dulled by the smoke; and below, on the flats behind the mill, are cluttered alleys, unsightly and unsanitary, the dwelling place of the Slavic

laborers. The trees are dwarfed and the foliage withered by
the fumes; the air is gray.[8]

The books of the Pittsburgh Survey blamed profit-driven business
interest for the squalor immigrants endured in their neighborhoods and the harm done to all Americans as industrialists exploited
workers.

Few readers might have confronted the details of the Byington
book or any of the other volumes of the Sage Foundation study,
but they did have a chance to get the same message in a popular novel of the era written in 1906. The fictional characters Ona
Lukoszaite, Jurgis Rudkus, Marija Berczyskas, and their Lithuanian
neighbors lived in Chicago's Packing Town, on the Near West Side,
in Upton Sinclair's novel *The Jungle*. Trapped in unsanitary homes,
laboring in repulsive workplaces, and gripped in the vise of corrupt
landlords who worked in tandem with the rapacious employers,
the immigrants, Sinclair wrote, saw themselves "tied to the great
packing-machine and tied to it for life." Only their churches and
their social halls, which resounded with the music and languages
of back home, provided any relief from the unending horror that
immigration to Chicago had brought them.[9]

In 1917 the Carnegie Corporation of New York, founded with
money from the millionaire Andrew Carnegie, an immigrant from
Scotland, who had made his fortune in steel production using
masses of immigrant male laborers, asked ten leading academics,
social workers, and reformers to document the ways the lives of immigrants changed after their arrival, and to chart their paths toward
Americanization.

Directly challenging the opponents of immigration, the Carnegie books, the ten-volume *Study of Methods of Americanization*,
pointed to the nearly universal process by which immigrants
adapted to their new American circumstances. Whereas the critics of the immigrants claimed that innate stubborn conservatism,
lack of a progressive outlook, and mental slowness kept newcomers
from learning American ways, the writers of the Carnegie books
showed the opposite, extensively covering immigrants' efforts to
transform themselves and how they set out to learn American ways
and adopt them.

One volume highlighted immigrant domestic life. Sophonisba Breckinridge, an associate of Jane Addams from Chicago and a professor at the University of Chicago's School of Civics and Philanthropy as well as an immigrant-rights activist, authored *New Homes for Old*, which appeared in 1921. Breckenridge looked into the corners of immigrants' homes and into the organizations, associations, and self-help projects immigrant women created for themselves and their families. How, Breckinridge asked, did immigrant women learn American techniques of child rearing, cooking, and other aspects of domestic life? How did they organize clubs to address their own needs? Breckinridge's book documented women's path to Americanization. She described, for example, Polish and Lithuanian women who "have become conscious of separate needs, and undertake to assist in the development of others of their sex." Breckinridge argued that immigrant women exerted agency, chose change selectively, and became familiar with predominant American ways of organizing their lives, communities, and homes, in contrast to the restrictionists' unfounded predictions that the wives of the Slavic peasants would continue to be abused by their husbands and would never develop any awareness of themselves as independent individuals.[10]

Some who questioned the rightness of the calls for restriction used hard scientific evidence to dismantle the prevailing truth that immigrants should be excluded along racial lines. The findings of Franz Boas, the founder of the field of American anthropology, challenged the prevailing racialist truth, which called for racially based restrictions. Boas, a Jewish immigrant from Germany, came to the United States in 1887 as a respected scholar, taught at Columbia University, and helped shape New York's Museum of Natural History. His research raised serious questions about the concept of race as a scientific category in general, and as a rationale for government policy. Race, he asserted, existed merely as a sociological category. People perceived it as meaningful for political reasons, but it did not exist in fact.

He wrote one of the forty-one volumes of the Dillingham Commission's report on immigration and race. His contribution stood apart from the others, which pointed to the immutability of racial traits in immigrant behavior. *Changes in Bodily Form in the Descendants of Immigrants,* which was based on Boas's research, offered scientific evidence pointing to the power of environment. Boas, an expert in physical and cultural anthropology, demonstrated that even the bodies of immigrants' children converged over time toward the native-born American norm. The American-born off-spring of immigrants whom he measured and weighed, regardless of place of origin, grew taller and bigger, and their heads became more "regular" than those of their parents, born and raised abroad. "The adaptability of the immigrant seems to be very much greater," concluded Boas, "than we had a right to suppose before our inves-tigations were instituted."[11] He compiled data on southern Italians, Bohemians, eastern European Jews, Scots, and Hungarians, con-fronting the widely accepted belief that immigrants considered by place of origin represented fixed racial types. American influences in diet, health care, and education affected the immigrants' children, who did not jeopardize American well-being.

The reality that immigrants and particularly their children nat-urally changed as a by-product of everyday life in a multiethnic soci-ety emerged as a theme in the silent films of the early twentieth cen-tury as well. It served as the plot line of the popular play *The Melting Pot,* which debuted in Washington, D.C, in 1908 and was attended by Theodore Roosevelt. Like many of the movies, it depicted the children of immigrants, having grown up in America, easily falling in love with and marrying someone from a different background and thereby transcending social boundaries and the premigration prejudices of their immigrant parents. The movies catered to the many immigrants who flocked to the nickelodeons and early movie theaters as places of inexpensive entertainment. These works em-phasized the malleability of identities and the impermanence of ra-cial types, as imagined and feared by the opponents of immigration.

Julius Drachsler, a professor of sociology at Smith College, con-firmed this in a scholarly book that came out in 1921 while members of Congress contemplated immigration restriction and the quota system. In *Intermarriage in New York City,* Drachsler presented his findings, having examined thousands of marriage licenses. He doc-umented statistically how the children of immigrants chose their life partners from beyond the narrow confines of their immigrant enclaves. They did not feel themselves limited to marrying only from within their own community but rather met, fell in love, and married across ethnic divides. By this ordinary behavior, Drachsler's work pointed out, new hybrid identities and new kinds of Americans would be born and take their place in the nation, shaping its future.

Progressive reformers wanted to manage the changes that they recognized happened inevitably with the passage of time in America. They believed that through education and social settlement work, the children of immigrants would become not just Americans, but good Americans, who would participate in civic life, embrace progress as defined in American terms, and strive for economic mobility.

But some of the progressive pro-immigrationists also did not want to see the cultural repertoires of immigrant parents, whether in terms of language, food, art, or religion, to be completely eradicated. The immigrants, they declared, in fact enriched America, and those riches should not be lost. Jane Addams evinced this in her Labor Museum and the work she organized in the pottery studio of Hull House, which focused on the aesthetically pleasing ceramics fashioned by the Mexican immigrants showing up in the Back-of-the-Yards neighborhood as workers in the slaughterhouses.

Horace Kallen, who arrived in the United States in the late 1880s as a child with his parents from Silesia, articulated this also in a way that gained the greatest attention of all such projects. The son of an Orthodox rabbi, Kallen studied philosophy at Harvard and received a doctorate in 1908, but by the 1910s he began to contemplate the effect of immigration on America. In 1915, in one of the most important pieces of writing on the subject, "Democracy versus the Melting Pot," he responded directly to what was probably the most respected and vociferous anti-immigrant text of the era, the sociologist E. A. Ross's *The Old World in the New*, a 1914 manifesto for radical restriction that asserted the racial inferiority of immigrants and described the risks they posed for real Americans.

Kallen's article took a very different tack. "All the immigrants and their offspring," Kallen wrote, "are in the way of becoming 'Americanized,' if they remain in one place in the country long enough—say, six or seven years. The general notion, 'Americanization,' appears to denote the adoption of English speech, of American clothes and manners, of the American attitude in politics. It connotes the fusion of the various bloods, and a transmutation by 'the miracle of assimilation' of Jews, Slavs, Poles, Frenchmen, Germans, Hindus, Scandinavians into beings similar in background, tradition, outlook, and spirit to the descendants of the British colonists, the Anglo-Saxon stock."[12]

Kallen asserted that all immigrants, whether "German" or "Hindu," would adapt in similar ways. Within a relatively short period of time they would pick up the language, dress, and politics of those descended from the "Anglo-Saxon" immigrants of the seventeenth century. Kallen worried, however, that American demands pressuring immigrants to give up all that they valued would be harmful.

He and the journalist Randolph Bourne, who had been influenced by Kallen's writings, advocated instead for cultural pluralism, a vision of America that honored immigrants for elements of their distinctive cultures, most of which, although not all, he believed could coexist within the general American culture. Kallen likened an ideal America to a symphony orchestra in which each section, brass and woodwind, string and percussion, retained its "timbre and tonality," as each cooperated with the others, producing a harmonious sound based on a shared score.[13] Bourne, like Kallen, argued that real definitions of *American* ought to have nothing to do with racialized ideas of Anglo-Saxon superiority. Rather, he wrote in 1916 in a piece titled "Trans-national America," the United States should honor and respect the various immigrant cultures. He envisioned a "cosmopolitan America," where the newcomers could be both American and whatever they had brought from their premigration homes.[14]

Bourne and Kallen were writing as the Klan was emerging into public consciousness with its diatribes against immigrants. The Klan frightened individuals and organizations. They wanted to respond to its highly charged words, such as its calls for a wall to keep immigrants out, and crafted narratives about immigrants in the United States accordingly.

Certainly, the single most widely cited and often recited paean to America as an optimistic, immigrant-welcoming nation, a tarnished vision even when Emma Lazarus had written it decades earlier, came from the pen of this young poet. In 1883, one year after the passage of the Chinese Exclusion Act, she wrote "The New

Colossus." Daughter of a comfortably situated, affluent New York Jewish family with deep American roots, Lazarus donated the poem to an auction of artistic and literary works sponsored by the "Art Loan Fund Exhibition in Aid of the Bartholdi Pedestal Fund for the Statue of Liberty." The funds raised would underwrite construction of the pedestal on which the massive statue would stand, as it arose in the waters of New York Harbor.

The Statue of Liberty, unveiled in 1886, had not been designed to celebrate immigration, to welcome immigrants, or to make Americans proud of their nation's absorption of millions of newcomers over the course of its history. Lazarus, however, who had worked as a volunteer at Castle Garden providing services to new Jewish immigrants, did see it that way. She called the statue "Mother of Exiles."

The sentiments of "The New Colossus" revealed much about the pro-immigrant ideology that it hoped would counter the growing calls for restriction and the increasingly ugly rhetoric against immigrants as racially defective. She wrote in the final stanza the words familiar to so many Americans:

> "Give me your tired, your poor,
> Your huddled masses yearning to breathe free,
> The wretched refuse of your teeming shore.
> Send these, the homeless, tempest-tossed to me.
> I lift my lamp beside the golden door!"

The stirring words of the sonnet set America apart as different, in fact as far better, than the "ancient lands" that she invoked at the beginning of the stanza, those lands from which the immigrants had come. Her poetic phrasing reflected a trope about immigrants common to much of the pro-immigration efforts of this era. The common thread involved the idea that the immigrants had come from backward and retrograde homelands. Those places represented ways of life very different from that in America, with its progressive, individualistic, and democratic culture. But Lazarus, like Addams, Boas, Kallen, and the other defenders of the immigrants, considered that the nation's absorptive capacities could raise the immigrants up to an American standard. They shared with the opponents of immigration an assessment that the immigrants came "tired," "poor," and even as "wretched refuse," but they parted company when it came to the origins of those problems or their intractability.

The opponents of immigration, who, however, constituted the emerging majority, considered the defects fundamental and innate. The children of the immigrants would only replicate their parents' wretchedness. They would continue to be poor and tired. But those who favored immigration believed that the American environment would transform the immigrants and certainly their children, making them better, healthier, less "wretched," and more American.

As World War I came to an end, opponents and skeptics of immigration increasingly justified their position by science, journalism, and popular culture, a project they had begun in 1882. They had spent these decades before 1920 trying to close the gates to the United States, with some success. In the Great War's aftermath, they continued this fight, with very different results.

Further Reading

Bannister, Robert C. *Social Darwinism: Science and Myth in Anglo-American Social Thought* (1979).

Gould, Stephen Jay. *The Mismeasure of Man* (1996).

Hester, Torrie. *Deportation: The Origins of U.S. Policy* (2017).

King, Charles. *Gods of the Upper Air: How a Circle of Renegade Anthropologists Reinvented Race, Sex, and Gender in the Twentieth Century* (2019).

Lissak, Rivka Shpak. *Pluralism and Progressives: Hull House and the New Immigrants, 1890–1919* (1989).

Perlmann, Joel. *America Classifies the Immigrants: From Ellis Island to the 2020 Census* (2018).

CHAPTER SEVEN
Closing the Gates
National Origins and the Great Depression

I N 1926 CLARA AND Tola Zacharjasz, Jewish twins from Poland, began a journey to the United States. They traveled to Montreal, where they lived for a few months before paying a smuggler to take them to the United States to reunite with their parents in New York City. On May 27 American authorities arrested the fourteen-year-old sisters in Bombay, New York, right over the border. The twins faced a government deportation order, but a Jewish immigrant aid agency took up their case and won a stay of their deportation for five years. The Zacharjasz girls, meanwhile, joined their parents in the Bronx. In 1931 the government let the twins leave the United States voluntarily and dismissed the original charges. Their father, meanwhile, had naturalized, which meant the two could legally enter the country.

The Zacharjasz twins joined millions of Europeans, Mexicans, Canadians, and those from the Caribbean who wished to enter the United States. In earlier decades they would not have faced huge barriers to entry and probably would have arrived without much notice. But after 1921 a new period in American immigration history began, one notable for the decline in immigrants coming to the United States. Two forces, the 1920s immigration laws and the Great Depression of the 1930s, created this profoundly anti-immigrant era.

In the early 1920s, virulent anti-immigrant sentiments coursed through American politics and culture, powered by economic uncertainty, fears of political radicalism, and concerns about the assimilation of newcomers. Congress responded by passing national origins quotas, effectively extending the barriers to Asian immigration to immigrants from southern, central, and eastern Europe. By severely limiting how many and who could enter, the federal government's new legal framework played the vital role in slowing the entry of newcomers.

The Great Depression struck another blow to immigration in the 1930s. The collapse of the American economy slowed the economic draw that had brought so many immigrants to the United States. Immigrant communities in the United States suffered greatly, reporting their dire circumstances to friends and family back home. State and local governments often proved unwelcoming. Some actively discouraged newcomers from settling and sometimes took steps to remove immigrants, approaches that the federal government enacted as policy at the national level. At times the economic troubles and their attendant anti-immigrant policies proved so all-encompassing that many recent migrants left the United States of their own volition. That repatriation alone, compared to previous decades, makes clear the momentous changes under way.

Immigration after the Great War

The Great War temporarily slowed immigration to the United States, but it bounced back by 1921, powered by a rush of southern and central European immigrants with geographic and religious demographics similar to those of immigrants who arrived in the early twentieth century (table 7.1).

Economic opportunity drove many of these newcomers, who for decades had heard family and friends tell tales of improved prospects in the United States. Rising nationalism, political radicalism, and the redrawing of national boundaries in the war's wake fostered political instability across central and eastern Europe and the Near East, creating the other major impetus to depart. By the middle of the 1920s, a full-blown refugee crisis of some 10 million displaced

Table 7.1. Immigrant Arrivals to the United States, 1918–1925

Year	Total Immigrant Arrivals	North-western Europe	Central Europe	Eastern Europe	Southern Europe	Asia	Americas
1918	110,168	12,499	508	4,335	13,721	12,701	65,418
1919	141,132	17,987	105	1,454	5,081	12,674	102,286
1920	430,001	85,997	11,480	5,664	143,154	17,505	162,666
1921	805,228	131,748	178,961	42,986	298,669	25,034	124,118
1922	309,556	61,506	75,929	32,154	46,796	14,268	77,448
1923	522,919	108,152	108,853	37,233	53,682	13,705	199,972
1924	706,896	128,255	136,597	34,091	65,396	22,065	318,855
1925	294,314	79,180	56,110	4,687	8,389	3,578	141,496

Source: Bureau of the Census, Historical Statistics of the United States, 1789–1945 (Washington, D.C.: Government Printing Office, 1949), 19–20, 33, 35.

Russians, Poles, Turks, and Greeks increased migration pressures and the desire to leave.[1] Finally, anti-Semitism flourished across eastern and central Europe, compelling some Jews to emigrate. Of course, for some individuals these factors worked in concert. Jews fleeing Russia and eastern Europe came to the United States for a combination of economic, political, and religious reasons.

The desire to reunite with family also drove immigration in these early postwar years. Before the Great War, men dominated the migration. The hostilities on the Continent made it more difficult for male immigrants to bring wives and children to the United States; the war even impeded their ability to send money to their overseas families to secure passage to the United States. The Russian Revolution and its subsequent civil war only extended these difficulties. Thus, when relative stability returned, wives and children came to the United States in greater numbers than in previous decades. In 1921 the number of female immigrants almost equaled the number of male immigrants, and females surpassed males in 1922.[2]

The decisions immigrants made to leave home for the United States often were complicated, demonstrating the various factors that shaped choices to migrate or not. In 1920 in Palermo, Sicily, a women named Francesca G. went to the police to ask them to prevent her husband, Ignazio, from emigrating to the United States.

Other women, though, eagerly came to the United States hoping to enjoy a life they could not in their homelands. Anna Kuthan, a domestic servant in Vienna, Austria, immigrated after the Great War and recalled, "When I came to this country, the first thing I see is those big stores. I said there is the Hecker's flour . . . there is the condensed milk!"[3]

Thousands of Canadians, West Indians, and Mexicans also arrived annually during the early postwar years. French-speaking Canadians resumed their resettlement in the mill towns of New England and the Midwest's industrial centers. Women, many from rural farming communities, made up about 40 percent of those arriving, and the majority of those who worked found employment in factories or as domestic servants. Anglo-Canadians migrated more widely across the United States, with roughly the same gender breakdown among newcomers as the French Canadians but with a greater percentage of professionals. Two French Canadians from Berthier County, just north of Montreal, illuminate the importance of jobs and family and friends in shaping immigration choices. Pauline Guthro, a single woman of twenty-two years who had worked in factories in her hometown, arrived in Woonsocket, Rhode Island, in 1926, drawn by the possibility of mill work but also, more important, by her brother-in-law, who already had settled there. Four years earlier, Lucien Dumontier, who had studied accounting, made the same journey after failing to find work in Montreal in that field. He, too, was drawn by connections to Woonsocket, in his case friends from his church.

In the early decades of the twentieth century, sometimes as many as ten thousand West Indians entered annually, settling in Miami and Tampa, Boston, and increasingly New York City. English speakers, the majority ended up in agricultural work, domestic service, or unskilled labor, but sizable numbers found jobs as craftsmen, professionals, or businessmen. West Indian communities thrived in the 1920s, even in the face of anti-Black racism. In New York City, West Indians helped craft the Harlem Renaissance, and Marcus Garvey, a Jamaican who came to the United States in 1916, articulated a Black nationalism that emphasized economic and political autonomy and a desire to return Africa to Black control. Louise Norton, born in the West Indies in 1897, found herself swept up in such forces. In 1917 she emigrated to Montreal to live with family, became a follower of Garvey, and in 1919 married a man, Earl Little, whom she had met in the movement. They lived in various U.S. cities and remained dedicated Garveyites, also starting a large family. In 1925 they had a son named Malcolm Little, who in the decades to come would practice his own Black nationalism under the name Malcolm X.

Finally, a new set of Mexican immigrants, increasingly from the west-central region of that country, moved first inside Mexico and eventually north of the border. Political turmoil caused by the Mexican Revolution (1910–1920), as well as wrenching changes in the socioeconomic structure of village life, led Mexicans to flee. Many came in search of employment and social and economic stability, the majority settling in the Southwest. Their daily wages in the United States were ten to twenty times greater than what they might earn at home. Agricultural work surpassed mining and railroad employment for Mexicans in the early twentieth century, as large-scale industrial farming boomed in the Southwest but suffered from labor shortages because of restrictions limiting Asian immigration.

Remarkable circumstances sometimes propelled Mexican immigration. In 1923, for instance, Pasquala Esparza quietly bundled up her belongings and with her two children, nine-year-old Jesusita and the infant Raquel, boarded a train in Durango state and headed for Ciudad Juárez. The plan was to get together the money for visas, cross into the United States, and settle with family in El Monte, California. What led to this extraordinary journey? Esparza's husband abused both his wife and Jesusita, so that the latter recalled years later, "I think the only way she could get away was to come over here."[4] When they finally got to El Monte, like so many other Mexican immigrants in the 1920s, Pasquala and Jesusita found work harvesting berries in the lush fields of Southern California.

Some estimates held that Mexicans crossed the border over 1 million times during the 1920s.[5] Mexicans often practiced circular migration: an individual worked in the United States for a time, returned home, and then repeated this process. But about 1.5 million Mexicans did permanently resettle in the southwestern United States between 1900 and 1930, costing Mexico one-tenth of its population.[6] By the 1920s, women—both single and some accompanying husbands—made up a larger proportion of the newcomers

Immigration interview at Angel Island, California, 1923.
National Archives, College Park, Maryland.

entering the United States than earlier in the twentieth century. This development gave those resettled communities a less transient and more permanent character.

Smaller numbers of Mexicans began to resettle during the 1920s in the urban Midwest, taking up jobs in industry. One earnest Mexican summed up the aspirations of many when he asked the Ford automobile company for a job: "I am a young Mexican, twenty-five years old, single, and I have left my home at Monterrey, Mexico to come up to Detroit. . . . I want to work for the Ford Motor Company because it is the best business on earth and there must be . . . permanent employment and a good future for a man who wants to work."[7]

Arguments about Immigrants in the Early 1920s

In the early 1920s, the powerful anti-immigrant sentiment of the preceding decades expanded. Scientific racism and anti-Semitism continued to flourish and presage attacks on immigrants. New editions of Madison Grant's *The Passing of the Great Race* came out in 1921 and 1923, and Lothrop Stoddard's 1920 book, *The Rising Tide of Color against White World-Supremacy*, which warned that people of color soon would engulf whites across the globe, found a large audience. Anti-Semitism accelerated, too, both with the postwar growth of the second Ku Klux Klan and through the work of powerful advocates like the automobile king Henry Ford. Ford used the *Dearborn Independent*, a newspaper he purchased in 1918, to attack Jews and what he believed was an international Jewish conspiracy to rule the world. Ford funded the distribution of nearly half a million copies of the "Protocols of the Elders of Zion," a notorious anti-Semitic text fabricated in 1903 by Russian czarists hoping to stymie the revolution and eventually proven to be completely fraudulent.

In addition to these long-standing concerns, particular postwar conditions also buttressed the anti-immigration case. A recession took hold in 1920 and 1921, when unemployment and inflation surged, economic productivity retreated, and agriculture faltered. Industrial workers, who joined unions in large numbers during the war, started making demands on management as the economy worsened. The resulting labor unrest put about 20 percent of the workforce on strike in 1919. The strikers faced management opposition and public disapproval, while internal divisions between immigrants and native-born Americans among the strikers weakened the effort. The economic distress fueled anti-immigrant sentiments in two ways. First, unemployment made workers in the United States wary of newcomers who might further inflate the labor supply. Second, recent immigrants often led the era's labor unrest, feeding accusations of immigrant radicalism. Or, as one newspaper put it, the strikes boiled down to "Americanism vs. Alienism."[8]

Likewise, in the postwar years long-standing fears of immigrant political radicalism surged. Law enforcement and many political and media leaders believed that the 1917 Russian Revolution threatened a proletariat revolution. American communists, socialists, and leftist political elements, strong in immigrant communities, drew energy from the revolution and sped their organizing and heightened their rhetoric. The backlash came swiftly. In the 1919–1920 Red Scare, the Department of Justice targeted leftists and labor, and the immigrants in those political communities. J. Edgar Hoover oversaw the so-called Palmer Raids, which arrested, often without warrants and with no guarantee of due process, 10,000 immigrants believed to hold radical political beliefs. The government deported some 500 of these detainees.

This fear of immigrant political and labor militancy reached its height in 1920 with the arrest of two Italian-American anarchists, Nicola Sacco and Bartolomeo Vanzetti, on charges of robbery and murder. Convicted and sentenced to death in a trial overseen by an anti-immigrant and antiradical judge, Sacco and Vanzetti's fate became a celebrated cause among many American intellectuals, but to no avail. Massachusetts executed the two men in 1927. The Sacco and Vanzetti saga reinforced the connection between immigrants and political radicalism, feeding anti-immigrant animus.

The pro-immigrant bloc responded to restrictionist thinking, but without the vigor it displayed earlier in the twentieth century. Some of the intellectuals known for their defense of immigrants before the Great War, such as Horace Kallen and John Dewey, largely stayed out of the debates in the early 1920s. Others blasted the scientific racism at the heart of anti-immigrant thinking, but to little effect.

A heartier defense of immigrants emerged in other forms. The most powerful explanation of the role of immigrants in American society arose from the newcomers themselves, who expounded on all that they brought to their new country in newspapers, magazines, and local community groups. The message only grew in import as the 1920s progressed. Some native-born Americans made parallel assertions, arguing that that immigrants made the nation stronger with their unique cultural backgrounds and desirable economic skills. By urging an acceptance of immigrants and their traditions, this approach essentially continued along the same lines taken by cultural pluralists like Kallen.

An interesting example emerged in the early 1920s with the Knights of Columbus, a Catholic fraternal order founded in the

1880s. The Knights decided to commission a project that would disseminate to its members and to the public the proposition that immigrants and other minority groups had contributed much to American history and would continue to do so in the future. The result was the Knights of Columbus Racial Contributions Series, a set of books that would tell the story of what immigrants and African Americans had contributed to America. An ambitious proposal, only three books were actually released, one on African Americans by the African American intellectual and historian W. E. B. du Bois, one on Germans, and one on Jews. The project's goals may have exceeded its accomplishments, but the organization hoped that the presentation of facts about immigrants could make a difference and sway the public from its drive toward restriction.

A different defense arose in groups such as the Syracuse Americanization League (and similar organizations in other cities) and the U.S. Army's program "Americans All." They aimed to Americanize European immigrants, scrubbing them of those ethnonational particulars that others lauded. As the "Americans All" program put it, "In this school, racial distinctions disappear almost over night— they are all Americans. . . . Every day, all day, the men live and work in an American atmosphere."[9] Much like Theodore Roosevelt's approach at the turn of the century, this stance demanded that newcomers assimilate to so-called American values and traditions. In focusing on newcomers of European descent, however, this version of pro-immigrant thinking had no room for individuals from Asia or Mexico.

Immigration Restriction's Triumph

The immigration debate reached a conclusion in the first half of the 1920s when opponents of immigration succeeded in enacting laws that trimmed the annual entry of newcomers and set up a system of admissions that favored immigrants from northwestern Europe.

Their first victory came with passage of the 1921 Emergency Quota Act. Under this law, each European country received an annual visa quota equal to 3 percent of the foreign-born of that country living in the United States in 1910, which capped total annual immigration from Europe at about 350,000. Within the quota system, immigrants who had begun the naturalization process and the wives and children of already naturalized immigrants gained preferential claim to visas. The law left in place the Asiatic Barred Zone created by the 1917 Immigration Act, and it did not place any limits on Western Hemisphere immigrants. The Emergency Quota Act expired in fourteen months, leaving Congress the task of passing a permanent reform that built on the 1921 legislation. The law achieved, for a time, its desired effect. European immigration to the United States plummeted in 1922 and then rose slowly to the legal limit by 1924 (see table 7.1).

Congress devised a permanent and more restrictionist law in 1924, the Johnson-Reed Act. It limited annual admissions to just over 185,000 Eastern Hemisphere immigrants; countries would receive visa quotas equal to 2 percent of their representation in the 1890 census. The use of the 1890 date, just before large numbers of southern, central, and eastern Europeans began to enter the United States, guaranteed that the quotas would favor newcomers from northwestern Europe. The Johnson-Reed Act reinforced the Asiatic Barred Zone, banning from immigration those who could not become U.S. citizens. Here the law drew from the recent Supreme Court cases *Takao Ozawa v. U.S.* (1922) and *U.S. v. Bhagat Singh Thind* (1923), in which the Court strengthened the color line in citizenship law by concluding that Asians were not white and could not naturalize. The 1924 law, then, closed a loophole that had allowed some Japanese to immigrate by means of the 1907 Gentlemen's Agreement.

Like the Emergency Quota Act, the law exempted Western Hemisphere immigrants from the quota system while making their entry requirements more stringent. Three factors led to this exemption. First, agricultural concerns in the Southwest needed access to Mexican labor, so they pushed for an open door on the southern border. Second, the State Department, concerned with how Mexico and Canada might react to restrictions, lobbied for the exemption. Third, a widespread assumption existed that Mexicans would eventually return home, so allowing Mexican workers into the country would not lead to their permanent settlement. Inherent in this thinking was the belief that Mexicans could not fit easily into the United States. Even some of the harshest critics of national origins policy, such as Representative Samuel Dickstein of New York, who led the effort to protect all European immigrants, supported this position: "One can not say, for instance, that a Mexican alien readily becomes Americanized, or is of the same blood or language with us."[10]

The Johnson-Reed Act dropped total immigration substantially, even below 1922 levels. It sorted immigrants into several tiers. Almost all Asians, ineligible for citizenship because of their nonwhiteness, were banned from immigrating to the United States. Mexicans could—and remained eligible for citizenship because the law considered them white—but faced formidable bureaucratic obstacles in trying to enter as immigrants with visas. Europeans were the most privileged, but the law's quota system sorted them into a hierarchy. Thus, while the law upheld whiteness as the key determinant of desirability, its treatment of southern, central, and eastern Europeans and Mexicans showed that restrictionist conceptions of whiteness contained gradations.

The political debate surrounding the 1924 law replayed the discussions of the early 1920s. Supporters argued that it guaranteed a proper mix of immigrants from desirable countries that safeguarded and perpetuated the United States' political and social ideals and structures. They also described the law as fair because it admitted white immigrants from across the Eastern Hemisphere. Congressman John Tillman (D-Arkansas) excoriated the mass immigration of the previous forty years: "We have admitted the dregs of Europe until America has been Orientalized, Europeanized, Africanized, and mongrelized to that insidious degree that our genius, stability, and greatness, and promise of advancement, and achievement are actually menaced."[11] Jasper Tincher, a Republican representative from Kansas, saw restrictionism as patriotic, representing "constitutional government; one flag, the Stars and Stripes."[12] Samuel Gompers, the head of the American Federation of Labor, echoed this patriotism, but he also feared that newcomers were flooding the labor market, hurting American workers.

Black Americans, with reservations, sided with the immigration restrictionists. During the Great Migration, Blacks had migrated from the South to take up industrial and manual labor jobs in the urban Midwest and Northeast. Those positions were a boon to social and economic mobility, but many Blacks knew that recent immigrants competed for those same jobs. In the postwar immigration debates, African Americans backed limiting entry despite qualms about supporting KKK-approved policies and curtailing migration for people of color from the Caribbean. Black intellectuals and media wrestled with these trade-offs, but they ultimately promoted restriction rather than challenging it.

Opponents of Johnson-Reed railed against it as racist, discriminatory, and un-American. They made the case, as Representative Ove Kvale from Minnesota did, that "these 'foreigners' and 'aliens' are the very people who have helped build America on farm, in shop and factory."[13] Others celebrated the patriotism of immigrants, who "fought loyally and valiantly in every war for the creation and preservation of this Union," a potent defense in light of the country's recent involvement in the Great War.[14] Representative John J. O'Connor of New York said simply of the discriminatory intent of the law: "That is not the America that I was brought up to love and to worship. That is not the America I want to be a part of."[15]

Recent European immigrants to the United States authored a more complicated approach toward immigration restriction. Some from northwestern Europe supported the restrictions and inveighed against southern, central, and eastern European immigrants. German Americans, after the scarring campaigns against them during the Great War, sat out the debates. But most immigrant communities did not follow these paths. Organizations representing nationalities and religions testified before Congress, lobbied lawmakers, and flooded politicians with constituent letters. Newspapers in immigrant communities published editorials attacking the national origins quota proposal. One Italian community in Chicago took the fight directly to advocates of restriction, burning down a Ku Klux Klan tent.

Most groups could not afford such spectacular opposition, and the fight illuminated cleavages in their communities. The American Jewish Committee slammed the racism at the heart of restrictionist thinking, but B'nai B'rith considered whether immigration restrictions might lessen criticism of Jewish communities perceived to be failures in assimilating quickly. Some Jewish groups calculated that in that political environment they should accede to the hemispheric cap while fighting for more generous quotas under national origins.

Italian Americans proceeded in a somewhat similar fashion, demonstrating the difficult political terrain. They blasted discrimination and restriction but also lauded the contributions of Italians in ways that validated the idea that racial groups had distinct qualities. The Order of the Sons of Italy in America described the Italian as "sober, thrifty and industrious[;] sound in mind and body, he constitutes an unimpeachable racial factor in the formation of the American race of the future."[16] *L'Italia*, a Chicago-based Italian immigrant paper, proudly celebrated "the people of the Mediterranean" who "had created the civilization of the white race."[17] This embrace of whiteness, and the willingness to work in restrictionist racial categories, demonstrated how weak the commitment to universalism was, even among immigration advocates.

The Johnson-Reed law had one peculiarity that played out over the rest of the decade. The initial quotas were based on the 1890 census, but the law held that a study of the national origins of the American population in 1920 would determine the quotas after 1927. A Quota Board led by a longtime Bureau of the Census statistician, Joseph Hill, would determine the ethnonational origins of the American people and use that assessment to create new, more scientifically accurate quotas. The effort floundered from the beginning. Incomplete census data and the instability of ethnic and national categories over time made the calculations nearly impossible. Hill even admitted his work included some "rather arbitrary assumptions."[18]

Congress rejected the first few reports of the Quota Board, delaying the unveiling of the national quotas. Nonetheless, when Congress and the president approved the quotas in 1929, immigration opponents had won the day. Great Britain (and Northern Ireland), Germany, and the Irish Free State earned large quotas, while countries in southern, central, and eastern Europe received pitiful quotas (table 7.2). In the course of the decade, restrictionists had remade the law, fashioning what came to be called the national origins quotas immigration system.

Table 7.2. 1929 National Origins Immigration Quotas

Country	Immigration Quotas on the Basis of National Origins, 1929
Great Britain and Northern Island	65,721
Germany	25,957
Irish Free State	17,853
Poland	6,524
Italy	5,802
Netherlands	3,153
Russia	2,784
Hungary	869

Source: U.S. Bureau of Foreign and Domestic Commerce, *Statistical Abstract of the United States, 1930* (Washington, D.C., 1930), 105.

The 1920s Laws in Action

After 1924, immigration to the United States collapsed. The Great Depression explains some of the drop, but the statistics in the pre-Depression years make clear the new law's importance. Between 1925 and 1929, 760,000 Europeans entered under the quota system, fewer than in any single year (except for 1909) between 1903 and 1915. Of those 760,000, the vast majority came from the United Kingdom, Ireland, and Germany. A comparison between two typical years, 1908 and 1928, draws the picture even more starkly (table 7.3). Even here, authorities probably undercounted Polish, Magyar, and Russian entrants in 1908 because they counted 103,387 "Hebrew" immigrants, mainly eastern and central European Jews, as a separate category.

Demand for visas did not dip after 1924. One estimate held that for every northern and western European who received a visa, three candidates were denied because of a full quota. For immigrants from southern, central, and eastern Europe and the Near East, a more daunting ratio emerged: one visa for every seventy-eight denied.[19] The same held for immigrants hoping to come from the Western Hemisphere. West Indians fell under the British quota, and, while there were plenty of available visas, U.S. authorities habitually denied them to Black West Indians. This effort, combined with the

Table 7.3. Comparison of Immigration Admissions, 1908 and 1928

Country	1908	1928
United Kingdom, Northern Ireland, Irish Free State	85,483	59,146
Germany	73,038	47,883
Italy	135,247	3,826
Poland	68,105	6,129
Russia	17,111	2,231
Magyar (1908)/Hungary (1928)	24,378	468

Sources: U.S. Bureau of Foreign and Domestic Commerce, *Statistical Abstract of the United States, 1916* (Washington, D.C., 1916), 98; U.S. Bureau of Foreign and Domestic Commerce, *Statistical Abstract of the United States, 1930* (Washington, D.C., 1930), 102.

Depression, reduced West Indian immigration well into the post-1945 era.

The way that immigrants entered the United States changed dramatically with these new laws. Before 1921, newcomers appeared at a port of entry where immigration officials conducted a series of interviews and medical exams to determine their eligibility to enter. In the vast majority of cases, the immigrant entered. This process made Ellis Island an icon of immigration to the United States. Under the quota system, this could no longer continue: if the quota was filled, then the potential immigrants would be in the United States but not legally able to enter, and they were forced to find a way home.

From then on, U.S. authorities would clear immigrants for entry to the United States, and assign quota visas, outside the United States. This required building up the federal government's immigration bureaucracy during the 1920s. The government merged the Consular Service and the Diplomatic Corps in the State Department, and consular officers working out of U.S. facilities overseas waded through thousands of visa applications from potential immigrants. Soon the U.S. Public Health Service joined consular officials overseas to weed out applicants who could not pass the health exam previously administered at the port of entry. Under this new system, prospective immigrants were required to disclose detailed background information and provide extensive documentation, including two photographs, military or prison records, and copies of any government records pertaining to the applicant. These amounted to real obstacles for many would-be immigrants, especially from eastern Europe, who had witnessed borders and governments shift under their feet after the war.

The 1920s brought into full relief the notion of "illegal" immigration. The development of exclusionary principles and devices meant that some immigrants entered via extralegal avenues, which immigration opponents saw as an affront. In 1924 Congress formally set up the U.S. Border Patrol within the Department of Labor. Relatedly, in 1929 Congress made first-time unauthorized entry a misdemeanor crime and second-time unsanctioned entry a felony offense punishable by jail time and a large fine. Staffed with forty men and charged with protecting the border and patrolling the borderlands to remove "illegal" arrivals, the Border Patrol grew by 1930 to 875 officers: 433 worked on the Canadian–U.S. border, 319 served on the Mexico–U.S. border, and the rest patrolled the coasts of Florida and the Gulf states. In its initial years, the Border Patrol focused on enforcing Prohibition and guarding the northern and southern borders to prevent the unauthorized entry of Europeans and Asians. The Border Patrol's predecessors had concentrated on halting the unauthorized entry of the latter group since the Exclusion laws of the late nineteenth century, but the quota laws made Europeans a target as well. Likewise, the ramped-up border security and entry requirements along the U.S.–Mexican border put Mexicans coming to the United States in the Border Patrol's sights.

The Experience of Immigration after Restriction

These changes affected how persons hoping to enter the United States experienced immigration. Immigrant networks on both sides of the Atlantic buzzed with information about the new laws that made coming to the United States more difficult. Families, in this country and in Europe, eagerly read newspapers, magazines, and personal correspondence that addressed immigration questions as they weighed whether their kin and friends should try to enter. Some decided to stay put, others decided on new destinations such as Canada or countries in South America, and others still tried to come to America, with or without a visa.

Those who chose to come to the United States experienced a journey different from their predecessors'. They met with more American officials, both in Europe and the United States, and these confrontations changed the way immigrants acted. Immigrants had for decades engaged in forms of performance at the border, but after 1924, when one immigration official crowed that newcomers now "looked exactly like Americans," these performances took on more importance.[20] The task of pulling together documentation such as birth certificates to satisfy immigration officials led one contemporary to describe the paperwork challenge as "the Eastern Jew's existential struggle against papers."[21] Individuals caught at the border attempting to obtain a visa with fraudulent papers often went to jail. One such unfortunate described his incarceration: "They hold us as if we were criminals, murderers, in dark stinking rooms with little to eat."[22]

The laws made immigration from Asia more difficult, but one group could still somewhat more easily enter the United States in the 1920s: immigrants from the Philippines. Living in a colonial possession of the United States, Filipinos could freely enter the country but were barred from citizenship, one of the strange ways that the formal American empire facilitated a certain type of immigration that provided workers for the economy but not new members of the nation. During the 1920s, about 14,000 Filipinos arrived in the continental United States from Hawaii, and 37,600 journeyed from the islands themselves.[23] They settled mainly on the West Coast, finding work in agriculture, where both white and Japanese American farmers recruited Filipino workers, as well as in domestic service and the service sector. In 1928 nineteen-year-old Mariano Catolico came to California from the Philippines and earned a living as a houseboy and by working on farms. He also continued his education, earning a master's degree from the University of California, Berkeley, before fighting in World War II. His intention in the 1930s was to return permanently to the islands, but he never did.

The United States' northern border, though, reflected the more restrictionist impulses of the era. Canadians entered steadily through 1926 before the pace slackened in 1927. New England textile mills needed less labor, which explains some of the drop, but immigration also slowed because crossing the border became more complicated. Canadians now had to decide whether they planned a permanent or temporary stay in the United States. Permanent relocation required applying for a visa, which involved visiting a consulate and perhaps staying a few days away from home, a real expense. And, while Canadians did not face quotas, they faced other restrictions, such as literacy tests, the "likely to become a public charge" clause, and medical and mental health inspections that turned away about 7 percent of migrants at the border in the decades before 1930.[24]

At the southern border, the immigration experience changed even more dramatically. After the 1920s reforms, Customs officials and immigration officers made passage across the 2,000-mile border more difficult with tougher health inspections, a literacy test, and a higher head tax. Border Patrol agents, drawn largely from the white working class, possessed little formal training, often lacked Spanish-language skills, and displayed little empathy for Mexicans. In El Paso, some border agents belonged to the local KKK, a not uncommon occurrence. Agents arbitrarily enforced immigration regulations and often harassed, sometimes violently, Mexicans crossing the border. One Border Patrol officer described his technique: "I was really in favor of banging a suspect over the ears with a sixshooter and then asking him when he crossed out of Mexico. This I found reduced the small talk to a few syllables and got a confession."[25] The Border Patrol, then, struck fear among Mexican immigrants, and, as it actively enforced the racial hierarchy in the Southwest, it helped cement the association between unauthorized immigrants and Mexicans.

The United States returned nearly 26,000 Mexicans between 1925 and 1929, a small number given the number of crossings, but with real, larger effects.[26] By threatening deportation, agricultural employers could ensure a more docile workforce. The Border Patrol's actions also produced a small unintended consequence. Facing greater scrutiny in crossing after 1924, some Mexicans decided to stay put in the United States, slightly slowing circular migration patterns.

And yet, Mexican immigration accelerated in the late 1920s. The Cristero War, a conflict between the government and Catholics in western-central Mexico, sent thousands to the north. Economic opportunities also beckoned. A 1925 advertisement read, "From one thousand to fifteen hundred Mexican laborers will be needed on these clearings, who, besides being employed for quite a while, will be able to maintain themselves until the coming cotton season."[27] Nothing encapsulated the difficult experience of immigration better than the 1920s ballad "El Deportado," in which a son describes leaving his mother to cross into the United States at Juárez. The lyrics portray a powerless immigrant encountering border agents who tell him that his money is worthless and, piercingly, that they control his body as they declare, "We have to bathe you."[28] Leaving the border with a labor recruiter, the youngster warns his listeners that his troubles have only just begun.

The Depression and Migration

The Mexican immigrant in the 1920s ballad entered a United States that was very different from that encountered by even his very recent predecessors. The main difference was the Great Depression, which began in 1929 and wrecked the economy through the next decade. The Depression reshaped immigration to the United States (table 7.4). Between 1931 and 1940, only 528,431 immigrants came to the United States, easily the lowest total in decades. From 1932 to 1935, more people left the country than arrived. During the 1930s, the number of nonimmigrant arrivals (especially newcomers from the Western Hemisphere and family members of U.S. citizens) who entered outside quotas but intended to stay permanently also slowed. Germany, Great Britain, Italy, and Poland sent the most immigrants in the 1930s, though only Italy came close to filling its annual quota. Fewer Canadians and Mexicans came during the 1930s, though the drop in Mexican immigration resulted from government policies than did the decline in Canadian immigration.

Two factors explain these dynamics. First, immigrants chose not to come to the United States as the allure of good jobs and thriving ethnic communities faded. Second, the United States actively discouraged the arrival of immigrants by tightening border controls to prevent entry and by removing newcomers who had recently arrived.

Table 7.4. Immigrant and Nonimmigrant Admissions, 1930–1939

Year	Immigrant Admissions	Nonimmigrant Admissions
1930	241,700	204,514
1931	97,139	183,540
1932	35,576	139,295
1933	23,068	127,660
1934	29,470	134,434
1935	34,956	144,765
1936	36,329	154,570
1937	50,244	181,640
1938	67,895	184,802
1939	82,998	185,333

Source: U.S. Bureau of the Census, *Statistical Abstract of the United States, 1943* (Washington, D.C., 1943), 101.

The Depression proved especially corrosive to elements that traditionally attracted immigrants to the United States. For instance, U.S. Steel's full-time workforce stood at 225,000 in 1929, but zero in the spring of 1933.[29] In Chicago, the manufacturing workforce shrank by half between 1927 and 1933, and manufacturing payrolls fell by 75 percent.[30] The payroll trend in the Windy City mirrored the national story. American manufacturers paid out $16 billion in wages in 1929, but only $7.7 billion in 1932.[31] One central European immigrant working in the auto industry scoffed at the 1929 stock market crash—"What t'hell does the stock market have to do with us Overland Hunkies? I ain't buyin' no General Motors common or Willys-Overland preferred, are you?"—but such a carefree attitude probably disappeared as the possibility of economic security for immigrant workers grew more remote.[32]

On the West Coast, where an unskilled, largely Mexican workforce made a living in the urban industrial areas such as Los Angeles, the Depression dried up jobs and pushed Anglos into the job market. In 1930 one of seven Mexican laborers in Los Angeles did not have a job, a ratio that soon worsened because employers, urged on by public opinion and in some cases by laws, looked to hire native-born or naturalized Americans.[33] At times, these employers locked out even native-born or naturalized citizens because they did not appear to be white. Such was the case in 1931 for one U.S. Army veteran, born to Mexican parents in the United States. He described going to "construction sites where the supervisors know me and always have given me a job. . . . Because I am of dark complexion I stay with people of my race and of course, do not get hired because the supervisor has the order to hire only the 'white people' and that is what he does."[34] If an American citizen and military veteran of Mexican heritage faced such long odds at finding work, immigrants from Mexico suffered even more.

Immigrants employed in America's fields encountered similarly dim circumstances. One story illustrates the era's desperation. A Mexican sharecropper in Mississippi named Timotea Arroyo pleaded with the Mexican consulate for help in 1930, as the Depression spiraled to new depths. She had children and an ill husband to care for, but she possessed no economic prospects to support her family. The consulate's solution: find a charity that would fund passage to the southwestern border, where the Mexican government would send her and the family home. While amenable to the plan, she could find no such help and endured, impoverished, in Mississippi.

Other immigrant farm laborers across America suffered like Arroyo. The Mexican migrant labor that increasingly worked in the sugar beet industry of the Plains and Midwest saw wages collapse from a pre-Depression rate of twenty-eight dollars per acre to ten dollars per acre.[35] These workers often fled for the Southwest in search of jobs, but the agricultural labor market was flooded with Mexican migrants, Mexican Americans, Filipino immigrants, and impoverished whites escaping the Dust Bowl and all competing for low-wage jobs. Only the California citrus industry, which employed tens of thousands of Mexican immigrants, weathered the economic storm decently, regularly producing annual revenues in excess of $90 million in the 1930s.[36] That money, though, almost never found its way to the immigrant workforce, who saw their wages frozen or slashed in the Depression decade.

The immigrant communities that had eased the settlement of newcomers in the early twentieth century came under stress during the Depression, dulling another attraction that encouraged migration. The locally owned groceries and theaters, and the community churches and fraternal organizations that sustained the European ethnic enclaves in urban America struggled to survive. Mexican, West Indian, and Canadian communities bowed under these same challenges. These communities showed incredible resilience as they gamely confronted the crisis. María Olazábal, living in 1931 in the Belvedere section of Los Angeles, declared, "It is frightening to see the misery endured by people ready and willing to work."[37] Her solution to some of the misery? She and a few neighborhood women began making and selling, at cost and not for profit, tamales to her community's hungry members. These efforts proliferated across Los Angeles's Mexican barrios. Wives creatively stretched household budgets and started informal businesses. Families relied on the church, as much for spiritual comfort as material aid (which the Catholic Church struggled to provide). Finally, although family bonds often disintegrated during the Depression, they also sometimes tightened as nuclear and extended families drew on each other for strength.

Policies toward Immigrants during the Depression

Immigrant communities needed to be resourceful because local, state, and federal governments often failed to alleviate their suffering. Given the tenor of 1920s immigration politics, this outcome was not surprising. Some Americans blamed immigrants for causing the Depression's brutal unemployment. The conservative Democratic Congressmen Martin Dies of Texas declared, "If we had refused admission to the 16,500,000 foreign-born who are living in this country today, we would have no unemployment problem."[38] Welfare policies during the Depression centered on providing for the deserving among the needy, and policy makers and politicians often placed immigrants into the undeserving category. Cries arose all over the United States to aid citizens and native-born first.

The New Deal's largesse, especially pertaining to immigrants, extended only so far. FDR's adviser Harry Hopkins, a liberal committed to expansive welfare programs, explained to Congress, "If we knew a man was here illegally, we would not take him on the relief rolls."[39] A variety of government programs practiced this thinking. The Works Progress Administration in 1937 banned unauthorized

immigrants as well as those authorized immigrants who had not begun the administrative process of becoming a citizen, from taking a
WPA job. Likewise, in the 1930s the federal government announced
that all its contractors could employ only U.S. citizens. The directive led, for instance, to a General Motors factory north of New
York City firing its noncitizen workers. States followed this national
policy. California, Arizona, and Colorado, among others, passed
laws requiring that public workers be American citizens, forcing
thousands from their jobs. Finally, the foundations of the modern
welfare state, like the Social Security Act and the Fair Labor Standards Act, excluded agricultural work, a profession that attracted
many Mexican and Filipino immigrants. California, then, had only
about 56,000 Mexicans enrolled in the Social Security program, a
pittance, because so many Mexicans worked in agriculture and thus
were ineligible.[40]

The New Deal occasionally did help immigrants and recently
naturalized Americans. Welfare and relief policies at times proved
generous, even to noncitizens. New Deal relief money, which
flowed into local and state governments in the mid-1930s, had to be
made available to both citizens and noncitizens. Yet access did not
mean equality. In Los Angeles in 1934, the average monthly check
to a needy Anglo family amounted to thirty dollars, but it was only
twenty dollars for a Mexican family.[41] No law affected European immigrant communities more than the 1935 Wagner Act, which offered federal government protection of unions' rights to organize
and collectively bargain. In industrial sectors, recent European immigrants flocked to unions (as did native-born workers), where they
rallied to the New Deal and became enthusiastic Democrats. These
unions, though, had less interest in organizing Mexican industrial
workers, largely out of racial and ethnic prejudice.

On the West Coast, immigrants, especially those from Mexico,
were vital players in the labor movements that sought to organize
those working in the fields and canneries. In a 1933 strike of cotton
workers in California's San Joaquin Valley, which saw over 10,000
workers fighting for a wage increase to one dollar per one hundred
pounds of cotton picked, about 95 percent of the union members
were Mexican.[42] The sense of unity was real. Enrique Vasquez led
nearly two weeks of protests for wages among grape pickers in 1933.

Mexican immigrant family, California, 1935.
Library of Congress, Washington, D.C.

He recalled years later how proud he was of his fellow strikers, "poor Mexicans" who forced their bosses to take them and their demands seriously.[43]

The federal government authored straightforward immigration control policies during the Depression. Both Democrats and Republicans endorsed the national origins quotas. Even President Roosevelt, who had incentives to support reform, never challenged the quota system, although his rhetoric valued the contributions of recent immigrants. Key policy changes during the Depression all signaled tougher border control. In 1929 Congress made it a felony (rather than a misdemeanor) to help an individual enter without authorization, and the State Department announced that it would restrict visa issuance to Mexicans by more rigorously enforcing existing regulations such as the literacy test, the ban on contract labor, and the "likely to become a public charge" (LPC) clause. In 1930 President Herbert Hoover ordered that immigration officers apply the LPC clause stringently to all visa applicants. The State Department explained that skyrocketing unemployment meant that "any alien wage earner without special means of support coming to the U.S. during the period of depression is, therefore, likely to become a public charge."[44] The policy expanded the LPC clause from a measure that targeted those who could not support themselves (like paupers) to one that forbade the entry of those who lacked substantial assets. Unsurprisingly, the redefined LPC clause deterred the entry of working-class immigrants. Legal migration from Mexico dropped from 40,000 to nearly 12,000 between 1928 and 1930, and after Hoover's 1930 directive, immigration to the U.S. dropped by 60 percent (see table 7.4).[45] President Franklin Roosevelt largely kept the expanded LPC policy in place. Officials rejected increasingly large numbers of applicants—from over 300,000 in 1933 to 750,000 in 1934—and half of those 1934 rejections cited the LPC clause.[46]

Deportation and Repatriation in the 1930s

Deportation and repatriation emerged as the other key aspects of immigration control. Deportation of individuals in the United States without authorization surged under Hoover (table 7.5). In the late 1920s, the United States annually deported around 11,000 individuals, but from 1931 to 1933 deportations hit about 19,000 annually. Secretary of Labor William Doak, who had a special bureau of twenty-one agents for the task, proudly claimed in 1932 "unremitting and devoted work in the deportation of aliens."[47] The deportations revealed precise targeting of Mexicans. FDR's Secretary of Labor Frances Perkins slowed deportations to around 8,500 per year for the rest of the decade, announcing that the administration would consider "human values, international amenities, and economic conditions."[48] The deportation numbers are undercounts in one important way. Many detained, unauthorized immigrants left

Table 7.5. Federal Government Deportation Statistics, 1928–1935

Year	Total Deportations	Deportations to Mexico	Deportations to European Countries
1928	11,625	2,830	5,021
1929	12,908	5,407	4,227
1930	16,631	8,438	4,502
1931	18,142	8,409	6,162
1932	19,426	7,116	6,530
1933	19,865	7,750	5,904
1934	8,879	3,883	2,418
1935	8,319	4,078	2,007

Sources: U.S. Congress, *Statistical Abstract of the United States, 1931* (Washington, D.C., 1931), 96; *Statistical Abstract of the United States, 1933* (Washington, D.C., 1933), 101; *Statistical Abstract of the United States, 1936* (Washington, D.C., 1936), 104; U.S. Bureau of Immigration, *Annual Report of the Commissioner General of Immigration, 1930* (Washington, D.C., 1930), 164; U.S. Bureau of Immigration, *Annual Report of the Commissioner General of Immigration, 1929* (Washington, D.C., 1929), 148–149.

the country either subject to a deportation case that had not yet begun or during their deportation proceedings. In 1934 the number of individuals in those circumstances amounted to just over 8,000, nearly the equal of those officially deported.[49]

Repatriation was more complicated because of the thin line between voluntary and forced repatriation, both of which occurred during the Depression; the latter sometimes resembled deportation in all but name. As the economy cratered, hundreds of thousands of immigrants, from Europe, parts of Asia, Canada, and Mexico, elected to return to their homelands. Mexicans underwent the most scarring repatriation experiences. Estimates of how many returned vary widely, but the most recent scholarship suggests around 500,000 individuals.[50] Some, especially early in the crisis, left of their own volition, as thousands of Mexicans living in Los Angeles did in 1929. These middle-class repatriates often traveled as families, and they sometimes arrived back in Mexico in cars loaded with consumer goods, planning to use their hard-earned capital to begin businesses after resettling. Others, though, chose to leave in the face of shrinking job prospects. One Mexican American in the economically ravaged industrial city of Gary, Indiana, remembered, "There was no other way out . . . we were happy to leave."[51]

By 1931 repatriation of Mexicans changed in two ways. First, those leaving were more likely to come from the working class or the poor; notable numbers of single men, born in Mexico, fled. They had few of the material resources of their predecessors, lacked the optimism that they could make a life anew in Mexico, and did not possess a reservoir of goodwill toward the United States. Second, the post-1930 repatriation efforts were far from voluntary, although the levels of coercion varied.

In cities across the United States, local governments and relief organizations frequently excluded from aid those of Mexican descent, even if they held American citizenship, leaving them no choice but repatriation. Some Anglo communities even solicited donations to pay for repatriation. A Mexican woman who departed made clear her sense of betrayal and frustration. "This is my country but after the way we have been treated I hope to never see it again," she explained. "As long as my father was working and spending his money in Gary stores, paying taxes, and supporting us, it was all right, but now we have found we can't get justice here."[52]

In Los Angeles, the city government led repatriation efforts after officials judged that paying for the removal of Mexicans cost less than providing welfare. Local agencies began in March 1931 to pay train passage for those who wanted to return to Mexico, a program that sent more than 13,000 south of the border by 1934.[53] In the three years after 1931, Texas, Arizona, and New Mexico repatriated nearly 32,000 Mexicans in similar state-funded programs of train voyages.[54] In a more nefarious 1931 program, Los Angeles officials publicized upcoming federal government deportation raids in foreign-language newspapers, the goal being to scare those of Mexican descent into leaving, which many did. Such tactics proved more effective than the raids, which swept up four hundred people, only seventeen of whom were detained.[55]

The Mexican government ambivalently addressed these repatriation and deportation schemes. They protested the treatment, especially the shadowy legal processes, of Mexicans facing deportation. But Mexican officials also encouraged repatriation and tried to manage the process, funding the travels of those of Mexican descent back to their mother country and organizing resettlement colonies. Life back in Mexico was hardly easy for most. One women explained: "Here it is harder. Cooking is more difficult. There we had gas ranges, but not here, and we used flour while here it is maíz."[56]

Repatriation slowed in 1934, especially in Los Angeles, even though officials wanted to continue removing those of Mexican descent. Indeed, as labor activism crested, many Anglos saw repatriation as a threat they could use to keep the Mexican agricultural workforce in line. Instead, the Mexican and Mexican American community brought an end to repatriation. By 1934 those Mexicans who wanted to leave had left. Once in Mexico, many reported back to colleagues in the States that life in Mexico offered no better options. The Roosevelt administration's de-emphasis on deportation and its slightly more generous relief programs encouraged more persons of Mexican descent to stay. Even when California officials offered cash bonuses and free rail transportation, Mexicans refused the offers. By the end of the 1930s, good numbers of the repatriated reentered the United States, often through nonlegal avenues. They took this route because officials had stamped their papers during repatriation, which was taken by officials later as running afoul of the LPC clause and thus constituted a blanket denial of entry to the United States.

Unsurprisingly, Mexicans and Mexican Americans who lived through these ordeals did not forget them. One recalled almost forty years later, "Even if they were citizens they had no rights and were treated like animals and put in cattle cars."[57] The Castañeda family moved from California to Mexico in 1934. Emilia Castañeda, born in the United States, was eight at the time of the move. She later recalled that her mother had passed away, leaving her father to care for the children as the Depression crested in the United States. When he could not find work and the family was surviving on welfare, he decided to return to Mexico with his kids. Back in Mexico, they moved in with a very large family, one of whose members taunted Emilia about coming to a country in which she had never lived, scarring her even decades later.[58] Finally, the deportations and repatriations left the Mexican community in the United States under the control not of the immigrant generation, but of their children. In the coming decades, they would lead a civil rights revolution.

The United States also tried to repatriate Filipinos. Racial prejudice, fears of miscegenation, and a mistaken belief that Filipinos took jobs from white Americans—they competed largely with Mexicans—fueled opposition on the West Coast. In 1934 Congress passed the Tydings-McDuffie Act, which transitioned the Philippines to independence over ten years and gave that nation an immigration quota of fifty, steeply reducing Filipino immigration.

In 1935, in the depths of the Depression, Congress funded a program to repatriate tens of thousands of Filipinos already in the United States. But if a Filipino agreed to repatriation, then he or she could reenter only as a quota immigrant, a near impossibility given the paltry quota. The government energetically advertised the program, avoiding the term *deportation*, but to no avail. During the program's five years, just over two thousand Filipinos repatriated, and the first who left did so largely because they had planned to return to the islands anyway and wanted the free government transportation back home.[59] Ultimately, the Filipinos generally stayed put. As one impoverished Filipino explained: "I would prefer to stay in America. I would rather go hungry and die here than go home with an empty hand."[60]

National origins policies and the Great Depression defined immigration to the United States during the 1920s and 1930s, as both created multiple barriers to entry. The politics of immigration in the United States, too, took a turn toward immigration restriction, even as many immigrants and their advocates offered impassioned defenses of the vital role newcomers played in the United States. As the 1930s came to a close, though, Americans turned their attention to gathering storms in Europe and Asia that would become another world war. Unlike the Great War, World War II touched the lives of almost all Americans and their society. The war also provoked changes in immigration, some of which reversed and some of which reinforced the changes of the previous two decades.

Further Reading

Balderrama, Francisco, and Raymond Rodríguez. *Decade of Betrayal: Mexican Repatriation in the 1930s*, rev. ed. (2006).

Fleegler, Robert. *Ellis Island Nation: Immigration Policy and American Identity in the Twentieth Century* (2013).

Garland, Libby. *After They Closed the Gates: Jewish Illegal Immigration to the United States, 1921–1965* (2014).

Hernandez, Kelly Lytle. *Migra! A History of the U.S. Border Patrol* (2010).

Ramirez, Bruno, with Yves Otis. *Crossing the 49th Parallel: Migration from Canada to the United States, 1900–1930* (2001).

Sánchez, George. *Becoming Mexican American: Ethnicity, Culture, and Identity in Chicano Los Angeles, 1900–1945* (1993).

CHAPTER EIGHT

Newcomers and World War II

S AILING THROUGH THE CARIBBEAN in 1939 on a ship called
the *St. Louis*, a ten-year-old German Jewish refugee, Liesel
Joseph Loeb, did not know where she might next call home.
Permitted to leave Germany, she and her family, and just over
nine hundred others, had hoped to land in Cuba, but that government prohibited them from disembarking in Havana. As the *St. Louis*
headed toward the United States, and possible landfall there, Loeb
remembered years later thinking: "America was a magic word. It was
the be-all and end-all. We knew America would not let us down."[1]
Of course, the United States did let Loeb and her fellow passengers
down, refusing to entertain their requests to immigrate to America.

Across the continent, Mexicans also wanted to enter the United
States, most often in search of better jobs, or as one song of the era put
it, "I go and come, come and go / Looking for bread for my children."[2]
Tens of thousands of Mexican workers entered the United States as
temporary workers during the war, and even more came without legal
authorization. Entering more easily than Loeb, those Mexicans still
found difficult conditions. "I came up here to support my family," one
commented, "but I have had a hard time with what I make."[3]

For Loeb, Mexican workers, and countless others, the United
States during World War II represented a future of personal and
familial security and economic improvement, the same possibilities
that had brought so many newcomers to the United States in the

191

centuries before. As their predecessors had discovered, that promise sometimes went unfulfilled, or proved more hollow than antic-
ipated. In this sense, the war fostered familiar immigration stories.

The war, though, also remarkably reshaped immigration. The
rise of fascist governments, especially Nazi Germany, created a
massive population of refugees. After taking very few steps to admit
refugees in the mid-1930s, the Americans admitted some by the decade's end before again cutting off entry once the country was fully
engaged in the hostilities. This record shadowed every U.S. engagement with refugees after 1945 and remains controversial to this day.

Rearmament efforts in the United States created a plethora of
well-paying jobs that immigrant communities, among others, eagerly
took up. The supercharged economy—in some sectors, jobs outpaced
job applicants—necessitated the importation of temporary workers
not only from Mexico (the braceros) but also from around the Carib-

Italian asparagus pickers, Pennsylvania, 1939.
Library of Congress, Washington, D.C.

bean. These workers found jobs, but they also encountered racism, discrimination, and a segment of the public eager to see them leave once the wartime emergency had ended. The most outrageous treatment fell not on immigrant workers, but on Japanese and U.S. citizens of Japanese descent who in almost all cases had lived in the United States for years. The U.S. government evacuated them from the West Coast and incarcerated them in camps in the country's interior.

Finally, the war led to significant changes in immigration law and policy, although in sometimes contradictory directions. In 1940 the federal government toughened screening and monitoring of immigrants. But later in the war, as the end came into sight, the U.S. government began to plan for European reconstruction and aid to refugees. Even more important, in 1943 the United States granted Chinese immigrants a small annual immigration quota. It was the first, albeit small, chip in the quota system.

The Refugee Problem of the 1930s

The first great refugee problem of the twentieth century came not with the rise of Nazi Germany and World War II, but in the aftermath of the Great War, which saw a refugee population numbering somewhere over 10 million by the mid-1920s.[4] Some of these individuals were displaced by the violence and destruction of the war. Others found themselves stateless after the peace settlement constructed new borders across Europe and the Near East. Political, ethnonational, and religious violence permeated these new states, forcing hundreds of thousands more to flee for their safety.

Herbert Hoover, charged by President Wilson with heading the U.S. government response, fairly energetically tackled the refugee problem in the war's immediate wake. Aided by a host of private organizations, Hoover spearheaded the United States' offers of material and financial aid. This ameliorated some of the suffering, but the effort withered as the 1920s wore on. Some exceptions existed, such as the high-profile advocacy by future Secretary of the Treasury Henry Morgenthau for Greek refugees fleeing Turkey. But with American immigration politics turning toward restrictionism, Americans did not offer in the 1920s to bring refugees to their shores.

The European refugee problem changed dramatically with the rise of the Nazis in Germany. When Adolf Hitler assumed control in early 1933, about 525,000 Jews lived in Germany, along with almost 300,000 Germans deemed to be of Jewish descent by the Nazis.[5] Some Germans, specifically Jews and political opponents of the Nazis, departed almost immediately after Hitler's rise. In 1933 and 1934, about 75,000 Germans (60,000 of them Jews) fled, mostly to Austria, Czechoslovakia, and France.[6]

During the mid- to late 1930s, two dynamics took root that created ever-larger numbers of individuals, especially Jews, seeking to escape the Nazis. First, the Nazi regime stepped up its persecution of Jews. In 1935 the Nuremberg Laws translated Nazi anti-Semitic thinking into law, and in 1938 the Nazis unleashed the infamous *Kristallnacht* pogrom, an act of state-supported terrorism that decimated Jewish communities throughout the country. Shortly after *Kristallnacht*, the Nazis sent 30,000 Jews to concentration camps, signaling how those camps, which had been used to punish political prisoners, now would be used to persecute large numbers of Jews.[7] From 1935 to 1937, in the face of heightening anti-Semitism and attacks, 70,000 Jews fled and many more hoped to depart.[8] These refugees differed from their predecessors in 1933 and 1934 in that they left Germany increasingly impoverished, a condition mandated by the Nazis, who expropriated the wealth of departing Jews.

Second, Hitler began his conquest of Europe, annexing Austria and the Sudetenland region of Czechoslovakia in 1938, invading Poland in September 1939, overrunning western Europe in May 1940, and launching a surprise attack against his former ally, the Soviet Union, in June 1941. As Hitler brought western Europe and large parts of eastern Europe and the Soviet Union under his control, the Jews in those regions, some of whom had recently left Germany to escape Hitler's wrath, became targets of Nazi policies. By the end of the decade, the refugee crisis sprawled across the continent.

The American Response to the Refugee Challenge

Observers in the United States paid attention to these developments. American media reported on the Nuremberg Laws and *Kris-*

tallnacht, as well as Nazi Germany's conquests in Europe. Jewish groups in the United States acutely understood the threat the Nazis represented to Jews. In May 1933 a leader of the American Jewish Committee, one of the country's key Jewish organizations, warned that German Jews faced "possible extermination" and that Nazi oppression was "not a passing episode. But one that threatens to be a problem for a long time."[9] Recognizing the threat, Jewish groups in the United States began to partner with like-minded politicians, with other religious organizations, and with traditional immigrant aid groups to raise awareness and to work with sympathetic government officials to find ways to bring German, and soon European, Jews to the United States. Those efforts, aptly described by one historian as "quietly building a refugee aid network," accelerated during the 1930s.[10]

American immigration law in the 1930s made no substantial special exceptions for aiding refugees. If a refugee from Nazism wanted to enter the United States, his or her best hope was to enter with a visa from the quota system, in which Germany had a quota of 25,957 and, after 1938, a quota of 27,370 in the wake of the annexation of Austria. No serious discussions of raising the quota occurred, even as the refugee crisis deepened. Restrictionists, triumphant in the battles over immigration policy and ascendant in the bureaucracy, held sway in politics and policy-making circles. Supporters of refugees and immigrants in Congress, especially liberal Democrats, concentrated more on battling the Depression than reforming immigration policy. In this environment, refugees from Nazism struggled in the years after 1933 to enter the United States by means of the quota (table 8.1). In 1934, 3,515 Germans entered with quota visas, a number that edged up slowly over the next four years.

The actions of the State Department, especially of those Washington officials and overseas consular officers charged with making and implementing visa policies, played a large role in the underutilization of the German quota. The State Department continued the Hoover administration's energetic application of the "likely to become a public charge" (LPC) clause, rejecting visa applicants on those grounds. State Department officials also rebuffed proposals from the Department of Labor and Jewish groups that would have helped refugees clear the LPC hurdle. U.S. officials often demanded

Table 8.1. Immigrants Admitted under the German Quota,
1934–1940

Year	Germans Entering the U.S. with Visas
1934	3,515
1935	4,891
1936	6,073
1937	11,127
1938	17,868
1939	32,759
1940	26,083

Sources: U.S. Bureau of the Census, *Statistical Abstract of the United States, 1941* (Washington, D.C., 1942), 112, and *Statistical Abstract of the United States, 1939* (Washington, D.C., 1940), 103.

that refugees provide all the necessary paperwork and meet all the precise legal requirements for entry, which time and again proved difficult for persecuted individuals merely looking to escape a government bent on their destruction. Finally, some anti-Semitic State Department officials, both in Washington and in various European consular offices, actively opposed the entry of Jews. This anti-Semitism surely helps explain, in some cases, the vigorous adherence to the LPC clause and the enforcement of the law to the exact letter.

The barriers to entry were substantial. For example, to gain a visa almost all immigrants had to provide an affidavit of support from someone in the United States, basically a guarantee that the sponsor would aid the newcomer upon his or her arrival. Consuls in Europe dealing with Jewish refugees from Germany scrutinized these affidavits and tended to approve affidavits submitted by family members. But since the Jewish population in the United States came largely from eastern Europe and not Germany (and thus had no family ties to German Jews), many German Jews found their affidavits and their visa applications deemed insufficient by the consuls. Other applications ran into different bureaucratic roadblocks on their way to the same outcome.

Not all U.S. government officials, even in the State Department, involved in immigration were anti-Semitic or opposed to the entry of refugees. A number of honorable men, some Jews and some not,

pushed back against the opposition to refugees and made heroic efforts to help refugees enter. But they sadly operated on this issue as
a distinct minority in the early and mid-1930s.

The tale of Hermann Kilsheimer, a nineteen-year-old German
Jew, shows the twists and turns an application for a visa might take.
Kilsheimer's sister lived in the United States, where she was married
to an American; she went with her brother to the Stuttgart consulate
in 1934 in the hopes that they could secure him a visa. They had
three affidavits of financial support from family members. But a U.S.
official, Charles Teller, refused Kilsheimer's application largely on
the grounds that those who supplied the affidavits did not have suffi-
cient weekly salaries (even though they each owned property) to support a young man planning to attend college. Stunned, Kilsheimer
and his sister were leaving the consulate, only to be recognized by
another consular official who had taken German language lessons
from the sister back in the United States! On the spot, he invited
the pair for another interview and secured a visa for Hermann, who
departed Germany in October 1934.

The European refugee crisis also brought together some nations and international organizations in attempts to develop solutions. On this front, the United States participated in, and even led,
a few efforts, none of which met with much success. In 1933 the
League of Nations set up a special High Commission on Refugees,
appointing an American, James McDonald, as its head. McDonald spent two years working tirelessly, and ultimately fruitlessly, to
find safe havens for those who wanted to leave Nazi Germany. His
greatest contribution came as he departed the position, when he
warned that inaction surely would produce a humanitarian disaster.
In 1938 President Roosevelt organized an international conference
at Évian-les-Bains, France, to tackle the refugee problem, inviting
leaders from Europe, Australia, Canada, and Latin America, as well
as a variety of nongovernmental organizations. At the conference,
the United States joined the other participants in speaking compas-
sionately about refugees but offering little in the way of commitments to allow refugees to enter. The conference's collapse served
to clarify that countries around the globe, and the United States,
shared in the failure to adequately address, much less solve, the
1930s refugee problem.

Wagner-Rogers, the S.S. *St. Louis*, and Refugee Admissions

To this rather depressing list of ineffective proposals and actions, two more episodes deserve to be added. In 1939 Senator Robert Wagner (D-New York) and Representative Edith Nourse Rogers (R-Massachusetts) crafted a bill to admit 20,000 German child refugees, outside the quotas, to the United States over two years. The Wagner-Rogers proposal had multiple backers, from former President Herbert Hoover to First Lady Eleanor Roosevelt, to the actress Helen Hayes, to a host of religious groups. It never even came to a vote in Congress. Polling revealed the public opposed the bill, and immigration restrictionists viewed it as an assault on the nation's immigration laws, even after some supporters—but not Wagner and Rogers, who dropped their backing—amended the proposal to have the children count against the quotas. The focus on child refugees, surely thought by the bill's supporters as strikingly humanitarian, even aroused some ire. Laura Delano, wife of the Immigration and Naturalization commissioner, remarked of the child refugees that "20,000 charming children would all too soon grow up into 20,000 ugly adults."[11] President Roosevelt, lobbied by his wife and some members of his administration to publicly support the proposal, demurred, writing "File No Action" on one request for his assistance.[12]

As the Wagner-Rogers bill floundered, the S.S. *St. Louis*, carrying just over 900 mostly Jewish refugees from Germany, wandered through the coastal waters of the United States. The ship was bound for Cuba, where all the passengers had permission to land and where the nearly 750 on a waiting list for American visas planned to bide their time until the United States officially admitted them. Other European refugees, especially Jews, used Cuba as a way station to the United States, so the path was not unfamiliar. The Cuban government, responding to domestic pressures, refused to let the *St. Louis* land. Despair set in among the passengers, one of whom remarked, "If we are returned to Germany it will mean the concentration camp for most of us."[13]

Jewish organizations and the U.S. State Department tried to find a place for the boat to dock and the passengers to disembark, either in the United States or elsewhere in the Western Hemisphere.

Some in the United States lobbied for the government to make an exception to take these individuals immediately, but those proposals proved legally and politically impossible. Eventually, the *St. Louis* returned across the Atlantic with what seemed a solution at the time: Britain, France, Belgium, and the Netherlands agreed to take the refugees. Of course, the Nazis overran those latter three countries within the next year, and ultimately 254 of the *St. Louis* passengers died in the Holocaust or the war.

Leopold and Johanna Dingfelder were two of those victims. They owned a meat shop in Plauen, Germany, and after their sojourn with their fifteen-year-old son, Rudi, aboard the *St. Louis*, they ended up in the Netherlands. The Nazis detained Leopold and Johanna in 1942 and sent them to Auschwitz, where they died. The Nazis also arrested Rudi, who toiled in various forced-labor camps for over two years. In spring 1945 Rudi and a handful of others attempted an escape near Schwerin, Germany. American forces eventually came upon Rudi, who returned to the Netherlands. In 1947 Rudi, almost a decade after the voyage of the *St. Louis*, came to the United States, settling in Detroit.

As the Wagner-Rogers and *St. Louis* episodes unfolded, refugees began to more easily enter the United States through the quota system (see table 8.1). The high point came in 1939, when 32,759 individuals from Germany and Austria entered. (The German and Austrian quotas were combined after the Nazis annexed Austria.) The key change came in the administration of immigration law and the process by which consuls overseas issued visas. The State Department ordered consular officials to relax their aggressive application of the LPC clause. One of these consuls described this as a "radical" policy revision, but also one truer to the law's origins because it "likely is to mean what is meant when the law was written."[14] Additionally, American officials began to allow those Germans on nonimmigrant visas, such as student or tourist visas, to remain in the United States instead of forcing them to return. Finally, the State Department agreed that private aid organizations, often Jewish groups, in the United States could vet affidavits of support. This change helped speed the entry of refugees and, in the long term, made aid organizations partners with the State Department in refugee policy, a relationship that continued in future years.

These policy changes originated with President Roosevelt. After his 1936 reelection, FDR operated in a political environment that freed him to push State Department visa policy in a more liberal direction. This signal moment, two leading historians assert, represented the "first time . . . the Roosevelt administration had done something decisive to help persecuted Jews escape from Germany," and it brought tens of thousands to safety.[15] But, as war descended on Europe in September 1939, passage from the Continent became much more difficult, and the escape valve from the Nazis closed considerably.

Assessing U.S. Actions in the 1930s

The catalog of American actions concerning refugees during the 1930s raises two questions. What forces in the United States shaped this response? And how generously, or critically, should we judge the United States' engagement with the refugee challenge?

A few factors shaped the American response. Most important, the refugee crisis unfolded against the backdrop of the rise of immigration restrictionism in the United States. The 1920s national immigration quotas severely limited how many Germans could enter the United States, which constituted a brake on how much the United States could help. A hypothetical demonstrates the point. If the refugee crisis had unfolded fifteen years earlier, German refugees surely would have encountered opposition, but not numerical limits. The coming of the national origins laws had two other effects. First, the laws revealed the larger, even dominant, anti-newcomer sentiment in American politics and culture as the refugee crisis began in the early 1930s. Second, the bruising immigration battles of the 1920s had made many Democrats and Republicans reluctant to wade into immigration policy again, even as circumstances drastically changed.

Other elements led to U.S. reticence to act in the face of a growing refugee population. The Depression's economic devastation magnified opposition to immigrants, as Americans viewed the refugees as competition for jobs, no matter their circumstances. Unsurprisingly, Roosevelt made the most headway in loosening immigration restrictions after the Depression started to recede a bit in the late 1930s. Foreign policy issues also helped form the American response. Isolationists held real power in American life in the mid- to late 1930s, and they counted on the support of many Americans who perhaps did not subscribe to the isolationist label, but skepti- cally viewed international commitments, such as helping refugees, that might entangle the United States more deeply in European af- fairs. This bloc forced internationalists like President Roosevelt to trim their sails on many foreign policy issues and thus approach the refugee crisis gingerly. Finally, it mattered that the vast majority of refugees from Europe in the 1930s were Jews. Anti-Semitism ran through many corridors of American society, not just the State De- partment. Father Charles Coughlin, the national radio figure and priest, harangued audiences with warnings about an international Jewish conspiracy, while others simply referred to the New Deal as the "Jew Deal." All this created a public atmosphere in which most Americans viewed refugees suspiciously, if not with outright hos- tility. Polling from the late 1930s bears out this sentiment. In mid- 1938, 67 percent of Americans opposed the entry of refugees from Nazism, a number that increased to 83 percent by April 1939.[16]

No single, or easy, answer appears to the question of whether to judge the American response to the refugee flows of the 1930s critically, with praise, or somewhere in between. That answer should not be easy. Conversations about this topic continue to this day, and they inform how Americans (and others) think about today's refu- gee problems, the responsibility of individual nations and the inter- national community to prevent or halt genocides, the past and fu- ture of the state of Israel, and the challenge of translating American ideals into action. All of us benefit from considering, and reconsid- ering, this question. Thus, instead of providing one answer, it seems prudent to sum up a few of the different perspectives.

The case for criticizing American actions begins with the ad- missions numbers. From 1933 through 1940, the United States ad- mitted 103,640 Germans (most of them Jews), but the quota system allowed for the possible entry of just over 210,000. Admissions did pick up late in the decade, but this was too little, too late. Ameri- can proposals to find other avenues to help German and European Jews, like the Wagner-Rogers bill and the Évian Conference, failed miserably. The State Department's leadership, as well as the officials in charge of approving or rejecting visa applications, for too long stood as major impediments to saving Jewish refugees, blinded by anti-immigrant attitudes and anti-Semitism. The American public shared these sentiments, compounded by Depression-era economic anxieties, and thus strongly objected to refugee admissions. The nation's elected leaders too often bowed to these currents rather than trying to shift them. On this front, President Roosevelt comes in for particular criticism for failing to exert his considerable persuasive powers, and his equally considerable political capital, to do more. FDR failed in the moment and the United States failed to live up to its ideals.

Defenders of the American record concede its imperfections, but they also argue that it was substantial both in comparison to other nations and given the domestic constraints. The more than 100,000 Germans who entered the United States through the quotas outpaced the admissions of Germans to any other single country in the 1930s. Those admissions represented a real achievement in the face of concerted opposition at home on multiple fronts. Moreover, as admissions accelerated in the late 1930s, and the role of private organizations changed in the entry process, these new procedures became the template for how refugee entry would work in the future. President Roosevelt, finally, earns better treatment. Dealt a poor hand politically, he waited until the first opportune moment to push the State Department and immigration bureaucracy. His gambit at Évian, while unsuccessful, proved a forerunner of postwar international cooperation on refugee issues.

Changes to Immigration during the Early Years of the War

The United States officially entered World War II in early December 1941, after the Japanese attack on Pearl Harbor. The country, though, had been on a war footing for a few years, which affected immigration policy and enforcement, as well as immigrant communities.

The federal government authored several immigration and border policy reforms as the United States became more entangled in the growing hostilities. In 1940 Congress passed the Alien Registration Act. This law toughened penalties for subversion, made it easier to deport aliens for subversive actions, and mandated that all aliens register with the U.S. government; fingerprints were obligatory for those over fourteen years of age. Five million complied with this order in 1940. The Registration Act followed closely on the transfer of the Immigration and Naturalization Service (INS, as the Bureau of Immigration and the Bureau of Naturalization were combined and renamed in 1933) to the Department of Justice to provide for "national defense."[17] That move also placed the Border Patrol in the Justice Department, increased the Border Patrol's budgets and personnel, and provided it with modern equipment such as airplanes and car radios. Between 1939 and 1941, the Border Patrol doubled to 1,531 officers.[18] The growth continued during the war, when new personnel were most often assigned to the Mexico–U.S. border. Their mission changed from a single-minded focus on Mexican immigration to protecting the United States from Axis saboteurs and spies. Both the Alien Registration Act and the Border Patrol's evolution show the increased emphasis on national security and the concern that resident aliens and immigrants represented a national security threat.

The building of U.S. military capabilities to aid allies and to strengthen American forces began in the late 1930s, annually infusing billions of government dollars into the economy through military contracts with industrial and manufacturing firms. This spending fully brought the country out of the Depression. It also proved a boon for immigrant communities, whose members increasingly found abundant jobs and healthy paychecks in these industries, eventually achieving a level of prosperity that many had never experienced.

The preparedness effort required huge amounts of labor, demands that only increased after the Selective Service Act initiated a draft in late 1940. In earlier decades, a steady flow of immigrants from Europe had helped solve these types of labor shortages. But the twin blows of the quota system and the near impossibility of travel from Europe to the United States because of the war cut off that labor supply. This scarcity of immigrant labor helped pave the way for two signal developments in World War II America: women entering the industrial workforce in huge numbers and African Americans migrating from the rural South to urban industrial and manufacturing centers to fill these jobs.

The Birth of the Bracero Program

Even then, jobs often outnumbered workers. In the fields in Southern California and parts of the Southwest, agricultural interests began loudly complaining about labor shortages. While some in the federal government dismissed the growers' warnings, they eventually addressed them, despite the objections of the labor movement. In 1942 the State Department and the Mexican government agreed that Mexican workers—males over the age of eighteen—could come to the United States during the war on contracts to fill jobs, but not to permanently settle. One year later, Congress approved this temporary guest worker program, which earned the name the bracero program (*bracero* coming from the Spanish word for arm, *brazo*). The United States negotiated similar arrangements that brought temporary workers from Canada, Honduras, Jamaica, Barbados, and the British West Indies, but the Mexico–U.S. agreement was the largest. About 300,000 Mexicans came to the United States during the war under its auspices.[19]

Almost three-quarters of these braceros worked in fields across the West and Great Plains of the United States, while significant numbers also labored as maintenance workers on railroads. All helped keep the wartime economy humming. During the war, the arrival of braceros in a town sometimes led the host community to hold a celebration, and employers of the braceros applauded the quality of their work. "We sure like these new Mexicans. They want to work all the time. Only trouble is when it rains or something and they have to lay off," remarked the wife of one farmer.[20] For their part, Mexicans embraced the program partly out of patriotism and opposition to fascism, but—more important—partly out of economic necessity. One investigation found that during the war, nearly three-quarters of braceros joined the program in search of better pay than they could find at home. Lucas Benítez, in fact, went to some lengths to become a bracero worker. Born in 1918 into a very poor family, Benítez worked in the mines with his father, and his mother was a street vendor. In 1942 Benítez learned of the bracero program, but he feared he did not look enough like a worker. He recalled: "The first thing they checked was the way of dressing, and show our hands, to see if we had calluses. Knowing that, I went to the places to exercise."[21] With some work, he got those calluses and found his way into the program.

In the agreement, the Mexican government won some concessions. The pact stated that bracero wages, and working and living conditions, should match those of native-born workers. U.S. employers paid for transportation of braceros and could not recruit in Mexico. Instead, the Mexican government selected those workers who headed to the United States, where braceros signed six-month contracts with the U.S. government and not with individual employers. Finally, the Mexican government won a requirement that automatically remitted 10 percent of the bracero's earnings to Mexico, where the worker could claim it later. The government hoped the wage garnishes guaranteed the return of the workers. Mexican leaders also hoped that back in Mexico that money would fund domestic economic development, which reveals how the agreement was part of the government's modernization program.

At times the Mexican government asserted its authority vis-à-vis the United States and the growers, as when it prohibited braceros from working in Texas from 1943 to 1947 because of that state's systematic discrimination against Mexicans. Of course, Texas circumvented this ban by recruiting Mexican workers who crossed the border through extralegal means. Too many times, however, the protections for Mexican workers failed. Wages and working conditions sometimes proved substandard during the war years, though not as horrific as they became during the postwar era. One bracero who picked cotton during the war declared: "The boss I worked for . . . robbed us of our pay, because he used crooked scales for weighing the cotton we picked. I came up here to try to support my family, but I have had a hard time with what I make."[22] A railroad worker named Adolfo Morales Matamoros complained about the food offered in the bracero camps: "The commissary obligates us to consume food that is completely vile and sickening that even dogs will not eat it. They fed us tripe, smelly liver, oatmeal that looked

like starch, and very little sugar."[23] Labor unions despised the bracero program, but the support of agricultural interests, their allies
in Congress, and the pressing wartime labor crisis blunted any critiques. Finally, and perhaps most important, the bracero program
long outlived the war, becoming a central part of U.S. migration
policy in the postwar era.

Mexican Immigrant Communities during the War

Mexican Americans and Mexican nationals had varied experiences
during the war. Some 500,000 Mexican Americans, many moved by
patriotism, served in the U.S. military.[24] One soldier commented on
an advantage of service: "It did not matter whether we were looked
upon as Mexicans; the war soon made us all *genuine* Americans, eligible and available to fight and to defend our country, the United
States of America."[25] These same communities wanted to contribute
on the home front in wartime industries, but they often found themselves blocked by rampant discrimination. At the war's beginning,
the shipyards of Los Angeles employed no Mexicans or Mexican
Americans, but by 1944 about 17,000 had found jobs there.[26] Other
defense industries saw similar growth in the numbers of Mexican
employees. The change arose not from government intervention, as
the Roosevelt administration expressly refused to support an investigation of discriminatory employment practices directed at those of
Mexican descent, but instead from the severe labor shortages.

One job advertisement especially revealed all the promise and
peril of the moment: "Martin Ship Service Company needs Mexican
Workers for repair and maintenance work. . . . We have Mexican
supervisors. You only need a birth certificate. You don't need to be a
U.S. citizen."[27] Martin's announcement pointed to the opportunities
that abounded for both Mexican Americans and Mexican nationals in
the United States. These jobs, though, came most often at the entry
level, such as "maintenance work," and with low wages. The "Mexican supervisor" job, with its relatively higher pay, rarely appeared.

And yet, for some in Mexican communities, these extraordinary
opportunities shone. Women of Mexican descent typically worked
in the agriculture or service fields before the war, but during it they

made a beeline to the factories. As one recalled, "The money was in defense."[28] Marie Echeverría, a Mexican immigrant living in Los Angeles, worked at a cannery that became a bomb factory, and she recalled the transformation in her finances with the new job: she went from struggling to "really [making] the money."[29] Her daughter Rose, meanwhile, joined an innovative program at her high school that had her doing four hours of schoolwork a day and four hours working for Avion, a company that made parts for bombers, at ninety cents an hour, much more than Rose had earned as store clerk. These women, despite facing sexual harassment from coworkers and superiors, loved these jobs that allowed an expression of economic and social independence and patriotism. Some even changed their immigration status to qualify for work. Lupe Purdy came to the United States in 1922, but applied for citizenship only as the war began in the hope of getting a wartime job. She explained: "I didn't go to work because I wanted more money. . . . It was hard work, very hard work. . . . I just felt very strongly that I should do my part."[30]

White Americans did not always acknowledge, much less respect, this commitment or patriotism in the Mexican American community. Some, like First Lady Eleanor Roosevelt, sounded the alarm about discrimination. Roosevelt, joined by luminaries such as the journalist Carey McWilliams and filmmaker Orson Welles, reacted with particular disgust after the so-called Zoot Suit Riots targeted Mexicans and Mexican Americans in Los Angeles in June 1943. The local media had been filled for months with reports of youth lawlessness and gangs in the Mexican communities throughout the city. While statistics showed no rise in serious crimes committed by Mexican Americans, the media's reporting stoked fears among white residents of Los Angeles.

The tension exploded in the early summer of 1943. A series of fights between Mexican American youth and white servicemen instigated the riots. Over one thousand white soldiers and sailors responded by marauding through the city and attacking Mexican Americans, as well as African Americans and Filipinos, who wore the stylish and distinctive zoot suit, a popular piece of clothing for hip youngsters of the day. As the violence crested, the Los Angeles police largely stood down. Only when the navy ordered its sailors out of Los Angeles did the rampage end.

Vincente Morales's experience was typical. On June 7, 1943, the teenager took his girlfriend to listen and dance to the music of Lionel Hampton, a jazz bandleader playing downtown. At the show, a pack of white servicemen assaulted Morales and later, outside the venue, beat him unconscious. They took his zoot suit, so his girl-friend gave him her coat, which he wore as the police arrested him for disturbing the peace. Lupe, a Mexican teenager, summed it up well: soldiers "beat up on any Mexican, whether there were young kids or older kids. . . . I remember because I saw it."[31]

While Eleanor Roosevelt and her liberal and leftist allies in la-bor, religious groups, and civil rights organizations, as well as some in the federal government, admirably defended Mexican Americans, the media and the majority of Anglos in Southern California blamed lawless youth of color for the riots. The Zoot Suit Riots and vi-olence, which occurred in Detroit, Philadelphia, and other urban centers in addition to Los Angeles, made clear the discriminatory challenges facing Mexicans and Mexican Americans in the United States.

Those trials extended to the border between the United States and Mexico during the war. The bracero program regulated and controlled some of the movement between the countries. Likewise, the Mexican government placed restrictions on who could apply for the program, prohibiting the sick, the aged, women, and rural land-holders. But many of those excluded still wanted to escape desper-ate conditions in Mexico. Looking to enjoy comparatively decent opportunities to the north, tens of thousands of Mexicans came to the United States through extralegal avenues during the war. The Border Patrol ramped up its interdiction efforts, using its new tools and enlarged personnel to crack down on unauthorized entry at the Mexican–U.S. border. Between 1943 and 1944, apprehensions by the Border Patrol doubled, and the total number of persons its forces questioned hit record highs between 1942 and 1944.[32]

"Enemy Aliens" and Incarceration

The German, Italian, and Japanese communities in the United States faced challenges of a different sort once the United States fully joined the war. Germans and Italians, either nationals of those countries or American citizens of those nationalities, did not encounter the virulent discrimination and attacks that the Japanese faced. Given what they had faced in the Great War, Germans had reason to fear. Likewise, the national origins quotas surely made Italians aware of their tenuous place in the nation. Yet most of the public, including the U.S. government, did not target the whole German and Italian, or German American or Italian American, populations in the United States. By the early 1940s, these groups had large numbers of U.S.-born citizens, had strong nationality-based organizations with ties to the country's political and religious institutions, and had lost some of their cultural and social insularity in the 1920s and 1930s. Finally, these groups plausibly claimed to be white, which others in the United States increasingly acknowledged. The Japanese had fewer of these advantages.

This difference between the relative sociocultural advantages and statures among these three groups played out in multiple ways during the war. In the realm of popular culture, for instance, American propagandists and leaders portrayed the Japanese as animals—often apes or monkeys, mimicking the portrayal of Germans during the Great War—bent on the destruction of civilization and its norms. Germans and Italians came under no such fire. Indeed, the heroic and patriotic Italian American GI emerged as a staple of Hollywood portrayals of the American fighting man in wartime films. Italians and Germans themselves made this case. In a St. Louis Italian American neighborhood, students protested when the principal replaced U.S.-born instructors with Italian nuns, which led one student to proclaim, "We want to be taught by Americans."[33]

The cultural currencies assigned to these groups played out in law and politics, especially when the U.S. government decided how to treat individuals living in the United States but with connections to enemy nations. After trading declarations of war with Germany, Italy, and Japan after Pearl Harbor, the U.S. government declared citizens of those nations living in the United States "enemy aliens," a legal designation that required registration with the government and the possession of identification papers. Within a year, FDR ordered Italians dropped from the "enemy alien" category, largely in deference to that group's support of him and the Democratic Party and the belief that Italians living in America had assimilated. The security agencies of the U.S. government detained about 14,000 German and Italian citizens in the United States on the grounds that they threatened the country and ordered about 5,000 to camps.[34] But the government rejected the suggestion of mass detention of these groups as impractical and because many in the public believed they had become integral to life in the United States.

For the Japanese, a different story unfolded. The Gentlemen's Agreement and 1920s laws shut down immigration from Japan to the United States, yet a thriving Japanese community lived in this country as the war approached. Nearly 200,000 individuals of Japanese descent (Japanese citizens and American citizens of Japanese descent) lived in Hawaii, and about 125,000 resided on the mainland.[35] Settling largely on the West Coast, they were a strong presence in agriculture. By 1940 almost two-thirds of those 130,000 of Japanese descent were of the second generation, born in the United States.[36] American law prohibited the remaining one-third from naturalizing, even though evidence suggests a good number would have eagerly taken that route.

During the war, federal authorities picked up over 2,000 Japanese—both American citizens and not—under suspicion of being national security threats, a policy similar to the one implemented toward Germans and Italians.[37] But, relying on the recommendations of the military and ignoring the objections of his attorney general and FBI head, President Roosevelt issued Executive Order 9066 in early 1942, which authorized the War Department to remove persons of Japanese descent from the West Coast. (The order exempted Hawaii and other regions of the United States from the removal program.) These West Coast Japanese then found themselves relocated to prison camps, run by the War Relocation Authority, in desolate sites in the interior of the country. Ultimately, the U.S. government incarcerated about 120,000 individuals of Japanese descent, about two-thirds of whom were U.S. citizens, for no other reason than their ethnonational background.[38]

The Iseri family shut their pharmacy in advance of their forced evacuation from Los Angeles, 1942. National Archives, College Park, Maryland.

Life in the camps was incredibly difficult on multiple fronts, as the story of Aiko Yoshinaga illustrates. A teenager graduating from high school in California, Aiko eloped with her boyfriend for fear they would be split up during the incarceration. The government shipped her and her new husband to a camp near Death Valley, California, while the Yoshinaga family ended up in Arkansas. Aiko described the conditions: "The only thing that was in the 'apartments' when we got there were army metal beds with the springs on it, and a potbellied stove in the middle of the room. . . . No chest of drawers, no nothing, no curtains on the windows. It was the barest of the bare."[39] After Aiko gave birth to a child, she learned her father was ill, so she traveled with the baby to Arkansas. Her father met his granddaughter as he was being taken to a hospital, where he died shortly thereafter. The incarcerated showed incredible resiliency throughout the ordeal, starting camp baseball teams, planting gar-den plots, organizing camp governance structures, publishing news-papers, and making stunning arts and crafts out of found materials. Even so, all the incarcerated paid emotional, mental, and financial costs for decades to come.

The Supreme Court approved these actions in a series of landmark cases, most notably in *Korematsu v. United States* (1944). Though the Court warned against detaining whole groups on the basis of their race or ethnicity, it then cited overriding national secu-rity concerns to justify FDR's actions. The public offered significant support for these policies, especially on the West Coast, where anti-Japanese sentiment had long roots. West Coast residents bought up Japanese-owned land, businesses, and belongings for pennies on the dollar. As one dairy farmer of Japanese descent remarked looking back: "Closed everything at a loss . . . which we never recovered from."[40] Many saw incarceration as necessary because, in the words of General John DeWitt, a leading advocate for the policy: "A Jap's a Jap . . . it makes no difference whether he is an American citizen or not. . . . I don't want any of them."[41]

The End of Chinese Exclusion

If the United States proved unwelcoming to those of Japanese back-ground, the Chinese found a different experience during the war. In the most important revision of American immigration law in nearly two decades, the U.S. government in 1943 dropped its ban on the immigration of the Chinese and instead placed China in the quota system with 105 annual visas and accompanying naturaliza-tion rights.

A number of factors brought about this reform. The Chinese stood as the United States' key and indispensable ally in Asia, and the United States' discriminatory immigration policies irked China. The decades-long educational exchange programs that brought thousands of Chinese to American universities effectively combated stereotypes of the Chinese as fit only for unskilled labor. Finally, the war also changed how many Americans viewed Chinese immi-grants, presenting them not as the so-called yellow peril but as brave, patriotic allies whose values were similar to Americans'. Thousands of Chinese worked in the defense industry, so that one Chinese observer commented: "For the first time among the Chinese there is an inter-racial contact, and for the first time, too, the average American has learned to know and highly regard his Chinese co-workers."[42] In American eyes, no figure better embodied this new China than Madame Chiang Kai-shek, wife of China's leader and a celebrity in the United States. One observer described her effect: "She has made Americans realize that the Chinese are like us: our differences superficial, our similarities fundamental."[43]

The war opened the path to reform, but it did not make it inevitable. Instead, a collection of allies did the hard work of political organizing and mobilization. Sympathetic American politicians, who coalesced into the so-called China Lobby in the postwar years, made the case in Congress. Private citizens, such as the publisher Henry Luce and the writer Pearl S. Buck, helped sway public opinion in middle America. Finally, members of the Chinese diaspora in the United States headed up organizations that expertly publicized these diplomatic and sociocultural rationales for the end of exclusionist policies.

The end of Chinese exclusion, while vitally important, had clear limits. Foremost, the reform doled out a truly paltry number of annual visas. Those visas, too, went not just to those born in China, but to anyone deemed of Chinese ethnicity even if he or she had never lived in China. Thus, it was just barely possible for Chinese to come to the United States after 1943. And yet the reform effort had cracked one of the most long-standing restrictions on immigration to the United States. Others soon began to fall. In 1946 Congress placed India and the Philippines, two American allies in the war effort, under the quota system, each with an annual allotment of one hundred visas, and allowed for naturalization. Less symbolic but more important in terms of numbers, the 1945 War Brides Act and amending legislation in 1946 and 1947 made it possible for American veterans to bring their wives and children, including individuals of Asian descent, to the United States outside the quotas. Over 9,200, mostly wives, from Asia—including 5,132 from China—entered the United States between 1946 and 1950.[44] The ban on Asian immigration crumbled, ever so slightly, during and immediately after the war, which paved the way for future possible reforms on larger immigration questions.

The U.S. and Refugees during the War

The refugee population grew as the war engulfed the globe in the late 1930s. The continuing brutality of the Sino-Japanese war displaced tens of millions, as did, on a smaller scale, the Nazi conquest of Europe. In Europe, the beginning of continent-wide hostilities in September 1939 made it that much more difficult for refugees to depart, effectively closing off entry to the United States through quota visas.

Still, the United States made some small efforts. In 1940 the government eased the entry to the United States of European refugees who had escaped to China, Portugal, or Africa. More strikingly, after France fell to the Germans, a group called the Emergency Rescue Committee, with the support of First Lady Eleanor Roosevelt, initiated a scheme to rescue Europeans of particular cultural, artistic, or intellectual importance, some of whom came to the United States. The challenge of getting them out of wartime Europe fell to an American named Varian Fry. In a series of covert operations, Fry offered aid to several thousand individuals, and he helped spirit another 1,500 persons, including the painters Marc Chagall and Marcel Duchamp, out of occupied Europe.[45]

The U.S. entry into the war in late 1941 made the goal of winning the war, not aiding refugees, paramount and singular among American objectives. In mid-1944 the United States initiated a program that transported 983 refugees from Italy to a camp in Oswego, New York. These mostly Jewish refugees of eighteen different nationalities largely stayed in the United States after the war's end.[46] More significantly, as the war moved to a conclusion, American leaders recognized the imminent arrival of a postwar refugee problem and began to set up the architecture of refugee aid efforts. The Americans played a key role in designing and funding the United Nations Relief and Rehabilitation Administration (UNRRA) in 1943 and supplied its first leader, Herbert Lehman. UNRRA, with vital U.S. support, eventually helped millions of refugees in the postwar world.

The war unleashed changes in immigration that reverberated in the postwar decades. World War II left behind a massive refugee population and a wrecked Asia and Europe that people wanted to depart, and it helped create the Cold War, in which the United States aimed to halt the gains of the Soviet Union. Each of these phenomena, sometimes intersecting, brought new dynamics to global migration that Americans had to confront after 1945. The American economy continued to grow in the postwar years. It both required and attracted labor from outside the country, which affected immigration patterns to the United States. Finally, the war both delivered and opened up the possibility for future liberal reform of restrictionist immigration policies. Driven by wartime exigencies, the U.S. government ended Chinese exclusion. Likewise, the majority of the public rejected the eugenic underpinnings of national origins policies, seeing them as too similar to Nazi ideology. These proved to be the opening salvo in a battle over the nation's immigration policies that lasted well into the 1960s.

Further Reading

Breitman, Richard, and Alan Lichtman. *FDR and the Jews* (2013).

Cohen, Deborah. *Braceros: Migrant Citizens and Transnational Subjects in the Postwar United States and Mexico* (2011).

Takaki, Ronald. *Double Victory: A Multicultural History of America in World War II* (2000).

Trachtenberg, Barry. *The United States and the Nazi Holocaust: Race, Refuge, and Remembrance* (2018).

Wu, Ellen. *The Color of Success: Asian Americans and the Origins of the Model Minority* (2013).

CHAPTER NINE

Prosperity, the Braceros, and
Cold War Refugees, 1945–1965

ESTHER LEGASPI DELGADILLO AND her boyfriend, Antonio Sanchez, came from a small town in central Mexico. In the late 1950s Antonio headed to the United States in search of work, where he remained for over a decade. Largely through Esther's efforts, the relationship did not die. Instead, Esther cultivated it by sending Antonio carefully choreographed photographs. In one photo, Esther appeared in her favorite necklace, which she had often worn on dates with Antonio before he left, to remind him, as she recalled, of the "memories of her at her most beautiful."[1] The separation took an immense emotional toll on Esther and Antonio, one that came to a happy end in 1970 when Antonio returned to Mexico to marry his sweetheart. The couple paid for their wedding ceremony in part from Antonio's savings from his work in the United States.

From across Europe, Asia, and the Americas, others joined Antonio. Between 1945 and 1964, about 4.5 million immigrants arrived in the United States.[2] The vast majority came from Europe and the Americas, as they had in previous decades. But by the early 1960s, the number of Europeans entering the United States declined and the numbers from the Americas, especially Mexico, increased. This trend strengthened in the following decades. And the numbers entering the United States, especially from Mexico, grow larger when taking into account the bracero program and unauthorized entry. All these arrivals occurred with the national origins immigration quotas still intact.

These newcomers had good reason to look to the United States. The country enjoyed a period of remarkable economic stability and growth. America's industrial and manufacturing sectors were the envy of the world and the heart of the nation's prosperity. Wages rose, unemployment stayed low, inflation remained manageable, and Americans—the "people of plenty"—consumed the abundance their economy produced.[3] That economy, buttressed by welfare state policies, spread its benefits fairly equally through the income structure. Even racial and ethnic minorities saw gains, though not as much as the white middle and working classes. One chronicler of the era described it as the "American High."[4]

The Cold War was the other key factor shaping immigration to the United States between 1945 and 1965. In the late 1940s, the United States confronted and tried to contain the Soviet Union through a host of diplomatic, economic, and military policies centered on anticommunism. The United States forged its immigration policies in this Cold War vortex. Soviet domination of Eastern Europe produced an exodus of refugees who hoped to resettle in the United States or other Western nations. The United States responded, in a reflection of the era's anticommunism, by admitting newcomers who serviced the country's Cold War objectives. This meant, necessarily, turning a blind eye to many of the world's displaced persons and refugees. Yet these Cold War refugee admissions did accomplish two objectives. They were another crack in the national origins quota system because they admitted Eastern Europeans and some Asians and they helped form a refugee law and policy regime that admitted hundreds of thousands of refugees by the end of the 1960s.

Immigrant Life in Postwar America

In the postwar decades, Italian Americans, Polish Americans, Hungarian Americans, Russian Americans, and even Chinese Americans, to name a few groups, became more fully a part of American life. This integration into the American mainstream resulted from multiple historical processes at work, in some cases stretching back a few decades. None was more important than the generational change under way in many immigrant communities as the children of the first generation of newcomers came of age. Jerry Delia Femina, from an Italian family in Brooklyn, New York, recalled of his upbringing in the 1950s: "I spoke not a word of English when I started school. But then why should I have? . . . I lived in a claustrophobically Italian neighborhood, everyone I knew spoke only Italian."[5] At school he learned English and settled years later into a career in advertising. Those like Delia Femina, the children of immigrants, made their ways in the world with language skills, educations, cultural knowledge, and employment opportunities that their predecessors had lacked. As this younger generation grew older, they necessarily altered their communities.

In the postwar decades, the dynamic between immigrants and the economy changed. Since the nation's founding, periods of extraordinary economic growth almost always relied on a steady stream of newly arrived immigrants to serve as the labor of economic expansion. In the 1950s and 1960s, new immigrants from Mexico, Canada, and the West Indies of course vitally contributed to the workforce. But the quotas continued to choke immigration to the United States and that traditionally large labor supply from Europe. Instead, the immigrant communities of Italians, Poles, and Hungarians, to name a few, that had settled in the United States in the years before the onset of immigration restriction helped fire postwar economic development. This work propelled many in these communities into solidly middle-class lifestyles in the suburbs and, not unrelatedly, the American mainstream.

Though not an industrial worker, Dennis Smith embodied a typical journey. A fireman from an Irish American family, he lived in New York City in a small, three-room apartment that must have been bursting at the seams with his wife and three children. With his wife's small inheritance and a steady salary from a good working-class job, Smith bought a home in the lower Hudson Valley. He explained, "After living in tenements all my life, I want to give my three sons a little more space than I had, a place where they can ride a bike and breathe clean air."[6]

Political activism and engagement, at both the state and national levels, helped speed those American children of European immigrants into the larger body politic. Immigrant organizations that began in the early twentieth century, such as the Japanese American Citizens League and the Sons of Italy, continued to operate after 1945. Religious groups like the American Jewish Committee, and labor unions like the CIO, also gave immigrants a political voice. European immigrants remained in the Democratic Party's New Deal coalition during these decades, although the Republican Party made strong efforts, usually involving foreign policy programs that promised to aid European immigrant communities' homelands, to win them over. Most important, the liberal state shaped urban (and increasingly suburban) immigrant communities in multiple, often unintended fashions. The GI Bill, federal housing programs, and tax policies brought immigrants (and their children) into the single-family homeowning middle class of the suburbs.

Finally, the Cold War shaped immigrant communities. The federal government's enormous Cold War military spending—government defense contracts in the last half of the 1950s totaled 10 percent of gross national product—powered the industrial economy in which recent immigrants and their children often found jobs.[7] Anticommunism ruptured American politics and the parties, and at times anticommunist zealots targeted political radicals in immigrant communities, just as they had in the Great War's aftermath. But anticommunism also was a tool by which immigrants, especially those from southern and eastern Europe, who only a generation earlier had been the targets of the discriminatory national origins quotas, demonstrated their loyalty to and fitness for the United States. Jerry Delia Femina looked back on the link between the Catholic Church, Italian Americans, and anticommunism: "There were no sermons to speak of. These were the salad days of 1947, 1948, and into the 1950s, the days of that hero of the Church, Senator Joseph McCarthy. McCarthyism was on its way and if we didn't heed the message, Godless Russia was going to swallow us up. Every Sunday we said a prayer for the conversion of Russia."[8]

Chinese immigrant communities played with similar Cold War dynamics that demonstrated their belonging. One Chinese American leader in the 1950s asserted, "In a world half slave and half free, we are determined to fight on the side of freedom,"⁹ a veritable pledge of allegiance. Strikingly, Chinese American and Chinese immigrant communities also displayed employment and educational mobility. The number of white-collar workers and professionals increased, and the number of service, agricultural, and blue-collar workers dropped. Meanwhile, education levels in Chinese communities in the United States equaled or surpassed those in white and Black communities. All this pointed to less isolation for Chinese communities and, yet, all was not equal. Wages in these communities sometimes lagged, and many faced discrimination. Sherman Wu, a student at Northwestern University, tried to join a fraternity in 1956, only to find himself blocked. Wu explained, "They told me that I degrade their house because I am Chinese."¹⁰ The incident gained some notoriety—the great folk singer Pete Seeger even wrote a song about it—but it highlighted the racism and discrimination that those from Chinese communities still faced.

These paths to upward mobility in the post-1945 United States were not available to everyone. Communities of Mexican immigrants faced systemic economic, legal, and social discrimination that did not lessen as braceros and unauthorized Mexican immigrants arrived in large numbers. Other Americans were disadvantaged by the same policies that helped recent immigrants of European descent. Urban African Americans, a growing population as the migration out of the South continued, found themselves locked out of the suburbs because of racist government and private-sector policies. This led to a fierce fight for scarce housing, often in or near urban immigrant neighborhoods, that then further helped spur the move of those white communities of European immigrant backgrounds to the suburbs. This racialized geography, which white immigrant Americans and their children participated in and helped construct, was at the heart of the suburban-urban divide in midcentury America.

European Immigration to the United States

The war ravaged Europe. Many lost families and friends, livelihoods and homes, and communities and social networks. The conflict produced a desperate population of tens of millions of displaced persons and refugees. With good reason, many Europeans, even those who managed to escape the worst of the war or those from countries on the "winning" side, yearned in the late 1940s and the 1950s for a new start.

Every European considering postwar immigration had a different story, many tinged with both hardship and joy. Aspasia Sonia Anyfantaki grew up on the island of Crete, survived the German occupation by fleeing her home with her family, and then after the war studied for a while in the United States, picking up a taste for Coca-Cola. Back in Crete, she went to a dance on a U.S. Air Force base—to "have a Coca-Cola and a little fun,"[11] she recalled later— and met an American Air Force serviceman, George Lang. A whirlwind courtship, speeded along because in Crete "we go straight from our parents' hearth to our husband's home,"[12] ended up in a wedding in November 1961. George headed to the States immediately thereafter, and Sonia joined him in spring 1962. She raised a family with George and became an artist.

Western Europe's recovery was under way by the early 1950s, but hundreds of thousands of Europeans still wanted to emigrate through that decade. Canada and South America were as popular as the United States as destinations for Europeans. Among Western European countries, Germany and Great Britain sent the most immigrants to the United States through the quota system in the 1950s (table 9.1), though the numbers of German (and Italian)

Table 9.1. Quota Immigrants Admitted, 1951–1960

Country	Immigrants Admitted
Germany	248,208
Hungary	17,812
Ireland	63,468
Italy	54,460
Poland	125,671
United Kingdom	230,948
Soviet Union	44,246

Source: U.S. Bureau of the Census, *Statistical Abstract of the United States, 1967* (Washington, D.C., 1967), 95.

newcomers were considerably larger when accounting for refugees arriving from those countries outside the quotas.

Only in the 1960s did the demand to leave Western Europe diminish. American financial aid such as the Marshall Plan and business investment sped Continental recovery while the postwar international economic system proved stable. Most important, a generation of Western European leaders guided the development of political economies that provided both welfare programs and capitalist economic expansion. Some in Western Europe, especially on the political left, worried about American dominance. But by the 1960s West Germany was on a path toward being a global economic powerhouse. France had developed a stable economy with a thriving consumer culture. Even Italy, long a developmental laggard, had achieved a degree of economic stability.

Eastern Europe faced even greater problems after the war. The Nazi and Soviet war machines had devastated the region, the Nazis had forcibly displaced millions through relocation policies, and millions more had perished. After 1945 the Soviet Union decisively shaped Eastern Europe's future. Early in the postwar years, the Soviets and their allies in Eastern Europe demanded the repatriation of former residents, a good number of whom had little interest in returning, setting up the first of many confrontations over migration with the West. As the Soviet Union slowly imposed effective control over the eastern half of the Continent, emigration from the Soviet empire proved incredibly difficult.

The United States brought in almost 100,000 Poles through the quotas in the 1950s, and smaller numbers of Czechs, Soviets, Latvians, and Lithuanians. Additionally, tens of thousands of refugees annually in the 1950s managed to head to the West in the hope of a new start, and the United States admitted many by means of special policies. Yet this decent-sized migration from Eastern Europe surely would have been larger but for the Soviet Union's fairly successful efforts to depress migration. Even then, leaving took a toll on some. One Polish immigrant who arrived after World War II voiced his regret about leaving his mother country: "As I see it today, it became not only political, but a moral issue to me. You shouldn't leave your mother or father in the critical moments of their lives, and you shouldn't leave your native country in the moment of crisis."[13]

Immigrants from Asia

Asian immigration to the United States slowly increased after 1945, even though American law still was largely inhospitable. In the 1950s about 153,000 Asians arrived, a rate that held into the early 1960s.[14] European and Western Hemisphere immigrants dwarfed these numbers from Asia, but they also represented real growth compared to the early twentieth century.

Much of this migration resulted from the United States' global responsibilities and its formal and informal imperial projects. Refugees, especially from Hong Kong and to a lesser degree from China and Korea, came in sizable numbers in the two decades after 1945. Servicemen stationed in Japan and Korea brought their spouses and children to the United States as nonquota immigrants, which meant that women outnumbered men in those migrations. Smaller numbers of Korean and Japanese also managed to come to the United States to study, and many found ways to stay as nonquota immigrants. In the case of the Philippines, not only did American servicemen in the islands bring their spouses and children to the United States, but the American government allowed Filipinos who had served in the World War II U.S. military to become citizens. Those men could then bring wives and children to the United States. In the two decades after 1945, just over 39,000 Filipinos arrived in the United States.[15]

After Pablo Mabalon earned his U.S. citizenship in 1946, he took advantage of legal procedures that allowed him to expeditiously bring his family from the Philippines. His wife and a son, whom he had not seen in more than fifteen years, arrived in 1947 and joined Pablo in Stockton, California, where a growing Filipino community had taken root. In the coming years, more of the Mabalon family arrived in the United States. At the same time, Pablo ran a flourishing restaurant in Stockton that afforded him a middle-class lifestyle. Pablo Mabalon's immigration story highlights an important dynamic that changed Filipino life in this country. Women and children dominated the Filipino migration in these years, which ended that community's male-dominated culture and produced, for instance, a skyrocketing number of married Filipinos in the United States in the 1940s.

The Chinese migration grew in the 1950s and 1960s too. About 8,800 Chinese arrived through the quotas between 1943 and 1960, and another 23,400 came outside the quotas. The wives of servicemen made up two-thirds of that latter group, and the rest consisted of refugees.[16] Foreign policy imperatives also eased the entry of thousands of Chinese students. After the communist victory on mainland China, the United States allowed Chinese students in U.S. universities to remain, and many settled into successful careers in academia and scientific fields. In this case, the Chinese benefited from the public's conviction that these newcomers were anticommunist and that their educational backgrounds would allow them to contribute to the U.S. economy.

C. Y. Lee was among thousands of Chinese who took this path. After arriving in 1943, he completed a masters in fine arts degree at Yale in 1947. The Chinese Civil War made a trip back to China impossible, so Lee stayed in the United States without authorization, working as a writer. He won a national writing contest, an accomplishment he mentioned to an immigration officer with the hopes that it might help him avoid deportation. It did more than that: immigration authorities presented Lee with a path toward permanent residency on the basis of his artistic skills. Lee became a citizen and authored the best seller *Flower Drum Song* in 1957, which became a Broadway musical and film.

Coming to the United States from the Americas

In the 1950s, 996,000 newcomers came from the Americas, a rate that jumped slightly in the early 1960s.[17] Mexico, Canada, and Cuba sent the most in the 1950s and 1960s. Only the Dominican Republic, in the 1960s, approached them. The Cuban migration consisted almost exclusively of refugees fleeing the political changes on the island. Likewise, the Dominican migration arose from a combination of U.S. government policies and internal political and economic events. The Dominican dictator Rafael Trujillo had severely limited emigration from the island, and coup leaders assassinated him in 1961. The new government, allied with the United States, permitted political dissidents to leave. Meanwhile, that government's socioeconomic program left many in the urban middle class desirous of better opportunities in the United States. In the mid-1960s the Americans agreed to speed the arrival of these Dominicans to keep the island politically stable. The coup and this policy change accelerated annual immigration to the United States during the rest of the decade, and family migration networks developed that soon would bring hundreds of thousands.

Mexicans, Canadians, and others from the Caribbean basin generally chased economic opportunity. Canadians coming to the United States in these years possessed high levels of education, and they came in search of higher wages and unique career opportunities, a contrast to the working and laboring classes that had arrived earlier in the twentieth century. From 1950 to 1955, over 65,000 Canadians with university degrees arrived, including 20 percent of all engineering graduates produced by Canadian universities in those years.[18] The talent heading south varied. Lorne Michaels, a graduate of the University of Toronto, worked in the mid-1960s for the Canadian Broadcasting Company before heading to Los Angeles in 1968 to write for television shows. In 1975 he created the television show *Saturday Night Live* and took up American citizenship in the 1980s. The Canadian migration slowed as the 1960s wore on, largely because of social unrest and economic challenges south of the 49th parallel.

Mexicans, too, pursued opportunities in the United States, but the circumstances of their arrival varied. This was José Vázquez's story. Born in Hermosillo, Mexico, in 1942, Vázquez began coming to the United States every few months as a youngster on shopping trips to Tucson, Arizona. At one particular department store, Vázquez and his mother developed a tight bond with the Mexican American owner, Alex Jácome. In 1963 Vázquez began attending the University of Arizona, graduating in 1967. He returned to Mexico and embarked on a career in engineering in Ciudad Obregón, a city in the Mexican state of Sonora. While a college student, he returned regularly to Jácome's store, which was a hangout for Mexican college and high school students. For those years, Vázquez lived a truly cross-border and privileged (compared to his countrymen and countrywomen) life.

During the 1960s, just over 450,000 Mexicans received an immigrant visa, a landmark because the country became the largest source of immigrants, a position it still holds today.[19] Tens of thousands of Mexicans came to the United States each year on temporary nonimmigrant visas, mainly as tourists, as students, on business, or to visit family. Some stayed after their visas' expiration and became unauthorized immigrants, sometimes staying for decades. Likewise, tens of thousands of unauthorized immigrants arrived each year. One estimate held that in the two decades after 1945, about six Mexicans came to the U.S. outside legal avenues for every Mexican who came through legal ones. Finally, the bracero program continued, sending over four million workers temporarily to the United States.

Between 1945 and 1965, working-age, single men, primarily farmworkers and laborers, constituted the majority of Mexican immigrants. While the braceros and unauthorized consisted of mainly younger working men, good numbers of women and children, sometimes approaching 50 percent in a year, entered with visas in the 1950s and presented largely as family members or individuals without an occupation. Several thousand skilled workers and professionals from Mexico also arrived with immigration visas each year.

Why did they come to the United States? A government-led industrialization program, increasingly mechanized agriculture, and an exploding birthrate in post-1945 Mexico meant that while GDP grew admirably, those gains did not find their way to many working- and laboring-class (semiskilled and unskilled) Mexicans. Rural Mexicans suffered especially, fleeing farmlands for urban areas in a too often unsuccessful search for employment. The Mexican government crushed most political discontent that arose from these circumstances. In dire straits, Mexicans headed north in search of jobs, surely recalling their family and friends who had preceded them. They settled mostly in the Southwest and West, as well as in some urban areas. They often found their way into existing Mexican communities, though the braceros discovered their ties to those communities strained for economic and social reasons.

With these options, how did Mexicans choose a path to the United States in the two decades after 1945? It is difficult to generalize because every individual confronted different personal circumstances, but a few general conclusions do emerge. Women and children who sought immigrant visas often aimed to reunite with family members, whereas men who used visas aimed to find skilled work. This group had the means, social capital, and time to navigate the visa application process. The bracero program attracted men coming to the United States for temporary, mostly agricultural work, who wanted to head north quickly to earn money. But they often needed connections in Mexico, or the ability to bribe Mexican officials, to get into the program. They also needed the strength to survive dehumanizing treatment from U.S. government officials as they entered the country and found their ways to the jobsites. For those Mexican workers who did not have the resources for the bracero program, or who needed employment quickly, or who did not want the hassle of dealing with the American authorities, unauthorized entry was the best choice. Braceros and the unauthorized shared one important piece of common ground. They probably understood that as agricultural or physical laborers, they had little chance of winning an immigrant visa from the United States, and they made their migration choices accordingly.

The Immediate Postwar Refugee Challenge

World War II produced the largest refugee and displaced person population in modern history, totaling 175 million, just over 7.5 percent of the global population (table 9.2). By comparison, the refugee populations that arose after the Great War and the Cold War each totaled less than 1 percent of the globe's population.

In late 1945 the United States' engagement with European refugees took a few forms. The nation was a vital source of funding

Table 9.2. Refugee and Displaced Persons Population, 1945

Location	Number
Europe	60,000,000
China	90,000,000
South Asia	20,000,000
Middle East	1,000,000
Other (including Hong Kong)	4,000,000

Source: Peter Gattrell, *The Making of the Modern Refugee* (Oxford: Oxford University Press, 2013), 3.

and leadership for a succession of international refugee aid agencies, especially the United Nations Relief and Rehabilitation Administration (UNRRA), the International Refugee Organization (IRO), and the United Nations High Commissioner for Refugees (UNHCR). Each worked, with different degrees of success, to shrink the postwar refugee population. They also, particularly UNRRA, engaged in morally dubious programs, such as the forced repatriation of the displaced from Western Europe back to Soviet-controlled Eastern Europe. By 1949 that policy ended, in part because about 650,000 Poles, Ukrainians, and Balts refused to go. They instead remained in refugee camps, mainly in West Germany. Closer to home, in late 1945 and early 1946 President Harry Truman ordered the Department of State and INS to bring about 5,000 European refugees and displaced persons to the United States.

One of those early arrivals was Egon Loebner, a Jew from Czechoslovakia. He was an engineering student in the 1930s when the Nazis sent him to various prison and labor camps, including Auschwitz. After liberation from Auschwitz, Loebner returned to his devastated village; he estimates that of the three thousand residents hauled away by the Germans, only eighty survived. He returned to school, worked to help Jews resettle across Europe and in Palestine, and in 1947 got a student visa to the United States to continue his education. After a Jewish immigrant aid organization put him in contact with Albert Einstein, Loebner switched his graduate work to physics. He became a U.S. citizen in 1952, under a provision of the 1948 Displaced Persons Act, and settled into a career at the electronics companies Sylvania and RCA and, later, Hewlett-Packard. Most famously, he helped design the technology for flat-screen televisions.

The European refugee population evolved in these early years, complicating the task of American policy makers. The Soviet domination of Eastern Europe, assured with the fall of Czechoslovakia's democracy in 1948 and the division of Germany shortly thereafter, sent refugees from the east to the west. Tens of thousands, and sometimes more, arrived annually in West Germany fleeing Soviet totalitarianism, while smaller numbers found their ways into other parts of Western Europe. These population transfers helped form the East-West divide and informed the ideological tensions that propelled the Cold War. Ultimately, the newcomers fleeing from the east made the refugee population in Europe like an amoeba: shrinking, expanding, and always moving.

The postwar refugee situation in Asia proved more grievous. The Japanese destruction of China internally displaced tens of millions and the Chinese Civil War's eruption in 1947 only caused the number to grow. In Korea, the end of the Japanese occupation led almost immediately to the partition of the country into a communist north and noncommunist south. UNRRA offered some developmental aid to China after 1945, and the U.S. military aided some 650,000 Koreans who fled from the north to the south as the borders began to set.[20]

The Cold War deepened the refugee challenges in Asia. When North Korea invaded South Korea, the war (1950–1953) displaced about 5 million in South Korea, and another 300,000 from North Korea traveled south.[21] The United Nations, led by the United States, took charge of refugee relief efforts. Even more significant refugee populations arose from the Chinese Civil War's end in 1949. With the communists and Mao Zedong triumphant, about 100,000 of the vanquished nationalists under Chiang Kai-shek's leadership fled to the island of Formosa, soon to be named the Republic of China and now referred to as Taiwan.[22] There, unlike most refugees in history, they soon took political power. Other nationalists fled to Burma, hoping to keep the fight going against Mao. Finally, the Chinese communists launched an effort to control Tibet, pushing some 70,000 Tibetans into India and Nepal by the end of the 1950s.[23]

The British colony of Hong Kong, located in southeast China, was the epicenter of refugee problems generated by the Chinese Civil War. Hong Kong's population in the early 1950s numbered about 2.5 million, of which 670,000 were recently arrived refugees. The arrivals continued in the 1950s, so that refugees made up one-third of Hong Kong's population in 1956.[24] Nongovernmental organizations and the UNHCR took the lead on refugee aid. The British government hesitated to label these people refugees for fear of offending the Chinese government, but it slowly acceded to that fact by pursuing integration of the refugees into Hong Kong. It helped that the refugees fueled Hong Kong's economic growth.

Early Cold War U.S. Refugee Policies

Refugees in Asia remained largely regional problems that international organizations and private groups, rather than the U.S. government, addressed. The United States did provide for small, targeted admissions. Refugees arrived from Hong Kong after passage of the 1953 and 1957 refugee laws and a 1962 program inaugurated by President Kennedy. Under the auspices of a CIA-supported nongovernmental organization called Aid Refugee Chinese Intellectuals (ARCI), the United States admitted about 2,500 highly educated Hong Kong refugees under those programs and laws.[25] The United States, however, did not admit large numbers of Asian refugees until the 1970s Indochinese refugee crises.

A different story emerged in Europe, where the U.S. government developed a slate of programs focused on refugee aid and admissions. The Displaced Persons (DP) Act allowed just over 400,000 refugees and displaced persons to enter between 1948 and 1952.[26] The program brought refugees from the war residing in International Refugee Organization (IRO; the successor agency to UNRRA) camps in Germany, Austria, and Italy, as well as Czechoslovakians fleeing the 1948 imposition of Soviet control in their country. Another part of the program permitted Chinese without immigrant visas, such as students, to apply for permanent residence, a program that over 3,600 Chinese took advantage of.[27]

Given restrictionist immigration policy and the absence of prewar refugee programs, the passage of the DP program was remarkable. Advocates argued that the measure was humanitarian, but also that it served U.S. Cold War imperatives by forging political, economic, and social stability in key allies and by demonstrating American ideals in contrast to Soviet barbarism. The ethnic and religious organizations, such as the National Catholic Welfare Conference and the Hebrew Immigrant Aid Society, that so adeptly lobbied for the DP program then partnered with the U.S. government to speed the resettlement and assimilation of the newcomers. This private-public partnership, as well as the Cold War rationales for refugee admissions, only strengthened in the coming years.

Many admitted through the DP program successfully carved out new lives in the United States. Walfred Reinthal came with his wife and two children, one of the first arrivals under the program. He quickly settled in as a professor of zoology at the University of Oklahoma. Edmund Nagy, his wife, and their daughter made a new life in Louisville, Kentucky, where Nagy was employed by a local oil company, a job related to his work back home in Hungary's oil fields. One resettlement expert who studied the DPs in the United States declared, "In addition to their skills and experience, they bring along their rich and heterogeneous cultural wealths which will greatly enrich our way of life and culture."[28]

But the DP program also exhibited considerable flaws. Refugees had to be in IRO camps by the end of 1945, which left Jews who arrived in Germany fleeing anti-Semitism in the east ineligible for the program, a perverse result given the recent trials of European Jewry. In the United States, some resettled refugees struggled. Thousands of DPs found themselves placed in low-wage, backbreaking work, picking cotton and chopping sugarcane in the South, harvesting fruit and sugar beets in the West, or toiling in sweatshops in urban America. One DP described his new life: "From early morning until late at night we pick cotton and pull heavy sacks on our stooped backs, our feet sinking deeply in mud. We have not had a bath for six months."[29] This transparent labor exploitation gave lie to the supposed humanitarianism and American ideals at the DP program's heart. One Latvian refugee-turned-sharecropper in Mississippi understood this perfectly, exclaiming: "Where is justice? Have we been punished by God?"[30]

Cold War Refugees

In the 1950s European refugees became more closely tied to the Cold War. In 1953 Congress passed President Eisenhower's Refugee Relief Act. It approved the admission, over three years, of 214,000 Europeans, mostly German and Italian refugees and nationals, as well as 7,000 refugees from Asia. President Eisenhower hoped the program would alleviate population pressures in Western Europe, producing economic, political, and social stability. He also believed the program demonstrated American humanitarianism, a sharp contrast to the Soviet Union. The program's advocates trumpeted that those entering the United States were ardent opponents of the Soviet Union and supporters of American ideals: "They understand the meaning of liberty . . . they would be only too happy to come here and understand, know, and appreciate all the more, freedom of speech, freedom of press, freedom of religion."[31] Unsurprisingly, the definition of refugee written into the law focused on those fleeing communism. Moreover, the law, reflecting 1950s Red Scare politics, put every applicant through a tough security screening designed to deny entry to communists.

The Refugee Relief Program (RRP) fell under the Department of State's Bureau of Security and Consular Affairs; its leader, Scott McLeod, was an ardent anticommunist charged with internal security at the State Department. Dedicated immigration restrictionists like Senator Patrick McCarran bragged that McLeod would slow the entry of refugees: "We haven't lost yet . . . we're going to administer the act."[32] And McLeod did this, forcing refugees through a series of background checks and interviews that one refugee advocate disdainfully called "a mystic maze of enforcement."[33] During the first eighteen months of the program, refugees trickled into the United States. Only when President Eisenhower removed McLeod did admissions pick up, and eventually almost all of the available RRP visas found recipients.

The RRP ended in late 1956, just as the Hungarian Revolution occurred. In October opponents of the Stalinist Hungarian government gained power and began to move the country away from the USSR's orbit and toward a social democratic government. In early November, the Soviet leader Nikita Khrushchev ordered his military into Hungary to restore a Soviet-allied government to power. Nearly 200,000 Hungarians fled the Soviet crackdown, mostly to Austria. Australia, Canada, Great Britain, and nations in South America all agreed to take in some refugees, and over the coming months the United States admitted about 38,000.[34]

One of those 38,000 Hungarian refugees was András Gróf, whose life story moved from ordinary to extraordinary. Gróf was a twenty-year-old supporter of the Hungarian uprising when the Soviets moved in to crush the independence movement. He recalled: "The idea of being taken away in a truck was ominous. . . . I needed to leave." He made his way to Austria with the clothes on his back, his school bag, and the equivalent of a few dollars. After a stop in Germany, he earned admission to the United States, arriving in New York in January 1957. Once in this country, he Americanized his name to Andrew Grove and completed his Ph.D. in the sciences in 1963. One year before that, though, he had managed to bring his parents from Hungary to the United States, alleviating one of his chief worries. Grove missed Hungary, but he realized, "I am fortunate I got out and have been able to live in a country that accepted me and gave me the opportunity to achieve." And achieve he did: in 1968 Grove and some colleagues started a computer company called Intel, which became the leading producer of semiconductors and microchips and a Fortune 500 company.[35]

Though the first few thousand arrived through the Refugee Relief Act, the Eisenhower administration paroled the vast majority into the United States. The parole power allowed the attorney general to admit an alien to the United States if that action fulfilled American interests. Parole was meant to admit an individual in an emergency, but the Eisenhower administration effectively used it to expedite mass admissions of refugees. In the case of the Hungarian admissions, the federal government worked closely with private refugee aid organizations to screen and resettle refugees, meaning the "mystic maze of enforcement" of the 1953 program receded.

The Refugee Relief Program and the Hungarian admissions campaign vitally shaped refugee policy. Coming after the Displaced Persons program, both efforts demonstrated the United States making a sustained, if ad hoc, commitment to refugee admissions. The Cold War justified these programs and informed the guiding principles that determined whom the United States would admit and the process by which they would enter the country. The programs also made clear the Eurocentric focus of admissions, given the small numbers of Asian and Middle Eastern refugees offered visas. Finally, the public largely acceded to these programs, a sharp contrast to the 1930s. Opponents of refugee admissions did exist, and these programs never polled superbly well among the public, as sizable minorities regularly opposed them. But the Cold War imperatives, a healthy economy that absorbed newcomers easily, and the focus on European admissions did much to limit opposition.

The next major turn in refugee policy began in January 1959, when Cuban revolutionaries overthrew the autocrat Fulgencio Batista. The Cuban Revolution ultimately produced the largest flow of refugees to the United States to that point. The refugees came in stages (table 9.3), and the U.S. government admitted almost all of them by parole under the reasoning that they fled Cuba as victims of communism. The movement of Cubans to the United States depended on the internal dynamics of Fidel Castro's revolution, conditions on the island, and the state of relations between the United States and Cuba, which deteriorated through the early 1960s. Indeed, Cubans sometimes took incredible (and controversial steps) to come to the United States. From 1960 to 1962, Operación Pedro Pan saw Cuban parents send about 14,000 Cuban children to the

Table 9.3. Stages of Cuban Refugee Arrival, 1959–1973

Years	Number of Refugees Arriving	Refugee Characteristics
January 1959	(in hundreds)	Political and economic elites; Batista allies
February 1959– January 1961	100,000	Upper- and middle-class Cubans who opposed Batista but disliked the Revolution's path
January 1961– October 1962	150,000	Middle-class Cubans
October 1962– November 1965	30,000	Middle-class Cubans, migration slowed by broken U.S.–Cuban relations after the Missile Crisis
November 1965– April 1973	260,000	Middle- and working-class Cubans, migration sped by U.S.–Cuban agreement

Sources: Carl Bon Tempo, *Americans at the Gate: The United States and Refugees during the Cold War* (Princeton: Princeton University Press, 2008), 107–112; Jorge Duany, "Cuban Migration: A Postrevolution Exodus Ebbs and Flows," Migration Policy Institute, July 6, 2017, https://www.migrationpolicy.org/article/cuban-migration-postrevolution-exodus-ebbs-and-flows.

Cuban refugees escaping to the United States, 1965.
National Archives, College Park, Maryland.

United States, largely out of fears for their future under Castro.[36] The U.S.–Cuban relationship stabilized in 1965, when the countries arrived at an agreement governing the departure of Cubans for the United States, which held until 1973.

All told, more than 500,000 Cubans came to the United States as refugees between 1959 and 1973. Carlos Eire, born in 1950, was one of the Pedro Pan children, coming to the United States at age eleven. He stayed with foster families in Miami at first, but then when his parents could not follow him to the states, he ended up in an institution, "an awful place . . . half the kids in the house had police records."[37] As a young man, Eire earned a Ph.D. from Yale University, became a professor, and authored an award-winning book on his migration experience, *Waiting for Snow in Havana*. But there has been pain: he never saw his father again, he has not returned to the island, and his book is banned in Cuba.

Federal government agencies, rather than private organizations, guided Cuban resettlement in the United States, and Cubans benefited from expansive welfare programs. But other than this change, the Cuban admissions displayed continuities with the programs that had brought European refugees to the United States. Parole was the vehicle for entry, most of the Cubans were "white" (and not drawn from the island's population with African backgrounds), and Americans supported entry because they believed the refugees were victims of communism and a valuable Cold War weapon. Ultimately, the Cubans helped cement an American commitment to refugees.

The American actions in refugee matters in the two decades after World War II, though, surely deserves criticism. First, the United States acted not out of a deep-seated commitment to humanitarianism, but primarily because refugee admissions aligned with its foreign policy and national security interests, and because refugees did not threaten economic prosperity. Second, some refugees, like the Latvian DPs, arrived and found themselves in the worst of the American economic and social environment. Third, the focus on those fleeing communism in Europe (at least until Cuba) left too many of the globe's refugees wishing for American help that never came. Finally, though the United States admitted hundreds of thousands of refugees and annually provided tens of millions of dollars in aid, it could have done more. The country's massive resources were beyond compare, and more generous admissions and aid were possible. Each of these critiques rings true, and they complicate, but do not invalidate, another conclusion. Between 1945 and the mid-1960s, American aid and admissions policies toward refugees grew more generous and substantial.

Continuing the Bracero Program

The bracero program long outlived World War II. The original arrangement ended in 1947, but the Mexican and U.S. governments kept the guest worker program operating until 1964. In total, the United States and Mexico executed 4.6 million bracero contracts, the overwhelming majority after 1945, which brought hundreds of thousands to this country.[38] (Many braceros signed multiple contracts.) The bracero program substantially changed U.S.–Mexican relations, the agricultural industry, life in the American Southwest, Mexican and Mexican American communities in the United States, and border control policies. Equally vital, the bracero program helped spur the entry, outside legal avenues, of Mexicans to the United States. The lure of jobs and reunification with family could not be contained within the bracero program, and Mexicans came to the United States, whether as legal migrants or not, to get those jobs and be with loved ones. And, of course, the bracero program affected life not just in the United States, but also in Mexico, where gender relations, family life, labor relations, and understandings of the nation evolved as Mexican men migrated north in search of temporary work.

In the postwar years, the program went through a few phases. From 1948 to 1951, the U.S. government and Mexico could not agree on a program extension. As a result, President Harry Truman issued executive orders, and the Department of Labor used an existing immigration law that allowed the continued entry of temporary workers. A good number of braceros in these years entered the United States outside legal avenues, were apprehended by the Border Patrol, and then placed into the bracero program, sometimes with the Mexican government's acquiescence and sometimes without. Once he was in the program, the authorities released the Mexican worker into the custody of his American employer, who could act with impunity in enforcing working conditions. For instance, instead of a six-month contract signed with the U.S. government, some braceros during these years signed forty-five-day contracts directly with the employer.

The Korean War's labor needs led to a new bilateral agreement between Mexico and the United States in 1951, which Congress approved one year later. After 1952, the contracts lengthened and Mexican workers signed them with the U.S. government, which provided transport from Mexico for the workers. The 1951 agreement and 1952 legislation also contained vague language about the Labor Department certifying the need for temporary foreign workers and braceros, receiving prevailing wages. The former principle aimed to protect American workers, while the latter supposedly protected both American workers and the braceros, but neither proved effective. Liberals in Congress, backed by their labor union allies, did win stronger penalties for those who helped or harbored those in the United States without authorization, but the law also declared that anyone employing a so-called illegal Mexican in the United States did not technically harbor that alien. That large loophole allowed employers to hire Mexicans crossing the border without authorization and outside the bracero program.

During the 1950s, the United States and Mexico made superficial changes that preserved the prerogatives of the U.S. government and American agriculture. The American desire for braceros, in whatever form the program took, continued unabated. Agricultural interests that owned huge farms and used the most up-to-date technologies to maximize yields needed large amounts of unskilled labor to harvest cotton, citrus, and vegetables. These farmers and their large-scale operations, which stretched across the Southwest from California to Texas, joined in their desire for cheap and, they hoped, relatively docile labor. The Truman administration came to see the guest workers as a necessary solution to production problems on the farms. It also hoped the agreement might regularize the migration of farm labor from Mexico, bringing under regulation practices that were long-standing.

During these years, Mexico saw a few advantages to the bracero program. The Mexican government believed the braceros would bring some cash back to the country, and they would return with new skills and techniques that might revitalize domestic agriculture. Because many of the braceros came from the indigenous population, long a scorned social and economic group, the Mexican government hoped the program would transform them into more useful citizens. The Mexican government, then, viewed the bracero program as part of modernization efforts in the mid-twentieth century.

In contrast, Mexican braceros joined the program in the 1950s in search of good jobs and pay. One survey revealed that 85 percent of the braceros went for the salaries and only 1 percent hoped to learn new farming techniques.[39] Tellingly, the number of braceros skyrocketed. In the late 1950s, over 400,000 braceros worked in the United States annually (table 9.4). Braceros made up somewhere between 5 and 10 percent of agricultural workers during the war, but

Table 9.4. Mexican Agricultural Contract Laborers in the U.S. and
Mexican Border Apprehensions, 1950–1962

Year	Mexican Agricultural Contract Laborers	Mexican Apprehensions
1950	67,500	458,215
1951	192,000	500,628
1952	197,100	534,538
1953	201,380	875,318
1954	309,033	1,075,168
1955	398,650	242,608
1956	445,197	72,242
1957	436,049	44,451
1958	432,857	37,242
1959	437,643	30,196
1960	315,846	29,651
1961	291,420	29,877
1962	194,978	30,272

Source: Mae Ngai, *Impossible Subjects: Illegal Aliens and the Making of Modern America* (Princeton: Princeton University Press, 2004), 157.

they at times constituted around 25 percent of the farm workforce during the 1950s.[40]

Unauthorized Immigration from Mexico

As braceros entered the United States in greater numbers in the 1950s, more and more Mexicans also came searching for work without legal permission to enter. One estimate holds that about half a million undocumented Mexicans crossed the border each year in the late 1940s and early 1950s, peaking in 1954 at one million. Apprehensions by the Border Patrol in the early 1950s sustain this assertion. The INS apprehended about 180,000 Mexicans entering outside legal avenues in 1947 and again in 1948, a figure that exceeded 500,000 annually by 1951 and 1952 (see table 9.4).

Several factors drove this unauthorized immigration of Mexicans to the United States. To win a slot in the bracero program, hopeful applicants often had to pay a bribe to a Mexican official of the equivalent of fifty U.S. dollars, a princely sum that led many to just head north for work. Moreover, the bracero program never had enough spots for all the workers who wished to come to the United States, so many Mexicans entered without authorization, eager to work for higher wages than they could get in Mexico. American employers happily greeted these unauthorized workers, whom they paid less than the braceros and without having to follow the bracero program's regulations. Indeed, many growers in the United States promised their braceros that if they came back to the country, but not in the program, they would be rehired. A Mexican worker described the logic: "As a wetback, alone, safely across the border, I may find a farmer who needs one man. He will pay me honestly, I think. But as a bracero, I am only a number on a paycheck . . . and I am treated like a number . . . not like a man."[41] Both American employers and Mexican workers, then, saw advantages to employment outside the bracero program.

If agricultural interests in the United States were pleased with this unauthorized workforce, other Americans objected to it. Unions protested about competition in the labor market, and humanitarian groups worried about the poor working conditions and pay that these unauthorized visitors were subject to. Some liberals in Congress pushed for substantial penalties for those who hired unauthorized Mexicans, but that effort almost completely failed. Instead, the Eisenhower administration in 1954 launched a program, Operation Wetback—*wetback* being a pejorative used by some Americans to describe Mexicans who crossed without authorization. Operation Wetback, which lasted into 1955, detained about 250,000 Mexicans, but its origins and motivations were more complex than border security.[42]

President Eisenhower asked his West Point classmate General Joseph Swing to oversee Operation Wetback, which had the trappings of a military operation. Hundreds of Border Patrol and immigration officers, cars and jeeps, and seven planes swarmed the U.S. border with Mexico, rounding up individuals suspected of being in the United States without authorization. Swing's forces also targeted Los Angeles, San Francisco, and Chicago, where unauthorized workers settled. Operation Wetback pushed some of the detained men into the bracero program and sent others back to

Mexico. The apprehensions and removals could border on the inhumane. In one raid on a day that registered 112 degrees, eighty-eight men perished, and an investigation described Mexicans being sent back home on an "eighteenth century slave ship."[43] Swing, though, lauded Operation Wetback, and the INS declared the so-called illegal immigration problem at an end.

This braggadocio marked the entire effort and concealed the policy's more prosaic origins, as the historian Kelly Lytle Hernandez has detailed. Swing and his allies, in search of a public-opinion victory, loudly proclaimed that they had surged enforcement personnel and equipment to the border and that they had returned around one million Mexicans south of the border.[44] They vastly overstated both claims. And, in fact, in the aftermath of Operation Wetback, they ratcheted down border enforcement. Nor did Swing and the U.S. government make clear the actual goal of the operation: they used the threat of detention and removal of unauthorized Mexicans to squeeze Texas agricultural interests to abandon their use of unauthorized Mexicans and instead rely on contract workers in the bracero and other temporary worker programs (and enrollments in those programs did increase in 1954 and 1955). Swing and the INS used Operation Wetback to discipline employers, not to control unauthorized border crossings. Still, Mexican workers bore the brunt of the effort.

Living as a Bracero

Hundreds of thousands of braceros came to the United States over more than two decades and worked in a variety of locations. Historians diligently have uncovered their stories, painting vivid portraits of the experiences of those temporary workers and their families, and of Mexicans who entered outside the program.

Every bracero's journey to the United States took on its own color. Ricardo Velazquez of Aguacaliente de Gárate, on the central-western coast of Mexico, decided to come to the United States because of the bracero program's promise of fifty cents an hour instead of the sixty-five cents a day he earned at home. It took two weeks for Velazquez and his friends to get the Mexican

*Authorities examine a bracero's hands at the Monterrey, Mexico,
Processing Center, 1956. Photo by Leonard Nadal, National Museum
of American History, Smithsonian Institution, Washington, D.C.*

government's approval to enter the program, but then things moved
quickly. They took a train to an INS facility in a Texas border town,
arriving at four o'clock in the morning. Authorities gave them a
short medical inspection and an interview and took photographs
and fingerprints. The INS worked quickly, wanting the men working as soon as possible. That afternoon the men signed contracts
with a farm and arrived at their work barracks that evening. The
next morning, they harvested melons. While every bracero's passage
differed, the emphasis on speeding workers to the fields and the de-

humanizing nature of their interaction with the authorities appear to have been routine.

Braceros never enjoyed ideal living and working conditions, and these deteriorated after 1945. Housing varied in the postwar years; some braceros lived in large barracks, some of new construction and some more worn, and others lived in shacks, tents, or even chicken coops. In the barracks, a man usually had a bed and a corner to store his belongings. Access to hot and cold water, as well as toilet and shower facilities, varied at bracero work sites. Sometimes, though, braceros marveled at the accommodations as "very well equipped . . . we were very comfortable there."[45] Braceros suffered through the substandard meals provided by their bosses, and the men sometimes chose to use their meager pay to purchase food, which introduced them to American staples less common in Mexico. The workday began as early as five o'clock and offered only hours of body-breaking labor harvesting fruit, vegetables, or cotton. After work, the men relaxed back in the camps, where radios offered what one man called "a circus of music."[46] Some left the camps in the evening to explore varieties of nightlife. One man summed up bracero life this way: "We worked together all day; we cooked together; we drank together; we slept together. We spent all our time together."[47]

Braceros' interactions with the people who ran these farms, as well as government officials, made clear the program's inherent economic and social hierarchy. At some camps, the supervisors obsessed over the bodies of the braceros, constantly urging them to shower and wash their hands before meals, and to put on weight and muscle for work in the fields. One supervisor complained that the braceros refused to use the indoor plumbing he had built: "They're just like animals. Now mind you, I'm not saying they're all like this. But even if it's just a few in each camp that's enough to make the camp into a pigsty overnight."[48] Others commented on the after-hours life of the workers, one noting approvingly, "A Mexican boy doesn't require much in the way of recreation or entertainment."[49] These employers viewed the braceros as beneath them and requiring social uplift, an attitude that meshed with the Mexican government's.

Unsurprisingly, farmers did not pay braceros decent salaries. One set of workers, promised a wage of $.50 per hour and $1.15 a day for food, ended up being paid $.30 per hour and about $.50 a day for provisions. The foreman told the workers that "he paid only thirty cents an hour, no more, and that if we did not want to work for thirty cents an hour that we could leave."[50] This exploitative labor system ultimately had a depressing effect on overall farm wages. In 1946 farm wages stood at 47.9 percent of manufacturing wages but by 1955 had fallen to 36.1 percent—a decline abetted in part by the availability of relatively cheap bracero workers.[51]

With wages so low, some braceros left to find work elsewhere, often in urban areas with industrial and manufacturing jobs. Some surveys show that 4 percent of braceros deserted their contracts, others show rates approaching 30–35 percent.[52] The choice to desert was thoroughly rational. One bracero recalled that the farm had paid $28 for a week of work, roughly what he earned in two days in industry.

Defying government's and management's hopes for a docile workforce, braceros did what they could to improve working and living conditions. Desertion was a form of protest. The U.S.–Mexico agreement provided official avenues for braceros to lodge complaints about their treatment. In the 1950s several thousand complaints (each authored by either a single worker or a group of workers) landed annually with the U.S. government, mainly claiming breach of contract on the grounds of low pay or inadequate housing. American officials usually just warned the employers and only very rarely terminated a contract. If braceros took their complaints to a Mexican consular office in the United States, and the consular officers alerted the U.S. government, the chances of remedial action in behalf of the braceros increased. Sometimes braceros took their complaints directly to their employers. This tactic could involve a onetime event at a work site—a group of men trying to improve living conditions by asking for changes in the camp—or an organized labor action that involved groups of men over a long period. In either case, the chances of success remained tiny.

When braceros left their living quarters in search of entertainment, companionship, or even just to shop, locals—be they Anglos, Mexican Americans, or Mexican immigrant communities—did not always react well. Renato Sandoval, who worked in Tulare, California, recalled that the locals, probably both Anglos and Mexican Americans, viewed the braceros as "inferior single men and unworthy of enjoying or interaction in family-oriented venues catering to town resident families on weekends."[53] Braceros and the Mexican American community often fell into conflict. Local Mexican Americans worried that the newcomers took job opportunities and put downward pressure on wages, which they did. Local domestic agricultural workers occasionally went on strike to protest their dwindling wages, but braceros proved a key obstacle in these campaigns because employers could call on the temporary workforce to keep the harvest going. Efforts to bridge this divide by building a transnational labor union of braceros and domestic workers to demand better pay and conditions in the fields largely failed.

Tensions spread beyond economic issues. Braceros came from some of the most marginalized groups in Mexico, especially the indigenous community. Often those of Mexican background in the United States looked down on them. Those cultural differences might flare up in restaurants, on dance floors, or in theaters, especially if the locals perceived the temporary workers as testing or breaking social boundaries. Finally, Mexican Americans, particularly those in California and Texas, understood that the braceros' presence increased nativism among white Americans toward any person of Mexican descent.

Though underpaid and overworked, braceros could earn more money in the United States than in Mexico. Braceros sent a much-needed $30 million back to Mexico in the 1950s.[54] And success stories did occur. Álvaro García recalled his time in the United States fondly, especially the battery-powered radio he brought back with him: "I liked that radio. . . . Only braceros had them. They were progress." García also came back with a small amount of savings, which he put toward a farm and, because he had learned to cut hair in his bracero quarters, a barbershop. The barbershop, which he ran into the 1990s, gave him prominence and standing in his community.[55]

Álvaro García's, though, was an exceptional story. The bracero program did not create a path to wealth or a guarantee of upward mobility. Most braceros earned too little to accumulate real savings, and they sometimes spent those earnings to settle their debts to those they had bribed to get into the program, or to pay for entertainment that made life in the United States, away from family and friends, bearable. And, as Esther Legaspi Delgadillo and her boyfriend, Antonio Sanchez, knew all too well, the weight of that separation was quite heavy.

Change was afoot in immigration by the mid-1960s. The rising numbers of newcomers from Mexico and the Americas, the slow growth of Asian immigration, and the slight drop in quota immigrants from Europe laid out the demographic path forward. Meanwhile, immigration advocates set their sights on two changes: ending the bracero program and destroying the hated national origins quota immigration system. Their work began in the 1950s and it culminated in the mid-1960s, when so much political and legal change came to the United States.

Further Reading

Bon Tempo, Carl. *Americans at the Gate: The United States and Refugees during the Cold War* (2008).

Hsu, Madeline. *The Good Immigrants: How the Yellow Peril Became the Model Minority* (2015).

Loza, Mireya. *Defiant Braceros: How Migrant Workers Fought for Racial, Sexual, and Political Freedom* (2016).

Marinari, Maddalena, Madeline Hsu, and Maria Cristina Garcia, eds. *A Nation of Immigrants Reconsidered: US Society in an Age of Restriction, 1924–1965* (2019).

Porter, Stephen. *Benevolent Empire: U.S. Power, Humanitarianism, and the World's Dispossessed* (2016).

Rosas, Ana Elizabeth. *Abrazando el Espíritu: Bracero Families Confront the US–Mexico Border* (2014).

CHAPTER TEN

The Age of Reform

Braceros, Immigrants, and Refugees

IN 1958 A YOUNG, Irish American, Catholic senator from Massachusetts named John F. Kennedy published a very slight book titled *A Nation of Immigrants*. Kennedy came to this project after the Anti-Defamation League of B'nai B'rith (ADL), a Jewish organization deeply involved in immigration, suggested it. Senator Kennedy, with the help of his aides, produced a book that extolled the virtues of immigration, claiming, "Everywhere immigrants have enriched and strengthened the fabric of American life."[1] *A Nation of Immigrants* also argued for reforming immigration law by ending national origins quotas. Kennedy wrote the book not only because of his commitment to that cause, but additionally to shore up his political standing and demonstrate his policy acumen in advance of a 1960 presidential run. The book and its success made clear the attention the immigration issue had earned and the deep desire of some to rethink immigration law. In time, they succeeded.

Between 1964 and 1980, immigration and refugee law and policies underwent major reforms. In 1964 the bracero program ended. One year later Congress, at President Johnson's urging, ended the 1920s national origins quota laws and erected a new legal system to regulate immigration to the United States. Finally, in 1980, the United States enacted the Refugee Act, which revised the definition of the term *refugee* and set up substantial annual admissions of refugees.

These changes came after decades of debates among supporters and opponents of immigrant entry, refugee admissions, and the bracero program. Foreign policy issues such as the Cold War, Vietnam and its aftermath, and the rise of a human rights movement played a role in some of these reforms, as did the large liberal majorities in Congress in the mid-1960s and a relatively healthy economy. Most important, the civil rights movement's fight against racial discrimination helped power an assault on national origins quotas and ethnonational bigotry. All these factors brought about a series of moments during which immigration and refugee advocates held the upper hand. These reforms were deeply a product of the times, but the times did not lead inexorably to reform. Opponents of immigration still held powerful sway in politics and political culture. The majority of Americans disliked the national origins quotas, but neither did they support allowing more immigrants and refugees to enter than were then permitted.

This age of reform, then, had a paradoxical quality. On the one hand, these reforms possessed a conservative nucleus. They did not return immigration to the more open-door approach of the late nineteenth century. The refugee law regularized annual admissions in the hope of ending large-scale paroles of persecuted individuals. Finally, few observers expected the laws to produce a surge in immigration to the United States, or even a drastic change in the origins of those newcomers. On the other hand, these laws did end national origins quotas and reset many of the ways the country engaged with newcomers, reforms that reverberated for decades.

Advocates of Immigration

By the late 1940s, supporters of more liberal immigration laws stood ready to fight. They included liberals in the Democratic and Republican parties, European American and Asian American lobbying organizations, mainline Protestant, Catholic, and Jewish groups, foreign policy internationalists from both parties, and business interests. American labor, supportive of restriction through most of the twentieth century, came aboard as well. While some immigration reformers conceded that the difficult political ground and powerful opponents might make modification of the quota system, rather than its elimination, the only possible option, they made no secret of their disgust with the 1920s laws.

Immigration advocates offered several powerful arguments. Foremost, they cited American ideals, contending that discrimination against particular ethnic groups had no place in the United States. The American Jewish Committee urged in 1955: "Let's junk the unfair quota system. . . . It runs contrary to all our ideals of liberty and equality."[2] Nearly a decade later Senator Robert Kennedy described national origins quotas as "totally alien to the spirit of the Constitution" and anathema in light of "our law, our traditions."[3] World War II's battles against totalitarianism, and especially the campaign against Nazi race thinking, had trumpeted American political and social ideals, making such appeals that much more potent.

Along these lines, the Cold War was yet another powerful immigration reform argument. In the face of the global confrontation with the Soviet Union and communism, reformers claimed that the United States could not afford to offend its allies in Asia and Europe with immigration bans and quotas. Walter Judd, a Republican and longtime opponent of the ban on Chinese immigration, attacked the 1920s laws and supported reform because it could "influence greatly the battle for men's minds and hearts that is going on between the two philosophies of life and government that are locked in mortal struggle in our world."[4] Liberalizers also touted the public diplomacy benefits of ending discriminatory quotas. Such a move, they believed, would illustrate the country's fidelity to ideals like equality and opportunity that it so loudly trumpeted in the Cold War. This proposition tracked with advocates of civil rights, who made similar cases about public diplomacy and national ideals.

In fact, as the push for Black civil rights gained steam, the case for eliminating national origins requirements from immigration law strengthened. This proved the major difference between the early 1950s failures to reform immigration law and the successful efforts to do so in the mid-1960s: immigration advocates could harness the moral and political arguments of Black civil rights to their cause. Hubert Humphrey, whose speech at the 1948 Democratic

Convention denouncing states' rights thinking marked a seminal first moment in liberals' fight against Jim Crow racism, offered an explanation of this dynamic in 1965: "We have removed all elements of second-class citizenship from our laws by the Civil Rights Act. . . . We want to bring our immigration law into line with the spirit of the Civil Rights Act of 1964."[5] Liberal after liberal echoed this line of thinking in the early 1960s immigration debates.

This argument highlights how liberals in the postwar era had moved beyond the economic concerns of the 1930s to acknowledge and address racial problems. Many liberals embraced a sort of racial universalism, best summed up by Lyndon Johnson in 1966: the United States "is one large island of earth inhabited by mortal men of many races, and many faiths, and many colors of skin. They all cry the same way. They all laugh the same way. If they are to build just and fruitful lives for themselves and their children, then they must do it here—and . . . together."[6] Universalism powered liberal efforts to end legal racial discrimination with the 1964 Civil Rights Act and the 1965 Voting Rights Act and it harmonized with opposition to discrimination in immigration affairs that was based on ethnicity and nationality.

These high-minded arguments stood next to self-interested appeals. Groups like the Sons of Italy and the Japanese American Citizens League, as well as religious organizations such as the American Jewish Committee and the National Catholic Welfare Conference, with their deep ties to ethnonational communities, flourished in the political and cultural pluralism of the 1950s and 1960s. Political pluralism conceived of democratic politics as the product of a variety of interest groups fighting for their agendas, while cultural pluralism held that society was made up of distinct ethnic, national, and religious groups whose traits gave the larger country its greatness.

In this environment, ethnic and religious groups blasted the quotas that so offended and affected their constituents. Judge Juvenal Marchisio, the national chairman of the American Committee for Italian Migration, criticized the quotas for keeping out Italians who would make good American citizens, pointing out that "in proportion to their number, less Italians have been convicted of crime than any other race, even as more Italians in proportion to their number fought and died in the Armed Forces of the United States

in the last war."[7] Likewise, so many European Americans found their
way into unions in the 1930s and 1940s that labor leaders—who
admittedly sympathized more with liberal causes in any event—saw
little choice but to oppose immigration quotas. After all, they ra-
tionalized, "despite the initial distrust of new peoples, the record of
adjustment, of integration, of accommodation is a glorious story."[8]
In response to all this political organizing and advocacy, politicians,
especially Democratic liberal politicians such as Harry Truman,
John Kennedy, and (later, after he became president) Lyndon Johnson responded to key voting blocs and pushed hard for immigration
reform.

Economic concerns had stymied immigration reform before, especially in the 1930s, but the relatively healthy economy of the postwar years waylaid the fiercest of such objections. But large portions
of the American working class, recent immigrants from Europe,
and their leaders in labor unions, as the polling showed, feared that
changes to immigration law might tighten the labor market. Thus,
supporters of immigration reform made a few strategic choices.
They promised that a new immigration system would eliminate the
quotas but would not increase total migration to the United States.
They made clear that a new admissions system would privilege those
with the education and skills needed in the United States. This preference for the well-educated and skilled arose from the long battle
against Chinese exclusion, where advocates touted these characteristics to combat charges that the Chinese migration brought low-
wage labor. In the larger immigration debates, it proved a key element in constructing an alternative to national origins as selection
criteria for newcomers.

Defenders of Immigration Restriction

Defenders of the national origins quotas in the postwar period resembled the group that devised the 1920s laws. Patriotic organizations like the American Legion and the Veterans of Foreign Wars
continued to support the quotas. They had allies in a group of conservative nationalist politicians housed in both parties, such as Senator Pat McCarran (D-Nevada), Senator Styles Bridges (R-New

Hampshire), and Representative Francis Walter (D-Pennsylvania). Elements of the "old right," the America Firsters and isolationists, and the "new right," including some writers at the *National Review*, regarded national origins policies favorably. Finally, white conservative Southerners in Congress, such as South Carolina's Senator Strom Thurmond and Louisiana's Senator Allen Ellender, formed the backbone of the restrictionist camp. McCarran in the Senate, Walter in the House, and the southern conservatives enjoyed one other powerful advantage: their seniority on Capitol Hill gave them control of key committees and the ability to stifle any immigration bill they opposed.

Two ideas fueled the thinking of this bloc: a belief in Anglo-Protestant white superiority and a fear of communism stoked by the Cold War at home and abroad. The restrictionists were willing to slightly alter the national origins system, but they largely stood by the quotas that greatly favored newcomers from northwestern Europe. In the post-1945 era, as opposed to the 1920s, most proponents of national origins quotas, even white Southerners, spoke less often in overtly racist vernacular. Instead, they adopted the less offensive terminology of protecting national cultural and social unity and assuring assimilation of newcomers, which they felt national origins quotas best guaranteed. Senator McCarran knocked any substantive reform because it would "in the course of a generation or so, change the ethnic and cultural composition of this Nation."[9]

But restrictionist concerns about race and nationality never fell too far below the surface. White Southerners were the strongest defenders of national origins theory, connecting the defense of African American segregation and white supremacy to the defense of an immigration policy that favored Anglo-Protestant migration. These restrictionists spoke for many white Americans who remained deeply invested in racial and ethnonational hierarchies that privileged them. They proudly interpreted history and contemporary affairs through that lens, and they defended the racial and immigration status quo as vital to the country. Robert Byrd, a Democratic senator from West Virginia and an ardent opponent of Black civil rights, made this link, noting, "It is indubitably clear that if the majority of Americans had sprung not from Western, central, and southern Europe, but from central Africa and southern Asia, we would today have a vastly different country."[10] Some southern white allies acceded to Byrd's position, a willingness to accept immigrants from all of Europe, if it meant forestalling any significant immigration from Asia or Africa. Even then, other white Southerners could not go that far. Senator Walter George, a Democrat from Georgia, made clear his wish that, in immigration policy, "the time had not come when one must apologize for being a hateful Anglo-Saxon."[11] When the final battle over the quota system took place in the Senate in 1965, fifteen of the eighteen votes in favor of sustaining the quotas came from the South.

Anticommunism and the Cold War also flowed through the restrictionist bloc's thinking. All members of the anti-immigration group shared these concerns, but especially key politicians like McCarran, Bridges, and Walter, buttressed by their allies in veterans' groups. McCarran orchestrated this line of defense. A Democrat, but a thorny critic of liberals like Presidents Roosevelt and Truman, McCarran from his perch in the Senate was the key legislative player in building the internal security state of the early postwar period. His Red Scare legislation, especially the 1950 Internal Security Act, aimed to identify and destroy the threat of communist subversion from both inside and outside the United States.

McCarran believed that the admission of immigrants and refugees represented a subversive threat to the United States during a very perilous period of the early Cold War, and he cautioned that the restrictive immigration system ought to remain. In 1953 he defined the purpose and value of the national origins system in a Cold War world: "I believe that this nation is the last hope of Western civilization and if this oasis of the world shall be overrun, perverted, contaminated or destroyed, then the last flickering light of humanity will be extinguished."[12] Though the Red Scare of the early 1950s had receded by the early 1960s, vigorous anticommunism still was a critical part of the worldview of the conservative right and white Southerners, and it shaped their thinking about immigration.

Postwar public opinion found itself buffeted by these crosscutting currents, arguments, and ideas. For most of the 1950s and early 1960s, public opinion might best be summarized as supporting reform of, and even, by 1965, the elimination of, national origins quotas. But the public also opposed any net increase in immigration to the United States. This dynamic made the politics of reform tricky and suggested that any changes to immigration or refugee laws would necessarily need to be conservative and somewhat cautious.

A Sort of Reform: The McCarran-Walter Act of 1952

The first major battle in postwar immigration law reform occurred in 1952. The pro-immigration bloc cautiously offered a reform bill that modified the national origins system but did not abolish the quotas. Their proposal went nowhere. Instead, Senator McCarran, Representative Walter, and their allies largely controlled the legislative process and produced a bill that left the quota system in place while slightly liberalizing aspects of it, toughened restrictions on entry of some immigrants, and made it easier to deport individuals. President Truman vetoed the McCarran-Walter bill with a blistering attack on national origins principles, but Congress resoundingly overrode the veto. The McCarran-Walter Immigration Act became law in late June 1952.

The 1952 debates occurred at the height of the Red Scare and McCarthyism, and in the midst of the Korean War and ongoing tensions in Europe, so the Cold War and anticommunism emerged as central issues. Truman's veto made the Cold War–inflected immigration liberalizer's case. He reminded Americans that "we have entered into an alliance, the North Atlantic Treaty, with Italy, Greece, and Turkey against one of the most terrible threats mankind has ever faced," but that national origins policy essentially declared to those allies: "You are less worthy to come to this country than Englishmen or Irishmen; you Italians, who need to find homes abroad in the hundreds of thousands—you shall have a quota of 5,645; you Greeks, struggling to assist the helpless victims of a communist civil war—you shall have a quota of 308; and you Turks, you are brave defenders of the Eastern flank, but you shall have a quota of only 225!"[13] Senator McCarran met Truman with a Cold War volley: "The times, Mr. President, are too perilous for us to tinker blindly with our national institutions."[14]

The McCarran-Walter law generally kept the basic structures of 1920s immigration law. The 1952 approach left the Western Hemisphere off the quota system, and it kept the quota system in place for Europe, slightly raising the total number of visas allocated to that region to 158,000 annually. Those quotas continued to favor northwestern Europe, which received 85 percent of the available visas. Within the quotas, individuals with skills needed in the United States received more visas, migrants whose children were adult U.S. citizens earned slightly fewer, and the spouses and offspring of permanent resident aliens were the final preference category. Overall, then, the 1952 admissions system tilted greatly toward northwestern Europeans with skills and family already in the United States as citizens or permanent residents.

The law came with a few new twists. First, it granted each Asian nation a quota of one hundred, but it capped the number of Asian visas in any year at two thousand. Additionally, the law changed citizenship laws to remove barriers to Asian naturalization, which in turn allowed naturalized citizens of Asian descent to bring family members to the United States without regard to the quotas (just as Europeans could do). Second, in the Western Hemisphere, colonies of European powers could now send only one hundred persons to the United States annually (and those visas were still charged to the colonial power's quota). This effectively choked off immigration to the United States from Jamaica and Barbados, two British colonies whose residents had come relatively freely to the United States under the large British quota before 1952. Critics correctly pointed out that this part of the 1952 law targeted people of African descent from the Caribbean. Third, the 1952 law increased the deportation powers of the federal government and gave the Border Patrol more tools to crack down on unauthorized entry and to fortify the U.S.–Mexican border. Finally, the 1952 law applied to immigration many of the 1950 Internal Security Act's measures combating political subversion, turning the immigration bureaucracy's attention toward the supposed problem of communist infiltration. These internal security provisions made it easier for the U.S. government to deny entry, even if the applicant wanted to visit for only a few days, to those it deemed political radicals.

The McCarran-Walter immigration law had both short- and long-term ramifications. In the short term, it generated immense political controversy. Truman's veto, the congressional override, and the Truman administration's publication of a pro-immigration report titled "Whom Shall We Welcome" showed both sides employing fiery rhetoric, which kept the issue alive and forced politicians to take sides throughout the 1950s and into the early 1960s. For instance, as a candidate and then as president, Eisenhower made clear his hope for thorough reform of the quota system. His administration failed to tackle the issue substantively, though, in large part because of energized congressional opposition led by Representative Walter, who emerged as the key restrictionist after McCarran's 1954 death. Finally, in terms of policy, the legislation offered a short-term victory for restrictionists: it kept the national origins principles enshrined in American law with only relatively minor changes.

But in the long term, the law's outcomes look different. The change to Asian naturalization policy proved most important, as it allowed tens of thousands of Americans of Asian descent to bring their relatives to the United States. Ultimately, this revision to naturalization law had many more ramifications than the largely symbolic elimination of bans on Asian migration. More important, criticism of national origins policy and the push for repeal of the quotas only picked up steam after 1952. In this sense, 1952 was the first step on the road to reform, and the last large victory for defenders of the 1920s quota laws.

The End of the Bracero Program

Before returning to the national origins quotas, the United States faced a final reckoning with the bracero program. After Operation Wetback was implemented in 1954, bracero workers arrived in even greater numbers. Labor unions, immigrant rights advocates in the Mexican American community, and religious and welfare organizations continued their criticism of the program. They argued that the braceros drastically undercut farm wages and tightened the labor market. They called into question the morality of a program that put workers in exploitative conditions. Moreover, by the 1960s the bracero program's opponents also effectively harnessed the language of rights, equality, and freedom coursing through American politics during the Black civil rights movement. As Henry González, a Democrat from Texas, thundered, "If we need the Mexican laborer, why not let him come here in freedom as our parents did and as a free man?"[15] These critiques found large and increasingly outraged audiences in prominent television, newspaper, and magazine exposés.

Support for the program collapsed along two fronts. First, the Kennedy administration and liberals in Congress took up the fight in Washington, D.C., no doubt influenced by the lobbying campaigns of the program's opponents. The growers won a two-year extension of the program in 1961, but Congress inserted new measures designed to protect the wages of U.S. farmworkers. The Kennedy administration also began to slow the admission of braceros, bringing it below 200,000 in 1962 for the first time in ten years (see table 9.4). Second, agricultural interests grew less dependent on and devoted to the program. They tired of the government's increasing regulations and oversight. More important, greater mechanization came to sugar beet, cotton, and tomato crop production in the early 1960s, meaning those farmers required fewer workers to get their harvests out of the fields. The agricultural industry, the principal supporters of the program, saw its need for braceros decline, and it acted accordingly.

The bracero program's demise came with a whimper. In 1963 the growers had the votes in Congress for only a one-year extension, which they won. But key political supporters in the Senate announced they would not ask for more. The bracero program ended in 1964. The idea behind the program, mainly the importation to the United States of temporary workers from poor countries to fill arduous, low-wage jobs, remained a part of conversations about immigration well into the twenty-first century, however.

The End of National Origins Quotas

After their defeat in 1952, immigration advocates continued to press their case. While they won few results over the next decade, they did hone their arguments and proposals and build support for reform. In 1965 they finally achieved their goal, and much like the bracero program's conclusion, that victory was a relatively quiet one.

A few factors explain the timing. Foremost, the civil rights movement, which made the eradication of discrimination on the basis of race the central political project of American society by the early 1960s, helped the cause. Immigration reformers, to use a racing term, drafted on that effort by arguing that the elimination of the discriminatory quotas naturally followed on the elimination of Jim Crow. Second, the establishment of postcolonial independent nations in Asia and Africa in the late 1950s and 1960s changed the thinking of American foreign policy makers. They now sought those nations as allies in the Cold War and thus had to consider their views on, and objections to, policies that discriminated against their Asian and African citizens. This dynamic made the case for eliminating discriminatory quotas that affected those nations that much more powerful, just as it made the case for ending racial segregation in the United States. Changes in American politics in the mid-1960s proved vital as well. Though Kennedy had a longer history of engagement on immigration issues, having emerged as a leading liberalizer in the Senate in the late 1950s, President Johnson proved a defter shepherd of legislation. He also benefited from the strongly liberal and Democratic Congress seated in 1965, a product of his overwhelming 1964 presidential election. Those congressional margins, and the liberal energy they represented, fueled the passage of his Great Society legislation, including immigration reform.

As the reform push came to fruition in 1964 and 1965, the elimination of national origins quotas was almost a foregone conclusion. But reformers also read the polls and knew that the public strongly hoped that overall immigration levels would remain steady under the new system. So immigration reformers quickly acceded to a cap on the total number of immigrants arriving from the Eastern Hemisphere, and to a preference system that once again favored potential immigrants with skills or with relatives already in the United States.

The discussion on immigration from the Western Hemisphere proved more of a sticking point. That region was not part of the quota system designed in the 1920s, though it operated under the preference system put in place in 1952. The State Department especially argued against a Western Hemisphere cap, fearing that it would anger American allies in the region. Immigration restrictionists countered that any reform ought to bring Western Hemisphere policies in line with the policies for the rest of the world, meaning a cap on total immigration from each hemisphere but no quotas. The fairness argument proved poor cover for the desire of immigration opponents to limit the arrival of people of color from the Americas. Even some immigration reform supporters, such as labor unions, agreed to a Western Hemisphere cap, though in the case of labor it had more to do with long-standing fears of increased competition in labor markets than it had to do with race. While the majority of immigration liberalizers probably hoped to avoid a Western Hemisphere cap, they chose not to sacrifice the quota system's destruction to that cause.

The reform proposal, called the Hart-Celler Bill after its two main sponsors, Senator Philip Hart of Michigan and Representative Emanuel Celler of New York, moved through both houses of Congress without much drama. One historian described the debates over the bill as "often flatulent."[16] The final legislation passed easily, and Johnson soon signed it on a sunny day underneath the Statue of Liberty.

President Johnson signs the 1965 immigration reform law.
Lyndon B. Johnson Presidential Library, Austin, Texas.

Table 10.1. Major Features of the 1965 Immigration Reform Law

Hemispheric visa quotas:	Eastern Hemisphere: 170,000 visas Western Hemisphere: 120,000 visas
Country limit (Eastern Hemisphere only, until 1976):	20,000 visas per one country annually
Preference system—percentage of visa allocations (Eastern Hemisphere only, until 1976):	Family reunification categories—74% Employment categories—20% Refugee category—6%
Exempt from the preference system:	Spouses, parents, and unmarried minor children

The new law, not slated to take full effect until 1968, had several basic elements (table 10.1). It set visa quotas for each hemisphere (170,000 for the Eastern and 120,000 for the Western) and allowed spouses, unmarried children under the age of eighteen, and parents of U.S. citizens to enter without counting against the hemispheric quotas. In the Eastern Hemisphere, the law limited how many visas any one country could claim in one year. Under the Eastern Hemisphere cap, it tweaked the existing preference system that guided allocation of those visas, with family reunification taking priority and employment categories and refugees accounting for the rest of the visa allocations. Those winning an employment-based visa in the Eastern Hemisphere needed certification from the Department of Labor. The refugee preference meant that just over 17,000 refugees from communism and the Middle East (as defined in the law) could enter each year, finally putting in place permanent, significant annual refugee admissions.

The Western Hemisphere did not have a preference system under the 1965 reforms, but all applicants for visas had to obtain labor certification from the Department of Labor. The process of labor certification was somewhat complicated. The Department of Labor published a list of occupations, mainly in the sciences and medicine, that did not require a certification. If a migrant worked in one of those professions, he or she could enter without a labor certification. But if he or she did not, then the migrant had to win from the Labor Department a certification that the United States lacked

workers in the field in which the migrant planned to find employment and that the migrant's addition to the labor force would not
cause wages or working conditions to deteriorate. The labor certification program, which almost all Western Hemisphere migrants
had to pass through, nodded to labor unions' fears of an influx of
migrants from Mexico and the Caribbean.

In the wake of the 1965 reforms, all observers believed the law
had ended the national origins quotas, but perhaps it had not accomplished much else that was revolutionary. Immigration liberalizers
celebrated the demise of the quotas, but immigration opponents
actually had something to cheer as well. They had won a Western
Hemisphere cap, a tool that potentially limited immigration from
Mexico and the Caribbean—though in the latter case the elimination of the 1952 law's limit on one hundred visas to each Caribbean
colony proved a boon. The new system promised to maintain overall legal immigration to the United States at levels roughly equivalent to those of the previous four decades. And they had managed to
prioritize family reunification in immigration. They reasoned that
a policy that favored newcomers with ties to families in the United
States, whose ethnonational makeup had been crafted by forty years
of the national origins system, would effectively perpetuate that
ethnonational makeup without national origins quotas. President
Johnson well summed up the thinking of the period, which would
in time prove incorrect: "This bill that we sign today is not a revolutionary bill. It does not affect the lives of millions. It will not
reshape the structure of our daily lives, or really add importantly to
our wealth or our power."[17]

With the 1965 law in place, Congress authored only small reforms to it in the 1970s, most of which consolidated or clarified
the basics of the new immigration system. In 1976 Congress extended the preference system for immigrants from the Eastern
Hemisphere to the Western Hemisphere, and it placed an annual
limit of 20,000 immigrants from any one country in the Western
Hemisphere, the same as for the East. In 1978 President Carter
signed legislation combining the Eastern and Western Hemisphere
quotas into a single global quota of 290,000. The law also established the Select Commission on Immigration and Refugee Policy
(SCIRP) to study immigration as well as refugee policies. In 1981

that bipartisan commission, headed by Notre Dame's President Theodore Hesburgh, produced its findings. It unequivocally endorsed legal immigration to the United States at current levels, but just as unequivocally it asserted that so-called illegal immigration represented a threat to economic prosperity and American sovereignty. Any changes to immigration law, the commission averred, ought to avoid the racial and ethnic discrimination that had marked earlier reform efforts and address, foremost, the "illegal" immigration issue. Indeed, Americans would spend much of the late twentieth century focusing on "illegal" immigration.

Vietnamese and Indochinese Refugees

As immigration laws and policies evolved in the 1960s and 1970s, refugees continued to arrive in the United States. And they entered even as major changes reset American engagement with refugees. Those changes began with the 1965 immigration law that set aside about 17,000 visas for refugees, but they soon accelerated beyond that relatively modest reform.

The key refugee problem of the 1970s from the American viewpoint sprang out of the Vietnam War and its aftermath. With the collapse of South Vietnam in 1975, the United States decided, relatively quickly, to bring many of its South Vietnamese allies to the safety of the United States rather than leave them to face what Americans believed would be vicious retribution from the victorious North. As a result, in April and May 1975, the United States admitted about 130,000 Vietnamese refugees. Republican President Gerald Ford, and many in the State Department and military who had developed close relationships with the South Vietnamese, spoke of an American responsibility to former allies as part of a larger diplomatic effort to demonstrate America's mettle even in the face of defeat. At the same time, Democratic Senator Edward Kennedy also vouched for the country's responsibility to Vietnamese refugees, but he instead framed it as a moral drive to alleviate suffering, a position clearly influenced by Kennedy's interest in human rights.

Kennedy's thinking quickly found another outlet in southeast Asia, as more refugees looked to escape the instability, chaos, and conflict of Vietnam and Laos, and the murderous regime of Pol Pot in Cambodia. In 1978 and 1979 tens of thousands of refugees from these nations fled each month, often on boats so rickety and danger- ous that around half of the crafts sank, giving these refugees their famous moniker, "the boat people." Estimates hold that around one- third of the boat people perished at sea, a death toll in the tens of thousands.[18] Phat Bui left Vietnam with family members, but not his mother or siblings, in 1979 at the age of seven because "there was no future for any of us."[19] Escaping by boat, Bui recalled, "you don't know if you're going to make it or not. It's pretty much a toss-up . . . either you survive the trip, or you don't."[20] Bui and his family made a decision to jump off their boat for an American oil rig, where they were rescued and sent to a refugee camp in Indonesia. Life in the camp was extremely difficult, as shelter and basic necessities were scarce. And yet Bui counted himself fortunate: others on the boat he left, he learned later, succumbed to starvation and the elements.

The boat people were not the only ones leaving Vietnam, Laos, and Cambodia. Hundreds of thousands of refugees also fled over- land into Thailand and China. In any event, the world witnessed this humanitarian catastrophe in real time on television, in magazines, and in newspapers. The international community responded with some help. Australia and France were generous in refugee admis- sions, and the international community helped provision the ref- ugee camps rapidly filling up in Southeast Asia. The United States offered the most aggressive response. In 1980 alone, the United States allowed 160,000 Indochinese refugees to enter through pa- role; about 300,000 came between 1978 and the early 1980s.[21] Phat Bui arrived in the United States in the early 1980s, resettling first with family in Port Arthur, Texas, and then in Chicago. Bui became a U.S. citizen around age eighteen, changed his name to Patrick Lam, and soon brought his mother and siblings to the United States The family excelled in the classroom: Patrick became a doctor, his sister an accountant, and another brother an electrical engineer.

Complicated thinking underlay the U.S. decision to admit the Indochinese. Several reasons existed for the United States not to pursue refugee admissions. The United States suffered from a weak economy in the late 1970s. After Vietnam, a significant portion of the public wished to wash the country's hands of southeast Asia altogether. Finally, the Indochinese did not have the racial backgrounds of other refugees the United States had helped over the previous decades. But American foreign policy leaders urged that aiding these refugees buttressed the American position in Asia and in world politics. Advocates for refugees, from Democratic President Jimmy Carter to neoconservative Jews, insisted that Indochinese admissions harmonize with notions of human rights, in effect making those abstract principles concrete.

The Indochinese admissions proved vital in a few ways. They broke the color line in American refugee admissions, as the country brought in large numbers of nonwhite refugees for the first time. By emphasizing human rights, they also showed that the justifications for refugee entry had moved beyond mere reflexive anticommunism. This triumph of human rights thinking had its roots in the rescue of South Vietnamese refugees, the efforts in the 1970s to help Jews fleeing persecution in the Soviet Union, and the support in the early 1970s for leftist dissidents trying to escape the brutality of the rightist Pinochet regime in Chile, but the Indochinese episode represented its apotheosis.

The Refugee Act of 1980

The Indochinese crisis also helped set the stage for a major overhaul of refugee policy. Public opinion about refugees in post-1945 decades grew more complicated. In the 1950s, with the Refugee Relief Program and the Hungarian admissions, the public essentially split, as supporters of refugee entry slightly outnumbered opponents. But by the late 1970s, as Congress contemplated vital changes to refugee law and admissions, a more complex picture of public opinion emerged. Strong majorities of Americans expressed doubts about refugee entry, especially of the Indochinese and Cubans. This was buttressed by general misgivings, based on economic fears, about immigrants. Even here, though, some hope for refugee advocates emerged. More Americans than not believed that refugees would be welcomed into their local community. Refugee advocates, like their immigration liberalizer colleagues, had to slalom through sometimes conflicting trends in public opinion as they contemplated reform.

That reform came with the Refugee Act of 1980. It secured a few major and long-standing policy objectives of refugee advocates like Senator Ted Kennedy, who played the key role in securing its passage. The law redefined a refugee as a person who cannot live in his or her home country because of persecution or a "well-founded fear of persecution" on the basis of "race, religion, nationality, membership in a particular social group, or political opinion."[22] The law, then, broadened the definition of refugee by emphasizing that refugees were victims of persecution regardless of political geography or ideology, a reform that both brought the U.S. definition of refugee more in line with international norms and partially unharnessed it from its origins in the early Cold War. Equally important, the 1980 legislation provided for the annual admission of 50,000 refugees. To determine those admissions, the president and State Department consulted with Congress each year about how those refugee visas would be allocated by region and country, though the Executive Branch retained final say. If the president determined that circumstances dictated refugee admissions greater than 50,000, he could consult with Congress on a larger number. Finally, the law provided for the allocation of 5,000 of those annual refugee visas to those seeking asylum. Asylees met the definition of refugee, but whereas a refugee made his or her bid for refugee status and protection outside the United States, an asylee claimed refugee status in the United States or at the U.S. border.

The law passed by comfortable margins in 1980. None of its drafters thought much of the asylum sections of the law, in part because so few individuals made such claims annually in the 1970s. Two other portions of the law garnered much discussion. Human rights supporters and refugee advocates pushed hard for the more capacious definition and the larger annual commitment to admissions, arguing that American global leadership required it and that the law demonstrated American fealty to human rights. Immigration restrictionists, who generally opposed refugee admissions, objected to both the mushy language about consultation, believing it granted too much discretion to the Executive Branch, and the 50,000 annual entries. Yet, in the midst of the Indochinese episode, they reasonably could look at the law as perhaps rationalizing refugee admissions and curtailing the mass paroles of refugees that had become common as the crisis exploded.

A boat carrying Cubans arrives in Florida during the 1980 Mariel refugee crisis. Wright Langley Collection, Florida Keys Public Library.

Implementation of the 1980 refugee law proved more difficult than any of those who had drafted the legislation might have imagined. In one sense, events rather quickly overtook the law. In the spring of 1980, Cuban refugees began departing, with Castro's approval, from the port of Mariel for the United States. About 125,000 made the passage over the rest of the year, many in unseaworthy boats, and landed mainly in Florida.[23]

Carlos de la Arena recalls the thinking among Cubans readying to leave: "There was so much discontent in Cuba in those days that many left everything they owned.... Their ideology—for or against the revolution—did not matter."[24] De la Arena was an automobile driver on the island, a job that he found unfulfilling but the only one he could hold because of the Cuban government's "system."[25] After a harrowing twenty-hour boat trip, de la Arena and his wife and young son arrived in Key West, the sight of which he later said was "almost like seeing God."[26] He adjusted well to life in his new country, eventually running a plumbing business in Florida, though he admits, "I still feel Cuban even after living in the United States longer than I lived in Cuba."[27]

The Mariel Cubans, or Marielitos, won less sympathy than their predecessors had. Castro unsurprisingly derided them as the trash of Cuban society. But some in the Cuban community in Florida rejected them as well, in part because these newcomers came from the lower classes and in part, it seems, because more of the Marielitos were Black or of mixed racial heritage than previous Cuban refugees. When the American media, echoing Castro, began reporting that large numbers of criminals, drug addicts, and homosexuals entered among the Marielitos, public support for their admission crumbled. Such portrayals even found their way into popular culture. The hit 1983 film *Scarface* starred Al Pacino as an equally ambitious and vicious Marielito who became a South Florida drug kingpin.

The challenge of the Cuban situation was compounded when, that same year, large numbers of Haitians fleeing the repressive rightist government of "Baby Doc" Duvalier began to land in Florida. Upwards of 12,000 arrived in 1980, a surge compared to earlier numbers.[28] One of them was Antoine (his pseudonym), a father of four in his late forties who had not worked in four years in his profession of mining. Antoine and about thirty other Haitians fixed up an old boat and sailed for eleven days, using the sun as navigation, before landing in the United States. When they arrived, American authorities apprehended them. Antoine explained how economic and political reasons intermingled in his decision to leave Haiti: "I went three years with my mouth closed. I could not talk about the government. If I did, I could get no job. When you are not part of the government family, you are not allowed to work or do anything."[29]

Haitians, of course, fled to the United States throughout the 1970s, landing and then trying, usually unsuccessfully, to claim asylum. Critics noted that, in sharp contrast, during the 1960s and 1970s another group of refugees fleeing a Caribbean island, the Cubans, almost automatically won admission. Supporters of the Haitian refugees in the NGO and legal communities asserted that the Haitians encountered both political bias (they fled a putative American ally) and racial discrimination, because most were Black. To fight what they saw as unjust treatment, refugee advocates in the late 1970s responded to the nearly blanket refusal of the U.S. government to admit Haitians by taking these cases to court to try to push for admission.

All this added up to one sticky situation for President Carter. The federal courts clarified Carter's options somewhat in the summer of 1980, ordering the government to revise its admissions process regarding Haitians and not to reject their asylum applications out of hand. Carter then decided to continue the American policy of admitting Cubans fleeing the island, even though most evidence suggested that those arriving in Florida, while not criminals, drug addicts, or gay, also did not qualify as long-standing political opponents of the regime but instead came north looking for economic opportunity. Likewise, Carter chose to admit Haitians who arrived before June 19, 1980 (a deadline soon pushed to October 11, 1980), while those who arrived after that last date had to pass through a new, and supposedly fairer, admissions process. Instead of admitting the Cubans and Haitians under the Refugee Act, the administration created a special category of "Cuban-Haitian entrant" and paroled them into the United States. Carter left it to Congress to resolve the immigration status of both groups, which it did a few years later by permitting them to apply for legal permanent residence. There was one final twist to the Haitian policy: in early 1981 the Reagan administration began intercepting Haitians on the ocean and returning them to the island, a policy called interdiction that aimed to deny them the chance to land and apply for asylum.

The Cuban and Haitian refugee populations, and the U.S. response to them, indicated two things as the United States engaged with other, future refugee populations. Cold War foreign policy considerations continued to play a key role in determining the admission of refugees, even after the Refugee Act. Equally important, the administration of the Refugee Act would prove quite controversial and challenging.

In time, the reform of immigration law in 1965 proved one of the great examples in American history of how new legislation can unleash a series of unintended consequences. Lyndon Johnson and others predicted no great changes in immigration, but the law contained loopholes and provisions that opened avenues for many more immigrants to come to the United States. The same might be said, on a smaller scale, of the Refugee Act of 1980. Moreover, because of global economic, political, and cultural changes, the majority of those newcomers came from different parts of the world than had previously sent immigrants and refugees to the United States. The changes encouraged by these laws helped create a new era in American immigration history as the twentieth century came to a close.

Further Reading

FitzGerald, David, and David Cook-Martin. *Culling the Masses: The Democratic Origins of Racist Immigration Policy in the Americas* (2014).

Kami, Hideaki. *Diplomacy Meets Migration: US Relations with Cuba during the Cold War* (2018).

Lindskoog, Carl. *Detain and Punish: Haitian Refugees and the Rise of the World's Largest Immigration Detention System* (2018).

Loescher, Gil, and John Scanlan. *Calculated Kindness: Refugees and America's Half-Open Door, 1945–Present* (1986).

Marinari, Maddalena. *Unwanted: Italian and Jewish Mobilization against Restrictive Immigration Laws, 1882–1965* (2019).

Tichenor, Daniel. *Dividing Lines: The Politics of Immigration Control in America* (2002).

CHAPTER ELEVEN

A New Open Door

Immigration in the Twentieth Century's Last Decades

RACHEL ARRIVED FROM THE Philippines in 1992. Trained as a nurse, she caught wind of American hospitals recruiting from her nursing school and eventually received a job offer. Nursing paid much better in the United States than the Philippines, so Rachel began sending six hundred dollars a month to her family. Even then, she had enough left over to spend on a car, good food, and clothes. Rachel, along with thousands of other Filipino nurses in the late 1980s and early 1990s, entered the United States through a program designed to help alleviate nursing shortages. The program allowed the newcomers to apply for permanent residence, which Rachel successfully did in 1994. Some of Rachel's countrywomen met a different fate. By the mid-1990s, hospitals no longer needed nurses and laid off the Filipinos. Without jobs, their permanent resident applications failed. Rachel counted herself lucky. Thousands of Filipino nurses lived unemployed and unauthorized in the United States, dreading a return home.

Rachel's story embodies some key themes in immigration to the United States from 1965 to 2000. She was a woman, and increasing numbers of female immigrants entered the United States, a reversal of earlier male-dominated migrations. She came because of a job, demonstrating how economic opportunity and labor needs still drove immigration. Rachel arrived with authorization and became a citizen, but some of her colleagues could not follow that path, which testifies to the shifting legal statuses that many immigrants held and to the growing presence of unauthorized immigrants. Perhaps most important, Rachel arrived from Asia. In these decades, Asia, Mexico, Central America, and the Caribbean became the major sources of newcomers to the United States, surpassing Europe. To a degree, this immigration from the Americas was unsurprising given the United States' deep ties to these places. Large-scale immigration from Asia, after decades of exclusion and discrimination, was a newer phenomenon, one that took on even more prominence in the twenty-first century.

The twentieth century's last decades, then, launched a new chapter in the nation's immigration history, but one with distinct links to the past. Though these immigrants arrived from different countries and in larger numbers than their predecessors, they came for many of the same reasons and had many of the same experiences in the United States as their forerunners. They were equally important in their contributions to the country, though they touched parts of the United States that previously had been shaped less by immigrants. Immigration at the twentieth century's end mixed the old and the new in fascinating ways.

Transformations

Transformations in the economy and global affairs had vital implications for immigration after 1970. American industry and manufacturing fell into steep decline, bleeding out jobs that newcomers had depended on for decades. Instead, the service sector, with its low wages, high turnover, and poor benefits, became the largest American employer. The finance and technology sectors also grew, generating wealth but not jobs for those lacking education and social advantages. Recessions and downturns damaged the economy as well. While the well-off survived this instability and even prospered in these decades, middle-class wages stagnated and working people suffered even more.

After 1970 the U.S. economy became even more globally integrated, increasing the flow in all directions of goods, money, and people across its borders. Economic relationships with Latin America and Asia, especially China, deepened. But this integration happened most spectacularly along the Mexican border with southern California, Arizona, and Texas. For example, the San Diego–Tijuana, Mexico, border region became an economic powerhouse. In 1990, $3.3 billion in American goods moved south through San Diego, while $3.8 billion in Mexican goods flowed in the opposite direction. About 50,000 Tijuanans worked in San Diego.[1]

The 1994 North American Free Trade Agreement (NAFTA), which created a free trade zone among Canada, the United States, and Mexico, sped this economic integration. NAFTA had an immigration component: it aimed to boost economic development in Mexico, alleviating the need for Mexicans to migrate north in search of better jobs. This proved incorrect. U.S. manufacturing jobs migrated across the border, but Mexican workers continued to move north, with authorization or without, to escape those horrible workplaces. Likewise, Mexico's domestic farming sector could not survive the NAFTA-driven importation of American agricultural products, and it sent more Mexicans to the United States.

The era offered a key lesson. If capital and goods proved mobile, so did labor. This lesson held for the highly skilled and educated in the workforce. In India, China, Eastern Europe, and across the developing world, those trained in medicine, computing, and engineering set off to the United States, Canada, and Western Europe, which for the most part happily received them.

Transformation also came to the international arena as the Cold War wound down between 1970 and 1990 and the Soviet Union collapsed. For many observers the Cold War's end made clear the triumph of liberal capitalism and free markets. The U.S.-led global economic order in the post–Cold War world, often called the Washington Consensus, embraced free markets, liberal trade and capital flow, and economic regulations and programs designed to foster this form of capitalism. Such thinking stood at the heart of the globalizing U.S. economy discussed above and in agreements like NAFTA.

American policy makers struggled in this new post–Cold War world. Issues like terrorism, failing states, genocide, and the Global South's economic development proved vexing. The Cold War's demise also reshaped global migration. The Iron Curtain's fall opened up migration from the eastern half of Europe. The Soviet empire's collapse reconfigured Eastern Europe and the Balkans, often involving massive population transfers that led some to leave permanently. Though not directly tied to the Cold War, post-1970 political transformations in Africa also led to huge population flows as the last vestiges of white settler colonialism fell and African states struggled with economic development and social stability. In this post–Cold War world, the movement of peoples became entangled with emerging policy issues such as the prevention of terrorism and molded the United States' immigration policy agenda.

Numbers and Origins

The immigration statistics for the last decades of the twentieth century are startling. Total authorized immigration to the United States grew steadily in these decades (table 11.1). Even more dramatically, the places of origin of these newcomers changed. The main sources of immigrants to the United States shifted from Europe to North

Table 11.1. Immigrants, by Region of Origin, to the United States, 1960–1999

Decade	Total Immigration	Regional Leaders
1960s	3,321,700	North and Central America: 1,351,100 Europe: 1,238,600 Asia: 445,000
1970s	4,493,300	North and Central America: 1,645,000 Asia: 1,633,800 Europe: 801,300
1980s	7,338,100	North and Central America: 3,125,00 Asia: 2,817,00 Europe: 705,600
1990s	9,000,000	North and Central America: 3,917,400 Asia: 2,892,200 Europe: 1,311,400

Sources: U.S. Bureau of the Census, *Statistical Abstract of the United States, 1993* (Washington, D.C., 1994), 11; U.S. Bureau of the Census, *Statistical Abstract of the United States, 2003* (Washington, D.C., 2003), 11.

and Central America (which in government statistics included the Caribbean) and to Asia. Immigration from Europe underwent a clear decline. As the economic recovery in Western Europe gained steam, Western Europeans had fewer reasons to migrate to the United States because the chance of a comfortable life at home, or elsewhere in Europe, was within reach. Eastern Europe took up only some of that slack in the 1990s after the end of Iron Curtain restriction on immigration and with generous U.S. refugee policies for Eastern Europe. At the same time, arrivals from Asia and North and Central America surged, more than making up for the European decline. Even immigration from Africa picked up in these years; 383,000 entered in the 1990s, about double the number from the previous decade.[2] In the twentieth century's last two decades, Mexico, the Philippines, Vietnam, China, and India sent the most immigrants, in that order, to the United States. Four of those countries were, of course, in Asia, a striking fact that hints at changes to come in the new century.

The overall number of authorized admissions, even discounting the refugees entering, who pumped up those total numbers, far surpassed the hemispheric, and then global, quotas established by the 1965 law and its subsequent amendments (see table 11.1). How? The 1965 law allowed immediate family members of American citizens to enter the United States outside the quotas, but they still counted as newcomers to the country. Thus, immigrants who became citizens could bring in family relatively easily. The 1965 reform also gave preference within the quotas to siblings of citizens, who, after they obtained citizenship, could then bring in immediate relatives outside the quotas. This dynamic, which some have called "chain" migration, was an unintended consequence of the 1965 reform. In 1995, a fairly representative year, 720,000 immigrants came to the United States, but just over 222,000 were immediate family members of citizens and thus outside the overall quota.[3] The historian Roger Daniels correctly notes a caveat to these admissions statistics. Annual admissions technically included tens of thousands of people already living in the United States, but without legal authorization, who then received permission (technically called an adjustment of status) that made them permanent residents. These people did not truly enter the United States because they already lived there, but their immigration status change qualified them as immigrants.[4]

Table 11.2. Estimated Unauthorized Population in the
United States, 1980–2000

Year	Estimated Unauthorized Population
1980	2.0 million
1986	3.2 million
1990	3.5 million
1995	5.7 million
2000	8.6 million

Sources: Pew Research Center, *Facts on U.S. Immigrants, 2018*,
"Unauthorized Immigrant Population," https://www.pew
research.org/hispanic/2020/08/20/facts-on-u-s-immigrants/;
Jeffrey Passel and Karen Woodrow, "Geographic Distribution
of Undocumented Immigrants: Estimates of Undocumented
Aliens Counted in the 1980 Census by State," *International
Migration Review* 18, no. 3 (1984): 645; Ruth Ellen Wasem,
"Unauthorized Aliens Residing in the United States: Estimates
since 1986," Congressional Research Service, September 22,
2011, https://trac.syr.edu/immigration/library/P5844.pdf.

Two other types of newcomers also came in greater numbers in
these decades. First, about 1 million refugees arrived in each of the
twentieth century's last two decades, a jump from the 539,000 admitted in the 1970s.[5] The largest numbers came from Indochina, Cuba,
and Central America. These particular refugees often fled political,
economic, or social instability, and sometimes wars fomented by the
U.S. government or American interests. Once in the United States,
many helped cement the larger change in the sources of newcomers
to the country because, as citizens, they could bring in relatives.

Second, the number of persons in the United States without legal authorization jumped during these decades (table 11.2). Almost
half of these unauthorized entries came from Mexico, though large
numbers also arrived in the 1980s and 1990s from El Salvador, Guatemala, the Dominican Republic, and Haiti. Smaller numbers came
from Columbia, Ecuador, China, and the Philippines.

The experiences of unauthorized immigrants varied. Some
entered legally, for example on a tourist or student visa, and then
stayed in the United States after that visa expired. Others entered
the country by means of legal procedures, but perhaps under false
pretenses or with fraudulent documents. Those who overstayed

tourist or student visas enjoyed a relatively easy crossing, while those who purchased documents faced a more stressful border entry. A study in the early 2000s posited that more than half of unauthorized migrants residing in the United States originally entered after successfully navigating an inspection at the border, numbers that probably held for the late twentieth century.

Large numbers of individuals also entered the United States by crossing the border without permission. Some made that frightening journey themselves or with family members. But in the late twentieth century, when the border was more well protected, many came to depend on smugglers. Mexicans and Central Americans worked with "coyotes," who charged at minimum a few hundred dollars for passage to the United States. Likewise, unauthorized entry of Chinese immigrants by smuggling picked up in the 1980s, especially from the Fujian province, which sent the vast majority of its migrants to New York City. By the mid-1990s, about 100,000 Fujian natives lived in New York, joined by another 10,000 annually, a significant percentage of whom in either case were unauthorized.[6] The Chinese smugglers, known as "snakeheads," established sophisticated transnational networks that provided illegal passage for a hefty price, sometimes as much as tens of thousands of dollars. Considering the dangers inherent in unauthorized entry, the draw of the United States must have been immense.

The upshot of these immigration changes was a more diverse United States at the twentieth century's end, when the foreign-born population stood at 10 percent, up from 5 percent in 1970. In 2000 the country was 75 percent white, 12.3 percent Black, 12.5 percent Hispanic, and 3.6 percent Asian.[7] (These figures tally to more than 100 percent because the census allowed individuals to claim two races.) No matter how problematic the categories, the Hispanic and Asian populations grew at astounding rates, spurred by immigration. The expansion in the arrival of Mexicans during the 1980s and 1990s underlay the larger Hispanic community's growth, of which Mexicans were the largest component. Yet Dominicans and Cubans also came in large numbers, a reminder of the Hispanic community's diversity. American cities especially emerged as multinational centers, but small towns and communities also often sported a diversity unimaginable earlier, all brought on by immigration.

Choosing to Come to America

Why did so many choose to come to the United States in these decades? Several structural factors spurred immigration to the United States. Improved global telecommunications allowed individuals to more quickly learn of new possibilities—jobs, housing, education, family developments—in this country, and then make the decision to come. Immigrants also benefited from more advanced transportation networks in their home countries and globally that eased passage. In the case of Mexico, Central America, and the Caribbean, U.S. economic and foreign policies very often introduced those technological and transportation developments. Those same policies also frequently fomented economic, political, and social instability that drove immigration. Thus, migration to the United States from those places needs to be seen at least in part as resulting from the United States' policies and its creation of an informal empire.

For the millions who entered the United States, though, that decision was, as it was for their predecessors, a deeply personal choice. Many came to improve their economic prospects and find a better job. José Martínez arrived in the fall of 1986 from central Mexico, after determining that he could earn much more money in the United States working as an agricultural laborer than he could at home. Martínez, working in North Carolina harvesting tobacco, stayed for about six months and then returned home. He repeated this migration pattern annually over the next few decades, although he began working in Illinois on a berry farm in the 1990s.

Others came for education that might secure a better future. Born on mainland China in 1955, Kwok-Wai (David) Chan moved with his parents to Hong Kong as a toddler, before coming to the United States at age nineteen with his parents and three siblings. Chan explained that education drove his parents' decision to come to the United States: "They believe we must have the high education to get a future, but in Hong Kong, we don't have that kind of chance."[8]

And still others came for family reasons. Maija Rhee immigrated because of love, but interestingly the relationship originated in a U.S. foreign policy program. Rhee was born in 1943 in Manchuria, but she ended up in South Korea for her childhood as an adoptee. After completing college in South Korea, she came to the United States for graduate work in 1965, eventually earning a degree in library science from the University of Minnesota. She returned to Korea to teach, but some Catholic priests at her university set her up with a U.S. Peace Corps volunteer. She recalled, "They ended up being an unofficial matchmaker for me."[9] She and Michael Devine married in November 1970 and came to the United States a month later.

Finally, some came to escape political volatility, violence, and social instability at home. Nineteen years old when the Khmer Rouge came to power in Cambodia in 1975, Samphoun Em and his family suffered almost unfathomable hardships. The government of Pol Pot forced them from their homes and into labor camps where starvation and torture were omnipresent until the Khmer Rouge's fall in 1979. In 1982 Em fled to a refugee camp in Thailand because he desperately needed medication to treat his asthma. After living in several camps in Thailand, Em came to the United States in the mid-1980s, settling in Minnesota.

Immigrants from countries large and small exemplified all these dynamics. Hundreds of thousands of citizens from the Dominican Republic migrated to the United States in the 1970s and 1980s. Most came for socioeconomic reasons, but some fled the government's political repression. In the 1970s the American-supported Balaguer government produced some macroeconomic growth, but it wrecked the rural agricultural sector. Rural Dominicans moved to urban areas, competing with the poor and the working class for jobs. A new government in the late 1970s incorrectly bet that industrial production and tourism would spark economic growth. By then middle-class, educated Dominicans struggled to find jobs too, and unemployment and poverty rates skyrocketed. In the mid-1980s, the minimum monthly wage in the United States stood six times greater than on the island, which Dominican communities in this country surely communicated back home.[10] The exodus to the United States accelerated, and it was incredibly heterogeneous. Split equally between men and women, the immigrants originated from rural and urban regions and had a variety of educational and employment backgrounds, though male blue-collar workers and laborers counted as the largest group. Educated middle-class Dominicans became more prominent in the 1980s migration.

Chinese immigrants came in larger numbers than Dominicans in the late twentieth century. About 1.5 million Chinese came
to the United States from 1960 to 2000, the pace quickening in
the 1990s.[11] This immigration, which made the Chinese the largest Asian group in the United States, rested on a few factors. The
establishment in 1977 of official relations between China and the
United States eased passage. The Chinese benefited from the 1965
immigration law, coming as students, as professionals, and as investors, all preferred categories. Others entered under family reunification principles, so much so that Chinese Americans nicknamed
the 1965 law the "Brothers and Sisters Act."[12] Finally, many Chinese immigrated after deciding they no longer wished to live under communist rule, especially in the wake of the 1989 Tiananmen
Square Massacre and the Chinese assumption of control of Hong
Kong in 1997.

Chinese immigrants, like their Dominican counterparts, were
extremely heterogeneous. They came from China, Hong Kong, and
Taiwan, and from the Pacific Rim's larger Chinese diaspora. They
were equally male and female. Some had university, or even advanced, degrees and commensurate work experiences. Many others,
though, lacked educational or employment credentials. Ultimately,
the Chinese, and other immigrants of this period, resembled, and
differed from, their newcomer predecessors. Like those who arrived
in the nineteenth and early twentieth centuries, they came largely
in search of economic opportunity. But unlike earlier immigrants,
those entering in the late twentieth century were more likely to be
female and highly educated, factors that shaped immigrant life in
fascinating ways.

Immigrant Experiences

Immigrant communities in the late twentieth-century United States
defied easy categorization. These communities mixed immigrants
who had become U.S. citizens, legal permanent residents of the
United States who maintained their citizenship in another country, individuals who entered the United States through authorized
means and planned to stay either temporarily or for the long term,

and unauthorized entrants. They also contained increasingly large numbers of children of immigrants, or the second generation.

Though every immigrant community had some combination of these groups, the mix in each differed. The Dominican community was one immigrant enclave where members held a variety of legal and citizenship statuses. About 250,000 Dominicans immigrated to the United States in the 1980s, and 340,000 in the 1990s.[13] Anywhere between 75,000 and 200,000 nonimmigrants arrived annually in the 1970s and early 1980s, as well as an unknown number of unauthorized entrants.[14] The Dominican community also included individuals who lived intermittently in the United States and the children born in the United States to Dominican immigrants. The legal status of these individuals clearly changed over time, at the behest of either the government or the individual.

The places where immigrants settled in the United States also changed. During the 1970s and 1980s, five states, and their major cities, received almost all immigrants: California (Los Angeles), Texas (Houston), New York (New York City), Illinois (Chicago), and Florida (Miami).[15] But in the 1990s, other states and regions became magnets for immigration.

Mexican immigrants for decades settled primarily in California and Texas, and smaller numbers migrated to the Midwest, mainly Chicago. But 1990s Mexican immigrants found their way to Nebraska and Iowa, the American South, and New York City. Even small towns attracted them. In Lexington and Schuyler, Nebraska, two towns that hosted meatpacking plants, the Latino, mainly Mexican, communities grew by over 1,000 percent in the 1990s.[16] José Martínez exemplified this trend, settling first in North Carolina before heading to work the orchards in Belleville, a town in southwest Illinois. Along these lines, Brazilians settled in large numbers in Framingham, a small city twenty miles outside Boston. This geographic dispersion surely arose from the availability of jobs, but the availability of affordable housing and a desire to reunite with family and friends also explains how immigrant enclaves grew so quickly and in places that previously had small populations.

Immigrants in these decades also increasingly stayed in the United States. Geography necessitated this decision for Asian immigrants, who had come halfway around the world. Some, like Samphoun Em from Cambodia, could not go back for fear of their own health and safety. More Mexican immigrants, too, eschewed the circular migration pattern of earlier decades. This change arose partly from an important demographic development: Mexican women and children made up a larger portion of the newcomers in the 1980s, although single men still predominated. These women and children came for better jobs and to join family, and they arrived both with and without authorization. Mexican communities, as a result, became more permanent and more structured around families. Large numbers of Filipino and Chinese women arrived too, with equal effects on their immigrant communities. As one Chinese female garment worker declared in 1992: "My husband dare not look down on me. He knows he can't provide for the family by himself."[17] Of course, exceptions occurred. José Martínez returned every year to his family in Mexico and then went back to Belleville, Illinois. He planned to retire in Mexico and saw his children's future there and not in the United States.

As these stories suggest, employment opportunities sustained these immigrant communities. Some did quite well. Immigrants with strong educational backgrounds, especially those from India, China, and Taiwan, moved into the technology sector often on temporary visas. Filipino doctors and nurses fortified health-care provision in the United States. Other immigrant groups embraced entrepreneurial opportunities and the autonomy and potential path to economic comfort they represented. Korean immigrants, whether because of a culture that valued individualism or because the average Korean entrepreneur arrived with about $14,000 in start-up funds, flourished as entrepreneurs.[18] David Chan fulfilled his parents' education goals—he got an accounting degree from the State University of New York, Buffalo—and after a few false starts got a business off the ground with two other partners. He opened a pharmacy that catered to the Chinese immigrant community, the first in New York City. His siblings followed in his successful footsteps, finding well-paying jobs.

The vast majority of immigrants at the twentieth century's end, though, found jobs that required more physical exertion and offered low pay and few benefits. Immigrants increasingly moved into semi- or unskilled positions in the textile, meatpacking, construction, hotel, and restaurant industries. Indeed, David Chan's parents worked in

*Chinatown, New York City, late twentieth century. Photographs
in the Carol M. Highsmith Archive, Prints and Photographs
Division, Library of Congress, Washington, D.C.*

jobs—at a restaurant and in the garment industry—in which so
many first-generation immigrants congregated. The agricultural
sector remained an important employer of recent immigrants, as
José Martínez demonstrated, even though mechanization steadily
eliminated jobs. Agricultural work was also no longer concentrated
in Florida and California at the century's end, as it had spread to
farms in Georgia, North Carolina, and New York.

Mexican immigrants, as just one example, found their way into
all these challenging jobs. In California's Central Valley, Mexican
immigrants picked fruit and vegetables. The work was backbreaking, low paying, inconsistent, and dangerous; in 1988 farmwork
rated as the most deadly profession. Immigrant farmworkers earned
between $3,500 and $5,000 annually during the agricultural season.[19] Mexican women toiled in Los Angeles's sweatshops, the cen-

ter of domestic apparel production. One estimate held that a $100 dress returned $6 in wages to the seamstress who made it.[20] Those Los Angeles jobs came at a price for a different immigrant group, though. Those positions had migrated to Los Angeles from New York City, where female Dominican immigrants in the 1970s and 1980s had taken those apparel industry positions only to see them disappear. Mexican immigrants flocked to the hotel industry as well, causing Mexican populations in resort areas like Las Vegas and Vail, Colorado, to surge between 1980 and 2000. This sector paid poorly and demanded vigorous labor. The same could be said for Mexican immigrants who joined the restaurant industry. Restaurants across the country happily hired Mexican immigrants, asking very few questions about legal status, and came to depend on them to undertake the difficult labor that makes every restaurant function.

Immigrants and Economic Mobility in the Late Twentieth Century

Did these jobs provide social and economic mobility for immigrants? Compared to the options in their countries of last residence, employment in the United States proved vastly preferable. But the degree of social and economic mobility experienced by immigrants in this country varied immensely. Education, acquired either overseas or in the United States, proved a key determinant of an immigrant's ability to climb the social and economic ladder. Some evidence suggests that Chinese, Indian, and Korean immigrant families pushed their children to achieve in school and find professional careers. This phenomenon had drawbacks, specifically in the "model minority" idea, but it also demonstrated the possibilities that the United States could afford newcomers.

Similarly, the historian José Limón reports the percentage of "Spanish origin" white-collar and skilled workers rose in Texas between 1950 and 1980, while the percentage of unskilled workers declined.[21] The U.S.-born children of Mexican immigrants fueled this growth, although recently arrived, mostly Mexican, immigrants surely played a role. Finally, Dominicans in New York achieved comparable successes in the 1980s. Many, even those living in or near poverty, still reported that they enjoyed a middle-class lifestyle. Roughly 20 percent of New York's Dominicans even sent a monthly remittance of about one hundred dollars to relatives on the island.[22]

Other statistics and stories offer a less sunny answer. Without education, immigrants could not secure high-paying, upwardly mobile jobs. Hispanic communities especially suffered because only about 5 percent of Hispanic immigrants graduated from college.[23] Even those newcomers with desirable credentials sometimes ran into problems. As the 1990s technology sector boomed, Mexican immigrants with competitive résumés encountered discriminatory work cultures and hiring practices.

Immigrants on the employment ladder's lower rungs confronted even more challenges as wages either fell or remained rock-bottom in several immigrant-heavy sectors. Thus, by the mid-1990s about 35 percent of New York City's Dominican community lived in poverty, whereas Mexican immigrants in Los Angeles, both male and female, lost substantial ground in income relative to native-born white men and women between 1960 and 1990.[24] But falling or depressed wages were not the only problems. Structural economic changes, inadequate public education and housing options in poorer neighborhoods where new immigrants often settled, and newcomers' ineligibility for government programs designed to help those struggling with economic, employment, or medical challenges all played a role, too. One peek at the camps of undocumented, mostly Mexican, immigrants in San Diego in the 1980s, living in the city's wooded ravines in plastic or cardboard makeshift dwellings, demonstrated the utterly precarious existence facing many newcomers.

No group better encapsulated these dichotomous experiences than Chinese immigrants. Chinese with training in engineering, medicine, computer science, and the law, as well as those of substantial means who looked to invest in the United States, did quite well, buying homes and supporting Chinese shops and restaurants in suburban communities. The Chinese had their share of entrepreneurial success stories. One restaurateur viewed his adaptability to an ever-changing market and clientele as a badge of honor. His restaurants shifted cooking styles and menus, moving from Cantonese to Sichuan to Taiwanese, over thirty years. Likewise, he first opened up shop in Houston in 1975, but by 2001 he owned an enormous pan-Asian eatery in Los Angeles.

The success of Chinese immigrants shone brightly in Monterey Park, about ten miles from Los Angeles's Chinatown neighborhood. In 1980 white Anglos dominated Monterey Park, and Asians made up 15 percent of the population. By 1995 Asians (mostly Chinese) accounted for 65 percent and the Anglo cohort had shrunk in half.[25] The transition came with problems, as Anglos disliked displays of Chinese culture. "Will the last American to leave Monterey Park remember to take the flag?" one resident wrote to the local paper.[26] Relations stabilized in the 1990s and the markers of American middle-class success emerged: housing prices boomed and the neighborhood worried about typical suburban issues. Monterey Park did have working-class and impoverished Chinese immigrants, of course, but its middle-class Chinese community dominated the landscape.

At the other end of spectrum, Chinese immigrants labored as restaurant and laundry workers, apparel makers, and domestics. In some cities, Chinese women dominated these jobs: in the 1990s, they made up 80 percent of the seamstresses in San Francisco and 85 percent of New York City's shrinking number of garment workers.[27] These women worked on the job, and as homemakers, a challenging double shift. All those in these jobs struggled to get by, and the unauthorized immigrants among them fared the worst. Huiling Zhao arrived as an unauthorized Chinese immigrant in 1985 and began work in a restaurant earning $700 a month. That was about $100 less than her legal Chinese coworkers, and she endured workplace bullying. Zhao's circumstances could not have been more different from those of the relatively affluent Chinese who lived in Monterey Park. An interesting symbiosis emerged, however. The Chinese entrepreneurs in labor-intensive industries, like restaurants, succeeded partly because they had access to the low-cost, constantly replenishing labor force of Chinese, especially female, immigrants.

Immigrants and Economic Growth in the United States

What role did immigrants play in the late twentieth-century economy? One interpretation, among those suspicious of authorized and unauthorized immigrants, held that the newcomers damaged the economy. Specifically, they either took jobs from native-born U.S. citizens or increased the supply of labor and thereby drove down wages for U.S. citizens.

This interpretation falters by designing a simple adversarial relationship between immigrants and American citizens. In fact, many U.S. employers needed this immigrant labor and often chose to pay it poorly. The ire of opponents of immigrant entry on this basis should focus on the employers willingly lowballing the wages and working conditions of their immigrant employees.

While some immigrants did loosen some labor markets and drive down some wages, these outcomes occurred in particular contexts. In most cases immigrants took jobs—in the fields, as domestics, and in sweatshops, to name a few—that U.S. citizens did not want, and certainly not at the low wages on offer. Downward pressure on wages in these sectors mainly hurt the various immigrants competing for these jobs. As one U.S. rancher who worked along the border for decades put it: "I would say that the jobs immigrants take—now and historically—have never been filled by those that are long-standing citizens. . . . I don't see a lot of gringos out there looking for jobs that are filled by these immigrants."[28] Well-trained immigrants did compete with native-born Americans for prized jobs in engineering, medicine, and the technology industry. But those jobs already paid well, so the wage competition did not produce such dire circumstances. Even here, immigrants sometimes took jobs Americans did not want. Immigrant doctors, for instance, provided care to rural, underserved communities as the twentieth century ended. Outside Springfield, Illinois, nearly a dozen Filipino doctors opened practices after one of their countrymen began working in the city in 1969.

Ultimately, the late twentieth-century U.S. economy could not have functioned as the vast majority of Americans expected it to without immigrant labor. Immigrants played too central a role in growing, harvesting, and making the food on American tables, building and maintaining American homes and workplaces, making clothes that Americans wore, and providing care and comfort to the sick and aged of the United States.

The revitalization of downtrodden communities often grew from immigrant economic activity. In Flushing, Queens, a borough of New York City, the streets bustled and stores and restaurants filled with Chinese immigrants, but also newcomers from Thailand, Vietnam, and Laos. That scene was repeated in San Francisco, Seattle, and northern Virginia, where immigrants from Asia supplied new verve to depressed corners of those urban centers. In previously overlooked upper Manhattan, Dominicans brought new economic and community vitality. Mexicans and other Central Americans, meanwhile, revitalized dusty, rural corners of the country. In rural agricultural areas, where Mexican and Central American immigrants came to pick crops, some set up restaurants, small retail shops and stores, and other businesses.

The rebirth sometimes came in unpredictable places. Between 1970 and 2000, about 90,000 Brazilians arrived in the United States from the Brazilian state of Minas, many following relatives northward.[29] They came searching for better economic prospects and eagerly sent money back home. In the mid-1980s, large numbers of these Brazilians, the majority unauthorized, started settling in Framingham and Marlborough, two towns twenty miles west of Boston. A decade later, nearly 12,000 lived there, probably the country's highest concentration of Brazilians.[30] In 1990s Framingham, nearly two hundred Brazilian businesses operated, and Brazilians worked in the gardening, housecleaning, and elder- and child-care fields. Many eventually earned enough to run their own businesses.[31]

Fernando Castro was one such immigrant. He began work in the United States in domestic service jobs like housecleaning and home repair, but he parlayed his savings from those jobs into a tax preparation business, One Stop Income Tax, in downtown Framingham. He bragged in 1997, "Of my customers, I guess maybe two hundred have already bought homes," testimony to their hard work and his sound financial advice.[32] The formerly moribund Framingham hummed. The Catholic church emerged as a community center, and Brazilians purchased and fixed up abandoned homes and buildings. The Brazilians' arrival came with costs, such as the expense of local schools' providing bilingual programs. But Framingham's building inspector at the time, Lew Colten, declared immigrants "are the solution, not the problem."[33]

Brazilians in Framingham crafted institutions that eased the adjustment of newcomers and proved their community's foundation. Other immigrant communities followed suit. Sometimes these efforts were informal and familial. Indian immigrants from Gujarat state entered the motel business in the United States in the 1940s, then came to dominate it by the century's end. Two families in particular, the Patels and Bhaktas, set up, or employed, Indian newcomers in the motel business across the country. In Minnesota in the late 1990s, the Hmong community faced a racist backlash after a teenage Hmong American committed infanticide. The Hmong organized Community Action Against Racism, which brought together sympathetic whites and people of color, to protest against those trafficking in discriminatory rhetoric. In Charlotte, North Carolina, which saw stunning growth in the Latino and Mexican communities in the 1980s and 1990s, the Latin American Coalition appeared in 1990. Its main work involved helping the impoverished in the Mexican community and protecting immigrant rights. These community organizations contained both authorized and unauthorized newcomers, and the former often supported the latter. Such help was necessary. The unauthorized often lived their first few years in the United States deeply isolated from family, friends, and social and economic institutions.

Harsh Greetings

Anti-immigrant sentiment surged during the twentieth century's last decades. This development was somewhat surprising. The 1965 reforms passed easily, and many in the political mainstream rejected overt racial and ethnonational discrimination. Yet immigration restrictionism's persistence throughout U.S. history made this surge unremarkable. Most important, the origins of post-1965 immigrants in Asia, Mexico, Central America, and the Caribbean fueled anti-immigrant sentiment. This backlash sometimes manifested as a fear that immigrant traditions perverted dominant cultural norms, a discomfort buttressed by, or based in, racial fears of newcomers who were not white. Worried about or dissatisfied with their jobs, many Americans also blamed the era's economic troubles on immigrants. Finally, though the anti-immigrant sentiment hit all newcomers, it focused on so-called illegal immigrants.

Public opinion polling showed restrictionism's strength. Only a small percentage (between 6 and 14 percent) of Americans between 1965 and 2001 wanted to increase immigration. But from 1977 to 2001 no fewer than 41 percent of those polled wanted immigration to decrease, and the percentage was usually slightly higher.[34] Americans repeatedly stated that too many Asian and Latin American immigrants entered the United States. On the "illegal" immigration issue, a clear majority in the twentieth century's last decades wanted the migrants removed from the United States.[35] In the mid-1990s immigration restrictionism peaked. Between 1993 and 1996, 65 percent of Americans argued for a decrease in immigration to the United States,[36] 62 percent protested that U.S. citizens lost jobs to immigrants, and 30 percent believed that "illegal" immigration was the country's chief challenge.[37]

The Black community split on immigration along these same lines. Black Americans only slightly intersected with immigrants through most of the twentieth century. Before 1920 the majority of Blacks lived in the South, but newcomers avoided the former Confederacy, worrying about lackluster economic opportunities and cultural dislocation. The Great Migration sent African Americans out of the rural South in the 1920s, but national origins policy severely limited immigration. Even so, some Black politicians and journalists in these decades feared economic competition between Blacks and immigrants.

As immigration surged in the twentieth century's last decades, sending newcomers to urban areas and the South, where African Americans resided in larger numbers, the Black community fully confronted the immigration question. Polling showed the majority of African Americans supporting immigration. Many Black leaders allied with immigration defenders, united by an understanding that racial and ethnonational discrimination had similar sources and ill effects. Thus, the Congressional Black Caucus in the 1970s and 1980s joined efforts to bat down anti-immigrant legislation, and

Black politicians such as Jesse Jackson invited immigrants to his movement. Black politicians more slowly came to sympathize with unauthorized immigrants.

But significant opposition to immigrants did exist in Black communities. Some African Americans feared economic competition from immigrants, a notion supported by some research showing that Black employment opportunities and wages dropped as immigrants entered labor markets. Others questioned why newcomers benefited from government resettlement aid while long-standing Black residents saw the social safety net slashed. African American Representative John Conyers (D-Michigan) explicitly raised this question about social welfare programs in 1975: "Should we spend them on Vietnamese 'refugees' or should we spend them on Detroit 'refugees'?"[38] The Black politician Barbara Jordan, a leading voice on immigration, expressed skepticism about unauthorized entries, a concern repeated by a significant minority of Blacks.

What energized immigration restrictionism in these late twentieth-century decades? One explanation stresses the public's economic and cultural fears of newcomers. The other emphasizes a variety of activists who stoked opposition to immigration. Both accounts are reasonable. Yet, to a striking degree, opposition to immigrants flowed from articulate, organized, and passionate interest groups and individuals.

Intellectuals and media figures played a vital role in this era's restrictionism. A varied lot politically, some proved merely suspicious of immigration and others launched blistering attacks. But they all feared that recent immigrants harmed American unity and traditions. Among political liberals, the historian Arthur Schlesinger's 1991 book, *The Disuniting of America*, held two divergent perspectives. Schlesinger rejected virulent anti-immigrant sentiment, writing, "No one wants to be a Know-Nothing."[39] But he also urged the assimilation of contemporary and future immigrants "to lead newcomers to an acceptance of the language, the institutions, and the political ideals that hold the nation together."[40] The last phrase tellingly revealed his worries that the American project might collapse. Schlesinger's unease about immigration displayed how some stalwart liberals, opponents of racial and ethnic discrimination in the 1960s, now wondered about pluralism's drawbacks.

On the political right, Patrick Buchanan was immigration's leading critic. A Republican political operative turned presidential candidate and media personality by the 1990s, the Irish Catholic Buchanan bemoaned the economic and cultural dislocation afflicting everyday Americans. Buchanan traced the former to globalization and trade deals like NAFTA and the latter to immigrants who arrived after 1965. In 1994 he called for a "time-out" on immigration to give the assimilation process time to work and thereby safeguard national unity.[41] In 2000 Buchanan sharpened these arguments during his presidential run, launching his infamous "meatball" campaign advertisement. It featured a middle-aged, middle-class white man choking on a meatball as he dialed 911 for help, only to find himself asked to select his language of choice from an unending menu of options. As the man was lying lifeless on the floor, the narrator intoned, "Immigration is out of control."[42]

A number of restrictionist groups organized supporters and lobbied lawmakers beginning in the late 1970s. Most important, the Federation for American Immigration Reform (FAIR) formed in 1979, led by the Michigan doctor John Tanton. Tanton participated in the early environmental movement and supported efforts to curtail population growth. Fears that too many humans degraded the earth's natural resources and environment led him to the immigration issue. When he failed to interest colleagues at the environmentalist Sierra Club in immigration restriction, Tanton formed FAIR with Roger Connor, another environmental activist. FAIR argued that "immigration is out of control and unchecked immigration complicates the solution to every important problem before the country," revealing how Tanton had moved beyond his beginning supposition that immigrants threatened the environment.[43] FAIR wanted to cut back on quota visas, greatly limit family exemptions, reduce refugee admissions, and crack down on unauthorized entries. FAIR also pushed for sanctions on employers who hired the migrants, more funding for border control, and national identification cards. By the 1990s FAIR's members numbered 70,000 and it had offices on both coasts.

Tanton left FAIR in the mid-1980s, but he stayed in the fight. He formed other anti-immigration organizations; one scholar called him "the godfather . . . of the contemporary anti-immigration movement."[44] Numbers USA focused on reducing immigrant admissions, relying on almost mathematical explanations of how immigration harmed the country. U.S. English, Inc., and Negative Population Growth laced their appeals with images of cultural decline brought on by immigration, sometimes deploying racial stereotyping that denigrated people of color and non-Europeans. As Tanton asked in the mid-1980s: "Will Latin American migrants bring with them the tradition of the *mordida* (bribe), the lack of involvement in public affairs . . . ? What are the implications of changes for the separation of church and state?"[45] FAIR, which sported a sheen of respectability because of its access to major media outlets and powerful politicians, forged connections with some racist extremist groups, and racists sometimes joined FAIR's public demonstrations and protests. FAIR and Tanton vehemently denied that race lay at the center of their immigration stances, arguing that their detractors labeled them racists to delegitimate them.

Immigration restrictionism also bubbled up locally, especially in California. In the 1980s a Tanton-led organization, U.S. English, successfully campaigned in California and a few other states to make English the official state language, though these victories proved hollow. By the early 1990s California suffered from a stale economy, its border regions saw repeated unauthorized crossings, its demography underwent rapid change because of immigration, and its welfare expenditures boomed. Pete Wilson, the incumbent Republican governor, faced a challenging reelection in 1994 as he struggled to tackle these problems. These elements combined to create a revolt against immigration in America's most populous state.

Wilson, who previously supported a guest worker program for California, consulted with FAIR and determined that his reelection rested on slamming unauthorized immigrants as a drain on state resources. Meanwhile, in November 1993, about ten anti-immigration activists, some connected to FAIR, formed a group called Save Our State. They drafted a ballot initiative designed to cut unauthorized immigrants off from California's welfare programs. One recalled the strategy: "It made sense to target the most objectionable recipients first—illegals. Then we could put the issue of too much legal immigration on the table."[46]

These efforts combined in the fall of 1994, when Governor Wilson and Proposition 187, nicknamed the Save Our State Initiative, appeared on the ballot. Prop. 187 proposed severely limiting the access of "illegal aliens" to state education facilities and to publicly funded nonemergency medical care, and it demanded that education and health-care officials verify the immigration status of students and patients. Prop. 187 unleashed a pitched political battle. Wilson promised to enforce it with alacrity. Prop. 187's opponents, a mix of California Democrats, minorities, churches, educators, and doctors, labeled it racist and inhumane. One anti-Prop. 187 poster proclaimed, "Ningun ser humano es ilegal," or "No human being is illegal."[47] Nationally, some Republicans, such as Jack Kemp, joined Democratic President Bill Clinton in condemning Prop. 187. While Clinton sympathized with voters' concerns about unauthorized immigration, he pled for time to allow the federal government to address the problem.

Californians made their preference clear in November. They passed Prop. 187, 59–41 percent, and Governor Wilson comfortably won reelection. Prop. 187's advocates immediately began planning to pass similar laws in other western and southwestern states. Then Prop. 187's momentum dissipated. Quickly, immigrant advocates successfully sued to block most of the initiative from taking effect. Over the next few years, the courts invalidated all its key measures.

Proposition 187 proved a signal moment. In response, California's Latino community began naturalizing in larger numbers. With the right to vote, Latinos moved decisively into the Democratic Party, making it dominant in state politics to this day. Prop. 187 revealed the depth of anti-immigration sentiment, channeled especially toward unauthorized immigrants, and how it could shape politics. National politicians took note. The Clinton White House, in the face of California's rebellion against immigration, moved to embrace its own restrictionist policies. Many Republicans, especially those with national ambitions, saw Wilson's political success and pushed the party toward anti-newcomer extremism. Finally, Prop. 187 foreshadowed the increased role that states would play in immigration policy and politics in the twenty-first century.

Advocating for Immigrants

The opposition to Prop. 187 demonstrated that immigration restrictionism did not go unchallenged in these years. Religious groups, civil and human rights organizations, some labor unions, immigrant communities, and lawyers led the charge against restrictive immigration laws and policies that limited the rights of authorized and unauthorized immigrants. Business interests and free-market ideologues joined the fight for liberal immigration laws, though they expressed less interest in immigrant rights.

Some of the most powerful advocates for immigrants helped Mexican and Central American newcomers. Cesar Chavez built a labor movement among exploited Mexican American and Mexican farmworkers in the fields of California in the 1960s and 1970s. Those workplaces presented two challenges: first, convincing individuals to join the United Farm Workers (UFW) in the face of threats to their employment, and, second, convincing growers to bargain in good faith. Chavez's campaigns, even in simple marches to rally workers, aimed to display the dignity of the Mexican American community and authorized Mexican immigrant workers. This distinction between authorized and unauthorized immigrants mattered. Chavez consistently viewed the latter as potential strikebreakers, even supporting UFW patrols of the border in the early 1970s that sometimes ended in vigilante violence against those crossing without permission. Others in the farmworker movement, even in his own family, disagreed, but the conflict demonstrated how unauthorized immigration roiled those who might sympathize with the UFW. Nonetheless, Chavez's championing of Mexican Americans and recent Mexican immigrants powerfully countered restrictionist thinking.

Latino and Mexican American organizations worked in the courts, in Congress, and in state legislatures to protect immigrant communities. Some, like League of United Latin American Citizens (LULAC), had been around for decades, whereas others, like the Mexican American Legal Defense and Educational Fund (MALDEF) and the National Council of La Raza, formed in the late 1960s. Those latter two groups began with Ford Foundation seed money and aimed to address deeply embedded political and legal discrimination against those of Mexican background.

MALDEF, in many ways analogous to the NAACP's Legal Defense Fund, which delivered the *Brown v. Board* decision, worked
successfully in education policy, achieving its biggest victory in
Plyler v. Doe (1982). A 1975 Texas law denied school districts funding to educate unauthorized immigrant children and permitted a
district to remove those children from school. Some districts even
charged these children a fee to attend public school. The law inevitably drove unauthorized immigrant children from Texas schools.
In 1982 a divided Supreme Court ruled in MALDEF's favor that the
Texas law violated the Fourteenth Amendment's equal protection
clause and that unauthorized immigrant children had a right to public education. The majority opinion saw education as the best way to
prevent "creation of an underclass of future citizens and residents."[48]

This activism occurred as Americans offered up multiple in-
terpretations of how immigrants contributed to society. President
Ronald Reagan celebrated assimilation when he declared that the
United States was a place "where the old antagonism could be cast
aside and the people of every nation could become one."[49] The liberal Democrat Shirley Chisolm lauded immigration by emphasizing pluralism. In "Unity through Diversity," a speech she regularly
gave in the early 1990s, Chisolm asserted: "We are nobody's melting
pot! We are a beautiful, giant salad bowl."[50] Chisolm and Reagan
approvingly started from the premise that immigrants contributed
immensely to the United States' past and present.

Chisolm's comments resonated with the "white ethnic revival"
of the early 1970s. In this phenomenon, descendants of European
immigrants, mainly those discriminated against by national origins
policy, rejected assimilation and adherence to Anglo-Protestant
norms. Instead, they saluted the cultural and social traditions of
their ethnicity. This ethnic revival, inspired partly by the Black civil
rights movement and its celebration of African American culture,
manifested itself across American life. For instance, *The Godfather*
movie series applauded Italian Americans, finding the roots of their
enviable traits like loyalty, dedication to family, and industriousness
in the old country.

White ethnics also began to commemorate their ancestors'
foods and recipes. In the 1970s, local immigrant enclaves sometimes published community cookbooks that memorialized favorite

recipes for future generations.[51] These books contained some outright paeans to heritage, and they often featured both obviously ethnic recipes and everyday family favorites with no antecedents in that specific national cuisine. But as the historian Donna Gabaccia notes, the publication of these community cookbooks arose out of the ethnic revival, cultivating and reflecting the authors' pride in their communities' roots.

By the twentieth century's end, some white ethnics demonstrated an interest in authentic foodways that at times bordered on an obsession. Authenticity was and remains a difficult term when applied to food and recipes. Sometimes it meant forging links back to first-generation immigrant communities, as when suburban Italian Americans headed into Little Italy in the Bronx in search of sausages and fresh mozzarella because "you can't get anything up there" in suburban groceries.[52] The authenticity impulse also came from a desire to reach back to the old country. One of this book's authors recalls the transformation of the Italian dish risotto in his family. In the 1980s the family risotto recipe involved regular rice cooked in tomato sauce and sprinkled with parmesan cheese. By the early 1990s the dish used chicken stock, an onion soffritto, and imported Arborio rice, which produced very different results. The explanation for the change, a simple "this is how they cook risotto in Italy," revealed the pride in heritage and the desire for authenticity.

A slightly different narrative emerged for Asian Americans. Chinese Americans fought immigration restrictions in the midcentury by emphasizing the educational accomplishments, job skills, and family structures of the Chinese, essentially demonstrating the value of Chinese immigration to American life. By the end of the 1960s, this thinking had solidified into a "model minority" trope that valorized Asian Americans, especially the Chinese and Japanese, as the best immigrants. The "model minority" idea in the twentieth century's last decades stressed education and hard work. Indeed, many from Asian immigrant communities succeeded in higher education at stunning rates. In 1990 one-third of California's high school graduates of Asian descent qualified for admission to the state's prestigious university system, compared to 13 percent of whites and about

5 percent of Blacks and Latinos.[53] By the twenty-first century, students of Asian backgrounds made up about one-third of the students in the University of California system.[54]

The model minority idea ambivalently shaped immigration. This narrative challenged the demeaning and racist portrayals of Asians, as well as some of the contemporary restrictionist charges that immigrants harmed the United States. Unsurprisingly, many white Americans lauded the model minority idea, insisting that other racial or ethnic minorities emulate Asian Americans.

Yet the dangers of the model minority idea were very clear. It offered a sweeping generalization of all newcomers from Asia, failing to account for the different national, gendered, and socioeconomic circumstances that powerfully shaped an immigrant's life and opportunities. Not every immigrant from Asia succeeded on the terms laid out by the model minority idea, and some struggled mightily in the United States. Too often, white Americans of European background used the model minority idea to criticize and discriminate against African Americans for failing to climb up the socioeconomic ladder as some Asians had. Finally, the notion that model immigrants possessed a certain educational background and job skills effectively denigrated other newcomers who lacked those hard-to-acquire characteristics but did have a willingness to work hard and in jobs that required physical labor. Critics of the model minority idea contended, then, that a model immigrant group came in many fashions and from many places.

The changes in immigration to the United States reshaped its economy, demography, culture, and social structures, affecting people living in communities large and small across the country. Equally important, the politics and policies surrounding immigration changed as well. In short, opponents and skeptics of immigration reclaimed the momentum in debates about newcomers. The question was whether they could shape immigration and refugee law and policy to their own ends. They certainly tried, the story we turn to now.

Further Reading

Gabaccia, Donna. *We Are What We Eat: Ethnic Food and the Making of Americans* (1998).

Hitchman, Virginia, ed. *La Frontera: Stories of Undocumented Immigrants Crossing the Border* (2014).

Massey, Douglas, ed. *New Faces in New Places: The Changing Geography of American Immigration* (2008).

Reimers, David. *Still the Golden Door: The Third World Comes to America*, 2nd ed. (1992).

Romo, Harriett, and Olivia Mogollon-Lopez, eds. *Mexican Migration to the United States: Perspectives from Both Sides of the Border* (2016).

Weise, Julie. *Corazón de Dixie: Mexicanos in the U.S. South since 1910* (2015).

Zhao, Xiaojian. *The New Chinese America: Class, Economy, and Social Hierarchy* (2010).

CHAPTER TWELVE

Immigration Politics and
Restrictionism, 1970–2001

ROGER CONNOR WAS ANGRY. He and the organization he helped lead, the Federation for American Immigration Reform (FAIR), had fought for years for substantial changes to immigration law. Congress finally delivered in 1986 with the Immigration Reform and Control Act (IRCA). That legislation promised to solve what many, Connor included, saw as the problem of "illegal" immigration. The ink had barely dried on the law when Connor, after reviewing the final product, offered this pithy verdict: "We wanted a Cadillac, we were promised a Chevy, and we got a wreck."[1]

FAIR and Connor were motivated by the incredible changes in the numbers and origins of immigrants in the twentieth century's last decades, literally the unintended consequences of the 1965 law. His comments, and the disappointment they reflect, bring into focus a central question about this period: Was this an age of restrictionism in the politics and policy of immigration and immigration enforcement or an era when the liberalizing tendencies of 1965 still held sway?

This chapter tracks the political, policy, and legal developments that governed who could enter the United States and under what conditions and, increasingly, their treatment once in the United

States. The bipartisan political alliances that for decades brought together some rather strange partners in the pro-immigration and anti-immigration blocs basically held in these years, though they produced increasingly restrictionist outcomes. The legislation of the 1980s, including the 1986 law that Connor disliked, exhibited both restrictionist and liberalizer impulses. But several laws and policies that arrived in the 1990s lacked that balance, instead displaying an animosity toward the arrival of newcomers and their rights once in the United States. Unauthorized immigrants, or who some called "illegal" immigrants, emerged as particular targets. Border policy and enforcement mirrored these changes, as the securing and militarizing of the U.S. border with Mexico continued apace. Refugee policy, too, remained a contested area; admissions fluctuated greatly during the two decades after 1980. Moreover, just as immigration policy makers struggled to appropriately address the migrants in the United States, refugee policy makers had their own vexation: those coming to the United States and applying for asylum.

And then, with immigration restriction and hostility to immigrants already powerful and several policy issues at full boil, the 9/11 terror attacks occurred. Predictably, the United States' response to 9/11 only accelerated these preexisting trends. The attacks further empowered restrictionists in politics and gave them new legal and policy tools with which to enact even more of their vision. The "War on Terror," then, beget attacks on immigrants, both authorized and unauthorized. By the early twenty-first century, Connor's complaining in 1986 looked somewhat silly. He and his allies had won some real victories in the last decade of the century that reoriented the United States' approach toward newcomers.

Political Alignments

Politics in the late twentieth century saw the rise of Republican conservatives and the weakening of the Democratic Party and its governing philosophy of liberalism. As the Democratic Party began to suffer setbacks in the late 1960s, conservatives in the Republican Party grasped this opportunity by offering a compelling economic and social program that seemed in tune with the times and brought electoral triumph. Between 1968 and 2000, Republican conservatives won six presidential elections and made significant headway in Congress. Democrats won, both nationally and at the local and state levels, when they openly questioned liberalism, a telling sign of the country's political temperature. In the process, American politics shifted in a decisively conservative direction.

Internally, both major parties remained heterogeneous on immigration questions. GOP conservatives split into a few, sometimes overlapping camps. Some stressed law and order, the sanctity of the border, and the need to control the arrival of newcomers in the name of national sovereignty. Others displayed suspicion of, and at times outright opposition to, post-1965 immigrants on the basis of their origins, race, or religion. Meanwhile, free-market conservatives welcomed the flow of immigrants as a boon to labor markets, and other conservatives, like President Reagan, embraced a sunny narrative about the United States being a home for immigrants. In short, no one conservative position on immigration existed. Democrats divided over immigration as well. Senator Ted Kennedy supported legal immigration and protecting immigrant rights, but Barbara Jordan, an African American and a Democratic former congresswoman who chaired a key immigration commission in the 1990s, joined him in the latter but also considered lowering legal immigrant admissions and cracking down on unauthorized entry.

The larger political transformations and these varying positions shaped the coalitions at the heart of immigration politics. As in the twentieth century, unlikely allies formed in the pro- and anti-immigration blocs, but now the configurations grew more scrambled as participants addressed complex questions surrounding legal immigration, "illegal" immigration, and the degree to which authorized and unauthorized immigrants could call on the welfare state. Thus, a conservative Republican like Senator Alan Simpson looked to decrease all forms of immigration to the United States, but he sympathized a bit more with protecting the rights of immigrants in the United States. His fellow conservative Ronald Reagan pushed to maintain or even increase legal immigration, never committed his administration to a crackdown on unauthorized immigration, and had little interest in immigrant rights—all of which resonated with his free-market principles. On the liberal and Democratic side, similar dynamics emerged. Even so, the key participants often compromised with each other. Simpson and Kennedy, for example, earnestly partnered to craft legislation.

Changing Immigration Laws

The small changes to immigration law in the 1970s, and especially the work of the Select Commission on Immigration and Refugee Policy (SCIRP), paved the way for a series of larger reforms in the 1980s and 1990s. Congress passed four major overhauls between 1986 and 1996, mixing restrictionist and liberalizer tendencies, though the former increasingly won out.

Following SCIRP's recommendation, Congress took up the "illegal" immigration issue in the early 1980s, an effort that culminated in the passage of the 1986 IRCA. The law provided for greater border enforcement to stem unauthorized entry. It penalized employers who "knowingly" recruited or hired those newcomers not permitted to work in the United States. IRCA also began what was called a diversity program, offering 5,000 visas in 1987 and 1988 for immigrants born in countries that found themselves disadvantaged by the 1965 reform. Supporters assumed the visas would go to Irish immigrants.

But IRCA's most important provisions addressed the more than 3 million individuals in the United States outside legal avenues. In keeping with the wishes of immigrant rights groups and employers, the law began three programs that set up a path by which those in the United States without authorization might gain legal status. First, immigrants living continuously in this country without authorization since January 1, 1982, could apply to be "lawful temporary residents" in the year after May 5, 1987, which almost all observers referred to as IRCA's amnesty provision. Second, the Seasonal Agricultural Worker (SAW) Program declared that unauthorized immigrants who had worked in agriculture for a minimum of ninety days between May 1985 and May 1986 could apply for legal status and eventually for citizenship. Third, fearing that the SAW Program might lead workers to leave the farms, the law provisionally set up programs to bring farmworkers from Mexico to the United States—with the possibility of permanent residency.

To assuage fears of immigrants with their newly won legal status taking advantage of federal welfare programs, the law placed a
five-year prohibition on applying for welfare for those legalized by
IRCA. The bill's authors, including the restrictionist Senator Alan
Simpson, believed the three programs would solve the unauthorized
immigration issue, but more ardent restrictionists were gravely dis-
appointed, believing IRCA rewarded lawbreaking.

In 1990 Senators Ted Kennedy and Alan Simpson, the leading
immigration supporter and skeptic, respectively, worked on tidying
up the laws surrounding the entry of legal immigrants to the United
States, a task that IRCA avoided in order to focus on unauthorized
entry. Simpson wanted to shift the preferences in the law away from
family reunification and toward employment skills, and to put hard
caps on immigrant and refugee entry. Kennedy acceded to portions
of this agenda, but other Democrats objected because, as one put it,
"for generations we only admitted white, European immigrants, and
then, after Asians and Latin Americans finally have an opportunity
to get in, there's this proposal to limit their numbers."[2] Republican
free-market conservatives, meanwhile, worried that hard immigration caps would deprive the economy of needed workers.

The result was the Immigration Act of 1990. It raised the global
annual cap for immigration to the United States to 700,000 until
1995, whereupon it dropped to 675,000. The annual per country
quota jumped slightly, from 20,000 to 25,620. The 1990 legislation
contained the now regular increase in funding for Border Patrol
and INS personnel, as well as for border fences. The preference system's reforms fell into three groups. First, family reunification visas
remained the most important category—480,000 of the 675,000
annual total. Lawmakers slightly changed which family members
might receive those coveted visas, but they did not eliminate the
ability of immediate relatives of citizens to enter outside the annual
quota. Second, the law doubled the annual employment-based immigration preference to 140,000. Third, the 1990 reforms greatly
enlarged the diversity program, ending its favoritism toward Irish
immigrants and mandating that recipients meet some work or education requirements.

Though it was not well noted at the time but would prove important in the coming years, the 1990 Immigration Act reformed

the H-1 nonimmigrant visa program, which temporarily brought skilled workers to the United States. The H-1 program had permitted businesses, without much difficulty, to bring in an unlimited number of skilled immigrants. The 1990 law capped the number of H-1s, defined them more thoroughly, and toughened oversight of the program. A new provision provided for 65,000 annual H-1B visas for workers with very specialized skills (and who had, at a minimum, a bachelor's degree), and for 66,000 annual H-2B visas for workers with slightly fewer skills and less education. Companies wishing to bring an employee to the United States through the H1-B program submitted to a rigorous application and screening process designed to make sure that the H1-Bs did not adversely affect the domestic labor market, or that these newcomers did not face substandard pay or working conditions. In the coming years, temporary workers of all kinds, not just those with prized educations and skills, came to the United States in larger numbers.

Two more vital laws came in 1996. They differed from the 1986 and 1990 legislation by addressing explicitly how the country treated newcomers and by reflecting the priorities of immigrant opponents. These laws arose from a particular mid-1990s political moment. A weakened President Bill Clinton, a moderate Democrat, confronted empowered conservative firebrands like House Speaker Newt Gingrich. Many Americans, meanwhile, supported shrinking social welfare programs, cracking down on crime, and reemphasizing individual responsibility. Such thinking, of course, found its way into conversations about immigration, especially in California's Proposition 187. The 1990s federal laws, in some ways, were a national version of the sentiments propelling Prop. 187 and the ends it tried to accomplish. Republican hardliners drafted these 1996 laws, which many Democrats supported for fear of looking soft on "illegal" immigration. As one of Clinton's advisers put it, "The illegal immigration legislation provides that same opportunity; . . . we can build up a strong Administration record on immigration."[3] Liberal Democrats and pro-immigration Republicans took small solace in mitigating some of the most objectionable measures.

The landmark 1996 Personal Responsibility and Work Opportunity Reconciliation Act most notably reformed welfare policy, but it also severely limited how deeply authorized immigrants, who paid taxes and contributed to the Social Security system, could call on the welfare state. The law banned immigrants from accessing the food stamp and supplemental income programs, and it allowed states to prohibit authorized immigrants from using Medicaid and the federal government's main antipoverty measure, Temporary Assistance for Needy Families. One critic of the law described these provisions as "mean" and unrelated to reforming welfare policy.[4] The immigrant provisions accounted for nearly half of the legislation's projected (and actual) budgetary savings, no small matter to the legislation's authors.

That same year Congress passed the Illegal Immigration Reform and Immigrant Responsibility Act (IIRIRA, pronounced "Ira-Ira"). Restrictionists retreated from key demands such as lowering the legal immigration cap and dropping the number of annual family reunification visas after businesses and pro–family reunification immigrant groups forged an alliance to blunt those proposals. Restrictionists hardly capitulated, though. To stem unauthorized crossings, the law provided for fourteen miles of fence along the Mexican border and funding for more than five thousand new Border Patrol officers over five years. Employers faced more stringent regulations regarding their responsibility to verify the immigration status of employees, and more penalties if they failed to do so. The law made it harder for authorized immigrants to adjust their immigration status or apply for government welfare programs, and it more severely limited the ability of "illegal" immigrants to do the same. Perhaps most important in the coming years, the legislation made it easier for the government to deport immigrants, both authorized and unauthorized. Congress swelled the crimes that made immigrants deportable and applied those changes retroactively. Unauthorized immigrants detained within one hundred miles of the border automatically entered the deportation process, without access to a legal hearing.

Implementing Immigration Laws

The 1986, 1990, and 1996 legislation did not recast immigration law as profoundly as the 1920s laws or the 1965 reform did. Yet these efforts shaped immigration enforcement, who entered and stayed in the United States, and the lives of newcomers. Likewise, the implementation of these laws proved tricky and often led to unintended consequences. Together, these laws clearly aimed to address the number of unauthorized entries and the growing population of unauthorized immigrants living in the United States.

The laws tried to curtail the ability of employers to hire unauthorized immigrants. The 1986 IRCA's employer sanctions proved nearly toothless, though. The Reagan administration had little interest in enforcing a regulatory regime on businesses when it embraced an antiregulatory orientation generally. The INS had a $100 million annual budget to administer these sanctions, but the agency rarely used half that allotment.[5] The money it did spend was focused on employer education rather than employer investigations. Some studies showed that Hispanic workers legally in the United States bore the brunt of the sanctions, as employers discriminated against them in trying to verify their citizenship status.

IRCA's employer sanctions proved so unsatisfactory that Congress returned to the issue with the Basic Pilot Program in 1996. It allowed employers to submit documentation electronically to the federal government to confirm an employee's eligibility to work in the United States. After starting in Florida, California, New York, and Texas (among others) in the late 1990s, it expanded in 2003 to all fifty states. In 2007 it gained a new name: E-Verify. Even then, Congress made participation in E-Verify voluntary, signaling its lack of interest in burdening businesses with paperwork and reporting, much less punishing them.

Business interests used these laws to secure workers. High-technology companies used the H-1B program, easily filling those visas in the mid-1990s as their booming industry required huge amounts of highly specialized labor. They looked mainly to Asia, where skilled workers could not find enough well-paid positions. In the 1990s India received half of the H1-Bs and Taiwan used about 10 percent.[6] As labor shortages grew, tech companies in the early 2000s lobbied Congress to push temporarily the number of H1-B visas to 195,000, ironically just as the high-tech bubble burst and labor needs dropped. A precedent had materialized, though: the tech sector looked overseas for labor and used the H-1B program to bring it to the United States. Indeed, this did much to speed entry of immigrants from certain parts of the world, especially India. Balraj Sokkappa, who arrived from India in the 1950s to do graduate work in electrical engineering and then stayed on to build a career in that field, marveled at the ease with which modern immigrants from India could get to the United States on H-1Bs. "They made the immigration laws much easier. A lot easier. . . . They got this so-called H-1 visa, and because of the computer technology, particularly for engineers and even doctors, if they couldn't hire somebody locally, they could give them an H-1 visa."[7]

These laws had complicated effects on those living in this country without authorization. On the one hand, the legislation contained punitive measures that effectively drew clearer lines between citizens and noncitizens by denying the migrants access to many social welfare programs. At times, officials walked back some of these measures. The Clinton administration in the late 1990s restored supplemental income payments to immigrants legally in the United States, the courts in New York made clear that immigrants could access Medicaid without regard to their arrival status, and more than twenty states set up antipoverty programs for immigrants cut out of the new 1996 welfare policy. All these moves effectively, but only partially, reversed the legislation's harsh elements.

The intended restrictionist effects of reform came to pass, and unauthorized immigrants bore welfare reform's burden. They made up only 9 percent of those households on welfare in 1994 but represented almost one-quarter of the drop in welfare rolls by 1997.[8] In the twenty-three states offering the most meager food benefits to immigrants, the percentage of the hungry among immigrant populations increased from 11.3 to 16.3 between 1994 and 1998, even as hunger rates for nonimmigrants declined.[9] In the five years after 1995, noncitizen children and their parents' participation in Medicaid dipped, as did their health insurance rates.[10] Finally, immigrants eligible for social programs sometimes chose not to enroll for fear of running afoul of regulations or endangering their unauthorized family members.

On the other hand, the 1986 law's amnesty provisions reconfigured the lives of millions of unauthorized individuals living in the United States. Angelica Dimas came to this country in 1981 without authorization, arriving in San Diego from Tijuana, Mexico, as a seventeen-year-old with dreams of a better life. She spent the next five years cleaning houses in Southern California, work that allowed her to stay out of sight of U.S. immigration authorities. She successfully legalized her immigration status under the 1986 law. That move changed her life, offering her access to a driver's license, a bank account, and credit. She embarked on a career as a school bus driver, declaring, "I was so happy, so excited. . . . I loved driving buses."[11] Amelia Cobarruvias, desperate to escape a stultifying family life in Mexico, went with her soon-to-be-husband, Florencio, to Oregon's lush Columbia River Valley in 1978, where they picked produce. Seven children followed, all of whom worked in the fruit orchards. With IRCA, the family earned legal immigration status. All seven children went to college, and the oldest, Maria Cobarrubias (her last name was misspelled at birth), became an immigration lawyer and now works in Salem, Oregon. Maria noted Amelia's pride in her children, remarking that her mom's "favorite gifts are now college T-shirts. And she has so many!"[12]

Though the Reagan administration attempted to administer IRCA's amnesty provisions in a restrictive fashion, it failed largely because the law's authors constructed these programs liberally, an interpretation the federal courts supported. Thus, nearly 1.8 million applied under IRCA's general amnesty program; 1.6 million won permanent residence, 40 percent of whom went on to naturalize. About 70 percent of the applicants came from Mexico and resided in either California or Texas, and the majority were male with a median age of twenty-nine.[13] The SAW Program, an afterthought at IRCA's passage, surprised almost everyone. About 1.3 million farmworkers applied, vastly more than expected. About 1.1 million won permanent residence, and nearly 25 percent of that group naturalized. Among the SAW applicants, 82 percent came from Mexico, the vast majority were men, the median age was twenty-seven, and most lived in California, Texas, or Florida.[14]

Of those who became permanent residents in these two programs, about 900,000 naturalized and became American citizens.[15] The effort to restrict access to social welfare benefits spurred this move, as did the Clinton administration, which worked assiduously to ease the process and the bureaucratic challenges accompanying it. For instance, the INS reduced the wait period between qualifying for naturalization to actually naturalizing from twenty-four to six months, and it made the language requirements for the civics test for naturalization less daunting. Naturalizations surged, then, in the mid-1990s, a long-term result of IRCA.

The Border . . . and Beyond

An emphasis on border security accompanied the public, political, and policy focus on unauthorized immigrants in the United States. The major immigration legislation of the era provided money for border control and policies meant to fortify the border and discourage unauthorized passage. But focusing on the 1986, 1990, and 1996 laws misses how other episodes and government actors pushed unauthorized immigration and the border to the forefront of immigration politics and policymaking.

The federal government's declaration of its War on Drugs was one such factor. Beginning in the 1970s, federal and state law enforcement emphasized curtailing the flow of illegal drugs across the southern border. By the 1990s powerful and more violent drug cartels in Mexico, often competing with each other, authored more sophisticated methods of shipping drugs. The United States deployed ever more personnel and resources to the border region to interdict the flow of drugs. The strategy achieved scant success, but it effectively fortified the border, making it more likely that immigrants trying to enter without permission would encounter American authorities. On the border, the War on Drugs and the effort to halt unauthorized immigration grew in tandem.

The Supreme Court also played a role, permitting the Border Patrol and INS to pursue unauthorized immigrants more vigorously. In the 1975 *Brignoni-Ponce* decision, the Supreme Court outlined several conditions that allowed immigration officers to conduct certain types of a "roving patrol" near the border to apprehend suspected unauthorized immigrants.[16] In 1976 the Court ruled in *Martinez-Fuerte* that the Border Patrol could set up a checkpoint on a well-traveled highway almost fifty miles from the border. In 1984 the Court further empowered the INS in two fashions. In the

Lopez-Mendoza case, the Court ruled that noncitizens contesting a deportation order in civil proceedings could not access the Fourth Amendment's prohibition on illegal search and seizure. In the *Delgado* case, the Court allowed the INS greater freedom to conduct workplace raids to arrest unauthorized immigrants. The Court clearly explained its thinking: facing an emergency at the borders, the INS and Border Patrol required extraordinary powers.

At the same time, the border control budget grew as part of the regular annual appropriations process, in addition to the expenditures authorized in this period's landmark legislation. In retrospect, the Border Patrol was fairly small in the 1970s. Its personnel did not grow much in that decade, and its budget stood in 1980 at $77 million, a relatively paltry figure. In the 1980s the Reagan administration and Congress swelled the Border Patrol budget by 130 percent and the number of personnel by just over 40 percent; the majority of those increases were targeted at enforcement. The trends continued in the 1990s. The number of Border Patrol agents more than doubled, from 4,200 in 1994 to 9,212 in 2000. Likewise, the Border Patrol's budget for the southwestern United States, its most vital area of operations, doubled from $400 million to $800 million between 1993 and 1997.[17]

The aggressive approach of U.S. authorities on the southern border had sometimes horrific consequences. In 1986 Ramón Celaya Enríquez and José Valle Rea left Mexico to come to the United States. They paid a smuggler to bring them across the border. The Border Patrol came across the two men, the smuggler, and fifteen others and as the group fled, the Patrol picked up Celaya and Valle. American border enforcement officials attacked the men; one of the agents ran over Celaya with his motorcycle and broke his arm, and both men were beaten and later forced to "voluntarily" depart the United States. Fourteen-year-old Luís Eduardo Hernández was not so fortunate three years later. He crossed without authorization in an attempt to reunite with his father, who had earned legal status under IRCA, but was struck by a Border Patrol vehicle and killed. The U.S. government later paid his family $50,000.

With more resources and legal support, immigration authorities more aggressively patrolled the border and monitored the country's interior, hoping to squelch unauthorized immigration. The

INS often raided workplaces or farms, and sometimes private residences or places where workers boarded. Furnished with warrants that named a few unauthorized immigrants, officials would sweep a site, detaining dozens of suspects for questioning. They sometimes found some, or none, of their targets. And the raids were dangerous. José Morales Sentalo, an eighteen-year-old unauthorized immigrant living near Boulder, Colorado, worked at a poultry operation. When the Reagan administration launched Operation Jobs, a series of raids supposedly targeting unauthorized immigrants in nine cities in 1982, Morales's workplace was swarmed by government authorities. As he fled, a cement truck struck him, killing him. The U.S. government called off the raids in Colorado after Morales's death, but not before deporting five hundred individuals from the state.

If swept up in the raid, the legal U.S. residents got a heart-stopping scare, and the unauthorized faced deportation. These raids caused real terror among immigrants. In 1981 Sara Saravia, in her early forties, came to the United States from El Salvador without authorization. She eventually became a U.S. citizen, but looking back on her life in the 1980s, she recalled worrying constantly about the immigration authorities sending her back. "You felt so afraid you couldn't even walk to the market," she remembered. In one instance, Saravia was eating her lunch when three men in uniform came near her. "I left my tacos on the table and took off running," not realizing they were security guards, not government officials.[18] One observer described the immigration officials as acting "like Hitler's police or the police in South Africa" during the raids. Immigrant advocates protested that officials racially profiled their targets. "They're looking for *brown-skinned people*, not any others," complained one lawyer.[19]

In 1994 the INS and Border Patrol embraced a new "prevention through deterrence" strategy to curb the entry of unauthorized immigrants from Mexico.[20] Authorities flooded key border crossing areas with agents, new fences, and equipment to deter unauthorized crossings by making the risk of apprehension so much higher. With traditional crossing routes well-guarded, authorities reasoned that migrants would, faced with traveling over much more inhospitable territory, choose to stay put. The Clinton administration, somewhat ambivalent about these operations, nonetheless supported them because of political pressure. One Clinton aide summed up the dynamic by referring to another country, Germany, where immigrants and newcomers in the 1990s suffered sometimes violent attacks: "There is a fear that unless the administration gets out in front, you'll see what you did in Germany: a violent reaction against immigrants."[21]

This enforcement regime took hold in the early 1990s. In 1993 the Border Patrol started Operation Hold the Line along the Mexican border at El Paso, Texas, placing several hundred agents and vehicles on a twenty-mile stretch of land where unauthorized crossings occurred regularly. Hold the Line's effects appeared immediately: there was an almost 90 percent drop in border apprehensions, which officials believed indicated that fewer individuals tried to cross the border.[22] Word of Hold the Line's success spread, and politicians urged wider adoption of the tactics.

A year later, the United States launched Operation Gatekeeper, which focused on the border between Mexico and San Diego. This roughly sixty-mile-long border region contained the San Ysidro entry point, the busiest land crossing in the United States, and was a shining example of economic integration. It also had the most unauthorized crossings of anywhere on the U.S.–Mexico border. In a show of deterrent force, Operation Gatekeeper put more border agents on patrol and constructed new barriers and warning systems.

The ramp-up in U.S. forces on the border made migration choices more difficult for Mexicans. In the spring of 1998, Julio Callejas and his wife, Josefina Mayoa, could not decide whether to cross without authorization to the United States. They desperately needed the money that could be made north of the border. And Callejas had jumped the border fence the previous fall, after having arranged for a car, at the cost of seven hundred dollars, to take him north to Indio, California, for work. But now the couple had a little baby, and Josefina worried, "It's too hard with the baby. It's very dangerous."[23] Wilfredo Cruz Hernandez had made up his mind, though. The seventeen-year-old had brothers in Michigan who told him about plentiful and well-paying jobs. Cruz wanted to cross but realized, "You don't know how to get past the migra. You don't know the roads."[24] (*Migra* is slang for the U.S. immigration authorities.) So he waited for his siblings to send him the money to pay a smuggler to take him across. Some were not so fortunate. José Luis Uriostegua left the Mexican state of Guerrero and crossed the border in the mountainous and inhospitable terrain east of San Diego in March 2000, hoping to avoid apprehension by the Border Patrol. Instead, the Patrol found the twenty-year-old's body. He had frozen to death.

Little wonder then that one immigrant advocate looked back on Gatekeeper on its twenty-fifth anniversary and said, "From a human rights vantage point, it was an utter failure."[25] The Mexican government estimated that 1,400 immigrants, forced to cross over more hostile territory, died between 1996 and 2000, a figure that others place even higher.[26] The casualties continued to mount in the twenty-first century as the government continued to employ Gatekeeper's tactics in the region. Indeed, the American authorities touted that crossings and apprehensions in San Diego plummeted because of Gatekeeper. As immigrants shifted their migratory paths to the east, the INS responded accordingly, moving resources to these areas.

Deportations spiked in these decades as well. In the 1980s and early 1990s, the United States annually removed (including those deported and excluded) between 20,000 and 40,000 individuals, while significantly larger numbers of apprehended unauthorized entrants chose to voluntarily depart.[27] But the 1996 IIRIRA gave government authorities more discretion to deport and widened the number of deportable offenses. The change registered most stunningly on the U.S.–Mexico border. In a typical year, 1999, the Border Patrol apprehended 1.579 million deportable persons at all the nation's borders; more than 97 percent of those apprehensions were on Mexico's border with Texas, California, and Arizona. Unsurprisingly, all but 43,000 of those apprehended were Mexicans.[28] Deportations followed apprehensions. The government never deported more than 50,000 Mexicans annually in the first half of the 1990s, but by 1997 deportations reached 100,000, and then 150,000 three years later.[29]

The stronger border measures, the IRCA legalization programs, and increased deportations, however, failed to shrink the number of persons living in the United States without authorization. The number of individuals entering outside legal avenues from Mexico increased a bit after IRCA, but then grew steadily in the 1990s. Immigration authorities asked those apprehended why they tried to enter the country, and most answered that they were looking for jobs. The unauthorized population also grew because those in the United States without authorization decided to stay rather than face stepped-up border enforcement if they should leave and try to return. This dynamic began in 1986 among those who did not qualify for IRCA's amnesty programs and increased in the 1990s as authorities fortified the border. By 2000 the United States had an unauthorized population of 8.6 million, and an estimated 4.5 million of those individuals were of Mexican origin.[30]

The United States and Refugees in the 1980s

The 1980 Refugee Act gave the United States a new tool with which to try to ameliorate the situation of the global refugee and displaced person population. But refugee affairs did not get any easier for two reasons. First, a political fight erupted that pitted the Reagan White House against liberals in Congress and their allies in refugee NGOs over the implementation of the Refugee Act. Second, a vexing refugee crisis emerged during the 1980s on the United States' southern doorstep, in Central America.

The global refugee population grew from about 2.8 million in 1975 to around 15 million by the close of the 1980s, complicating U.S. choices under the Refugee Act.[31] The Reagan administration's first refugee admissions proposals came in at 140,000, well over the 50,000 proposed under the Refugee Act. In the following years, the administration shrank proposed admissions (67,000 in 1986) before inflating them again in Reagan's last years.[32] With these policies, the administration seemingly heeded restrictionist sentiments in American life. As Colorado's Governor Richard Lamm put it, "One refugee is a symbol; a million refugees . . . constitute a major demographic event."[33] By stressing repatriation and resettlement in regions from which refugees came, Reagan officials demonstrated their goal of shrinking overall admissions.

Equally controversial, the administration consistently allocated Refugee Act visas to those fleeing communism. Europeans escaping communism received more visas than those fleeing communism in Africa or the Middle East, who did better than individuals not flee- ing communism at all. Even then, European refugees from behind the Iron Curtain saw available visas shrink in the 1980s as part of the larger trend outlined above. Congressional liberals protested vigor- ously, but to no avail. Besides, they had more pressing concerns: the Central American refugee crisis.

Central America suffered in the 1980s from political unrest and violence, war, and stunted economic development. U.S. foreign pol- icy interventions designed to blunt the supposed rise of communism in the region caused many of these problems, as did efforts to impose American economic hegemony. By the end of the 1980s, the region's refugee population reached just over 2 million, mainly Guatemalans and Salvadorans.[34] Many were internally displaced, refugees in their own countries, but hundreds of thousands fled across borders. Many headed to Mexico, which did not want them. From there tens of thousands of refugees crossed into the United States, some filing asylum claims and others entering without authorization.

One of those fleeing was Armando, who entered without autho- rization in 1990 at age twenty. He offered a harrowing description of Guatemala: "Everyone was in danger . . . we faced a dilemma be- cause the army could conscript us, but if we were in either the army or civil police, then the guerillas would kill us. If instead we were not in the army and they stopped us, they might decide that we were guerillas and then the army (or police) might kill us or imprison us. So my family and I and my parents . . . decided that I would come to this country."[35] To travel from Guatemala to the United States took one month and cost about $1,600, including $600 to a coyote who brought Armando across the U.S.–Mexican border.

The Reagan administration was generally inhospitable to indi- viduals like Armando who might make an asylum claim. Huge back- logs of cases developed because the overloaded asylum adjudication system could not handle tens of thousands of applications. Salvado- rans who had their asylum cases heard found only a 4 percent suc- cess rate in the early 1980s—and that excludes the thousands whose cases did not get a hearing. In 1984 Salvadorans and Guatemalans won about 3 percent of their asylum cases. Critics accused the immi- gration authorities of rejecting these claims out of hand, especially after learning that Iranians, Afghans, and Poles won about one-third of their asylum cases.[36] Nicaraguan refugees had better luck in asylum cases than other Central Americans, and even those who lost their asylum claim often won an administrative reprieve from the Justice Department called Extended Voluntary Departure (EVD), which allowed them to stay in the United States.

The Reagan administration ultimately had little interest in helping Salvadorans and Guatemalans, who fled from governments the United States supported as bulwarks against communism in the region. The Nicaraguans, meanwhile, fled from Reagan's antagonists, the leftist Sandinistas, and thus received a warmer welcome. One Reagan official explained that most of the Central Americans were not fleeing political persecution, and thus were not refugees, but instead were "fleeing poverty and seeking better lives."[37] Advocates for Salvadorans and Guatemalans pointed to cases like Armando's to combat such claims. They also noted that immigration authorities at the border actively discouraged their clients from filing asylum petitions to win refugee status.

Reagan's Central American policies, and his treatment of refugees, exploded in domestic politics. The administration almost immediately decided to aid the Nicaraguan rebels fighting the Sandinistas and to provide military and economic assistance to rightist governments in El Salvador, Guatemala, and Honduras, ignoring their often atrocious human rights records. American liberals, but especially human rights activists and religious groups, excoriated Reagan's policies as amoral and dangerous. Reagan touted them as necessary, which became crystal clear when the administration became embroiled in illegal efforts, known as the Iran-Contra Affair, to ship arms to the Nicaraguan opposition.

For the opponents of Reagan's policies, the treatment of Central American asylum seekers clearly demonstrated the administration's ill intent. Reagan's critics decided that aiding those asylum seekers demonstrated support for human rights, highlighted their opposition to the president's Central American policies, and was morally correct. The Sanctuary Movement, made up largely of religious groups, immigration lawyers, and Central American communities in the United States, did just that. It provided support for those who entered without authorization: 150 congregations offered their houses of worship as sanctuary from the authorities, and thousands of other religious groups pledged support.

Manuel Hernandez, a young man and student from Guatemala, took sanctuary in the Community Church of Boston in late 1983, living with Reverend William Alberts and his family on an upper floor of the church building. Hernandez had fled his homeland after Guatemala's government, supported by the United States, began a war against leftist political groups whom it labeled subversives and communists. Guatemalan forces occupied Hernandez's small village in the late 1970s, terrorizing its residents and, eventually, targeting Hernandez. He came to the United States without authorization shortly thereafter, but he chose not to apply for asylum, judging that the United States would not award it to him and would instead very probably deport him. This Boston religious community offered him sanctuary, and he stayed for two years. In 1985 he won asylum in Canada.[38]

The Justice Department successfully prosecuted some leaders of the Sanctuary Movement, but the legal challenges to Reagan's asylum policy filed by immigration lawyers proved the bigger story. In the 1990 settlement to the *American Baptist Churches v. Thornburgh* case, the U.S. government agreed to reexamine previously denied asylum cases of Salvadorans and Guatemalans who entered before the fall of 1990, to let refugees who had been scared of, or dissuaded from, filing for asylum do so, and to allow asylum applicants to work in the United States. Meanwhile, as part of Congress's 1990 revision of immigration law, liberals won a provision called Temporary Protected Status (TPS), a successor to Extended Voluntary Departure, which the president could grant to groups in need of safe haven. TPS and the *American Baptist Churches* decision opened a path for Salvadorans and Guatemalans (including Armando) to stay in the United States. A 1997 law cleared the way for them to apply for permanent residence.

Refugee Policy after the Cold War

By the Central American refugee episode's resolution, the Cold War had ended. Its conclusion complicated refugee affairs by removing the "lens," as the historian María Cristina García put it, through which Americans interpreted refugee crises and justified action (or inaction).[39] That lens distorted American priorities at times, but it did serve an important interpretive function. Without the Cold War framework, new issues and orientations shaped refugee admissions after 1990.

Most important, the global refugee population stood at over 14 million during the 1990s.[40] The number of internally displaced stretched into the tens of millions. Asia, Africa, and the Middle East had the most severe crises, tied, at least in the American public's view, to intractable ethnonational political conflicts (such as the disintegration of Yugoslavia and the genocide in Rwanda). War (including the Iraqi Wars of the 1990s) and political violence (in China in the aftermath of Tiananmen) also produced refugees.

The Refugee Act continued as the United States' chief vehicle for admitting refugees. The refugee quota peaked in 1993 at 142,000, and admissions spiked in the early 1990s as well, but both declined (sometimes by 50 percent) in the second half of the decade.[41] Refugees from European communist or formerly communist nations received the largest allocations; the states of the former Soviet Union sent the most refugees until the decade's end. At times the United States took other concrete steps to help refugees. The George H. W. Bush administration, bowing to intense lobbying from Congress, in 1989 and 1992 put in place policies allowing mainland Chinese in the United States before April 1990 to become permanent residents instead of going back to a post-Tiananmen China. A few years later, the Clinton administration eased the entry to the United States of Hong Kong natives, mostly professionals, who did not want to stay in that city as the Chinese assumed control from Britain. At other times, like Rwanda's implosion in the early 1990s that was the central event in what one observer termed "Africa's World War," a genocide and immense refugee crisis had little influence on U.S. politics, as only paltry efforts to halt the killing and help the victims were made.[42]

Those refugees who won entry generally possessed strong domestic political support, often from members of their nationality living in the United States, or their admission flowed from American foreign policy considerations. These same dynamics, though, could work against admission. Domestically, the restrictionist turn in immigration politics made refugee admissions harder to win, as did the charge that those seeking entry as refugees actually sought economic opportunity instead of escape from persecution. Foreign policy concerns were even more daunting. Some quarters of the public, and some leaders, hoped to retrench diplomatically and militarily, a sort of post–Cold War restructuring that augured a retreat from engagement with the world and from refugee admissions. Bilateral relations proved problematic too, as when the Bush administration hesitated to aid the Chinese students after Tiananmen for fear of upsetting delicate relations with Beijing. Finally, in the wake of the 1993 World Trade Center bombing, in which anti-American terrorists from the Middle East attempted to use a truck bomb to bring down the twin towers, policy makers focused increasingly on terrorism and feared that terrorists might sneak into the United States as refugees.

The Agonies of Asylum Policy

Asylum remained another major avenue by which the persecuted might enter the United States in the twentieth century's last decades. Asylum applications surged in the late 1980s; there were 235,000 new applications between 1988 and 1990 alone, which resulted in a backlog of nearly 300,000 cases by 1992.[43] Any individual case might prove difficult to resolve because of incomplete evidence, the difficulty in weighing that evidence, and the judge's subjective role in deciding whether the claim met asylum qualifications. In any event, the asylum bureaucracy was too small to deal with this many cases and their complexity. The number of cases grew so large that even those who won their asylum claim got stuck in limbo because the 1980 Refugee Act provided for only 5,000 asylum visas annually. Thus, one could win asylum but then wait for legal admission.

No one thought the asylum system worked. Restrictionists viewed it as a backdoor into the United States that immigrants abused. They pointed out that some of the 1993 World Trade Center bombers had entered the United States claiming asylum, which introduced terrorism into the politics of asylum policy. Meanwhile, asylum lawyers believed the system needlessly abused their clients, who in many cases had already suffered greatly.

Two kinds of changes came in the twentieth century's last decade. The United States did take some steps to make asylum function more effectively and humanely. The 1990 immigration law provided for 10,000, instead of 5,000, annual visas for asylees in the hopes of reducing the wait time for admission. Likewise, throughout the first part of the decade the number of asylum officers and immigration judges increased, as did the former's training. But other policies and laws had the opposite effect. The 1996 immigration law effectively raised barriers to claim and win asylum. It required that an individual file an asylum claim within one year of coming to the United States, and it gave more power to immigration officers at the border to order potential asylum seekers removed from the country before they could establish their claim. Under this system, asylum seekers needed to provide their own interpreter, a small but vital element to a successful case. Asylum advocates decried these policies as punitive and a betrayal of the country's history as a haven for asylum seekers. As intended, asylum applications dropped in the late 1990s to about 38,000 in 1999, well below the 147,000 made in 1995.[44] That 38,000 did not count individuals removed before they could file a claim.

The Haitians and Cubans demonstrated the complexities of late twentieth-century asylum law and policy. In Haiti the Duvalier regime fell in 1986, succeeded by a number of unstable governments before the 1990 election of the reformist Jean-Bertrand Aristide. In September 1991 the military and economic elites overthrew Aristide. With the exception of the Aristide interregnum, Haitians continuously fled for the United States, often in unseaworthy crafts. In the months after the anti-Aristide coup, the United States rescued almost 35,000 Haitians at sea.[45] Americans often viewed the Haitians as economic migrants and thus supported the U.S. government's policy of interdiction, in which the Coast Guard intercepted Haitians on the seas and returned them to Haiti or, in some cases, to the American base at Guantanamo Bay for screening. Between 1991 and 1994 the United States interdicted about 67,000 Haitians. In 1994 Aristide returned to power, and the number of Haitians leaving the island dropped dramatically. During the 1990s only about 6,000 Haitians received asylum in the United States and another 6,000 entered as refugees, testimony to the U.S. government's unwillingness to provide relief to the Haitians.[46]

American policy toward Cuban refugees proved just as vexing. The island's economy collapsed after Soviet aid disappeared and the government launched a new campaign against political dissidents, pushing thousands to cross the Florida Straits to the United States. That movement quickened with Castro's 1994 announcement that anyone who wanted to leave could. The Clinton administration ordered the Coast Guard to interdict Cubans at sea and, rather than offer them entry to the United States as refugees as past U.S. governments had done, take them to Guantanamo. They then faced a choice of returning home or immigrating to another country. This tough line angered Cuban Americans, who also objected to the crisis's resolution. In 1995 the Cuban government stopped encouraging its citizens to leave for the United States on boats and agreed to take back Cubans (without punishment) who wished to return. The United States, in turn, promised Cubans as many as 20,000 annual visas. The 20,000 Cubans detained at Guantanamo, though, refused to go back and could not find acceptable third-country alternatives, so the Clinton administration eventually paroled them into this country.

This maneuvering produced the "wet foot, dry foot" policy. Cubans interdicted at sea ("wet foot") by the United States were sent back to the island unless they showed a legitimate asylum claim. Those Cubans who landed in the United States ("dry foot") could apply for residency after one year of parole status. As a result, unauthorized Cubans predictably started entering the United States via Mexico to take advantage of the "dry foot" provision. Supporters of Central American and Caribbean refugees howled in protest at the advantages accrued to Cuban asylum and refugee cases.

Once in the United States, these refugees and asylees encountered job markets and experiences much like those faced by other immigrants. In one key difference, even as Congress chipped away at authorized and unauthorized immigrants' access to welfare programs, refugees retained access to more, though not all, of those initiatives.

Refugee and Asylee Experiences in the Late Twentieth-Century United States

In many cases, refugees and asylees adapted well. Armando, who escaped from Guatemala, started work almost immediately in California for an electrician, and in the early 2000s he set up his own electrical business. Across the country, Armando's story repeated itself as refugee and asylee communities revitalized stale neighborhoods and these newcomers crafted new lives and futures. One of the great success stories came in the Washington, D.C., area. For instance, Mount Pleasant, Adams Morgan, and Columbia Heights, a cluster of neighborhoods in the northwest quadrant of Washington, D.C., attracted Salvadorans in the 1970s and 1980s, who helped lead the area's economic and social turnaround. But two other groups authored even more remarkable stories.

Many Vietnamese refugees settled in northern Virginia, within sight of the nation's capitol, in the mid-1970s. They opened a number of shops in a run-down part of Arlington, Virginia, called Clarendon. Nguyen Van Hoan opened a department store, called Pacific, that sold Vietnamese groceries and assorted items on the first floor and had a coffee shop and billiard hall above. Hoan explained the success of the store and other surrounding shops in Clarendon: "The Vietnamese like to stay together, because living in America they feel isolated. . . . Coming to Clarendon makes them feel less lonely."[47] When Clarendon became too expensive in the early 1980s, a group of Vietnamese investors purchased an abandoned shopping mall nearby and named it Eden Center, after a mall in Saigon. Patrons flocked to a host of jewelry and electronics shops, restaurants, bakeries, and grocery stores, and in the center of the parking lot a Republic of Vietnam flag flew. "The flagpole at the Eden Center reminds us constantly of our heritage," one Vietnamese commented.[48]

In the 1990s another refugee group announced its presence in the Washington, D.C., region: Ethiopians. Their story began in the 1970s, when political instability and violence at home foreclosed the possibility of return for a small number of businessmen, students, and tourists. Getachew Metaferia arrived in the United States in 1973 to study at an American university. He had the same plan as others: he "wanted to get the knowledge and go back to Ethiopia

A Vietnamese store in Arlington, Virginia, 1977.
Library of Congress, Washington, D.C.

and help in building the nation." But his plans changed when "the 1974 revolution took place, followed by human rights abuses—killing right and left. So I wanted to stay here until the situation improves, but that didn't happen."[49] Metaferia stayed in the United States, becoming a professor of political science at Morgan State University. The Ethiopian community grew in the 1980s and 1990s as troubles in Ethiopia multiplied and American policies allowed them to stay as refugees. In the 1990s, the United States admitted nearly 50,000 Ethiopians.[50] Two of these were the brothers Yared and Henock Tesfaye, who came to Washington, D.C., in 1994 from Ethiopia's capital city, Addis Ababa. Yared got two jobs, in real estate and as a parking attendant, but he and his brother saved up enough money to buy a restaurant for their mother, who had cooked Ethiopian cuisine professionally for nearly two decades. The brothers worked at the restaurant, named Etete—their mom's nickname. Yared explained their goals for Etete: "We want to bring a lot of people, not just Ethiopians, but tourists to this block."[51] Their food and hospitality won accolades across the city.

Washington, D.C., and suburban Maryland became the hub of Ethiopians in the United States. In particular, the Ethiopian refugees revitalized the Shaw neighborhood (home of the restaurant Etete), one of the epicenters of the crack problem in D.C. in the 1980s, and the so-called U Street Corridor, the historic center of Black culture in the city that had been laid low by the unrest and riots of the 1960s. By the end of the twentieth century, both areas had bounced back, well on their way to gentrification in the early twenty-first century, which ironically forced Ethiopians to move to the suburbs in Virginia and Maryland.

9/11 and After

This era's final reset of immigration and refugee policies came in the wake of the terrorist attacks of September 11, 2001. Members of the terrorist group Al-Qaeda hijacked four jet planes, crashing two of them into the World Trade Center towers in New York City and one into the Pentagon in Washington, D.C. The fourth plane crashed in Pennsylvania after the passengers attempted to retake control of the craft. Nearly three thousand died in the attacks, the damage climbed into the billions and, some estimated, trillions of dollars, and the United States' triumphalist psyche, nurtured in the aftermath of the Cold War, took a severe blow. The administration of President George W. Bush reoriented U.S. foreign policy in response, ultimately launching major wars in Afghanistan and Iraq and countless smaller antiterrorism operations around the globe. These measures often proved destabilizing, fostering more terrorism and creating large populations of refugees and the displaced.

The 9/11 attacks also reconfigured domestic governance and its priorities. The antiterrorist capabilities of the U.S. government grew with the creation of the Department of Homeland Security (DHS), the passage of the U.S.A. PATRIOT Act, and the construction of domestic monitoring systems like the National Security Entry-Exit Registration System (NSEERS). These antiterrorism efforts had profound effects on immigration. The Bush administration employed these legal, bureaucratic, and administrative maneuvers to harden the borders, control immigration into the United States, and monitor recent newcomers living in this country.

Homeland Security created three entities—Customs and Border Protection (CBP), the United States Citizenship and Immigration Service (USCIS), and Immigration and Customs Enforcement (ICE)—to formulate and enact immigration policy. Their creation accompanied small bumps in the immigration and border security budgets and personnel, which dramatically increased in 2007. Under DHS's leadership, bureaucracies like ICE amassed power and resources in the new century, employing 20,000 personnel in 400 offices with a budget of $6 billion by 2019, and performing a variety of immigration enforcement and removal actions.[52] Equally important, moving the immigration and border policy portfolios to Homeland Security signaled the further securitization of these issues.

These new immigration bureaucracies deployed powerful, and sometimes new, measures as they sought to monitor immigration more closely. The Antiterrorism and Effective Death Penalty Act, a Clinton-era law, allowed the Bush administration to detain immigrants it suspected of terrorism or even just breaking the law. The U.S.A. PATRIOT Act, which overwhelmingly passed Congress immediately after 9/11, put more money into border security. It gave the government more leeway to detain immigrants in the name of preventing terrorism. And it permitted the attorney general to deport anyone he or she suspected of potentially committing terrorist acts, without a hearing or presentation of evidence. Finally, the State Department put sixteen- to forty-five-year-old male visa applicants from twenty-six countries in the Middle East, Africa, and South and Southeast Asia under special scrutiny. Officials paid increased attention to those applying for permanent residence in the United States, and also to those such as businessmen, students, and tourists hoping to enter on temporary, nonimmigrant visas.

All those entering the United States in the years after 9/11, whether on a permanent basis or not, ran headlong into a much more sophisticated tracking system that attempted to catalogue who entered and why. Such monitoring extended to some of those newcomers already in the country. The center of this effort was the Justice Department's creation in mid-2002 of NSEERS. It demanded that males aged sixteen and older from North Korea and twenty-four largely Muslim nations entering the United States, and some nationals from those countries already in the United States with visas, register with the government and submit to fingerprinting and questioning. Critical observers quickly named the policy "the Muslim registry." The Bush administration rolled back some of these requirements in 2003, but the program continued until 2011, when the Obama administration effectively discontinued it.

NSEERS totally failed in identifying terrorists. By the end of 2003, it had catalogued 83,000 individuals, and the government charged none of them with terrorism. Authorities accused only eleven of having terrorist links, without even clarifying what that meant or the circumstances of those cases (whether they involved people living in the United States, people entering at the border, or people living overseas). The registry proved much more effective as a deportation instrument: the government placed 14,000 of the 83,000 in deportation proceedings.[53] Indeed, by the end of the registry program, one official remarked, "We looked at what kind of benefit, what kind of leads were being generated by the domestic registration, and it was minimal in number."[54] A cabdriver from Morocco now living in Chicago surely agreed: "They make foreigners who spent so many years here working hard, getting up early every morning, trying to live the American dream, they make these people feel insecure in order to make the American people feel secure."[55]

In many of these antiterrorism efforts, the Bush administration built on parts of the 1996 immigration law. Specifically, the administration expanded the use of a technique called 287(g) agreements, in which the federal government used local authorities to enforce immigration laws. Indeed, some evidence suggests that the Bush administration encouraged states and localities to write their own laws and policies governing immigrants in their communities. This shift, inviting vastly more local and state participation in immigration enforcement, ran counter to decades of practice, and it shaped immigration policies in the new century in vital fashions.

Refugee policy and admissions ran parallel to immigration during the George W. Bush years. After 9/11 the State Department quickly tightened screening procedures, making prevention of the entry of terrorists a priority and slowing an already arduous admissions process. Refugee advocates howled about the misapplication of resources. "You have to be a pretty dumb terrorist to decide that the way you're going to get to the U.S. is to go to Pakistan, sit in a refugee camp for six years and hope the U.S. selects you for admission," Jana Mason of the U.S. Committee for Refugees pointed out.[56]

The results of these changes to immigration and refugee policies and laws quickly became apparent, especially to any person attempting to enter the United States who encountered a bulked-up entry regimen. As one historian described it, the daily implementation of these immigration laws created "blatant ethnic profiling" that singled out immigrants from the Middle East and South Asia, especially Muslims.[57] Unsurprisingly, the number of nonimmigrant visas from those regions fell precipitously in 2002 and 2003. The effects on refugee admissions also intensified. In 2001, about 70,000 refugees entered the United States, a number that dropped below 30,000 in 2002 and 2003.[58] It began to crawl upward in the years that followed, but not enough to keep pace with the refugee crises that exploded in Afghanistan and Iraq, where American interventions brought forth under the guise of a "War on Terror" displaced hundreds of thousands. In a particularly cruel irony, large numbers of Iraqis and Afghans who aided or supported American forces and now faced persecution for their actions tried to enter the United States, only to run into the bureaucratic blockade.

In retrospect, the U.S. government clearly chose to make immigration and refugee policy and procedures a major front in the post-9/11 War on Terror. Other nations, especially in Europe, followed roughly this same path. They, too, in the early twenty-first century put more emphasis on border security and devising ways to both limit and track immigrants. In the United States, Bush and others lauded these developments, while critics saw mainly an assault on civil liberties and a further securitization and militarization of the border and immigration.

The attack on 9/11 was a shocking event. Thousands of people living in the United States died that bright, sunny morning, and it led the United States into two wars that cost the lives of many more. The effects on the United States' engagement with immigrants and newcomers were more predictable, though. The post-9/11 crackdown on newcomers in the United States, and those in other lands hoping to join them, grew from restrictionist and anti-immigrant policy and political and sociocultural trends already well under way. Those post-9/11 policies were extreme, to be sure, but they were not rootless. As the new century proceeded, more shocks and more continuities emerged in U.S. society and in the country's relations with newcomers.

Further Reading

Coleman, Sarah. *The Walls Within: The Politics of Immigration in Modern America* (2021).

García, María Cristina. *The Refugee Challenge in Post–Cold War America* (2017).

Goodman, Adam. *The Deportation Machine: America's Long History of Expelling Immigrants* (2020).

Mittelstadt, Michelle, et al. "Through the Prism of National Security: Major Immigration Policy and Program Changes in the Decade since 9/11." Migration Policy Institute, August 2011.

Nevins, Joseph. *Operation Gatekeeper and Beyond: The War on "Illegals" and the Remaking of the U.S.–Mexico Boundary,* 2nd ed. (2010).

CHAPTER THIRTEEN

The Era of Border Security

Immigration after 9/11

UNTIL 2017 ALEJANDRA CONTRERAS lived something approaching the American dream, given all that she had endured. She and her young son entered the United States from Honduras in 2004 without authorization. The Border Patrol apprehended her, but, following its policy, released her in advance of a deportation hearing, one that she claims she never received notification of. Contreras moved to Michigan, had two daughters, joined a church, and started working. In 2013 a car accident, not her fault, brought her to the immigration authorities' attention, who noted that she had missed her deportation hearing. Authorities granted her a routine temporary stay of removal, but in 2017, as the Trump administration's policies maximized deportations, Immigration and Customs Enforcement (ICE) deported her. Contreras flew back to Honduras with her two young girls, their first trip to a country they had never visited.

Contreras's story is a window onto the issues that made immigration a central political, cultural, and social issue in American life in these years. Between 2016 and 2020, largely because of Donald Trump, it was *the* issue roiling the country, a prominence unknown in American history. This chapter explains this rather incredible development.

The United States, with its promises of economic opportunities and political freedoms, acted like a magnet to newcomers in the twenty-first century's first decades, just as it had for centuries. The magnet pulled in different newcomers, though, as immigration from Asia surpassed that from Mexico in the middle of the 2010s. Nonetheless, not everyone could get in and not everyone could stay. In these decades the desire of newcomers to come was somewhat mismatched with the country's immigration system, which increasingly made the entry of newcomers more difficult and their policing and removal easier. Significant portions of the American public and government focused even more on border security, immigration enforcement, and limiting not just unauthorized, but also authorized, immigration. Supporters of newcomers, as they had in the late twentieth century, pushed back hard, organizing public defenses of immigrants and refugees rarely seen in the preceding hundred years.

This state of affairs had long roots, generated in the decades leading up to, and through, 9/11, but a variety of new episodes fueled it immensely. The arrival of Central American refugees in the Southwest and the large number of unauthorized immigrants living in the United States brought even more attention to border policies and immigrant communities. Federal, state, and local officials honed their monitoring and enforcement techniques, targeting especially unauthorized populations. As a result, newcomers, and policies and laws addressing them, became a heated issue that energized both immigration advocates and opponents in communities around the country.

At the national level, meanwhile, immigration affairs shifted dramatically. The bipartisan basis of immigration politics, which emphasized compromise between liberalizer and restrictionist proposals, ended in the twenty-first century. The two major parties polarized and homogenized on immigration: the GOP fervently embraced nativism and anti-newcomer politics, its immigration advocates effectively silenced; the Democratic Party contained more diversity on immigration admissions and border policy, but it stood in favor of immigrant rights and strongly against the demonization of authorized and unauthorized newcomers. With this sorting, immigration became an issue each party could define itself by, amping up the rancor in immigration discussions. Donald Trump, the most anti-newcomer president in U.S. history and the head of a party with a significant nativist component, entered this environment, pushing immigration politics in new directions.

Who Came?

The number of newcomers and their origins in the early twenty-first century mostly resembled those who came in the late twentieth century. These immigrants, while still settling in traditional regions and states, also found their way in larger numbers to communities in Idaho, South Carolina, and Tennessee that had not attracted many immigrants in decades, if they ever had. Finally, several categories of newcomers, crafted in large part by the 1965 law and its later revisions, lived in the United States, hinting at the complexity of immigration in the new century.

Each year about 500,000 individuals arrived in the United States with authorization and became legal permanent residents. (This excludes the slightly larger number of individuals already in the country who annually adjusted their immigration status to become legal permanent residents.)[1] Among the new arrivals, immediate relatives of those already living legally in the United States made up the largest category (and they led in the adjustment-of-status cases, too), followed by entrants under family preference prerogatives, and then, trailing badly, employment preferences. As in the late twentieth century, those settling permanently in the United States benefited from some sort of family connection.

Among these authorized entrants, newcomers from North and Central America, the Caribbean, and Asia dominated, continuing trends begun in the 1980s. And yet some changes emerged. Recent arrivals from Mexico easily outstripped those from India and China in the early twenty-first century. But beginning in 2013, more of the recently arrived in the United States—as legal permanent residents, as unauthorized entrants, and even as temporary nonimmigrants—came from China (147,000) and India (129,000) than from Mexico (125,000).[2] The change resulted from the slowing of Mexican, and the steady rise of Indian and Chinese, migration to the United States.

Refugee admissions after the post-9/11 decline slowly returned to between 70,000 and 80,000 annually by 2009 and even bumped up in 2016. Again, a shift to Asia (which includes the Middle East in government statistics) occurred in admissions. European and African refugees claimed the most refugee admissions until 2007, but thereafter refugees from Asia earned the most spots; Iraq and Burma led the way. Foreign policy and domestic considerations determined which refugee groups won admission. Many of the Iraqi refugees had helped the American military during the Iraq War (2003–2011), which added to the pressure to admit them.[3]

Grants of asylum stood in the 20,000–25,000 range from 2003 to 2016. Slightly more than half of those admissions were affirmative cases—where the individual declared his or her intention of applying for asylum at the border—rather than defensive cases, in which the applicant requested asylum while under removal procedures after entering without authorization.[4] Asylum remained difficult to obtain. After 2010 the number of applications increased each year, hitting over 180,000 in 2016, as claims from Mexico and Central America spiked. The surge stretched U.S. government capabilities, leading to a huge backlog of cases. In the century's first decade, Chinese asylees won the most admissions, but by 2014 El Salvador and Guatemala joined China and Egypt in receiving the most asylum grants.[5]

The population of unauthorized immigrants fluctuated in the early twenty-first century, declining with the 2008 recession and with increased border security (table 13.1). Mexicans were the single largest part of the unauthorized population, though they dipped from nearly 7 million in 2007 to 4.9 million in 2017. As the number of unauthorized entrants from Asia and Central America grew, Mexicans for the first time in a few decades accounted for less than half of the unauthorized population by 2017.[6]

Immigrant Attractions

Immigrants came to the United States in the new century to work, to escape difficult conditions at home, to be reunited with family members already in the country, and to enjoy political and social freedoms unavailable where they lived. In other words, they came

Table 13.1. Estimated Unauthorized Population
in the United States, 2006–2016

Year	Estimated Unauthorized Population (in millions)
2006	11.6
2007	12.2
2008	11.7
2009	11.3
2010	11.4
2011	11.5
2012	11.2
2013	11.2
2014	11.1
2015	11.0
2016	10.7

Source: Pew Research Center, "Unauthorized Immigrant Population Trends for States, Birth Countries and Regions," June 12, 2019.

for the same reasons immigrants came in earlier centuries. Work was especially important. As in the late twentieth century, the jobs that recent immigrants took fell into two categories. Immigrants with technology or computer skills, or an advanced degree, could find well-paying and less physically taxing jobs in finance, high technology, or the upper levels of the service sector. Immigrants without education or training found jobs in the service sector or as manual laborers. Unauthorized immigrants, defying conventional wisdom, worked in all these economic sectors.

The news, of course, was not all good. Larger structural factors, especially the 2008 recession and its aftermath, burdened immigrants' lives. The housing market's collapse in 2008 particularly crushed immigrant communities (authorized and unauthorized alike), especially Latinos. They invested heavily in their homes (and not the stock market, for instance) and so took huge losses. Equally troubling, they depended on the construction and home-care industries for employment, sectors particularly hard hit after 2008. Thus, poverty and unemployment rates spiked higher in Latino communities, which included many immigrants, during and after the recession, compared to national averages. And though the wealthy recovered quickly from the downturn, the recession's wounds lingered for many immigrants. During the recovery, Latinos saw unemployment drop slowly, wages rise too little, and wealth accumulation fail to recover, which signaled the precarious position of recent newcomers.

Mexican, Chinese, and Central American immigration illustrate the many forces in operation. Diana, a Mexican woman whose husband entered the United States without authorization in 2003, explained: "My husband doesn't have any education. . . . He couldn't get work, and when he did, the most he could earn here is 450 to 500 pesos a week. My husband doesn't want to be [in the United States] but we need to save some money to build a house [in Mexico]." In the United States, Diana's husband earned $350 a week, and she visited him on a tourist visa.[7] Others in Mexico moved for different reasons. The prevalence of violence in Mexico's border regions with the United States surely accelerated immigration. Deaths and danger spiked after the Mexican government in 2006 stepped up military maneuvers against the country's drug cartels. The cartels fought the government, and each other, for dominance. In the face of violence, Mexicans moved.

Vicente Burciaga and his family left in 2010: "They are killing people over there who have nothing to do with drug trafficking. They kill you just for having seen what they are doing."[8] One study found that twice as many Mexicans moved because of "public insecurity" in 2010 compared to 2007.[9] Those fleeing often came from the middle classes, and they had better economic and educational backgrounds than the average late twentieth-century Mexican immigrant. Moreover, the violence in Mexico made it less likely that those living in the United States might choose to return home.

At the same time, other factors somewhat deterred Mexican immigration. Birthrates in Mexico, which began to decline in the 1970s, continued to do so into the twenty-first century. The Mexican economy, meanwhile, slightly improved, offering more and somewhat better jobs. More jobs paired with a declining labor pool resulted in slightly fewer Mexicans coming north in search of jobs. In the United States, the 2008 recession destroyed jobs and a key attraction for Mexican immigrants. The U.S. government's stricter border policies, including more aggressive deportations, discouraged some from immigrating. Notably, tougher American border policies began before the economic downturn and did little to discourage immigration. Economic conditions, then, were paramount in the twenty-first century slowdown.

If Mexican immigration plateaued and then slowed, Chinese immigration grew continually. More than any other country, China used employment-based visas available through regular annual admissions. The unauthorized Chinese population grew too—from about 115,000 in 2000 to just shy of 362,000 in 2016—many of whom came in search of jobs.[10] While good numbers of Chinese also entered by means of asylum claims and took advantage of policies that allowed U.S. citizens of Chinese descent to bring in their relatives, economics ultimately chiefly drove Chinese immigration to the United States.

Lao Wu and his wife, Fei, arrived in the United States in the early 2000s. Wu was a factory worker in Tianjin before he and his wife sold their home and borrowed money to enter the United States with documents that won them a temporary visa. An initial two years in New York City working in a restaurant did not suit Wu—he despised "being bossed around and bullied day after day"—so he and Fei headed to Los Angeles, where he found work in carpentry and his wife worked, for a time, as a nanny.[11] The work, for both of them, was difficult and only sometimes rewarding. Wu hoped he might win a carpenter's license, and since the couple's children remained in China, they "would ask for nothing more if our children could attend college in the United States."[12] As of 2010 the couple's petition for asylum in the United States still awaited resolution. Similarly, Qiming Lui, an artist with a degree from Sichuan Fine Arts Institute, settled in 2018 in Queens, New York, with his family. His artistic talents had won him his visa, but his art career floundered in the competitive New York scene. Qiming paid his bills by selling merchandise on the web to people back in China. Lui's and Wu and Fei's stories resemble those of millions of other immigrants who scraped by in their new country, a mixture of dreams delivered and deferred.

The motivations of refugees and asylees were more straightforward: escaping to safety. The global displaced person population held steady at around 40 million between 2000 and 2013, before exploding to reach 68 million in 2017. Of those 68 million, 25 million were refugees (meaning displaced outside their home country), asylum seekers made up 3 million, and 40 million were displaced in their home countries. The vast majority of the world's displaced came from the Global South and tried to find safety in the Global North, and children accounted for roughly half of the displaced in 2017. Large populations of refugees and internally displaced persons could be found in the Middle East, Africa, and Central America in the twenty-first century's second decade.[13]

Syria was a particular problem, accounting for almost 20 percent of those 68 million, split evenly between refugees (6.3 million in 2017) and internally displaced. Those 12 million individuals fled the horrific Syrian civil war, which the United States and the international community protested but failed to stop. Syria's neighbors, Turkey and Lebanon, took in 3.5 million and 1 million of those refugees, respectively.[14] In 2015 the Syrian catastrophe entered a new phase when its victims began to seek safety in Europe in large numbers. Asylum applications spiked in 2015: some 378,000 applied for asylum in the European Union in that year alone, joined by hundreds of thousands of Afghans and Iraqis. Facing a rising number of refugees unlike anything the Continent had seen since the 1930s and 1940s, the European Union struggled to respond adequately.[15]

The United States experienced these dynamics firsthand in 2013. Unaccompanied children and families with young children fleeing from Guatemala, Honduras, and El Salvador began to arrive on the southern border in significant numbers. Surely some hoped to find jobs or to reunite with family. But, like many Mexicans, most Central Americans were escaping drug wars and gang violence at home. One woman described the horrors in El Salvador: gang members murdered her police officer husband in 2015, "then they came, they raped my kid and chased me from my house. They said I should leave, or they would take my kids. I had no other choice."[16] Thousands of others told similar stories. The number of arrivals from Mexico and Central America was overwhelming and unprecedented. In the year after fall 2013, U.S. border officials took into custody about 70,000 children and an equal number of persons traveling in family groups.[17] The U.S. government struggled to respond to this refugee crisis in its own backyard just as it struggled to solve other global refugee and displaced person situations.

Temporary Immigrants

The phenomenon of temporary immigrants to the United States came into sharper relief in the twenty-first century as well. Students and family members had been arriving in the United States for over a century, and immigration law, especially in the 1980s and 1990s, became more specific about the types of workers who could receive a temporary visa. In the early twenty-first century, smaller numbers arrived using this path, about 1.5 million temporary workers and students (and families of both).[18] By the end of that decade, almost 2.8 million nonimmigrants (workers, students, and their families) entered annually, a figure that held into the second decade of the twenty-first century.[19] Those on temporary visas shaped newcomer life in two ways. First, some of those temporary immigrants overstayed their visas and became unauthorized immigrants. Second, students and workers on temporary visas often intermingled with, and lived in, immigrant communities. They helped shape and flavor the experiences of immigrants, authorized and unauthorized, in America.

China and India were two important sources of temporary immigrants, especially students and workers, in these years. In 2015, over 300,000 Chinese students matriculated to American universities, which eagerly recruited them and their tuition payments.[20] The Chinese also generously used nonimmigrant employment visas, such as the H1-B for scientists and engineers and the L-1 for managers with special knowledge or skills. The Indian higher education system, meanwhile, produced highly skilled graduates who, facing bleak prospects at home, came to America. By 2000 U.S. companies feverishly recruited highly skilled technology workers from India, so much so that three scholars dubbed this century's Indian immigrants the "IT Generation."[21] By 2015 the country ranked first in the number of H1-B visas and second in L-1 visas. Like China, India also sent huge numbers of students to U.S. universities.

The United States offered new starts for those on temporary visas, but not without peril. In 2008 Pavitra (last name not reported) arrived in Atlanta with her husband, the holder of an H-1B visa that got him a plum job at a tech firm. Pavitra, a graduate of an Indian university, held an H-4 visa, which allowed her to pursue a graduate

degree in the United States. That path closed when no school recognized her Indian undergraduate degree. The H-4 also prohibited
her from working in this country. With these prospects, her mental
and physical health suffered as she struggled in the United States, a
familiar circumstance for all types of newcomers adjusting to life in
a new country.[22]

Political Alignments over Immigration

Immigration in the twenty-first century was deeply intertwined in
the ongoing reordering of the major political parties. The Republican Party moved from Reagan's free-market, anticommunist, optimistic conservatism of the 1980s toward, by 2010, a much more
darkly nationalist, socially traditionalist, and populist vision that often manifested itself as a politics of grievance—and especially white
grievance. The GOP maintained a remarkable ideological homogeneity as it moved further to the right. Christian evangelicals and a
business-friendly donor class remained at the party's base, joined by
large numbers of working-class whites and older white Americans.
The Democrats, a fairly heterogeneous lot, counted conservative,
moderate, and liberal factions that offered different economic and
foreign policy positions but found more comity on social issues. The
Democrats, despite those moderates and conservatives, in the 2010s
moved slowly to the left but still maintained strong attachments to
the pragmatism and moderation of figures like Barack Obama and,
later, Joe Biden.

The parties increasingly differed on immigration, though. Since
the 1980s, Democrats had willingly accepted more border security
measures in exchange for the maintenance of some relatively liberal
admissions policies. But as Republican willingness to strike such a
bargain disappeared, as GOP anti-immigration rhetoric heated up,
and as Latinos emerged as more important Democratic voters, immigration activists pushed the Democrats to more liberalizing positions. Activists critiqued President Obama's policies, rejected efforts
to compromise with restrictionists, and urged more aggressive executive actions to protect unauthorized immigrants. Democrats divided on border security, especially early in the new century, when a

good number supported stepped-up enforcement. No major figures in the party called for open borders. But by Obama's second term, many Democrats believed that border security received too many resources and was too militarized. By the Obama presidency's end, the Democratic Party held a near-consensus about protecting the rights of immigrants in the United States, helping the unauthorized legally reside in the country, and maintaining legal immigration at present levels.

The GOP underwent an even more dramatic transformation. President Bush, and his allies on immigration like Senator John McCain, generally valued immigrant contributions, from the authorized and the unauthorized, to the country. But the ground shifted during Bush's presidency, as immigration hardliners such as Representatives Tom Tancredo and Steve King, joined by senators like Jeff Sessions and Jim DeMint, reflected the party's will. They supported more border security, the removal of unauthorized immigrants, and a rethinking of the preference system that guided annual immigrant admissions. These restrictionist immigration positions, motivated to different degrees by racial and cultural concerns, became a vehicle for the GOP's grievance politics.

This party's transformations brought an end to the peculiar partnerships that had guided immigration for over a century. The liberalizer and restrictionist blocs became much more partisan: Democrats were in the former and Republicans in the latter. While some Democratic skeptics on immigration remained, the real change came in the GOP. It became nearly impossible for Republicans with liberalizer instincts, such as Florida's Governor Jeb Bush or Senator Lindsey Graham of South Carolina, to hold that position and retain power in the party. This fundamental change immensely altered immigration politics and lawmaking.

American Reactions to Immigration

Immigration restrictionists organized vast and impressive networks of supporters. Specialized anti-immigrant interest groups, such as the Center for Immigration Studies (CIS) and the Federation for American Immigration Reform (FAIR), continued to craft a case against immigration, as they had in the 1980s and 1990s. FAIR increasingly stepped into more controversial areas. Its representatives regularly appeared on conservative talk radio, and many of its members loudly questioned the validity of President Obama's birth certificate (a phenomenon known as the "birther" movement). FAIR took funding from a group advocating theories of white genetic superiority.[23] A more important funding source was conservative donors like the Scaife family, who had bankrolled conservative causes for decades. FAIR, CIS, and others increasingly immersed themselves in, and built connections to, conservative political outfits, funders, and media. In cementing these alliances, anti-immigration groups found new and larger audiences and moved from the fringes to the center of politics, a journey with immense political and policy consequences.

Anti-immigrant organizations flourished in local communities. Self-styled volunteer defenders of the border, the Minutemen, appeared in the American Southwest around 2005 and then spread to other parts of the country. Along the border, the Minutemen stood watch and, upon spotting someone entering, called the Border Patrol. In suburban Virginia, the Minutemen surveyed sites where Latinos gathered to pick up work, hoping to intimidate potential employers and employees. The Minutemen cited economic concerns and the supposed strains newcomers put on social services to justify their actions. But one Virginia Minuteman also remarked, "It comes back to their culture. . . . I spent some time in Rio when I was in the Navy. They urinated on streets, they threw trash, bottles. . . . When you come here, you're going to do what you did in your culture."[24] In the policy arena, the Minutemen demanded that Congress reject any legislation that gave permanent residence to unauthorized immigrants.

A group of insurgent Republicans, the so-called Tea Party, that coalesced in 2009 also expressed a powerful suspicion of newcomers. Largely middle- and upper-middle-class older whites, the Tea Party promised to "take the country back." Tea Party members blamed many people of color, the young, and supposedly lazy Americans for leaching the nation's wealth by accessing social programs they did not deserve. Republican leaders struggled to control the Tea Party, but its energy propelled the GOP to victories in the 2010 elections.

Often overlooked at the time, opposition to newcomers, especially unauthorized entrants, helped define the Tea Party. "Illegal" immigrants, Tea Party adherents believed, too often did not work and consequently overwhelmed the social safety net, leaving less for those Americans who deserved such aid. Tea Party members seemed unaware that unauthorized and authorized immigrants—except refugees—could not legally participate in key social welfare programs. But, as two keen observers noted of Tea Party rank and file, "virtually all want government to police immigrants."[25]

The diverse supporters of newcomers crafted a compelling counternarrative. The National Immigration Forum, the American Immigration Council, and the National Immigration Law Center worked tirelessly to educate the public about the importance of immigrants to American life. Refugee aid and resettlement organizations like the International Rescue Committee trumpeted examples of refugees restarting their lives to great economic and social success. Additionally, as refugee entry plummeted after 9/11, they argued for admissions as a global expression of American ideals. Religious organizations of many faiths provided material aid and comfort to individuals crossing the inhospitable U.S.–Mexico border, sometimes even saving lives.

Separately, free-market ideologues and think tanks joined businesses and their lobbying organizations to support immigration in an effort to loosen labor markets. This approach was not just the province of lobbyists, corporations, and intellectuals. As a manager at a chicken processing plant that employed large numbers of Guatemalans, both authorized and unauthorized, who oversaw some fairly abusive work conditions, put it, "At the end of the day, we need labor in our plants; we're not looking to get rid of these folks."[26]

This business community's thinking and actions put it at odds with immigrant rights groups and some labor organizations. The National Council of La Raza (renamed in 2017 UnidosUS) and others aimed to maintain the open door and to protect authorized and unauthorized immigrants. They partnered with sectors of the labor movement, especially after 2000, when the AFL-CIO leadership finally wholeheartedly endorsed liberal immigration laws and policies. This sea change at the AFL-CIO resulted from decades of work by service-sector unions. The Service Employees International Union

A pro-immigrant demonstration in Houston, Texas, 2006.
National Archives, College Park, Maryland.

(SEIU) and UNITE HERE, unions whose members worked in the hotel industry and elsewhere, brought recent immigrants into their memberships, a vital task because many newcomers took up these service jobs. These unions led protests and provided legal defense to workers targeted by government immigration authorities. Finally, SEIU and others made efforts to put Latinos in leadership positions.

Many of these pro-immigrant organizations flexed their muscles in politics. National registration and voter-turnout efforts among Latinos helped Barack Obama to his presidential victories and protected vulnerable congressional Democrats. With this electoral clout, pro-immigration groups pressured politicians to enact policies friendlier toward immigrants, especially during the Obama presidency. Many of Obama's executive actions on immigration, such as the Deferred Action for Childhood Arrivals program (DACA), which addressed minor children brought to the United States by their parents, grew from this lobbying.

Just as many local pro-immigrant organizations emerged in cities and, increasingly, in smaller communities. Facing restrictionist activism, these groups vigorously defended the contributions of recent immigrants to the country's social fabric. On May 1, 2006, hundreds of immigrants and their allies launched nationwide "Day without an Immigrant" protests that involved economic boycotts and walkouts from schools and jobs. The numbers were stunning: 300,000 marched in Chicago, 400,000 demonstrated in Los Angeles, and 12,000 formed human chains in New York City. Without workers, Tyson Foods closed a dozen plants for a day, and Cargill meats did the same in six states.[27] These "Day without an Immigrant" protests became a key tactic of the pro-immigrant movement. But the most telling comment, demonstrating both pride and weariness, came from an immigrant advocate in 2006: "I think people have to realize that enough is enough. . . . We can't be the scapegoats for everything that happens in this country. We're just as American as everyone else."[28]

Bush and Immigration

Against this backdrop, and in 9/11's shadow, national leaders contended with immigration policy and law. President George W. Bush's approach reflected his personal and political inclinations. Bush, a Texan, was comfortable with Latinos and his religiosity pushed him toward an inclusive worldview. He envisioned a North American political economy in which goods and labor passed easily across the Mexican–U.S. border. Bush and his political adviser Karl Rove believed that a relatively liberal immigration policy would allow the GOP to court Latinos and bring a good portion of them permanently into the Republican coalition—not an unreasonable thought given Bush's ability to win Latino votes in his gubernatorial and presidential runs. Bush, then, envisioned an approach to immigration that involved hardening the border, maintaining high levels of "legal" immigration, possibly beginning a guest worker program,

The border between San Diego (left) and Tijuana,
Mexico (right), 2007. Wikimedia Commons.

and constructing a path for those in the United States without authorization to normalize their status. Bush crafted a deal with Mexico's President Vicente Fox along these lines, but then Al-Qaeda
launched the 9/11 attacks.

   The potential U.S.–Mexico agreement fell by the wayside, replaced by border and immigration control policies that aimed to
identify security threats among those entering the United States.
The Bush administration's deportation and removal policies embodied this shift. Early in Bush's presidency, border officials very
often returned those apprehended entering the country without authorization, but they kept no record of those individuals, nor did
they file criminal charges. After 2005 border officials more regularly
placed individuals entering without authorization into formal removal proceedings, creating an official record of their apprehension
and detention. Those removed—rather than returned—could not
legally immigrate to the United States for five years (in some cases
longer) and could be subject to prison time if apprehended again

entering without authorization. During the Bush years, the government removed 2 million unauthorized immigrants, with a spike in removals in 2006 and 2007, versus 8.3 million returned cases.[29]

Legislation took a restrictionist turn, too, and against Bush's wishes. In 2005 House Republican immigration hardliners passed a harsh bill that, for instance, jailed those who entered the United States without legal authorization. Immigrant advocates launched the "Day Without an Immigrant" demonstrations in response. Moderate Senate Republicans, supported by Bush, countered with a proposal that heightened border security, set up a guest worker program, and offered unauthorized immigrants a path to stay legally in the United States. Those House Republicans rejected the moderate approach, pushed to that position in part by the conservative media that derided two GOP Senate supporters of the bill, John McCain and Lindsey Graham, as "Amnesty John and Lindsey Gomez."[30]

As 2007 ended, immigration legislation stalled in Congress. But two things became clear in the next few years. First, Latino voters in 2008 abandoned the GOP in droves, mimicking nationally what happened in California in the 1990s during the Republican push for Proposition 187. Second, the death of Bush's immigration approach at the hands of GOP hardliners made clear who controlled the party's immigration agenda. That uncompromising position grew more popular in the party in the early 2010s. In 2012 Republican presidential candidate Mitt Romney advocated "self-deportation," a term immigration hardliners used to describe the process of making life in the United States so inhospitable to unauthorized immigrants that they just choose to leave.

Obama and Immigration

Barack Obama ran for president as a problem solver promising to overcome national political dysfunction. He sought, like Bush, a bargain on immigration that addressed border security and a path to legal status for the migrants. Not coincidentally, organized labor and Latino voters, two of his voting blocs, wanted this second goal. Obama did not tackle immigration immediately, but he judged in his first term that immigration reform involved walking a political and

policy tightrope. Thus, he continued Bush's policy of placing detained unauthorized immigrants into removal proceedings. Obama
reasoned that taking a hard line on unauthorized arrivals would
convince congressional conservatives of his commitment to border
control and thus win their acceptance of a path to legal residence
for the migrants. From 2009 through 2014, the Department of
Homeland Security deported through formal removal procedures
some 2.4 million persons. This figure is exclusive of the 1.95 million
individuals in the United States without authorization who were
apprehended and returned to their home country (usually Mexico)
without being placed in formal removal procedures.[31]

Immigrant rights groups and Latinos detested this deportation regime, especially the reliance on formal removal procedures
that exceeded those achieved by both the Clinton and George W.
Bush administrations. Some blamed President Obama personally;
the National Council of La Raza in 2014 famously derided him as
the "deporter in chief."[32] Obama countered this criticism with other
moves, ordering DHS to draw down its participation in the 287(g)
agreements with state and local authorities, which some argued
produced racial profiling and abuses. Instead, Obama ramped up
a Bush-era pilot program called Secure Communities that coordi-
nated federal and local immigration information and enforcement.
None of this broke the political logjam, where the strategy of winning over recalcitrant Republicans failed to get a 2010 bipartisan bill
through Congress.

By 2012, with a presidential election looming, Obama shifted his
approach. At the behest of immigrant advocates and hoping to secure Latino votes, Obama announced the DACA (Deferred Action
for Childhood Arrivals) executive action. DACA directed the DHS
to halt deportations of about 1.2 million persons who arrived in the
United States as children (under the age of sixteen) of unauthorized
immigrants. To qualify for DACA those 1.2 million needed to have
graduated from high school or served in the military, not run afoul
of the law, and lived in the United States for the previous five years.
The legal fate of these children, the "Dreamers," had been stalled for
years in Congress in a piece of legislation called "The Dream Act."

As hopes for a grand bargain on immigration with the GOP
again faded in 2012 and 2013, Obama instituted more changes.

The president suspended the Secure Communities effort. DHS placed slightly fewer individuals in formal removal deportation proceedings and fairly drastically reduced the practice of returning apprehended unauthorized immigrants. DHS also began to focus on deporting criminals and those who recently crossed the border without authorization rather than pursuing unauthorized entrants living lawfully in American communities. Thus, deportations at the border remained high, but deportations in the country's interior—in immigrant communities—dropped. The president also turned even more to executive actions. In November 2014 Obama expanded DACA, covering another 300,000 individuals, and announced the Deferred Action for Parents of Americans (DAPA) program. DAPA allowed parents of U.S. citizens or legal permanent residents who had entered or stayed without authorization to avoid deportation if they had lived in the United States for more than five years and not committed crimes. DAPA affected about 3 million unauthorized immigrants. Some Republican state attorneys general legally challenged the enlarged DACA and DAPA orders, and lower courts put both programs on hold. The Supreme Court in June 2016, down to eight members after Justice Antonin Scalia's death, deadlocked on the case, leaving the lower courts' suspensions in place.

Refugee policy also vexed the Obama administration. During Obama's first term, the United States set annual refugee admissions at 70,000–80,000, comparable to Bush's targets, but filled more of those spaces than the Bush administration.[33] The global refugee population swelled after 2012, and the Syrian situation dominated the agenda. The United States responded to Syria's crisis with about $4.5 billion in humanitarian aid from fiscal year 2012 through fiscal year 2015,[34] but it resettled only about 1,850 Syrian refugees in those same years.[35] Critics urged more Syrian refugee admissions, and in 2015 the administration proposed larger annual refugee caps for the next two years, aiming to resettle 10,000 Syrians in the country in 2016. The United States exceeded that goal by about 20 percent, but critics noted that Canada accepted 25,000 that year.[36] U.S. officials responded that resettlement was complicated and that moving aggressively would further fuel a xenophobic backlash.

That backlash complicated the U.S. response to the Central American refugee crisis of 2013 and 2014. Unaccompanied Mexican children arriving at the border received an interview with a Border Patrol officer, who determined if the child possessed a credible fear of persecution. If so, the child entered the asylum adjudication system; if not, the child could be returned to Mexico. Unaccompanied children from El Salvador, Honduras, Guatemala (or other nations not contiguous with the United States) went within seventy-two hours into the custody of the Department of Health and Human Services, which then tried to place them with a relative. Meanwhile, the children's asylum cases proceeded through the immigration system. The families presenting at the border, numbering as many as the unaccompanied children, entered the regular asylum process if they claimed to be victims of persecution. The DHS detained many of these families in government facilities while processing their asylum claims, which immigration lawyers decried as inhumane.

In 2014 the sheer number of children and families proved challenging. The system could accommodate about 8,000 children, not the 70,000 unaccompanied children who arrived.[37] The migration's magnitude, and the dire situations many fled, put the Obama administration in a difficult spot. It put more personnel on the border to process these cases, worked with the Mexican government to slow the arrivals, launched a public relations campaign in Central America to discourage migration, and sent $250 million in aid to Central America in hopes of stabilizing the region. As the summer of 2014 ended, the migration slowed largely because of aggressive enforcement actions from Mexican authorities. By then, immigration opponents had weaponized the episode, claiming that the United States had lost control of its borders.

Policies and Laws: States and Communities

Immigration politics and policy controversies percolated in states and local communities, a continuation of trends begun with California's Prop. 187 and the 287(g) programs. In southwestern and southern communities where growing numbers of newcomers arrived, immigration opponents and skeptics claimed that they sat on the front lines and had to turn to local and state action as the federal government, in their view, did nothing. Between 2005 and 2009, the number of state and local immigration laws quintupled. Those laws, addressing education, employment, and driver's licenses and state or local identification, often focused on identifying a newcomer's legal status.

Arizona emerged as the center of state-level anti-immigration activism. It was home to Joe Arpaio, the notorious, media-savvy, and anti-immigrant sheriff of Maricopa county. The Justice Department later deemed his racial targeting of immigrants, and his outdoor prison camp, as gross violations of civil rights. In 2010 the Republican-controlled legislature, with the backing of Republican Governor Jan Brewer, passed SB 1070, the Support Our Law Enforcement and Safe Neighborhoods Act. The legislation ramped up monitoring of unauthorized immigrants in Arizona in the hope that the scrutiny would drive them from the state. It criminalized being in Arizona without immigration papers or applying for, or holding, a job without proper immigration status. It required the police to verify the immigration status of anyone they arrested and empowered police to arrest suspected unauthorized immigrants. Brewer deemed the law necessary to combat an "illegal immigration" crisis. Her opponents decried it as anti-immigrant fearmongering and an attack on civil liberties that led to racial profiling.

Other states joined Arizona. In Georgia in 2010, the Republican-controlled state legislature pushed the Georgia Board of Regents, which ran the state's public universities, to prohibit unauthorized immigrants from attending Georgia's five top public universities. The board also announced that unauthorized immigrants had to pay out-of-state tuition, double the in-state rate, at Georgia's other thirty public universities. Nearby South Carolina and Alabama had similar policies. One supporter of Georgia's effort explained: "We can't afford to have illegal immigrants taking a taxpayer-subsidized spot in our colleges."[38] In 2016 the Georgia State Supreme Court upheld the Regents' policy.

These state and local efforts generated resistance. In Georgia, talented students chose scholarship offers at other universities, abandoning their home state, which many pointed out only hurt the state's economic future. For those who could not leave, four University of Georgia professors set up a covert "Freedom University" to educate some of those shut out of the state's public universities.

Freedom University consciously echoed the 1960s Freedom Schools set up by civil rights activists to confront Jim Crow. It also led to a memorable, double-entendre-laden T-shirt, featuring the slogan "FU Georgia."[39]

Resistance to Arizona's SB 1070 emerged locally and nationally. President Obama decried it, the mayor of Phoenix blasted the law as "discriminatory" and an embarrassment to the state, and some local law enforcement refused to implement its provisions.[40] In 2012 the Supreme Court found, by a 5–3 margin in *Arizona v. United States*, that three of the law's key sections intruded on the federal prerogative to control immigration, and it severely curtailed another section of the law. All in all, the Court shredded SB 1070. Equally important, SB 1070, and Arpaio's policies, encouraged young Arizona Latinos to enter politics and organize their communities, shifting state politics in ways Brewer and her allies had never expected.

Some communities learned that no laws could halt the dynamics behind immigration. Hazelton, Pennsylvania, in 2006 passed one of the earliest laws to deter Latino immigrants, especially the unauthorized, from settling in the town. The Supreme Court twice voided the law, but something else happened in Hazelton. The lure of good housing, schools, jobs, and family proved too powerful, as they had for centuries. In Hazelton, Latinos kept arriving, and longtime white residents moved away. The 2016 population was 46 percent Latino (versus 5 percent in 2000) and dying downtown Hazelton began to revive, a dynamic that echoed throughout the country and over the last centuries.[41]

Trump and Immigration

Running for the Republican nomination and then the presidency, Donald Trump made immigration a centerpiece of his campaigns. He lauded immigrants from northwestern Europe and labeled refugees from the Middle East, and immigrants from Muslim countries, likely terrorists. He asserted that newcomers, especially the unauthorized, stole jobs from Americans and led to surges in crime and drug trafficking. He lashed out at immigration from Mexico: "When Mexico sends its people, they're not sending their best.

. . . They're sending people that have lots of problems, and they're bringing those problems with us. They're bringing drugs. They're bringing crime. They're rapists. And some, I assume, are good people."[42] While Trump saw almost all newcomers as undesirable, he targeted largely immigrants of color. That his assertions were untrue—crime rates plummeted in the twenty-first century and most of the migrants did not commit crimes for fear of attracting police attention—mattered little to his supporters. Unsurprisingly, Trump's solutions to these so-called problems always involved reducing immigrant entry and immigrant rights.

Politics underlay this focus on immigration. Trump symbolized, and responded to, the powerful nativist segment of the Republican Party suspicious of newcomers and immigration. For good reason, Trump was the candidate of the GOP's hardline immigration restrictionists, like Senator Jeff Sessions. Trump did not so much execute a hostile takeover of the Republican Party as he understood better than other leaders where the majority of the party's voters stood, especially on immigration, and how to harvest their votes in this particular environment. Trump and his advisers also calculated that these positions would appeal to Americans who disliked or feared the social, economic, cultural, and demographic changes wrought, in part, by modern immigration patterns. Immigration in the Trump campaign became a way to explain, stimulate, and address the grievances of some in the white working class and older white Americans, important parts of Trump's voting coalition. In doing so, Trump willingly deployed racist imagery and rhetoric, unsurprising given his embrace of birtherism during the Obama presidency. These gambits also brought him the open support of white nationalists and supremacists.

As president, Trump stocked his administration with anti-immigration hardliners like Jeff Sessions (as attorney general) and Stephen Miller (who assumed the White House immigration portfolio), and set out to remake the U.S. approach to newcomers of all types. During his four years in office, real opposition emerged to his immigration agenda. But Trump also remade key aspects of immigration, refugee, and asylum law and policy to deeply restrictionist ends. In doing so, Trump set two novel marks. He established himself as the most anti-newcomer president in all American history, and he, as president, stood at the head of a nativist movement.

Some of Trump's memorable pledges on immigration fell flat. Trump planned to end DACA and DAPA and find a humane solution to the fate of the so-called Dreamers. In June 2017 the administration killed DAPA. It tried to end DACA too, but the Supreme Court in June 2020 ruled, 5–4, that Trump officials failed to follow proper administrative procedure in terminating DACA, so it survived. Despite some public pledges expressing sympathy for the Dreamers, Trump did not expend any political energy to find a legislative solution. While his moves on DACA failed, much to the relief of the Dreamers and their allies, the program's fate remains tied to presidential support.

President Trump's signature promise to build a wall between Mexico and the United States produced mixed outcomes. Mexico, unsurprisingly, refused to pay for the wall. Congress balked too, which led to a budget battle between the White House and congressional Democrats in December 2018 that resulted in a thirty-five-day government shutdown and very modest funding for "existing technologies" for border security—a defeat for President Trump.[43] The administration then cleverly decided to build the wall largely using funds allocated from the Pentagon budget, a move the Supreme Court let proceed in July 2019. By January 2021 the administration had erected about 450 miles of border wall, but the vast majority of it replaced existing structures. Total costs ran to over $15 billion, two-thirds of which came from the defense budget.[44] Observers have questioned both the effectiveness of the border wall and the quality of construction.

President Trump and his allies had more success making it difficult for newcomers to enter the United States. The immigration bureaucracy ramped up background checks and paperwork for those trying to secure immigrant, and nonimmigrant, visas. Most stunningly, the administration relied on the public-charge clause in immigration law, which allowed officials to deny entry to immigrants who it believed might use public assistance programs, to cut back on immigration. Under the Trump administration, the circumstances that officials might label in violation of the public-charge codicil expanded. These moves, tellingly, revealed the Trump administration's goal of slashing legal immigration to the United States and its willingness to use controversial policies, like the public-charge law, to do it.

President Trump had success with his border security and enforcement agenda, though he was unable to deliver on the promise of deporting millions. The Department of Homeland Security reported nearly 360,000 removals in fiscal year 2019, along with just over 171,000 returns of migrants, figures that exceeded those of the Obama administration's last years but were below levels reached earlier under Obama.[45] Likewise, the arrest and deportation of unauthorized immigrants away from the border, called interior removals, pushed upward under Trump after dipping in the last years of the Obama administration because Trump ended the Obama-era policy of removing only those with criminal records. Finally, Attorney General Sessions revived the 287(g) and the Secure Communities programs, partnering local and state law enforcement with the federal government to police immigrants and share data.

One of Trump's border security policies provoked the greatest controversy: separation of children from their parents. The story began with the administration's decision to charge those crossing the southern border without authorization with a crime, rather than just removing them to Mexico or releasing them in the United States in advance of deportation hearings. In the summer of 2018, as unauthorized crossings along the Mexico–U.S. border increased, the administration began to separate families it apprehended, placing the adults in criminal proceedings and the children, including babies and toddlers, in government facilities run by the Department of Health and Human Services. DHS Secretary Kirstjen Nielsen flatly denied such a policy existed, but the images, reporting, and then documents told a different story. The appalling situation saw immigrant children living in cages, instances in which sexual predators attacked the confined children, and parents and children psychologically scarred. In January 2020 the government stated that 4,368 children were separated from their parents or guardians, though NGOs said the number was higher.[46] Between September 2018 and May 2019, six children died in the custody of immigration authorities.[47] (Some were unaccompanied minors and not forcibly separated from their parents.) Because of the public uproar and court orders, the administration partially retreated from the policy, though it retained (and used) the power to separate children from parents. In fact, the government had so poorly accounted for these children and parents that it struggled to reunite them.

President Trump defended the separation policy as necessary, even asserting that past presidents had separated families at the border. On this point, Trump seriously misrepresented the policy's history. Bush and Obama had separated families only when the immigrant in question possessed a serious criminal record or seemed to threaten the child, both of which proved rare. The Trump administration, though, separated families as a deterrent to entry and as a matter of policy. Trump was right that history mattered in the child separation policy episode, just not how he thought. Child separation should be understood as part of a larger policy architecture, erected over the preceding three decades, to discourage unauthorized entry by making entry much more difficult and costly. The viciousness of child separation was extreme, but the logic corresponded to earlier efforts.

President Trump made even more significant changes to refugee and asylee policy. Days after the inauguration, he issued an executive order that suspended all refugee resettlement programs for four months, blocked entry of Syrian refugees indefinitely, and tightened refugee admissions procedures. That order, also known as the "Muslim ban," prohibited the entry of anyone from seven mostly Muslim-majority countries. Though the order was halted for a time in the courts, the Supreme Court ruled in favor of the administration's revised executive order in the summer of 2018.

President Trump also drastically shrunk the annual admissions caps under the 1980 Refugee Act. Trump administration officials repeatedly denied the global refugee problem's existence and outlined a goal of admitting only refugees with close ties to the United States as they justified this approach. Such thinking departed significantly from previous administrations', which ran U.S. refugee programs as a strategic, diplomatic, and humanitarian tool. Moreover, the administration did not worry when those caps went unfilled. The administration starved refugee programs of resources by, for instance, failing to put officials in the field to conduct necessary interviews and security checks. At the same time, the administration ordered

Table 13.2. Refugees Resettled in the United States, 2016–2020

Fiscal Year October 1–September 30	Refugee Admission Ceiling under 1980 Refugee Act	Refugees Resettled
2016	85,000	84,995
2017	50,000	53,716
2018	45,000	22,533
2019	30,000	30,000
2020	18,000	11,814

Note: For 2017, President Obama proposed in September 2016 a ceiling of 110,000. In March 2017 President Trump issued an executive order reducing the ceiling to 50,000.

Sources: Jeanne Batalova et al., "Frequently Requested Statistics," Migration Policy Institute, February 14, 2020; Mark Greenberg et al., "As the United States Resettles Fewer Refugees, Some Countries and Religions Face Bigger Hits Than Others," Migration Policy Institute, October 17, 2019; "U.S. Annual Refugee Resettlement Ceilings and Number of Refugees Admitted, 1980–Present," Migration Policy Institute (n.d.); Pew Research Center, "U.S. Resettles Fewer Refugees, Even as Global Number of Displaced Grows," October 12, 2017, https://www.migrationpolicy.org/programs/data-hub/charts/us-annual-refugee-resettlement-ceilings-and-number-refugees-admitted-united.

more in-depth interviews of refugees applying for resettlement. Slower processing meant lower annual admissions, the Trump goal (table 13.2).

The officials overseeing refugee admissions managed to cut admissions while targeting certain groups for entry. The Democratic Republic of Congo, Burma, and Ukraine (in that order) saw the most refugees resettled in the United States in 2018 and 2019. Yet, given the regional targets within the annual cap, only European refugees surpassed their 2018 target, as Christian, often evangelical, refugees from the former Soviet Union entered relatively easily. Why did they get such favorable treatment? Observers pointed out these refugees were European, white, and Christian.

The Trump administration just as aggressively remade the asylum system, which the president held in special contempt. Administration officials argued that asylum law allowed individuals backdoor—and therefore illegitimate—entry, which led to the administration's conflation of asylum seekers with so-called illegal immigrants. Unsurprisingly, the Trump immigration team took several steps to curtail asylum. They constricted the path to asylum for Central Americans by narrowing the definition of persecution attached to asylum claims. The administration expanded a tactic called metering, which lowered the number of asylum cases processed at the border each day, to make applying for asylum slower and more burdensome. Finally, the administration tried to mandate that the government would accept asylum claims only at the border or a port of entry, a policy the courts rejected.

Most important, the administration and Mexico in late 2018 agreed to a pilot program called the Migrant Protection Protocols (MPP), wherein asylum seekers from Honduras, Guatemala, and El Salvador, after reaching the U.S. border and presenting an asylum claim, were shipped back to camps in Mexico to await a U.S. court date to adjudicate their claim. MPP (and the threat of U.S. tariffs on Mexican goods) paved the way for a larger 2019 agreement between the two countries wherein Mexico acceded to MPP practices along the whole border and promised to use its National Guard to slow unauthorized migration from its territory. In turn, the United States agreed to process asylum claims more quickly and to send development money to Central America in the hopes of slowing departures of asylum seekers. From January 2019 to December 2020, the United States sent 70,000 asylum seekers to Mexico, where they encountered often dangerous living and working conditions.[48] Predictably, asylum cases backed up in the United States so that in April 2020 about 20,000 cases had either not been heard or were still in process.[49] The larger point is clear: by forcing asylum applicants at the southern border to "remain in Mexico" rather than allow them into the United States, President Trump dramatically altered asylum practice.

If President Trump's policies on newcomers were predictable, so was the massive pushback that developed in response. This opposition became spectacularly clear only a week into Trump's presidency. On January 28, 2017, the day after President Trump issued his "Muslim ban" executive order, word spread on social media of refugees stuck in limbo at John F. Kennedy Airport in New York City. They expected admission to the United States under the refugee program, but authorities denied them entry. A small demonstration in the morning grew by the afternoon to hundreds of chanting and shouting protesters flooding the terminal entrance. New York City cabdrivers showed their support by refusing to work at JFK. Inside the airport, lawyers who specialized in refugee law huddled on the floor with their laptops and cell phones, plotting how best to assist those in limbo. The world watched it all unfold on TV and the web—and the scene repeated itself at other U.S. airports.

The JFK protests set the tone for the next four years. Some localities refused to cooperate with the Justice Department's immigration agenda, most notably when several communities declared themselves "sanctuary cities" and offered protection to unauthorized immigrants. Immigrant rights and civil rights organizations, such as the American Civil Liberties Union and the Texas Civil Rights Project, combated the deportation and child separation policies. Finally, everyday Americans opposed to Trump's immigration policies kept up the pressure. This resistance to restrictionism began not at JFK Airport, but in the early twenty-first-century protests (the "Day Without an Immigrant" marches) and networks of resistance. Some of this was political theater, as when some restaurants chose not to serve administration officials who made immigration policy. Some of it revealed a rethinking of border policy among liberals, best exemplified by the "Abolish ICE" movement, which detested ICE for its role in deportations and family separations. But all made clear they viewed Trump's policies as unacceptable and un-American.

The COVID-19 Pandemic and Immigration

The turmoil of the Trump years, in immigration and otherwise, only accelerated with the COVID-19 global pandemic of 2020. COVID-19, which is caused by the highly contagious coronavirus, was a global public health challenge that led to lockdowns restricting activity and movement, destroying economies around the world. In the United States, as the virus raged in April through major cities such as New York, Washington, D.C., Seattle, and Detroit, as well as high-density rural communities that housed meat-processing plants, the country shut down and unemployment skyrocketed as economic activity collapsed. Surges in the virus pummeled different regions of the United States through the rest of the year; nearly 345,00 Americans perished from COVID-19 in 2020.[50] Blacks and Latinos, including those in immigrant communities, proved especially prone to contracting the virus (because of their work and living environments) and dying from it (because of their lack of adequate health care).

The meatpacking industry, which was a key employer of newcomers, illustrates sharply how the pandemic affected immigrant communities. Guadalupe Paez came to the United States as a young man in the 1980s, winning a green card and eventually settling in Green Bay, Wisconsin. He was working at a cattle-processing plant—backbreaking work for a sixty-two-year-old—when he got the coronavirus and had to be hospitalized. He recovered to almost full strength, but he probably will not return to work. His daughter explained, "He's traumatized."[51] At the same Sioux Falls pork processing plant that employed Achut Deng, the Sudanese refugee introduced in this book's first pages, the Kebede brothers encountered similar troubles. They arrived in the United States in 2020, joining their mother, who had settled in South Dakota. But in South Dakota the best jobs for new immigrants with sparse English language skills came in the pork plant—and the men eagerly took up the jobs. Then COVID-19 decimated the factory as the workforce fell sick, including the brothers. Fearing for their jobs, the Kebede brothers were reluctant to speak about their experiences.

These individual stories of lives upended multiplied exponentially as the pandemic upended immigration and immigrant communities across the country and around the globe. President Trump responded by restricting travel from China, then Iran, and then much of Europe. The United States, Mexico, and Canada also agreed to shut their border crossings for all except essential personnel. Trump's xenophobia appeared when he referred, to cheers at campaign rallies, to the coronavirus with the anti-Chinese slur "Kung Flu," a strong echo of the late nineteenth- and twentieth-century association between Asian immigrants and disease.[52] The president ordered the suspension of quota immigration under certain family and employment preferences through 2020, the cornerstone categories governing who can enter the United States. He also suspended the issuance of non-quota visas for tourists and some temporary workers (like the H1-B visas that went to high-tech employees). The government did exempt other temporary workers in medical, agricultural, and food service industries critical to the pandemic response. Finally, Trump barred from work those waiting for their asylum cases to be adjudicated, and he began deporting, without a hearing, those seeking asylum or presenting as unaccompanied minors at U.S. borders.

President Trump cited public health rationales and, calling on his "America First" rhetoric, asserted that these moves protected U.S. workers in what he hoped would be a quick economic recovery. Economists, the U.S. Chamber of Commerce, and high-tech companies like Google challenged him, arguing that any economic restart required talented foreign labor, and public health experts did the same. It was clear that Trump and his allies had rolling back these immigration programs as a goal before the pandemic, and these COVID-19 policies were thus consonant with the president's larger immigration agenda. The arch-restrictionist and Trump ally Mark Krikorian admitted as such: "This is a victory for the immigration hawks within the White House. Maybe it took the pandemic to help them overcome the pressure from lobbyists to keep the cheap labor coming."[53] The global pandemic, then, presented Trump another opportunity to enact his vision of immigration, refugee, and asylum policy.

Public opinion polling showed that a majority of Americans in 2020, even during the pandemic, saw immigration as a net benefit for the country and wanted to see immigration continue at current levels or increase. Those same polls also showed Democrats and Republicans lining up on different sides of the question. Yet the first two decades of the twenty-first century also made clear that a determined minority can shift policy and law in stunning ways. At the start of the century's third decade, immigration, and newcomers more generally, stood at the center of American politics and debates about the shape of society. And the country's politicians, as well as the public, found little common ground to address the questions springing from immigration.

Further Reading

Coleman, Sarah. "A Promise Unfulfilled, an Imperfect Legacy: Obama and Immigration Policy." In *The Presidency of Barack Obama: A First Historical Assessment*, ed. Julian Zelizer (2018).

Gerstle, Gary. "Minorities, Multiculturalism, and the Presidency of George W. Bush." In *The Presidency of George W. Bush: A First Historical Assessment*, ed. Julian Zelizer (2010).

González, Liliana M., and Michael Feil. "Public Insecurity and International Emigration in Northern Mexico." In *Mexican Migration to the United States*, ed. Harriet Romo and Olivia Mogollon-Lopez (2016).

Pierce, Sarah, and Jessica Bolter. "Dismantling and Reconstructing the U.S. Immigration System: A Catalog of Changes under the Trump Presidency." Migration Policy Institute (July 2020).

Ruiz Soto, Ariel G. "One Year after the U.S.–Mexico Agreement: Reshaping Mexico's Migration Policies." Migration Policy Institute (June 2020).

Sheridan, Lynnaire. *I Know It's Dangerous: Why Mexicans Risk Their Lives to Cross the Border* (2009).

Past, Present, Future

B Y THE END OF the twenty-first century's second decade, a
new wrinkle in the story of newcomers in the United States
became clear: migration and climate change. Nowhere was
the dynamic more on display than in Guatemala. Celso, a
sixteen-year-old from a rural community in Cuilco, was the oldest
of five children. He and his family worked in the nearby cornfields,
but in 2020 a snowstorm—in Guatemala!—destroyed the crop. His
family plunged into extreme poverty, and after consulting with his
father, "we both decided that I should go to get help."[1] Paying a
smuggler $8,000, Celso settled in Florida and got a ten-dollar-per-
hour job at a construction site. Jorge A. and his son had a similar
story. They fled Guatemala for the United States after a five-year
drought followed by a flood destroyed their crops. Jorge paid a coyote several thousand dollars to take only part of his family north, out
of a country whose social and economic structures were collapsing
under climate change.

Experts understandably now sound warnings about the convergence of climate change and migration, specifically the creation of
climate refugees. In the less well-developed world, some regions in
the last decades have become hotter and drier, and rural residents
cannot make a living farming, as they have done for years. Searching
for safety, they move to urban areas in their home countries, which
already suffer from overcrowding and poor infrastructure, offer

little economic opportunity or public safety, and buckle under their own climate challenges. With no future in these dense cities, many choose to move across national borders. This story repeats itself in the Middle East, Southeast Asia, the African Sahel, and—most relevant for the United States—Central America.

Climate change, then, is already altering migration patterns and forcing those in wealthy, developed countries, especially the United States, to contemplate their responses to this steadily growing crisis. Climate change, though, is just one reason Americans must be ready to think smartly, now and in the future, about immigration. To do this, we believe that Americans should think about immigration history. In particular, we can think of three themes from this history that seem to us to be the ones with which to best arm our readers as the story of immigration and the United States continues to unfold.

Immigrants came to North America in search of a better life. In almost every case, immigrants made this courageous choice at some risk, taking a veritable leap into the unknown. The exact circumstances that led many tens of millions to come to the United States, instead of elsewhere, depended on the individuals. And they changed over time. For some, the opportunity to reunite with family sparked immigration, whereas others left in search of a safer home. Many immigrants desired the political and religious freedoms the United States offered. But, over and over, people moved to the United States in search of economic opportunities in the form of better jobs, more work, more pay, and more chances to provide for an existing or future family.

Immigrants chose to come to the United States in the face of a variety of challenges at home, and they hoped that the United States would provide new beginnings. That lure of a better life, and especially the possibility of a better economic life, stands as the single most important reason tens of millions arrived on American shores. As immigration to the United States ebbs and flows in future years, this attraction stands as the starting point for understanding who is coming, from where, and why they hope to enter the country.

Throughout American history, the state, that constellation of federal, state, and local governance, shaped immigration. It regulated, or chose not to regulate, entry to the United States. It outlined who could stay, and who could become a citizen, and as such the state held great powers to shape the decisions of those immigrating. It encouraged, or failed to encourage, economic development, religious freedom, and political and civil rights that potential newcomers found attractive. Its relationships with other nations sped, or retarded, immigration. The American state grew more deeply involved in immigration toward the end of the nineteenth century, a trend that grew in the twentieth century.

The American state, of course, existed and evolved largely as a product of politics. How Americans conducted their politics, and how their politics addressed and framed social, economic, cultural, foreign policy, racial, gendered, and class concerns, gave the American state its meaning and its direction. Political concerns also gave the state's role in immigration its meaning and direction. The role of borders illustrates the point. Americans and their representatives made choices in the late nineteenth century that demanded that the state and its agents monitor all and restrict some of those who came to the United States. The state's greater attention to borders, and who passed over them, arose out of a political moment. Americans practiced a politics in the twentieth century that more often than not increased state scrutiny at the nation's border, sometimes to restrict who entered and sometimes to ease their entry. That scrutiny ultimately played out differently on the northern border than on the southern one; the latter became a site of fear and loathing, increasingly militarized and securitized, qualities not associated with the former. But at all its borders the state did scrutinize, and continues to today, at the behest of the American people and their representatives.

Ultimately, there can be no disengaging of the history of immigration and the United States from the history of the state and its politics. As the future unfurls, the connection between the state, politics, and immigration will do much to carve the path forward.

Immigrants are like us. Let us finish with a simple, but nonetheless important, observation: life is complex. The big decisions individuals make every day require sifting through, understanding, and balancing multiple factors. Reflecting on this process leads to the unmistakable conclusion that life is complicated. The point certainly holds true of people today, and also those who lived before us, though of course different concerns, dangers, and opportunities buffeted their lives.

And it serves as a useful reminder about immigrants. Economic opportunities brought many, many newcomers to the United States, but their lives ought not to be reduced to economics. Too often, contemporary discussions of immigrants revolve around their very real importance to economic life in the country, just as discussions of immigrants in American history focus on the role newcomers played in building the American economy. The lives of immigrants, though, involved much more than their experiences as workers, as laborers, or as statistical inputs into the gross national product. They led, and continue to lead, complicated lives, contributing to the fabric of the United States in multiple ways.

Indeed, we cannot imagine music, theater, sports, the visual arts, and food in the United States, not to mention churches, school groups, local sports leagues, or the American military, without immigrants. Any discussion of immigrants and the United States in future years should embrace their intricate and multifaceted experiences and avoid economic essentialism for a simple reason. They and their descendants helped create the United States, in all its beautiful, inspiring, and terrible complexity. Grappling with that past and present, we believe, can light a better and more honest way to the future.

Notes

Introduction. Immigration

1. John W. Nordstrom, *The Immigrant in 1887* (Seattle: Dogwood Press, 1950), 15.
2. "One Meat Plant, One Thousand Infections: Revisiting Achut Deng," *New York Times "The Daily,"* podcast, hosted by Michael Barbaro, July 15, 2020, https://nyti.ms/2ZrPUOi.
3. Adam Goodman, *The Deportation Machine: America's Long History of Expelling Immigrants* (Princeton: Princeton University Press, 2020).
4. U.S. Bureau of the Census, *Historical Statistics of the United States, 1789–1945* (Washington, D.C.: Government Printing Office, 1949), 19.

Chapter One. Founding Immigrants

1. John Harrower, *The Journal of John Harrower, an Indentured Servant in the Colony of Virginia, 1773–1776*, ed. Edward Miles Riley (New York: Holt, Rinehart and Winston, 1963), 14–19, 38–42.
2. Thomas S. Kidd, *American Colonial History: Clashing Cultures and Faiths* (New Haven: Yale University Press, 2016), 231.
3. Bernard Bailyn, *The Peopling of British North America: An Introduction* (New York: Random House, 1986), 149–150.
4. Maldwyn A. Jones, *American Immigration*, 2nd ed. (Chicago: University of Chicago Press, 1992), 34, 36.
5. Maldwyn Allen Jones, "The Scotch-Irish in British America," in *Strangers within the Realm: The Cultural Margins of the First British Empire*, ed. Bernard Bailyn and Philip D. Morgan (Chapel Hill: University of North Carolina Press, 1991), 284–313.
6. Bailyn, *The Peopling of British North America*, 39–40.

7. James T. Lemon, *The Best Poor Man's Country: A Geographical Study of Early Southeastern Pennsylvania* (Baltimore: Johns Hopkins Press, 1972), 154.

8. The scattered nature of the data and the multiple sources of the numbers are discussed in detail in an appendix, "The Number and Distribution of Indentured Servants," in Abbot Emerson Smith, *Colonists in Bondage: White Servitude and Convict Labor in America, 1607–1776* (Chapel Hill: University of North Carolina Press, 1947), 307–337.

9. Frederick Jackson Turner, "The Significance of the Frontier in American History," *Annual Report of the American Historical Society* (1893): 197–227.

10. Bailyn, *The Peopling of British North America*, 121.

11. "New France circa 1740," in *The Atlas of Canada* (Ottawa: Natural Resources Canada, 2002).

12. *A Discourse Concerning Western Planting, Written in the Year 1584 by Richard Hakluyt*, ed. Charles Deane (Cambridge, Mass.: J. Wilson, 1877), 7–8.

13. Thomas T. McAvoy, *A History of the Catholic Church in the United States* (Notre Dame, Ind.: Notre Dame University Press, 1969), 50–51.

14. Eli Faber, *A Time for Planting: The First Migration, 1654–1820* (Baltimore: Johns Hopkins University Press, 1992), 4.

15. Benjamin Franklin, *The Autobiography and Other Writings*, ed. Ormond Seavey (New York: Oxford University Press, 1993), 251–252.

16. Quoted in Kidd, *American Colonial History*, 71.

17. Cited in Bailyn, *The Peopling of British North America*, 10.

Chapter Two. Opening the Door to Europe's People

1. Hector St. John de Crèvecoeur, *Letters from an American Farmer* (1782; repr., New York: Fox, Duffield, 1904), 52, 54, 90.

2. George Washington, "Address to the Members of the Volunteer Association and Other Inhabitants of the Kingdom of Ireland Who Have Lately Arrived in the City of New York, December 2, 1783," in *The Writings of George Washington*, ed. John C. Fitzpatrick, 39 vols. (Washington, D.C.: U.S. Government Printing Office, 1931–1944), 27:254.

3. "From George Washington to the Hebrew Congregation in Newport, Rhode Island, 18 August 1790," *Founders Online*, National Archives, https://founders.archives.gov/documents/Washington/05-06-02-0135. Original source: *The Papers of George Washington*, Presidential Series, vol. 6, *1 July 1790–30 November 1790*, ed. Mark A. Mastromarino (Charlottesville: University Press of Virginia, 1996), 284–286.

4. Quoted in Hasia Diner, *A Time for Gathering: The Second Migration, 1820–1880* (Baltimore: Johns Hopkins University Press, 1992), 37.

5. "Alexander Hamilton's Final Version of the Report on the Subject of Manufactures, [5 December 1791]," *Founders Online*, National Archives, https://founders.archives.gov/documents/Hamilton/01-10-02-0001-0007. Original source: *The Papers of Alexander Hamilton*, vol. 10, *December*

1791–January 1792, ed. Harold C. Syrett (New York: Columbia University Press, 1966), 230–340.

6.　John Melish, *Information and Advice to Emigrants to the United States* (Philadelphia: John Melish, 1819), 90–91.

7.　Quoted in Maldwyn A. Jones, *American Immigration*, 2nd ed. (Chicago: University of Chicago Press, 1992), 55.

8.　Jones, *American Immigration*, 54.

9.　Quoted in Richard A. Bartlett, *The New Country: A Social History of the American Frontier, 1776–1890* (New York: Oxford University Press, 1974), 131.

10.　Hibernian Society of Baltimore, http://www.hiberniansocietyofbaltimore .org/.

11.　Deposition of Samuel B. Martin (1832), in *The Committee on the Judiciary of the Senate of the United States Made by the Honorable John MacPherson Berrien on January 27 and March 3, 1845, with Testimony Relating to the Violation of the Naturalization Laws* (Washington, D.C., 1845), 132.

12.　Quoted in Seth Rockman, *Scraping By: Wage Labor, Slavery, and Survival in Early Baltimore* (Baltimore: Johns Hopkins University Press 2009), 30, 86.

13.　Art. IV, sec. 2, U.S. Constitution.

14.　Madison and Hamilton both quoted in Richard A. Easterlin, David Ward, William S. Bernard, and Reed Ueda, eds., *Immigration* (Cambridge: Belknap Press of Harvard University Press, 1982), 81.

15.　Quoted in Marilyn C. Baseler, *"Asylum for Mankind": America, 1607–1800* (Ithaca: Cornell University Press, 1998), 256.

16.　*Annals of Congress*, Senate, 1st Cong., 2nd sess. (1790), 124.

17.　Quoted in Thomas T. McAvoy, *A History of the Catholic Church of the United States* (Notre Dame, Ind.: University of Notre Dame Press, 1969), 50–51.

18.　Quoted in Gordon S. Wood, *Empire of Liberty: A History of the Early Republic, 1789–1815* (New York: Oxford University Press, 2009), 247.

19.　William Smith Shaw to Abigail Adams, May 20, 1798, *Founders Online*, National Archives, https://founders.archives.gov/documents/Adams/04 -13-02-0018. Original source: *The Adams Papers*, Adams Family Correspondence, vol. 13, *May 1798–September 1799*, ed. Sara Martin et al. (Cambridge: Harvard University Press, 2017), 44–45; emphasis in original.

20.　Quoted in Marion R. Casey, "The Limits of Equality: Racial and Ethnic Tensions in the New Republic, 1789–1836," in *The Columbia Documentary History of Race and Ethnicity in America*, ed. Ronald Bayor (New York: Columbia University Press, 2004), 153.

Chapter Three. From Two Continents, Bound for Two Coasts, 1820–1882

1.　Reprinted in Thomas Dublin, ed., *Immigrant Voices: New Lives in America, 1773–2000* (Urbana: University of Illinois Press, 2014), 77–78.

2. Sylvia Sun Minnick, "Never Far from Home: Being Chinese in the California Gold Rush," in *Riches for All: The California Gold Rush and the World*, ed. Kenneth N. Owens (Lincoln: University of Nebraska Press, 2002), 143.

3. Quoted in Hasia R. Diner, *Erin's Daughters in America: Irish Immigrant Women in the Nineteenth Century* (Baltimore: Johns Hopkins University Press, 1983), 34.

4. Quoted in Ronald L. Lewis, *Welsh Americans: A History of Assimilation in the Coalfields* (Chapel Hill: University of North Carolina Press, 2008), 38–39.

5. Timothy Guinnane, "The Great Irish Famine and Population: The Long View," *American Economic Review* 84, no. 2 (1994): 303.

6. Roger Daniels, *Coming to America: A History of Immigration and Ethnicity in American Life* (New York: HarperCollins, 1990), 146.

7. Quoted in Elizabeth Sinn, *Pacific Crossing: California Gold, Chinese Migration, and the Making of Hong Kong* (Hong Kong: Hong Kong University Press, 2013), 51.

8. Quoted in Hasia R. Diner, *A Time for Gathering: The Second Migration, 1820–1880* (Baltimore: Johns Hopkins University Press, 1992), 39.

9. Whitaker quoted in Rowland Berthoff, *British Immigrants in Industrial America, 1790–1950* (Cambridge: Harvard University Press, 1953), 19; seamstress quoted in Arnold Schrier, *Ireland and the American Emigration, 1850–1900* (Minneapolis: University of Minnesota Press, 1958), 38.

10. Quoted in Lars Ljungmark, *Swedish Exodus*, trans. Kermit B. Westerberg (Carbondale: Southern Illinois University Press, 1979), 16.

11. Quoted in Berthoff, *British Immigrants in Industrial America*, 19.

12. Quoted in Walter D. Kamphoefner, Wolfgang Helbich, and Ulrike Sommer, *News from the Land of Freedom: German Immigrants Write Home*, trans. Susan Carter Vogel (Ithaca: Cornell University Press, 1991), 413.

13. T. W. Hancock, "On the Remittances from North America by Irish Emigrants. Considered as an Indication of Character of the Irish Race," *Journal of the Society for Social and Statistical Inquiry of Ireland*, 1873, 280–290.

14. Dean B. Mahin, *The Blessed Place of Freedom: Europeans in Civil War America* (Washington, D.C.: Brassey's, 2002).

15. M. Mark Stolarik, ed., *Forgotten Doors: The Other Ports of Entry to the United States* (Philadelphia: Balch Institute Press, 1988).

16. Quoted in Diner, *Erin's Daughters in America*, 89–90.

Chapter Four. Americans React, Regulations Begin, 1820–1882

1. Abraham Lincoln, State of the Union Address, December 8, 1863, http://www.let.rug.nl/usa/presidents/abraham-lincoln/state-of-the-union-1863.php.

2. Lyman Beecher, *A Plea for the West* (New York: Leavitt, Lord, 1835).

3. Philip Hone, *The Diary of Philip Hone, 1828–1851* (New York: Dodd, Mead, 1889), 64.

4. Quoted in Robert Ernst, *Immigrant Life in New York City, 1825–1863* (New York: King's Crown Press, 1949), 53.

5. Hidetaka Hirota, *Expelling the Poor: Atlantic Seaboard States and the Nineteenth-Century Origins of American Immigration Policy* (New York: Oxford University Press, 2017).

6. Hirota, *Expelling the Poor.*

7. Quoted in Hasia R. Diner, *Erin's Daughters in America: Irish Immigrant Women in the Nineteenth Century* (Baltimore: Johns Hopkins University Press, 1983), 123.

8. Quoted in *Complete Works of the Most Rev. John Hughes, D.D., Archbishop of New York, Comprising His Sermons, Letters, Lectures, Speeches, Etc. Carefully Compiled from the Best Sources, and Edited by Lawrence Kehoe*, vol. 2 (New York: Lawrence Kehoe, 1866), 270.

9. Quoted in William S. Bernard, "A History of U.S. Immigration Policy," in *Immigration*, ed. Richard A. Easterlin, David Ward, William S. Bernard, and Reed Ueda (Cambridge: Belknap Press of Harvard University Press, 1982), 85.

10. Morgenthau and Drachman are both quoted in Hasia R. Diner, *A Time for Gathering: The Second Migration, 1820–1880* (Baltimore: Johns Hopkins University Press, 1992), 198.

11. Quoted in Ernst, *Immigrant Life*, 67.

12. Arnold Schrier, *Ireland and the American Emigration, 1850–1900* (Minneapolis: University of Minnesota Press, 1958), 106.

13. Roger Daniels, *Coming to America: A History of Immigration and Ethnicity in American Life* (New York: HarperCollins, 1990), 239–242.

14. McDougal is quoted in Michael Miller Topp, "Racial and Ethnic Identity in the United States, 1837–1877," in *The Columbia Documentary History of Race and Ethnicity in America*, ed. Ronald H. Bayor (New York: Columbia University Press, 2004), 231.

15. Mary Elizabeth Brown, "Dennis Kearney (1847–1907): 'The Chinese Must Go!'" in *The Making of Modern Immigration: An Encyclopedia of People and Ideas*, ed. Patrick J. Hayes, 2 vols. (Santa Barbara, Calif.: ABC-CLIO, 2012), 2:468.

Chapter Five. The Masses Arrive as the Door Starts to Close, 1882–1921

1. Mary Antin, *The Promised Land* (Boston: Houghton, Mifflin, 1912), 163.

2. Lara Putnam, "Sentiment and the Restrictionist State: Evidence from the British Caribbean Experience, ca. 1925," *Journal of American Ethnic History* 35, no. 2 (Winter 2016): 5–31.

3. Roger Daniels, *Coming to America: A History of Immigration and Ethnicity in American Life* (New York: HarperCollins, 1990), 273.

4. Katherine Benton-Cohen, *Inventing the Immigration Problem: The Dillingham Commission and Its Legacy* (Cambridge: Harvard University Press, 2018).

5. Louis Adamic, *Laughing in the Jungle: The Autobiography of an Immigrant in America* (New York: Harper and Brothers, 1932), 10.

6. Quoted in Ewa Morawska, *For Bread with Butter: The Life-Worlds of East Central Europeans in Johnstown, Pennsylvania, 1890–1940* (New York: Cambridge University Press, 1985), 187.

7. Quoted in Hasia R. Diner, *Hungering for America: Italian, Irish, and Jewish Foodways in the Age of Migration* (Cambridge: Harvard University Press, 2001), 48.

8. Jack Glazier, *Dispersing the Ghetto: The Relocation of Jewish Immigrants across America* (Ithaca: Cornell University Press, 1998).

9. Sucheng Chan, *Entry Denied: Exclusion and the Chinese Community in America* (Philadelphia: Temple University Press, 1991).

10. Quoted in M. Vartan Malcom (Malcolm Vartan), *The Armenians in America* (Boston: Pilgrim Press, 1919), 118.

Chapter Six. What Americans Said about the Immigrants, 1882–1921

1. "Speech by Ellison Du Rant Smith, April 9, 1924," *Congressional Record*, 68th Cong., 1st sess. (Washington, D.C.: Government Printing Office, 1924), 65:5691–5692.

2. Quoted in Thomas Gossett, *Race: The History of an Idea* (Dallas: Southern Methodist University Press, 1963), 306.

3. Francis A. Walker, "Restriction of Immigration," *Atlantic*, June 1896.

4. Linda Gordon, *The Second Coming of the KKK: The Ku Klux Klan of the 1920s and the American Political Tradition* (New York: Liveright, 2017).

5. Gibbons is quoted in Richard Linkh, *American Catholicism and European Immigrants, 1900–1924* (Staten Island, N.Y.: Center for Migration Studies, 1975), 168–177. Eugene Weare, "Our Immigration Problem," *America* 39 (May 5, 1923): 55.

6. Booker T. Washington, "The Atlanta Exposition Address," delivered September 18, 1895, in Atlanta, quoted in *The Booker T. Washington Papers*, ed. Louis R. Harlan, vol. 3 (Urbana: University of Illinois Press, 1974), 583–587.

7. Jane Addams, *First Report of the Labor Museum, at Hull House, Chicago, 1901–1902* (Chicago: Hull House, 1902), 1.

8. Margaret Byington, *Homestead: The Households of a Mill Town* (New York: Charities Publication Committee, 1910), 3.

9. Upton Sinclair, *The Jungle* (New York: Doubleday, Page, 1906), 106.

10. Sophonisba P. Breckinridge, *New Homes for Old* (New York: Harper and Brothers, 1921), 215.

11. U.S. Immigration Commission, *Changes in Bodily Form of Descendants of Immigrants* (Washington, D.C.: Government Printing Office, 1910), 2. ("Based on investigations by Franz Boas, chiefly among Sicilians and East European Hebrews in New York public schools.")
12. Horace Kallen, "Democracy versus the Melting Pot," *Nation*, February 25, 1915, 192.
13. Kallen, "Democracy versus the Melting Pot," 220.
14. Randolph Bourne, "Trans-national America," *Atlantic*, July 1916, 86-97.

Chapter Seven. Closing the Gates

1. Aristide Zolberg, *A Nation by Design: Immigration Policy in the Fashioning of America* (Cambridge: Harvard University Press, 2006), 247.
2. U.S. Department of Commerce, *Statistical Abstract of the United States, 1925* (Washington, D.C., 1926), 75, table 70.
3. Quoted in Elizabeth Ewen, *Immigrant Women in the Land of Dollars: Life and Culture on the Lower East Side, 1890–1925* (New York: Monthly Review Press, 1985), 66.
4. Quoted in Vicki Ruíz, *From Out of the Shadows: Mexican Women in Twentieth-Century America*, rev. ed. (Oxford: Oxford University Press, 2008), 3–4.
5. Kelly Lytle Hernandez, *Migra! A History of the U.S. Border Patrol* (Berkeley: University of California Press, 2010), 26.
6. Francisco Balderrama and Raymond Rodríguez, *Decade of Betrayal: Mexican Repatriation in the 1930s*, rev. ed. (Albuquerque: University of New Mexico Press, 2006), 9.
7. Quoted in T. H. Watkins, *The Hungry Years: A Narrative History of the Great Depression in America* (New York: Henry Holt, 1999), 396.
8. Eric Foner, *Give Me Liberty! An American History*, 5th ed. (New York: W. W. Norton, 2016), 2:770.
9. Quoted in Robert Fleegler, *Ellis Island Nation: Immigration Policy and American Identity in the Twentieth Century* (Philadelphia: University of Pennsylvania Press, 2013), 19.
10. Quoted in Fleegler, *Ellis Island Nation*, 31.
11. Quoted in Fleegler, *Ellis Island Nation*, 21.
12. Quoted in Fleegler, *Ellis Island Nation*, 22.
13. Quoted in Fleegler, *Ellis Island Nation*, 23.
14. Quoted in Fleegler, *Ellis Island Nation*, 24.
15. Quoted in Gary Gerstle, *American Crucible: Race and Nation in the Twentieth Century* (Princeton: Princeton University Press, 2001), 117.
16. Quoted in Thomas Guglielmo, *White on Arrival: Italians, Race, Color, and Power in Chicago, 1890–1945* (Oxford: Oxford University Press, 2003), 70.
17. Quoted in Guglielmo, *White on Arrival*, 74.

18. Quoted in Mae Ngai, *Impossible Subjects: Illegal Aliens and the Making of Modern America* (Princeton: Princeton University Press, 2004), 34.

19. Zolberg, *A Nation by Design*, 264.

20. Quoted in Libby Garland, *After They Closed the Gates: Jewish Illegal Immigration to the United States, 1921–1965* (Chicago: University of Chicago Press, 2014), 134.

21. Quoted in Garland, *After They Closed the Gates*, 129–130.

22. Quoted in Garland, *After They Closed the Gates*, 134.

23. Ngai, *Impossible Subjects*, 103.

24. Bruno Ramirez with Yves Otis, *Crossing the 49th Parallel: Migration from Canada to the United States, 1900–1930* (Ithaca: Cornell University Press, 2001), 132.

25. Quoted in Hernandez, *Migra! A History of the U.S. Border Patrol*, 63.

26. Hernandez, *Migra! A History of the U.S. Border Patrol*, 63.

27. Quoted in Julia Young, *Mexican Exodus: Emigrants, Exiles, and Refugees of the Cristero War* (New York: Oxford University Press, 2015) 32n56.

28. Quoted in George Sánchez, *Becoming Mexican American: Ethnicity, Culture, and Identity in Chicano Los Angeles, 1900–1945* (New York: Oxford University Press, 1993), 15.

29. William Leuchtenburg, *Franklin D. Roosevelt and the New Deal, 1932–1940* (New York: Harper & Row, 1963), 19.

30. Lizabeth Cohen, *Making a New Deal: Industrial Workers in Chicago, 1919–1939*, 2nd ed. (New York: Cambridge University Press, 2008), 217.

31. Watkins, *The Hungry Years*, 44.

32. Quoted in Watkins, *The Hungry Years*, 37.

33. Sánchez, *Becoming Mexican American*, 210–211.

34. Quoted in Sánchez, *Becoming Mexican American*, 211.

35. Balderrama and Rodríguez, *Decade of Betrayal*, 92.

36. Matt García, *A World of Its Own: Race, Labor, and Citrus in the Making of Greater Los Angeles, 1900–1970* (Chapel Hill: University of North Carolina Press, 2001), 157–158.

37. Quoted in Sánchez, *Becoming Mexican American*, 209.

38. Quoted in Salvatore LaGumina, "The New Deal, the Immigrants, and Congressman Vito Marcantonio," *International Migration Review* 4, no. 2 (1970): 60–61.

39. Quoted in LaGumina, "The New Deal, the Immigrants, and Congressman Vito Marcantonio," 63n21.

40. Balderrama and Rodríguez, *Decade of Betrayal*, 107.

41. Balderrama and Rodríguez, *Decade of Betrayal*, 95.

42. Vicki Ruíz, *Cannery Women, Cannery Lives: Mexican Women, Unionization, and the California Food Processing Industry, 1930–1950* (Albuquerque: University of New Mexico Press, 1987), 49.

43. García, *A World of Its Own*, 117.

44. Quoted in Daniel Tichenor, *Dividing Lines: The Politics of Immigration Control in America* (Princeton: Princeton University Press, 2002), 156.
45. Zolberg, *A Nation by Design*, 268.
46. Zolberg, *A Nation by Design*, 269.
47. Quoted in Daniel Kanstroom, *Deportation Nation: Outsiders in American History* (Cambridge: Harvard University Press, 2007), 165.
48. Quoted in Kanstroom, *Deportation Nation*, 165.
49. U.S. Deparatment of Commerce, *Statistical Abstract of the United States, 1935* (Washington, D.C., 1935), 104.
50. Adam Goodman, *The Deportation Machine: America's Long History of Expelling Immigrants* (Princeton: Princeton University Press, 2020), 46.
51. Quoted in Watkins, *The Hungry Years*, 399.
52. Quoted in Watkins, *The Hungry Years*, 400.
53. Watkins, *The Hungry Years*, 401.
54. Zolberg, *A Nation by Design*, 270.
55. Sánchez, *Becoming Mexican American*, 214–215.
56. Quoted in Sánchez, *Becoming Mexican American*, 218.
57. Quoted in Sánchez, *Becoming Mexican American*, 224.
58. Interview with Emilia Castañeda, "Stories and Legacies," *Fighting Mexican Removal since the 1930s*, Boyle Heights Museum, https://www.boyleheights museum.org/five.
59. Ngai, *Impossible Subjects*, 122.
60. Quoted in Ngai, *Impossible Subjects*, 122.

Chapter Eight. Newcomers and World War II

1. Quoted in Sarah Ogilvie and Scott Miller, *Refuge Denied: The* St. Louis *Passengers and the Holocaust* (Madison: University of Wisconsin Press, 2006), 23.
2. Quoted in Ronald Takaki, *Double Victory: A Multicultural History of America in World War II* (Boston: Little, Brown, 2000), 94.
3. Quoted in Takaki, *Double Victory*, 94.
4. Aristide Zolberg, *A Nation by Design: Immigration Policy in the Fashioning of America* (Cambridge: Harvard University Press, 2006), 247.
5. Zolberg, *A Nation by Design*, 272.
6. Zolberg, *A Nation by Design*, 273.
7. Richard Breitman and Alan Kraut, *American Refugee Policy and European Jewry, 1933–1945* (Bloomington: Indiana University Press, 1987), 53.
8. Zolberg, *A Nation by Design*, 277.
9. Quoted in Zolberg, *A Nation by Design*, 274.
10. Quoted in Stephen Porter, *Benevolent Empire: U.S. Power, Humanitarianism, and the World's Dispossessed* (Philadelphia: University of Pennsylvania Press, 2016), 54.
11. Quoted in Roger Daniels and Otis Graham, *Debating American Immigration, 1882–Present* (Lanham, Md.: Rowman & Littlefield, 2001), 28.

12. Daniels and Graham, *Debating American Immigration*, 28.

13. Quoted in Barry Trachtenberg, "Did U.S. Anti-immigrant Hysteria Doom the Passengers on the 'St. Louis'? It's Complicated," *Tablet*, February 27, 2017, https://www.tabletmag.com/sections/news/articles/immigrant-hysteria-st-louis.

14. Quoted in Breitman and Kraut, *American Refugee Policy and European Jewry*, 49–50.

15. Richard Breitman and Alan Lichtman, *FDR and the Jews* (Cambridge: Belknap Press of Harvard University Press, 2013), 95.

16. Porter, *Benevolent Empire*, 54.

17. Daniel Tichenor, *Dividing Lines: The Politics of Immigration Control in America* (Princeton: Princeton University Press, 2002), 165.

18. Kelly Lytle Hernandez, *Migra! A History of the U.S. Border Patrol* (Berkeley: University of California Press, 2010), 106.

19. Mae Ngai, *Impossible Subjects: Illegal Aliens and the Making of Modern America* (Princeton: Princeton University Press, 2004), 138–139.

20. Quoted in Erasmo Gamboa, *Mexican Labor and World War II: Braceros in the Pacific Northwest, 1942–1947*, 2nd ed. (Seattle: University of Washington Press, 2000), 62.

21. Lucas Edmundo Benítez Cárdenas, interview by Alejandra Valles, 2008, "Interview no. 1335," Institute of Oral History, University of Texas at El Paso, https://scholarworks.utep.edu/cgi/viewcontent.cgi?article=2347&context=interviews, 6.

22. Quoted in Takaki, *Double Victory*, 94.

23. Quoted in Erasmo Gamboa, *Bracero Railroaders: The Forgotten World War II Story of Mexican Workers in the U.S. West* (Seattle: University of Washington Press, 2016), 92.

24. Takaki, *Double Victory*, 83.

25. Quoted in Takaki, *Double Victory*, 88.

26. Takaki, *Double Victory*, 96.

27. Quoted in Takaki, *Double Victory*, 98.

28. Quoted in Takaki, *Double Victory*, 99.

29. Quoted in Elizabeth R. Escobedo, *From Coveralls to Zoot Suits: The Lives of Mexican American Women on the World War II Home Front* (Chapel Hill: University of North Carolina Press, 2013), 74.

30. Quoted in Escobedo, *From Coveralls to Zoot Suits*, 76.

31. Luis Alverez, "Zoot Violence on the Home Front: Race, Riots, and Youth Culture during World War II," in *Mexican Americans and World War II*, ed. Maggie Rivas-Rodriguez (Austin: University of Texas Press, 2005), 153–154.

32. Hernandez, *Migra! A History of the U.S. Border Patrol*, 120–121.

33. Quoted in Gary Mormino, *Immigrants on the Hill: Italian-Americans in St. Louis, 1882–1982* (1986; repr., Columbia: University of Missouri Press, 2002), 239.

34. David Kennedy, *Freedom from Fear: The American People in Depression and War*, 2 vols. (New York: Oxford University Press, 2004), 2:750–751.

35. Kennedy, *Freedom from Fear*, 2:748; Erika Lee, *The Making of Asian America: A History* (New York: Simon and Schuster, 2015), 211.

36. Kennedy, *Freedom from Fear*, 2:749; Takaki, *Double Victory*, 151.

37. Kennedy, *Freedom from Fear*, 2:749.

38. Lee, *The Making of Asian America*, 212.

39. Quoted in Lauren Migaki, "At 92, a Japanese-American Reflects on the Lessons of Internment Camps," NPR, December 7, 2016, https://www .npr.org/2016/12/07/504602293/at-92-a-japanese-american-reflects-on -the-hardships-of-internment-camps.

40. Quoted in Lee, *The Making of Asian America*, 230.

41. Quoted in Kennedy, *Freedom from Fear*, 2:752.

42. Quoted in Ellen Wu, *The Color of Success: Asian Americans and the Origins of the Model Minority* (Princeton: Princeton University Press, 2013), 43.

43. Madeline Hsu, *The Good Immigrants: How the Yellow Peril Became the Model Minority* (Princeton: Princeton University Press, 2015), 90.

44. Philip Wolgin and Irene Bloemraad, "'Our Gratitude to Our Soldiers': Military Spouses, Family Re-Unification, and Postwar Immigration Reform," *Journal of Interdisciplinary History* 41, no. 1 (2010): 32.

45. Roger Daniels, *Guarding the Golden Door: American Immigration Policy and Immigrants since 1882* (New York: Hill and Wang, 2004), 84; "Varian Fry," *Holocaust Encyclopedia*, United States Holocaust Memorial Musuem, https://encyclopedia.ushmm.org/content/en/article/varian-fry.

46. Breitman and Kraut, *American Refugee Policy and European Jewry*, 199; Daniels, *Guarding the Golden Door*, 86.

Chapter Nine. Prosperity, the Braceros, and Cold War Refugees, 1945–1965

1. Quoted in Ana Elizabeth Rosas, *Abrazando el Espíritu: Bracero Families Confront the US–Mexico Border* (Berkeley: University of California Press, 2014), 119.

2. Tabulated from the table "Immigration to the United States: Fiscal Years 1820–2000," in Department of Homeland Security, *2000 Statistical Yearbook of the Immigration and Naturalization Service* (Washington, D.C., 2002), 18.

3. David Potter, *People of Plenty: Economic Abundance and the American Character* (Chicago: University of Chicago Press, 1954).

4. William O'Neill, *American High: The Years of Confidence, 1945–1960* (New York: Free Press, 1986).

5. Quoted in Joshua Zeitz, *White Ethnic New York: Jews, Catholics, and the Shaping of Postwar Politics* (Chapel Hill: University of North Carolina Press, 2007), 17.

6. Quoted in Joshua Freeman, *Working-Class New York: Life and Labor since World War II* (New York: New Press, 2000), 170.

7. James T. Patterson, *Grand Expectations: The United States, 1945–1974* (New York: Oxford University Press, 1996), 314.

8. Quoted in Zeitz, *White Ethnic New York*, 85.

9. Ellen Wu, *The Color of Success: Asian Americans and the Origins of the Model Minority* (Princeton: Princeton University Press, 2013), 138.

10. Quoted in Wu, *Color of Success*, 148.

11. "An Interview with Sonia Lang," by Carol Esarey, October 25, 2010, transcript, Abraham Lincoln Presidential Library, *Immigrants' Stories* Oral History Project, https://www2.illinois.gov/alplm/library/collections/OralHistory/ImmigrantStories/Documents/LangSon/Lang_Son_4FNL.pdf, 28.

12. Lang interview, 31.

13. Quoted in Danuta Mostwin, "Post–World War II Polish Immigrants in the United States," *Polish American Studies* 26, no. 2 (1969): 9.

14. U.S. Department of Commerce, *Statistical Abstract of the United States, 1980* (Washington D.C., 1980), 93.

15. Erika Lee, *The Making of Asian America: A History* (New York: Simon and Schuster, 2015), 260.

16. Madeline Hsu, *The Good Immigrants: How the Yellow Peril Became the Model Minority* (Princeton: Princeton University Press, 2015), 133.

17. U.S. Department of Commerce, *Statistical Abstract of the United States, 1970* (Washington, D.C., 1970), 93.

18. Reginald Stuart, *Dispersed Relations: Americans and Canadians in Upper North America* (Baltimore: Johns Hopkins University Press, 2007), 90.

19. U.S. Department of Commerce, *Statistical Abstract of the United States, 1980*, 94.

20. Peter Gatrell, *The Making of the Modern Refugee* (Oxford: Oxford University Press, 2013), 182.

21. Gatrell, *The Making of the Modern Refugee*, 182–183.

22. Gatrell, *The Making of the Modern Refugee*, 186.

23. Gatrell, *The Making of the Modern Refugee*, 179.

24. Gatrell, *The Making of the Modern Refugee*, 186–187.

25. Hsu, *The Good Immigrants*, 148.

26. Stephen Porter, *Benevolent Empire: U.S. Power, Humanitarianism, and the World's Dispossessed* (Philadelphia: University of Pennsylvania Press, 2016), 102.

27. Hsu, *The Good Immigrants*, 123.

28. Quoted in "Good Report Given on DPs in US," *New York Times*, July 16, 1950, 32.

29. Quoted in Porter, *Benevolent Empire*, 101.

30. Quoted in Porter, *Benevolent Empire*, 101.

31. Quoted in Carl Bon Tempo, *Americans at the Gate: The United States and Refugees during the Cold War* (Princeton: Princeton University Press, 2008), 44.

32. Quoted in Bon Tempo, *Americans at the Gate*, 47.

33. Quoted in Bon Tempo, *Americans at the Gate*, 34.

34. Roger Daniels, *Coming to America: A History of Immigration and Ethnicity in American Life* (New York: HarperCollins, 1990), 337; Bon Tempo, *Americans at the Gate*, 85.

35. Lilli Tnaib, "Fifty Years On," *Refugees* 144, no. 3 (2006), https://www.unhcr.org/4523cb392.pdf, 12–13.

36. Roger Daniels, *Guarding the Golden Door: American Immigration Policy and Immigrants since 1882* (New York: Hill and Wang, 2004), 195.

37. Constance Parten, "Escape from Havana: Personal Stories," September 13, 2013, https://www.cnbc.com/2010/05/25/Escape-From-Havana:-Personal-Stories.html.

38. Mae Ngai, *Impossible Subjects: Illegal Aliens and the Making of Modern America* (Princeton: Princeton University Press, 2004), 138.

39. Deborah Cohen, *Braceros: Migrant Citizens and Transnational Subjects in the Postwar United States and Mexico* (Chapel Hill: University of North Carolina Press, 2011), 26.

40. Cohen, *Braceros*, 24–25; David Reimers, *Still the Golden Door: The Third World Comes to America*, 2nd ed. (New York: Columbia University Press, 1992), 43–44.

41. Ngai, *Impossible Subjects*, 146.

42. Kelly Lytle Hernandez, "Largest Deportation Campaign in US History Is No Match for Trump's Plan," *The Conversation*, March 8, 2017, https://theconversation.com/largest-deportation-campaign-in-us-history-is-no-match-for-trumps-plan-73651.

43. Ngai, *Impossible Subjects*, 156.

44. Kelly Lytle Hernandez, *Migra! A History of the U.S. Border Patrol* (Berkeley: University of California Press, 2010), 171–173.

45. Reimers, *Still the Golden Door*, 48.

46. Quoted in Cohen, *Braceros*, 120.

47. Quoted in Cohen, *Braceros*, 120.

48. Quoted in Reimers, *Still the Golden Door*, 48.

49. Quoted in Cohen, *Braceros*, 120.

50. Quoted in Ngai, *Impossible Subjects*, 142.

51. Ngai, *Impossible Subjects*, 139.

52. Ngai, *Impossible Subjects*, 147.

53. Quoted in Rosas, *Abrazando el Espíritu*, 67.

54. Ngai, *Impossible Subjects*, 142.

55. Cohen, *Braceros*, 1–2.

Chapter Ten. The Age of Reform

1. Quoted in John F. Kennedy, *A Nation of Immigrants* (1958; repr., New York: Harper Perennial, 2008), 3.
2. Quoted in Robert Fleegler, *Ellis Island Nation: Immigration Policy and American Identity in the Twentieth Century* (Philadelphia: University of Pennsylvania Press, 2013), 127.
3. Quoted in Fleegler, *Ellis Island Nation*, 161.
4. Quoted in Roger Daniels, *Guarding the Golden Door: American Immigration Policy and Immigrants since 1882* (New York: Hill and Wang, 2004), 116.
5. Quoted in David Tichenor, *Dividing Lines: The Politics of Immigration Control in America* (Princeton: Princeton University Press, 2002), 215.
6. Lyndon B. Johnson, "Remarks to the Delegates to the White House Conference 'To Fulfill These Rights,'" June 1, 1966, American Presidency Project, https://www.presidency.ucsb.edu/node/238890.
7. Quoted in Fleegler, *Ellis Island Nation*, 127.
8. Quoted in Fleegler, *Ellis Island Nation*, 133.
9. Quoted in Gary Gerstle, *American Crucible: Race and Nation in the Twentieth Century* (Princeton: Princeton University Press, 2001), 260.
10. Quoted in Fleegler, *Ellis Island Nation*, 162.
11. Quoted in Daniels, *Guarding the Golden Door*, 121.
12. Quoted in Judith Gans, Elaine M. Replogle, and Daniel Tichenor, eds., *Debates on U.S. Immigration* (Thousand Oaks, Calif.: SAGE, 2012), 544.
13. Harry S. Truman, "Veto of Bill to Revise the Laws Relating to Immigration, Naturalization, and Nationality," June 25, 1952, American Presidency Project, https://www.presidency.ucsb.edu/node/231060.
14. Quoted in Gerstle, *American Crucible*, 260.
15. Quoted in Tichenor, *Dividing Lines*, 211.
16. Quoted in Daniels, *Guarding the Golden Door*, 133.
17. Quoted in Daniels, *Guarding the Golden Door*, 135.
18. Thomas T. Phu, "Refugees and Boat People," *Encyclopedia of the Vietnam War: A Political, Social, and Military History*, ed. Spencer Tucker, 2nd ed. (Santa Barbara, Calif.: ABC-CLIO, 2011), 3:965–966; Michael Pugh, "Drowning Not Waving: Boat People and Humanitarianism at Sea," *Journal of Refugee Studies* 17, no. 1 (2004): 51.
19. "Interview with Dr. Patrick Lam," by Edward Cunningham, August 14, 2014, *Immigrant Stories* Oral History Project, Abraham Lincoln Presidential Library, https://www2.illinois.gov/alplm/library/collections/OralHistory/ImmigrantStories/Documents/LamPat/Lam_Pat_4FNL.pdf, 3.
20. "Interview with Dr. Patrick Lam," 4–5.
21. Carl Bon Tempo, *Americans at the Gate: The United States and Refugees during the Cold War* (Princeton: Princeton University Press, 2008), 150–151.

22. Refugee Act of 1980, Public Law 96-212, 96th Cong., March 17, 1980, https://www.govinfo.gov/content/pkg/STATUTE-94/pdf/STATUTE-94-Pg102.pdf.

23. Roger Daniels, *Coming to America: A History of Immigration and Ethnicity in American Life* (New York: HarperCollins, 1990), 347.

24. José Manuel García, *Voices from Mariel: Oral Histories of the 1980 Cuban Boatlift* (Gainesville: University of Florida Press, 2018), 44.

25. García, *Voices from Mariel*, 44.

26. García, *Voices from Mariel*, 50.

27. García, *Voices from Mariel*, 50.

28. Bon Tempo, *Americans at the Gates*, 180.

29. Quoted in Ward Sinclair, "Haitian Boat People: Flotsam in an American Sea of Plenty," *Washington Post*, April 19, 1980, https://www.washingtonpost.com/archive/politics/1980/04/19/haitian-boat-people-flotsam-in-an-american-sea-of-plenty/30b0503f-4012-4afa-8912-b8c130e62fb2/.

Chapter Eleven. A New Open Door

1. Joseph Nevins, *Operation Gatekeeper and Beyond: The War on "Illegals" and the Remaking of the U.S.–Mexico Boundary*, 2nd ed. (New York: Routledge, 2010), 101–102.

2. U.S. Bureau of the Census, *Statistical Abstract of the United States, 2003* (Washington, D.C., 2003), 11.

3. U.S. Bureau of the Census, *Statistical Abstract of the United States, 2000* (Washington, D.C., 2000), 9.

4. Roger Daniels, *Guarding the Golden Door: American Immigration Policy and Immigrants since 1882* (New York: Hill and Wang, 2004), 249–250.

5. U.S. Bureau of the Census, *Statistical Abstract of the United States, 2003*, 11; U.S. Department of Commerce, *Statistical Abstract of the United States, 1990* (Washington, D.C., 1990), 11.

6. Zai Liang and Wenzhen Ye, "From Fujian to New York: Understanding the New Chinese Immigration," in *Global Human Smuggling: Comparative Perspectives*, ed. David Kyle and Rey Koslowski (Baltimore: Johns Hopkins University Press, 2001), 190–191.

7. U.S. Census Bureau, *Population Profile of the United States: 2000*, https://www.census.gov/prod/2001pubs/p23-profile2000.pdf, 2-2.

8. Kwok-Wai "David" Chan, interview by Mary Lui, Museum of Chinese in America, April 17, 1993, http://ohms.mocanyc.org/viewer/viewer.php?cachefile=1994_007_006_1529529080.xml.

9. "Interview with Maija Rhee Devine," by Mark DePue, August 29, 2013, *Immigrant Stories* Oral History Project, Abraham Lincoln Presidential Library, https://www2.illinois.gov/alplm/library/collections/OralHistory/ImmigrantStories/Documents/DevineMaija/Devine_Mai_4FNL.pdf, 89.

10. Sherri Grasmuck and Patricia Pessar, *Between Two Islands: Dominican International Migration* (Berkeley: University of California Press, 1991), 46.

11. Erika Lee, *The Making of Asian America: A History* (New York: Simon and Schuster, 2015), 288.

12. Lee, *The Making of Asian America*, 288.

13. U.S. Bureau of the Census, *Statistical Abstract of the United States, 2004–2005* (Washington, D.C., 2005), 10.

14. Grasmuck and Pessar, *Between Two Islands*, 21.

15. Charles Hirschmann and Douglas Massey, "Places and Peoples," in *New Faces in New Places: The Changing Geography of American Immigration*, ed. Douglas Massey (New York: Russell Sage, 2008), 2–3.

16. Ronald Mize and Alicia Swords, *Consuming Mexican Labor: From the Bracero Program to Nafta* (Toronto: University of Toronto Press, 2011), 136.

17. Quoted in Lee, *The Making of Asian America*, 290.

18. Barbara M. Posadas, *The Filipino Americans* (Westport, Conn.: Greenwood Press, 1999), 80.

19. Philip Martin, "Good Intentions Gone Awry: IRCA and U.S. Agriculture," *Annals of the Academy of Political and Social Science* 534, no. 1 (1994), https://migration.ucdavis.edu/cf/more.php?id=198_0_2_0.

20. Mize and Swords, *Consuming Mexican Labor*, 123–124.

21. José Limón, "Transnational Triangulation," in *Mexico and Mexicans in the Making of the United States*, ed. John Tutino (Austin: University of Texas Press, 2012), 240.

22. Grasmuck and Pessar, *Between Two Islands*, 70–71.

23. Mike Davis, *Magical Urbanism: Latinos Reinvent the US City* (New York: Verso, 2000), 117.

24. Ramona Hernández, *The Mobility of Workers under Advanced Capitalism: Dominican Migration to the United States* (New York: Columbia University Press, 2002), 98.

25. Joel Millman, *The Other Americans: How Immigrants Renew Our Country, Our Economy, and Our Values* (New York: Viking, 1997), 259–261.

26. Quoted in Millman, *The Other Americans*, 260.

27. Lee, *Making of Asian America*, 290.

28. Quoted in Virginia Hitchman, ed., *La Frontera: Stories of Undocumented Immigrants Crossing the Border* (Newman, Calif.: La Frontera Press, 2014), 37.

29. This figure is drawn from U.S. Bureau of the Census, *Statistical Abstract of the United States, 2004–2005* (Washington, D.C., 2005), 10, and U.S. Bureau of the Census, *Statistical Abstract of the United States, 1993* (Washington, D.C., 1994), 11; see also Millman, *The Other Americans*, 213–214.

30. Millman, *The Other Americans*, 219–220.

31. Millman, *The Other Americans*, 229.

32. Quoted in Joel Millman, "Newcomers," *New Republic*, November 24, 1997, 18.

33. Quoted in Millman, "Newcomers," 18.

34. Roger Daniels, *Coming to America: A History of Immigration and Ethnicity in American Life* (New York: HarperCollins, 1990), 438; see also the compendium of immigration polls by Gallup at http://news.gallup.com/poll/1660/immigration.aspx.

35. Niskanen Center, "Americans Support Immigration," June 10, 2015, 6, chart 7, https://www.niskanencenter.org/wp-content/uploads/old_up loads/2015/06/Niskanen-Americans-Favor-Immigration.pdf.

36. See the compendium of immigration polls by Gallup at http://news.gallup.com/poll/1660/immigration.aspx.

37. Nevins, *Operation Gatekeeper and Beyond*, 111.

38. Quoted in Carl Bon Tempo, *Americans at the Gate: The United States and Refugees during the Cold War* (Princeton: Princeton University Press, 2008), 171.

39. Arthur Schlesinger, *The Disuniting of America: Reflections on a Multicultural Society* (1991; repr., New York: W. W. Norton, 1998), 127.

40. Schlesinger, *The Disuniting of America*, 147.

41. Patrick Buchanan, "Immigration Time-Out," October 31, 1994, https://buchanan.org/blog/immigration-time-out-163.

42. The campaign advertisement can be seen on YouTube at https://www.youtube.com/watch?v=4-KkiYcK7IA.

43. Quoted in David Tichenor, *Dividing Lines: The Politics of Immigration Control in America* (Princeton: Princeton University Press, 2002), 237.

44. Quoted in Peter Schrag, *Not Fit for Our Society: Nativism and Immigration* (Berkeley: University of California Press, 2010), 178.

45. Quoted in Schrag, *Not Fit for Our Society*, 179.

46. Quoted in Tichenor, *Dividing Lines*, 276.

47. Poster, "No al 187," ca. 1994, Oakland Museum of California, http://collections.museumca.org/?q=collection-item/2010546538.

48. Quoted in Linda Greenhouse, "Breathing While Undocumented," *New York Times*, April 26, 2010.

49. Quoted in Robert Fleegler, *Ellis Island Nation: Immigration Policy and American Identity in the Twentieth Century* (Philadelphia: University of Pennsylvania Press, 2013), 196.

50. Quoted in Charles Fishman, "Shirley Chisolm," *Orlando Sentinel*, October 25, 1992.

51. Donna Gabaccia, *We Are What We Eat: Ethnic Food and the Making of Americans* (Cambridge: Harvard University Press, 1998), 184.

52. Quoted in Gabaccia, *We Are What We Eat*, 199.

53. Diane Seo, "Growing Asian Enrollment Redefines UC," *Los Angeles Times*, December 27, 1995, VYA1.

54. University of California, "Fall Enrollment at a Glance," https://www.universityofcalifornia.edu/infocenter/fall-enrollment-glance.

Chapter Twelve. Immigration Politics and Restrictionism, 1970–2001

1. Quoted in Hugh Davis Graham, *Collision Course: The Strange Convergence of Affirmative Action and Immigration Policy in America* (New York: Oxford University Press, 2002), 119.
2. Quoted in David Tichenor, *Dividing Lines: The Politics of Immigration Control in America* (Princeton: Princeton University Press, 2002), 269.
3. Quoted in Dara Lind, "The Disastrous, Forgotten 1996 Law That Created Today's Immigration Problem," *Vox*, April 28, 2016, https://www.vox .com/2016/4/28/11515132/iirira-clinton-immigration.
4. Peter Edelman, "The Worst Thing Bill Clinton Has Done," *Atlantic*, March 1997, https://www.theatlantic.com/magazine/archive/1997/03/ the-worst-thing-bill-clinton-has-done/376797/.
5. Tichenor, *Dividing Lines*, 262–263.
6. Bill Ong Hing, *Defining America through Immigration Policy* (Philadelphia: Temple University Press, 2003), 110.
7. Balraj Sokkappa, interview by Julie Kerssen, January 14, 2005, South Asian Oral History Project, University of Washington, https://digitalcollections .lib.washington.edu/digital/collection/saohc/id/14/rec/7.
8. Aristide Zolberg, *A Nation by Design: Immigration Policy in the Fashioning of America* (Cambridge: Harvard University Press, 2006), 419–420; Audrey Singer, "Immigrants, Welfare Reform, and the Coming Reauthorization Vote," Migration Policy Institute, August 1, 2002, https://www .migrationpolicy.org/article/immigrants-welfare-reform-and-coming -reauthorization-vote.
9. Amanda Levinson, "Immigrants and Welfare," Migration Policy Institute, August 1, 2002, https://www.migrationpolicy.org/article/immigrants-and -welfare-use#IMPACTOFWELFAREREFORM.
10. Levinson, "Immigrants and Welfare."
11. Quoted in Erin Siegal, "Immigration Reform: What the Last 'Path to Citizenship' Did for Immigrants," *Christian Science Monitor Weekly*, April 8, 2013.
12. Quoted in Siegal, "Immigration Reform."
13. Daniels, *Guarding the Golden Door*, 229; Zolberg, *A Nation by Design*, 371–372.
14. Philip Martin, "Good Intentions Gone Awry: IRCA and U.S. Agriculture," *Annals of the Academy of Political and Social Science* 534, no. 1 (1994), https://migration.ucdavis.edu/cf/more.php?id=198_0_2_0.
15. Nancy Rytina, U.S. Immigration and Naturalization Service, "IRCA Legalization Effects: Lawful Permanent Residence and Naturalization through 2001," October 25, 2002, https://www.dhs.gov/xlibrary/assets/ statistics/publications/irca0114int.pdf, 3.

16. United States v. Brignoni-Ponce, 422 U.S. 873 (1975), https://www.loc
    .gov/item/usrep422873/.

17. These figures are drawn from Joseph Nevins, *Operation Gatekeeper and
    Beyond: The War on "Illegals" and the Remaking of the U.S.–Mexico Boundary*,
    2nd ed. (New York: Routledge, 2010), 5, 44, 84, appendix F.

18. Quoted in Ruben Vivas, "Illegal Immigration: Return of the Workplace
    Raid?" *Los Angeles Times*, January 15, 2017, B1.

19. Quoted in Hing, *Defining America through Immigration Policy*, 151; empha-
    sis in original.

20. Nevins, *Operation Gatekeeper and Beyond*, 2.

21. Quoted in Nevins, *Operation Gatekeeper and Beyond*, 110.

22. Nevins, *Operation Gatekeeper and Beyond*, 111.

23. Quoted in Ken Ellingwood, "Border Battle's New Hot Spot," *Los Angeles
    Times*, May 10, 1998, 1.

24. Quoted in Ellingwood, "Border Battle's New Hot Spot," 1.

25. Quoted in Kristina Davis, "Turning Point at the Border," *Los Angeles
    Times*, September 30, 2019, B1.

26. Mike Davis, *Magical Urbanism: Latinos Reinvent the US City* (New York:
    Verso, 2000), 42.

27. Department of Homeland Security, *Aliens Expelled: Fiscal Years 1892–2004*,
    "Immigration Enforcement Actions 2004 Data Tables," table 40, https://
    www.dhs.gov/immigration-statistics/enforcement-actions.

28. Department of Homeland Security, *Aliens Expelled*, "Immigration En-
    forcement Actions 2004 Data Tables," tables 40 and 38.

29. U.S. Bureau of the Census, *Statistical Abstract of the United States, 2004–
    2005* (Washington, D.C., 2005), 198.

30. Jeffrey Passel and D'Vera Cohen, "U.S. Unauthorized Immigrant To-
    tal Dips to Lowest Level in a Decade," Pew Research Center, Novem-
    ber 27, 2018, https://www.pewresearch.org/hispanic/2018/11/27/u-s
    -unauthorized-immigrant-total-dips-to-lowest-level-in-a-decade/.

31. U.N. High Commissioner for Refugees, *The State of the World's Refu-
    gees, 2000: Fifty Years of Humanitarian Action* (January 1, 2000), 105–106,
    https://www.unhcr.org/3ebf9bafo.html.

32. Migration Policy Institute, "U.S. Annual Refugee Resettlement Ceil-
    ings and Number of Refugees Admitted, 1980–Present," https://www
    .migrationpolicy.org/programs/data-hub/charts/us-annual-refugee
    -resettlement-ceilings-and-number-refugees-admitted-united.

33. Richard Lamm, "The U.S. Accepts Too Many Refugees," *New York Times*,
    December 15, 1985, sec. 4, p. 23.

34. Roger Daniels, *Coming to America: A History of Immigration and Ethnicity in
    American Life* (New York: HarperCollins, 1990), 382.

35. Quoted in Virginia Hitchman, ed., *La Frontera: Stories of Undocumented Im-
    migrants Crossing the Border* (Newman, Calif.: La Frontera Press, 2014), 3.

36. Bon Tempo, *Americans at the Gate: The United States and Refugees during the Cold War* (Princeton: Princeton University Press, 2008), 190; Daniels, *Coming to America*, 382–383; Susan Gzesh, "Central Americans and Asylum Policy in the Reagan Era," Migration Policy Institute, April 1, 2006, https://www.migrationpolicy.org/article/central-americans-and-asylum-policy-reagan-era.

37. Quoted in Bon Tempo, *Americans at the Gate*, 190.

38. William Alberts, "Opening Tombs and Resurrecting Lives," *Counterpunch*, April 17, 2019, https://www.counterpunch.org/2019/04/17/opening-tombs-and-resurrecting-lives/.

39. María Cristina García, *The Refugee Challenge in Post–Cold War America* (New York: Oxford University Press, 2017), 1.

40. García, *The Refugee Challenge in Post–Cold War America*, 8.

41. Migration Policy Institute, "U.S. Annual Refugee Resettlement Ceilings and Number of Refugees Admitted."

42. Gérard Prunier, *Africa's World War: Congo, the Rwandan Genocide, and the Making of a Continental Catastrophe* (New York: Oxford University Press, 2009).

43. García, *The Refugee Challenge in Post–Cold War America*, 159, 163.

44. García, *The Refugee Challenge in Post–Cold War America*, 168.

45. García, *The Refugee Challenge in Post–Cold War America*, 52.

46. García, *The Refugee Challenge in Post–Cold War America*, 59–60.

47. Quoted in Kim A. O'Connell, "Echoes of Saigon: Vietnamese Immigration and the Changing Face of Arlington," Virginia Foundation for the Humanities, https://virginiahumanities.org/wp-content/uploads/2016/09/Echoes-of-Little-Saigon.pdf, 12.

48. Quoted in O'Connell, "Echoes of Saigon," 22.

49. Quoted in Matthew Schwartz, "Why Is There Such a Large Ethiopian Population in the Washington Region?" WAMU Radio, April 21, 2016, https://wamu.org/story/16/04/21/how_did_the_dc_region_become_home_to_the_largest_population_of_ethiopians_in_the_us/.

50. Solomon A. Getahun, "Africans and African Americans from East Africa, 1940–Present," in *Immigrants in American History*, ed. Elliott Barkan, 4 vols. (Santa Barbara, Calif.: ABC-CLIO, 2013), 3:692.

51. Quoted in Walter Nicholls, "Washington's Little Ethiopia," *Washington Post*, May 18, 2005.

52. These figures are from U.S. Customs and Immigration Enforcement, "History of ICE," https://www.ice.gov/history.

53. Cam Simpson and Flynn McRoberts, "U.S. Ends Muslim Registry," *Chicago Tribune*, December 2, 2003, https://www.chicagotribune.com/investigations/chi-0312020136dec02-story.html.

54. Quoted in Simpson and McRoberts, "U.S. Ends Muslim Registry."

55. Quoted in Simpson and McRoberts, "U.S. Ends Muslim Registry."

56. Quoted in Bon Tempo, *Americans at the Gate*, 205.

57. Quoted in Aristide Zolberg, *A Nation by Design: Immigration Policy in the Fashioning of America* (Cambridge: Harvard University Press, 2006), 445.

58. See the 2001–2003 spreadsheets at the Refugee Processing Center, "Refugee Admissions Report," https://www.wrapsnet.org/admissions-and -arrivals/.

Chapter Thirteen. The Era of Border Security

1. Department of Homeland Security, *2016 Yearbook of Immigration Statistics* (Washington, D.C., 2016), 5–7, tables 1 and 2.

2. Muzaffar Chishti and Faye Hipsman, "In Historic Shift, New Migration Flows from Mexico Fall Below Those from China and India," Migration Policy Institute, May 21, 2015, https://www.migrationpolicy.org/article/historic -shift-new-migration-flows-mexico-fall-below-those-china-and-india

3. Department of Homeland Security, *2016 Yearbook of Immigration Statistics*, 39, 40–41, tables 13, 14; Department of Homeland Security, *2009 Yearbook of Immigration Statistics*, 40–41, table 14.

4. Department of Homeland Security, *2016 Yearbook of Immigration Statistics*, 43, table 16.

5. Nadwa Mossad and Ryan Baugh, "Refugees and Asylees: 2016, Annual Flow Report," January 2018, https://www.dhs.gov/sites/default/files/ publications/Refugees_Asylees_2016_0.pdf, 7.

6. Jens Manuel Krogstad, Jeffrey Passel, and D'Vera Cohn, "5 Facts about Illegal Immigration in the U.S.," Pew Research Center, June 12, 2019, https://www.pewresearch.org/fact-tank/2019/06/12/5-facts-about-illegal -immigration-in-the-u-s/.

7. Quoted in Lynnaire Sheridan, *"I Know It's Dangerous": Why Mexicans Risk Their Lives to Cross the Border* (Tucson: University of Arizona Press, 2009), 34.

8. Quoted in James McKinley, "Fleeing Drug Violence, Mexicans Pour into U.S.," *New York Times*, April 17, 2010, A1.

9. Liliana M. González and Michael Feil, "Public Insecurity and International Emigration in Northern Mexico," in *Mexican Migration to the United States: Perspectives from Both Sides of the Border*, ed. Harriet Romo and Olivia Mogollon-Lopez (Austin: University of Texas Press, 2016).

10. For the 2000 figure, see U.S. Bureau of the Census, *Statistical Abstract of the United States, 2004–2005* (Washington, D.C., 2005), 9; for the 2016 figure, see Carlos Echeverria-Estrada and Jeanne Batalova, "Chinese Immigrants in the United States," Migration Policy Institute, January 15, 2020, https:// www.migrationpolicy.org/article/chinese-immigrants-united-states-2018.

11. Quoted in Xiaojian Zhao, *The New Chinese America: Class, Economy, and Social Hierarchy* (New Brunswick: Rutgers University Press, 2010), 133.

12. Quoted in Zhao, *The New Chinese America*, 134.

13. UNHCR, "Forced Displacement above 68M in 2017, New Global Deal on Refugees Critical," June 19, 2018, https://www.unhcr.org/afr/news/press/2018/6/5b27c2434/forced-displacement-above-68m-2017-new-global-deal-refugees-critical.html.

14. UNHCR, *Global Trends: Forced Displacement in 2017*, https://www.unhcr.org/5b27be547, 6, 14.

15. Phillip Connor, "Number of Refugees to Europe Surges to Record 1.3 Million in 2015," Pew Research Center, August 2, 2016, https://www.pewresearch.org/global/2016/08/02/number-of-refugees-to-europe-surges-to-record-1-3-million-in-2015/, 2.

16. Quoted in Doctors Without Borders, "Forced to Flee Central America's Northern Triangle," May 11, 2017, https://www.doctorswithoutborders.org/what-we-do/news-stories/research/report-forced-flee-central-americas-northern-triangle, 24.

17. Dara Lind, "The 2014 Central American Migrant Crisis," *Vox*, October 10, 2014, https://www.vox.com/2014/10/10/18088638/child-migrant-crisis-unaccompanied-alien-children-rio-grande-valley-obama-immigration.

18. Elizabeth Grieco, "Temporary Admissions of Nonimmigrants to the United States in 2004" (Washington, D.C.: U.S. Department of Homeland Security, 2005), tables 3, 4.

19. Randall Monger and Macreadie Barr, "Nonimmigrant Admissions to the United States: 2009," Department of Homeland Security, April 2010, https://www.dhs.gov/sites/default/files/publications/Nonimmigrant_Admissions_2009.pdf, tables 2, 4; Bryan Baker, "Nonimmigrants Residing in the United States: Fiscal Year 2016," Department of Homeland Security, March 2018, https://www.dhs.gov/sites/default/files/publications/Nonimmigrant_Population%20Estimates_2016_0.pdf, tables 1, 2.

20. Douglas Belkin and Mariam Jordan, "Heavy Recruitment of Chinese Students Sows Discord on U.S. Campuses," *Wall Street Journal*, March 17, 2016, https://www.wsj.com/articles/heavy-recruitment-of-chinese-students-sows-discord-on-u-s-campuses-1458224413?tesla=y.

21. Narayan Lakshman, "For Indian Women in America, a Sea of Broken Dreams," *The Hindu*, July 5, 2016, https://www.thehindu.com/news/international/for-indian-women-in-america-a-sea-of-broken-dreams/article3697211.ece.

22. Chakravorty Sanjoy, Devesh Kapur, and Nirvikar Singh, *The Other One Percent: Indians in America* (New York: Oxford University Press, 2016), xii.

23. Jason DeParle, "The Anti-Immigration Crusader," *New York Times*, April 17, 2011.

24. Quoted in Michael Leahy, "Crossing the Line," *Washington Post*, March 19, 2006.

25. Theda Skocpol and Vanessa Williamson, *The Tea Party and the Remaking of Republican Conservatism* (New York: Oxford University Press, 2012), 46–56.

26. Quoted in Michael Grabell, "Exploitation and Abuse at the Chicken Plant," *New Yorker*, May 8, 2017.

27. Ines Ferre et al., "Thousands March for Immigrant Rights," CNN.com, May 1, 2006, http://www.cnn.com/2006/US/05/01/immigrant.day/.

28. Quoted in Nancy Trejos and Aruna Jain, "Organizers Expect Crush for Immigrants Rights Rally," *Washington Post*, April 10, 2006.

29. Dara Lind, "Removals vs Returns: How to Think about Obama's Deportation Record," *Vox*, April 11, 2014, https://www.vox.com/2014/4/11/5602272/removals-returns-and-deportations-a-very-short-history-of-immigration.

30. Ryan Lizza, "Getting to Maybe," *New Yorker*, June 17, 2013.

31. These figures are tabulated from Department of Homeland Security, *2018 Yearbook of Immigration Statistics* (Washington, D.C., 2018), https://www.dhs.gov/immigration-statistics/yearbook/2018/table39, table 39, "Aliens Removed or Returned: Fiscal Years 1892 to 2018."

32. Seung Min Kim and Carrie B. Brown, "The Death of Immigration Reform," *Politico*, June 27, 2014, https://www.politico.com/story/2014/06/how-immigration-reform-died-108374.

33. Migration Policy Institute, "U.S. Annual Refugee Resettlement Ceilings and Number of Refugees Admitted, 1980–Present," https://www.migrationpolicy.org/programs/data-hub/charts/us-annual-refugee-resettlement-ceilings-and-number-refugees-admitted-united.

34. USAID, "Syria Complex Emergency—Fact Sheet #1 (FY 16)," December 11, 2015, https://www.usaid.gov/crisis/syria/fy16/fs01.

35. Jie Zong and Jeanne Batalova, "Syrian Refugees in the United States," Migration Policy Institute, January 12, 2017, https://www.migrationpolicy.org/article/syrian-refugees-united-states-2017.

36. Deborah Amos, "U.S. Is on Target to Accept and Resettle 10,000 Syrian Refugees," NPR, August 5, 2016, https://www.npr.org/sections/thetwo-way/2016/08/05/488896247/u-s-is-on-target-to-accept-and-resettle-10-000-syrian-refugees.

37. Dara Lind, "The 2014 Central American Migrant Crisis."

38. Quoted in Jonathan Blitzer, "An Underground College for Undocumented Immigrants," *New Yorker*, May 22, 2017.

39. Blitzer, "An Underground College."

40. Muzaffar Chishti and Claire Bergeron, "New Arizona Law Engulfs Immigration Debates," Migration Policy Institute, May 17, 2010.

41. Michael Matza, "10 Years after Immigration Disputes, Hazelton Is a Different Place," *Philadelphia Enquirer*, April 1, 2016, https://www.inquirer.com/philly/news/20160403_10_years_after_immigration_disputes__Hazleton_is_a_different_place.html.

42. Katie Reilly, "Here Are All the Times Donald Trump Insulted Mexico," Time.com, August 31, 2016, https://www.yahoo.com/news/times-donald-trump-insulted-mexico-153525059.html.

43. Katelyn Burns, "Trump Is Diverting Another $7.2 Billion in Military Funds to Build His Border Wall," *Vox*, January 14, 2020, https://www.vox.com/2020/1/14/21065352/trump-diverting-military-funds-border-wall-construction.

44. Christopher Giles, "Trump's Wall: How Much Has Been Built during His Term?" BBC News, January 12, 2021, https://www.bbc.com/news/world-us-canada-46748492; Paul Sonne and Nick Miroff, "Pentagon to Divert $3.8 Billion from Its Budget to Build More of Trump's Border Barrier," *Washington Post*, February 13, 2020.

45. These figures were tabulated from Department of Homeland Security, *2019 Yearbook of Immigration Statistics* (Washington, D.C., 2019), https://www.dhs.gov/immigration-statistics/yearbook/2019/table39, table 39, "Aliens Removed or Returned: Fiscal Years 1892 to 2019."

46. Kristina Davis, "U.S. Officials Say They Are Highly Confident to Have Reached a Tally on Separated Children: 4,368," *Los Angeles Times*, January 18, 2020.

47. "Six Migrant Children Have Died in U.S. Custody," *Los Angeles Times*, May 24, 2019.

48. American Immigration Council, "Fact Sheet: The 'Migrant Protections Protocols,'" January 22, 2021, https://www.americanimmigrationcouncil.org/research/migrant-protection-protocols, 2.

49. Alicia Caldwell, "Trump Administration Program Nearly Ended Asylum. Now Coronavirus Has Halted It," *Wall Street Journal*, April 25, 2020.

50. Centers for Disease Control and Prevention, "Provisional Mortality Data—United States, 2020," April 9, 2021, https://www.cdc.gov/mmwr/volumes/70/wr/mm7014e1.htm.

51. Quoted in Stephen Groves and Sophia Tareen, "Meatpacking Relies on Immigrants. But Coronavirus Fears, Border Moves Could Trigger Labor Shortage," *Chicago Tribune*, May 26, 2020.

52. Bruce Y. Lee, "Trump Once Again Calls Covid-19 Coronavirus the 'Kung Flu,'" Forbes.com, June 24, 2020, https://www.forbes.com/sites/brucelee/2020/06/24/trump-once-again-calls-covid-19-coronavirus-the-kung-flu/?sh=6f6edec71f59.

53. Quoted in Nick Miroff and Tony Romm, "Trump, Citing Pandemic, Orders Limits on Foreign Workers," *Washington Post*, June 22, 2020.

Epilogue. Past, Present, Future

1. Quoted in Kevin Sieff, "The Reason Many Guatemalans Are Coming to the Border? A Profound Hunger Crisis," *Washington Post*, April 1, 2021.

Index